THE BEST LETTER BOOK EVER!

THE BEST LETTER BOOK EVER!

Business Letters by
Marya Holcombe

Personal Letters by
Nate Rosenblatt and Judi Barton

Round Lake Publishing
Ridgefield, Connecticut

Round Lake Publishing Co.
31 Bailey Avenue
Ridgefield, CT 06877

Printed in the United States of America

0   9   8   7   6   5   4   3

ISBN 0-929543-55-6

What this Book Will Do for You

Many bright people, perhaps you're one of them, go to great lengths to avoid writing letters. Even when they need to make sales, straighten out credit problems or deal with difficult people, the threat of facing a blank page or a bare computer screen can be so daunting that they never write that important letter.

Just the thought of getting started can strike terror! How should I open the letter? What information should I include (and what should I leave out)? Which approach and tone will be most effective, and what closing will bring the action or reaction I want? Sometimes the challenge presented by these issues is so overwhelming that the letter that is finally composed misses the mark completely or undermines the writer's intended purpose. *The Best Letter Book Ever* solves these problems by providing you with the finest model letters for all your business and personal correspondence.

Here are some of the features that make this book truly *The Best Letter Book Ever*.

A very wide variety of letters. More than 830 letters provide the greatest wealth of letters ever assembled in one book. 42 thank you letters...31 congratulatory letters...39 complaint letters...31 job search letters...64 sales and marketing letters...16 collection letters...28 sympathy and condolence letters. And these are just a small sampling of the hundreds of letters available in *The Best Letter Book Ever*.

Quality—not just quantity. Three experts with more than 60 years of combined writing experience produced this monumental work. Their letters represent the highest quality of writing available. People with little letter-writing experience will vastly improve their communications skills by using this book. And, as *The New York Times* has said, "Even a glib executive could benefit from these letters."

Easy to find letters, whatever the subject. Thanks to a comprehensive table of contents and two indexes (one by letter title and one by key word), it takes only a few seconds to find exactly the letter you want.

Written in today's style. All of the letters in *The Best Letter Book Ever* are written in today's conversational style. No longer do we need to use phrases like "Per your request" or "enclosed herewith please find..." The letters are written in the same language we speak when we converse face-to-face with others—a far more natural sounding, compelling approach to communications, and one that writing experts highly recommend.

Step-by-step hints accompany each letter. Imagine a writing coach sitting by your side as you prepare a letter. With *The Best Letter Book Ever,* you have the benefit of expert help with the hints that accompany each and every letter. The hints explain what to include in your letter for maximum effectiveness, how to customize it to *your individual needs*, and how to phrase each letter to ensure that it conveys exactly what you want it to.

Expert guidance on starting and ending each letter. Each letter was carefully written to grab the reader's attention, convince or explain a particular subject, and then call for a specific action. The opening and closing sentences provide the reader with the skill and confidence to make every letter a highly successful one.

Every letter category introduced with professional advice. The opening pages of each chapter contain concise guidance on how to write the types of letters found in that chapter. This means that for a given area of letter writing you have not only dozens of concrete examples ready to use, but the full understanding of what makes that kind of letter work most effectively.

Preface

With *The Best Letter Book Ever*, letter writing will be an easy (even pleasant) task, as well as a rewarding one. Before you start using these letters, read this preface to get the most out of your letter writing activities.

Before you begin, decide whether you should be writing at all. Ask yourself "What do I want the reader to do?" "Or how do I want the reader to feel after reading my letter?" If you can't answer this question, perhaps you shouldn't be writing at all.

Don't write:

- When a quick phone call will do the job as well or better than a letter, *and* a written record is *not* required.
- When your reason for writing is to congratulate yourself. If your objective is to let someone know how great you are, think again. It's better to *show* your worth to people than to *tell* them about it.
- When you're emotionally upset. If you're in a rage or emotionally overwrought, take some time to cool down before you begin to write. The letter will be better thought-out, and you'll avoid saying things you may regret later on.

Do write:

- When a permanent record is necessary to guard against misinterpretation or to protect both writer and reader from the memory lapses that come with the passage of time.
- When the reader needs time to understand and absorb a message— for example if the material is complex or technical, or if it packs an emotional punch.
- When you need a polite way to get someone's attention. For example, when you've been trying to reach a potential customer, or your landlord by phone, with no success.
- When writing a letter demonstrates that you've made a special effort.

Be prepared! Whether you're writing for business or personal reasons, you need to give the purpose of your letter some preliminary thought before you begin to write. Focus on the reader, the person who will act or react to whatever you say, and write with that person in mind. The best way to achieve this is to picture the person in your mind as you write.

Be direct. Establish the main point of the letter by asking yourself, "What is the one thing I want the reader to remember?" Start with a sentence that compels the reader to continue reading, and then quickly make the main point or points. Don't save important information for late in the document. The reader may never get that far.

Be brief. If your letter is well organized, you won't be tempted to run on. Most readers are just as busy as you are. They won't read pages and pages of explanation or analysis. Keep business letters, memos, and executive summaries to one page, if possible, and keep your paragraphs short.

The exception to the rule of brevity is for newsy letters to family or friends, but even here, try to keep from drawing your letters out needlessly, or repeating information.

Be forthright. Hedging fools absolutely no one. By qualifying the statements you make, you come off sounding insecure and insincere. Avoid phrases such as, "There is a possibility that" or "In my estimation it seems as if" whenever you can. Use the active voice ("he did it" rather than "it was done") for the same reasons—it's shorter and more forceful.

Be positive. If you can state something positively, do so. Saying "We can't fill your order" is honest enough, but offering to "substitute Product X, a superior version of the product you ordered" is much better. The same is true when transmitting personal information. Try to focus on the positive, rather than the negative aspects of your message.

Be natural. Use your own "voice" when you write. Letter writing doesn't have the stilted, formal sound it once did. Don't use slang, but do write in a conversational style, similar to the way you speak. Even contractions like "I've" and "let's" accurately reflect the way people converse, and are perfectly acceptable in today's communications. Read your letter. If it sounds stiff, it probably is! Change it so that it sounds more natural.

Customize the letters to your needs. Many of the letters in this book require very little customizing to make them appropriate for other situations, while some will need additional editing. The more complex letters provide excellent examples of how to handle particularly difficult situations.

When creating your own documents, consider combining paragraphs from several letters within the same category. This is particularly helpful when your needs fall somewhere between two model letters.

Review your letter when you finish to be sure you have changed all the information necessary to make the letter correct for your purposes. And, of course, proofread it to be sure there are no typographical errors or misspelled names.

Contents

Contracts and Government Regulations

Chapter 2   ADVERTISING AND PUBLIC RELATIONS

Dealing with Advertising Agencies and Rate Requests

Announcements to Customers

Public Relations Companies and Fees

Press Releases

Chapter 3   CUSTOMER RELATIONS

Chapter 4   HANDLING CUSTOMER COMPLAINTS

Chapter 5   CREDIT AND COLLECTIONS

Chapter 6   DEALING WITH SUPPLIERS

Compliments and Suggestions

Payment

Request Permission to Return Item/Shipment

Chapter 7   PERSONNEL RELATIONS

Hiring

Problems

Chapter 8   MANAGING YOUR BUSINESS

Business Plans, Help, and Housekeeping

Reservations and Rentals

Chapter 9   INTERNAL COMMUNICATIONS

Meetings and Planning

Suggestions, Reports, and Recommendations

Chapter 10   COMMUNITY SERVICE

Chapter 11   FAXES

Chapter 12 NETWORKING

Chapter 13 LETTER FORMATS AND FORMS

Chapter 14 APOLOGIES

Chapter 15   COMPLAINTS

Chapter 16   CONGRATULATIONS

Chapter 17   CORRESPONDENCE TO FAMILY AND FRIENDS

Reminders

Holiday Correspondence

Chapter 18   DEALING WITH BANKS, CREDIT, TAXES

Banks

Credit

Taxes

Chapter 19   EMPLOYMENT

Chapter 20   EXPRESSING OPINIONS

Chapter 21   GIFT CARD ONE-LINERS

Gift Cards

Chapter 22   INTRODUCTIONS AND REFERENCES

Introductions

References

Chapter 23   INVITATIONS

Chapter 24   LETTERS TO BUILDERS AND LANDLORDS

Chapter 25   LETTERS TO PROFESSIONALS

Chapter 26   PRAISE AND THANK YOU'S

Thank You's from Adults

Thank You's from Children

Thank You's in Business

Thank You's to Organizations

Chapter 27   REQUESTS FOR INFORMATION AND ASSISTANCE

Requests to Colleges and Board of Education

Requests from Charitable Organizations

Requests to Civic Organizations

Requests to Companies and the Federal Government

Requests to Local Government

Chapter 28   SENSITIVE ISSUES

Saying No

Chapter 29   SYMPATHY AND CONDOLENCES

Sympathy

Condolences

Sales and Marketing 1

Sales and marketing are the lifeblood of most companies. Written communications cover many different kinds of activities in these areas. All of them are crucial to the success of a company, primarily because they are directly responsible for generating income or, in the case of communicating with the sales force, dealing with those who generate the income. The effectiveness of the written word is critical in all of these endeavors.

Sales letters. Although all business communications should be persuasive, persuasion is usually the *sole* reason for sales letters. While a face-to-face encounter provides a sales person with the ability to establish rapport with the customer, sales letters long have proven themselves powerful marketing tools as well. They are personal, command undistracted attention and can be precisely targeted to a market. Methods have been developed over the years which, when followed, yield highly productive results.

The alternative to the salesman's warm smile and sincere handshake is the "grabber." It captures the reader's attention and gives him a compelling reason to continue reading. The headline or opening sentence should involve him immediately. Among the time-proven grabbers are free offers, announcements of new or improved products, provocative statements and attention-demanding questions.

The body of the letter should demonstrate a need and then show how your product or service meets that need. Next, persuade the reader to make a purchase decision. The easier you make that decision for him, the more successful the letter will be. A reduction of the selling price or offering a money-back guarantee are strong inducements to purchase. Finally, ask for action: mail the order card, phone today. Keep the ordering instructions simple and clear.

Follow-ups. The cardinal rule is always to leave a "thread" that leads to the next contact, to a continuation of the relationship. Ending a letter with "Please call me if you have an interest in any of our products" will seldom elicit action. Much better is "I will call you in a week to hear your reaction to this proposal." Imagine that the steps preceding a sale are a dance and that you are leading.

Following up also means thanking people who give you leads or information about potential customers. Report your progress to date, if appropriate, and always let them know if you make the sale. It's simple courtesy.

Communicating with the sales force. Because most salespeople are on the road or unavailable, managers must communicate with them by memo or letter. The key is to be straightforward and to use a civil tone. Salespeople are no less sensitive to nuances than any other human beings. With their distance from the office, they may be prone to misunderstanding communications that aren't carefully worded.

Orders and shipping. Orders and shipping issues are part of the sales process in many organizations, since the salesperson will often also be responsible for fulfillment. The touchstone is to be pleasant and honest, particularly if there are difficulties in fulfilling the order.

Proposals, bids and quotations. Whether writing proposals, confirming terms, or changing terms and specifications, these letters have contractual ramifications. You may want to have them looked at by an attorney if significant amounts of money are involved. As with all customer correspondence, be clear, concise and polite.

Welcome to the Area (1-01)

Dear Mr. and Mrs. Hawkins:

Congratulations on your new home and welcome to the Easton area! We wish you many happy years in this new location.

We at Chim, Chim, Cheree have been serving customers in Easton for over 50 years, and we would like to add your name to our list of satisfied customers. We are specialists in chimney cleaning, damper repair, masonry repair, and chimney cap installation. Please call me at 281-5333 to arrange an appointment for a **complimentary** fireplace inspection and consultation with one of the professionals from our staff. I've included our brochure, which tells you more about our company and services.

Again, welcome to Easton. I look forward to hearing from you.

Sincerely,

- Explain who you are and the services you provide.
- If possible, give an incentive for the customer to try your services (premium, discount, complimentary visit, etc.).
- Clearly indicate how you may be reached.

Welcome to the Family (1-02)

Dear Ms. Johnson:

Thank you for choosing AAAble Rents for your first catering job. I heard that it was a great success. The staff and I wish you and Mrs. Jones the best success with your new service.

At AAAble, we are ready when you need us. In addition to chairs, tables, china, silverware, table linens, and glasses, which you have already rented from us, we can also supply you with tents, candelabra, hollowware, party decorations, dance floors, and many other party supplies. Please call us soon!

Best regards,

- Thank them for the business.
- Offer any additional services that you might have.
- Solicit more business.

Welcome, Brochure with Company Terms (1-03)

Dear Mr. Siegler:

Thank you for your order of last Tuesday; we appreciate new clients, as they are the lifeblood of our business. I am enclosing our latest company brochure, which describes our capabilities and terms of sale. I think you will find the section on small motors particularly interesting.

Our regional sales representative, Chuck James, will contact you next week to set up an appointment. At that time he can explain our products more fully and answer any questions you might have.

We look forward to serving you again.

Very truly yours,

- Thank them for the business.
- Explain what you have enclosed and why.
- Establish the mechanism for doing more business with the customer, whether by mail, phone, or in person.

Welcome, Catalog Enclosed (1-04)

Dear Mr. Zimmerman:

Thank you for your order for carving chisels. You'll find that our tools will enhance your work and pleasure in woodworking. They are well-crafted, enduring, useful, and unique—the best that money can buy.

I'm enclosing a copy of our latest catalog. We have expanded into gardening tools in addition to our line of woodworking tools.

We look forward to hearing from you again soon.

Very truly yours,

- Express appreciation for the business.
- Explain anything new or different in your catalog.
- Say that you're looking forward to doing more business.

Follow-up to Sales Call: First Follow-up to New Client/Customer (1-05)

Dear John and Fran:

It was a pleasure meeting you last week, and I thank you for the opportunity to introduce you to our insurance plans. I hope you have had the chance to look over the information on family protection, retirement income, and education plan that I left with you.

I will call you Thursday evening to see if you have any questions about our services. I hope to have the opportunity to work with you in planning your family's financial security and other insurance needs.

Sincerely yours,

> • Thank them for the initial meeting.
>
> • Establish a time when you will next contact them (at which time you can try to set up a meeting to close the sale).

Follow-up to Sales Call: Inactive Customer (1-06)

Dear Mr. Johns:

It was a pleasure meeting with you last Friday. I'm glad we had the opportunity to discuss and, I hope, resolve some of the problems you had with our toy shipments three years ago. As I mentioned, we've upgraded our delivery system in the past year, which should prevent any recurrence of late shipments and shipping errors.

I will call you in two weeks, after you've had the chance to look over our new catalog.

We look forward to doing business with you again.

Sincerely,

> • Express appreciation for the client/customer's time.
>
> • Follow up with what you discussed during the sales call (answer questions raised, send material requested, etc.). If the customer stopped doing business with you because he or she was dissatisfied, state how the problem has been, or can be, fixed.
>
> • Always leave a thread—a link to your next contact.

Solicitation of Additional Business to Current Customer (1-07)

Dear Toni and Marshall:

Because of the rapid appreciation of housing (and replacement costs) here in Southern California, we need to make sure your current homeowner's policy of $300,000 provides sufficient protection before we renew the policy on May 30. We are generally suggesting that our accounts increase their policies 10-15%.

If you've made significant improvements to your house in the last year, you'll need to think about an additional increase to the policy amount.

I'll call you next week to discuss your coverage.

Best wishes,

- If you're seeking additional business or an increase in an account, be sure to give a reason that makes sense to your reader.

- Leave the ball in your court—"I'll call you..." is much more appealing to a busy customer than "please call me."

Solicitation of Former Customer (1-08)

Dear Mrs. Tovar:

We were sorry to see that your name has not been on our list for service contract renewals for the past two years. If you have had a problem with Friendly Air Conditioning, we would like to remedy it.

We have also expanded and improved our service fleet in the past year, and our prices have remained very competitive. We now have servicemen on call 24 hours a day and can guarantee that one will be at your place within an hour of your call.

I'll telephone you next week to see if I can answer any questions you might have about our new services. We would very much like to welcome you back as a Friendly Air Conditioning customer.

Sincerely,

- Highlight any improvements in your products or services that have occurred since you last did business.

- Try to find out why they stopped doing business with you.

- Let them know that you would like their business back.

Response to Request for Information (1-09)

Dear Mr. Green:

Thank you for your request for more information on American Adjustable Frequency AC Motor Speed Control products.

American has been producing quality AC motor controls since 1974, and we have over 14,000 units in operation throughout the world. We have an excellent reputation for quality, reliability, and service, and all our products are designed, engineered, and manufactured in the U.S.A.

I've enclosed a catalog that describes our products. Please contact me for more sales information and application assistance. I would like to be of further service to you.

Again, thank you for your interest in American Controls.

Sincerely yours,

- Express thanks for their interest in your product or services.
- Let them know you're interested in providing more information and try to find out more about what they're looking to buy.

Request to Use Name As Reference (1-10)

Dear Mr. Handel:

May I use your name when prospective clients ask for a reference? You have been a valued client for over ten years, and you are well-known and respected as a piano teacher in our community—a perfect reference for a piano-tuning business!

I will call you in a few days for your answer. Thank you very much.

Sincerely,

- Express how you appreciate their business.
- Make it sound like an honor and privilege to be "selected" as a reference. (Saying complimentary things usually helps.)
- Arrange to follow up.

Thank You for Permission to Use Name As Reference (1-11)

Dear Mr. and Mrs. Walker:

Thank you very much for allowing us to use you as a reference for prospective clients interested in our window-washing service. We appreciate your time and value you as a client. As a token of our appreciation, I have enclosed a coupon good for 10% off our regular rates for our next visit.

Again, thank you.

Sincerely,

- Express your appreciation for the referral permission and for their business.
- When possible, include some token of appreciation for the use of their name.

Lead Generation, Consumer Services (1-12)

Dear Homeowner:

Now that fall is here and you are getting things ready for the winter, it's time to think about your driveway. Does your driveway have cracks? Is it in need of sealing?

East Coast Seal Cote Co. specializes in asphalt driveway refurbishing. We seal cracks, large and small, and apply two coats of premium rubberized sealer to the entire surface. Our finish is guaranteed for two years.

If you would like a free, no-obligation estimate, please call 572-7800. You don't even have to be home for the estimate; we will leave it in your mailbox.

We look forward to helping your driveway look better and last longer.

Yours very truly,

- Explain your services.
- Make it easy for them to respond.
- Ask for action—a response, an order.

Lead Generation, Industrial Products (1-13)

Dear Maintenance Manager:

- Do you have concrete floors in your manufacturing area?
- Do they require maintenance in heavy traffic areas due to cracking?
- Would you like to end this maintenance headache?

If your answer is yes to these three questions, we suggest that you try Glass-Coat brand sealer/resurfacer. Glass-Coat is a reinforced polycarbonate coating that goes on like paint and stands up even to heavy forklift traffic. It resists most chemicals and is nontoxic in the event of a fire.

We feel so strongly that once you try Glass-Coat you'll want it in all your problem areas that we will send you a free sample to use as a test. If this sounds good, give me a call at 1-800-555-3871 for the name of our representative in your area.

Sincerely,

- Explain your product.
- Direct it to the most likely buying influence.
- Ask for a response.

Flyer (1-14)

SPRING CLEANUP

Dread cleaning up your yard this spring? We will do it for you at a price you can't afford to pass up!

Full cleanup: Rake out entire lawn; rake out dead grass, leaves, branches and debris from garden and flower beds; clean all lawn and driveway areas and pile debris neatly at the curb for city pickup.

Small-average lot	$60-75
Larger than average or small corner lot	$85-150
Large corner lot	$150-up
X-large lot	Call for estimate

Mini cleanup: Same work done as above except no beds are touched. Cost is 1/2 to 3/4 of above prices, depending on size of lot and lawn area.

For quick, reliable service, please call
Steve, Pete, or Joe Jetson
39 Provinceline Road
Princeton, NJ 08540
(609) 555-0111

All work done on first-come, first-served basis. References available upon request. Gift certificates available.

> * Outline your services and quote typical rates.
>
> * Make sure they know who to contact and where you can be reached.
>
> * Distribute widely and frequently in targeted area.

Contest (1-15)

Name Our New Ice Cream Sundae Sensation!

Come in and taste our latest ice cream treat, a luscious concoction of mango, papaya, and coconut ice cream topped with chocolate and pineapple sauces, whipped cream, and candied grapefruit bits. Then dream up a name for this sundae sensation and fill out one of our entry forms.

If your entry is selected, you win a $25 gift certificate available for use at any one of our three Robert's Ice Cream Parlor locations: Landsdowne Square (downtown), West Road Mall, or South Landsdowne.

Hurry! The contest ends June 5. Be a winner, name a winner!

> * Outline contest rules, deadlines, and awards.
>
> * Contest should be geared to promote your business traffic (e.g., involve people coming to your store).

Discount Offer (1-16)

Dear Mr. and Mrs. Humphries:

This year we are again offering to our customers our prepayment option of a 5% cash discount on our seasonal mowing contract (April through November). Many of our customers prefer the seasonal mowing contract because of the convenience of writing one check and using one stamp.

If you decide to take advantage of this offer, please send us your check for $171.00 for the full year's mowing by April 30. If you decide to pay monthly, the seasonal charge will total $180.00.

If you have any questions concerning prepayment or your cost, please call me at 484-9333.

Sincerely,

- State clearly the advantages and terms (including deadline of the offer) of the discount.
- Encourage your customers to call you directly. Giving a person's name is always better than saying "please call our office."

Premium Incentive (1-17)

Dear Mr. and Mrs. Long:

As a special offer to new customers, we will clean your living room, dining room, and hall carpets for a flat fee of $49.95. And that's not all—we will also clean any one of your bedroom carpets **at no added cost.** This offer is good through May 31.

We are extending this low, low price to you to demonstrate the fine quality of work we do, with the hope that you will join the list of the many satisfied customers we service.

I've enclosed a description of our company, our services, and our regular rates. You may be particularly interested in quotes from some of your Farragut Hills neighbors (p. 3 of the brochure). Please take a minute to call me at 773-4592 and schedule an appointment. I'm sure you'll be very satisfied.

Sincerely,

- Outline your offer clearly. People are very skeptical about offers like this and you must be very explicit.
- If you can get testimonials, use them in your promotional literature and refer to them in the letter.

Trade Show Announcement (1-18)

Ameritherm Temperature Controls invites you to the National Plastics Exposition and to the windy city of Chicago on November 2 and 3. You can view the full range of our temperature controllers for plastics manufacturing equipment at our company display in:

Booth number 164, 2nd floor of McCormick East

Our product specialists and sales representatives will be on hand to answer any questions you might have.

Our temperature controllers are also installed on the extruders in the following manufacturers' booths:

Davis Standard	Booth number 27
Wellex	Booth number 53
NRM	Booth number 71
Husky	Booth number 82
Glouster	Booth number 99
HPM	Booth number 125

We look forward to seeing you.

- Indicate what products you have on display.
- If your booth is in a difficult-to-find location, provide directions or a map.
- If your product is also part of other equipment at the show, indicate where it can be found (name of company and booth location).

Store Opening, Special Offer (1-19)

Dear Beachwood Resident:

The Frameworks is opening a new store in the Beachwood Mall on June 1. To celebrate and to welcome you to our new store, bring in this letter and we'll take 25% off any ready-made frame or 15% off any custom frame you purchase before July 15.

We specialize in all kinds of metal, wood, and plastic frames and have over 300 different styles to choose from in our store.

Please stop in and see us soon.

Sincerely,

- Make sure you can determine how the person heard of your offer (so you can determine the effectiveness of the campaign).
- Offer some enticement for responding quickly.

Workshop Promotion (1-20)

Dear Ms. Rouse:

If you are looking for a truly unique spouse activities program for your national sales conference in June, I believe my workshop, "The Beauty of Ikebana" (Japanese flower arranging), would provide a memorable experience.

The four-hour workshop offers insight into the meaning of particular ikebana arrangements, the history of the flowering arranging art in Japan, and an opportunity for participants to make and take home a small arrangement of fresh flowers. I bring to the workshop several arrangements to illustrate examples of different styles.

I've enclosed a brochure with color photographs, a description of my experience and education in ikebana, a client list, and a fee schedule to give you a better idea of what I can offer you. I will call you next week to discuss your program needs and answer any questions you may have.

Sincerely,

- Tie your seminar to a result the reader wants—i.e., an interesting and memorable program.
- Include supporting information (brochures, etc.) to give details and arrange to follow up.

Announcement of Sales Program, Consumer Goods (1-21)

To: Boston Area Foodwell Stores

For the Fourth of July this year, we will be running a special promotion on O'Grady's "Fire Breathing Barbeque Sauce." There will be a special point-of-sale display, coupons in the local papers, and radio advertising. This sauce has done well in test markets in New Hampshire and Virginia and should help sell chicken and pork in addition to beef.

The program will run from May 21 to July 9. We hope to move 40,000 bottles in this time period. Our sales representative, Dean Phillips, will contact you next week to give you further details of the program and to answer any questions you might have.

Sincerely,

- Explain the elements of the sales program.
- State the duration and objectives of the program.
- Indicate who the contact person is for the program.

Announcement of Sales Program, Industrial Products (1-22)

To: Lumi-Co Distributors

Lumi-Co is pleased to announce the expansion of last year's growth program to include our new line of indoor and outdoor sodium lighting.

The program will run throughout this year and has a quarterly discount that gets better as the year progresses—provided you meet the agreed-upon sales levels. Our sales representative will be contacting you to review the details of this plan. Together we can make this year a "bright" year for everyone!

Yours very truly,

- Explain how the program works and what is included.
- State the duration of the program.
- Solicit participation.

Announcement of Advertising Campaign, Consumer Goods (1-23)

Subject: Spring/Summer Advertising Campaign

We are starting our Billie's Better Burger campaign in your area on April 21. This will coincide with national TV advertising during the Monday night baseball games.

The primary advertising in your area will be on WQOX and WNNB radio stations, as well as weekly ads and coupons in the Chicago Tribune.

We expect excellent response to this program, so plan your supplies accordingly. The program will run through June 30.

Let us know if there are any questions. Please have the weekly coupon totals ready to report with your weekly sales figure. Thank you and good luck!

- State when the campaign starts and ends.
- Describe how the advertising will be done; clearly state what actions you expect of the recipient of the letter.
- Have a feedback mechanism to record the success of your program.

Announcement of Advertising Campaign, Industrial Products (1-24)

Dear Distributor:

Frampton Gear Reducers is embarking on a large-scale advertising campaign for its new line of offset parallel gear reducers. We are targeting primarily the paper, stone and gravel, and chemical industries. We will be running full-page ads in *Chemical Age*, *Pulp and Paper Digest*, and *Gravel and Trap Rock News*. We will also be running similar advertising in Power Design. Ads will start in June and run through December.

We will make reprints available that are suitable for imprinting and mailing to your customers. We hope that this will stir up a lot of leads, and we are ready to help you close orders.

Good luck and good selling!

Yours very truly,

- Indicate who is targeted.
- State what advertising vehicle(s) will be used.
- Describe how long the program is to last.

Announcement of New Product/Service
to Former Customer (1-25)

Dear Customer:

We at North Shore Home Remodeling have been known for the past seven years for our excellent craftsmanship. Last year—the best in our history—more than 200 home-owners became North Shore customers. We look forward to continuing to serve the five towns on the North Shore.

This spring, we are expanding and will be starting our new division, North Shore Aluminum Siding, Refinishing, and Brick Cleaning. I'm enclosing a brochure that explains our new products and services. If you have been pleased with a remodeled kitchen or bath that we've built for you, you will love the way we can make the exterior of your home look brand new. Please call us at 790-6345 for a no-obligation consultation and quotation.

Sincerely,

- Establish the quality of your present product/service.
- Explain your new product/service.
- Make a tie between the old and the new product/service.
- Ask for action (quote, meeting, or order).

Explanation of Change in Prices to Sales Force (1-26)

Subject: Price Increase

On May 1, Powerflo will announce a 7 1/2% price increase on all plastic pumps and a 9 1/2% increase on the combination plastic/cast-iron pumps, effective June 1. Both prices are the result of increased PVC prices.

Orders entered before June 1 with shipment dates prior to July 1 will be priced at the old levels, and any orders entered after May 31 will be increased accordingly.

Please call me if you have any questions.

- Give as much advance notice as possible for a price increase, since the salespeople will want to prepare their customers.
- Give the amount of the price change, the date it will take effect, and a brief reason that salespeople can use with their customers.

Update on Product Specifications (1-27)

Subject: Power Mate Gear Reducers

Starting with shipments in June, all Power Mate gear reducers will have new and improved shaft seals. We have made the popular double lip seal standard across the line. This superior sealing system stands up to tough applications two and a half times better than the previous single lip seal systems.

We are offering this added feature at no additional cost. Please use the attached data sheet to explain the features and benefits of this new seal to your customers. We will be happy to help you work through any non-standard applications.

Thank you for your support. Please call me if you have any questions.

- Tell how the product has changed and how to apply the change to get sales.
- Solicit feedback and offer further assistance.

Introduction of New Salesperson to Sales Force (1-28)

Subject: Fred Porter Joins Our Team

It is with great pleasure that I introduce our newest sales engineer, Fred Porter. Fred has an extensive background in computer systems, particularly in positioning systems software.

Fred and his wife, Barbara, will be relocating to Richmond, where he will be joining our Southern office, handling accounts in Virginia, Kentucky, North Carolina, and South Carolina starting July 1.

Welcome aboard, Fred!

- Emphasize introduction in subject line.
- Give a short description of the person's background.
- Say when and where the person will locate.

Explanation of Changes in Territory Assignments (1-29)

Subject: New Territory Assignment

As you know, Jim Fitzpatrick is leaving us next month, which will leave us one person short in the Boston office. I am asking you to assume responsibility for part of his territory, specifically southern New Hampshire, for the time being.

Please get together with Jim before he leaves. He and I have discussed the transition, and he plans to allow enough time so that he can introduce you to all his major accounts. I want you to make especially sure that we have a smooth transition of the Milekin Company account. We have spent a lot of time and effort developing this account, and we want to pass the baton with professional grace.

I will be in your office next Friday to see how things are going. We have every faith that you will handle this new territory in your usual highly professional manner. Good luck!

- Smooth transitions are vital to keeping customer goodwill. Give specific direction; ensure that the outgoing rep and the newly assigned rep talk to each other, and follow up.

Explanation of Bonus/Commission Program (1-30)

Subject: Fourth Quarter Bonus Bonanza

The last quarter of the year is traditionally our slowest quarter. To make things more exciting this year, we are offering an expanded bonus program. For orders placed in the fourth quarter, we will pay sales representatives an additional 1% commission on orders for immediate shipment. All product categories qualify, and bonus payments will be made on December 15th!

Get out there, stir up sales, and earn a nice Christmas bonus.

- Be specific about how the bonus works and to what products it applies. Also state time frames, limitations, and when the bonus will be paid.

Request for Meeting to Review Sales Performance (1-31)

Subject: Second Quarter Performance

I've been reviewing your region's performance, and last quarter it was excellent! Certainly, 115% of plan is an outstanding result.

Your team posted over-plan sales in all product categories but two—chain and line. Is there a reason why these two groups were only 87% and 71% of plan respectively? I'll be in your area the first week of next month and would like to have dinner with you to discuss how we can help you get these two products on track.

My secretary will call yours to arrange a date.

- Be specific when you're talking about performance—generalized platitudes don't motivate anyone.
- Congratulate good performance first; suggest corrective actions for areas that need improvement later on.
- Take a problem-solving, rather than a punitive, approach.

Cover Letter for Questionnaire (1-32)

Dear Executive:

We need the information requested in the enclosed questionnaire in order to prepare The Marketer's Reference Guide. Please take a minute and help us.

The Marketer's Reference Guide is a resource book highlighting the multitude of marketing and support services that businesses use in the greater Phoenix area. It's a valuable reference for your company because it indexes the local talent available to meet your marketing needs.

Whether your organization is in the market for direct-mail consulting, graphic-design help, a brochure writer, or an advertising/marketing agency, you can find what you need by looking through the 162 different categories of suppliers of services in this book.

We will send you future editions of The Marketer's Reference Guide free-of-charge if you return the questionnaire by September 30. Alerting us to your needs (by filling out and returning the questionnaire) will also enable us to invite you to specific trade shows geared to your interests.

Thanks for taking the time to complete and return the enclosed questionnaire. We promise that you will be the ultimate beneficiary.

Sincerely,

P.S. If you would like an additional copy of The Marketer's Reference Guide or need additional copies for other departments, you may order them for $19.95 ($10.00 off the cover price of $29.95) simply by enclosing with this questionnaire a check made payable to The Marketer's Reference Guide.

- It's very difficult to get people to return questionnaires. (Some people go so far as to enclose dollar bills with their requests.) Here the offer is a free reference book and invitation to trade shows.
- The P.S. will get read—and may get sales even if the questionnaire isn't filled out.

Thank You for Answering Questionnaire (1-33)

Dear Mr. Swan:

Thank you for the information you provided for our 1998-1999 marketing campaigns questionnaire. As always, your cooperation has helped ensure the success of this project.

Your copy of the findings is enclosed. Please note that some of this information is extremely sensitive and should be treated as confidential.

We'll be back to request an update in September. In the meantime, we welcome any changes or corrections, which we will incorporate in our July newsletter.

Sincerely,

> • Questionnaires are marketing tools. Providing results to respondents rewards them for participation and gives you another chance to get their attention. People who have a long history of cooperation should be thanked and commended, even in a form letter.

Questionnaire about Salespeople (1-34)

Dear Customer:

Thank you for visiting The Stork's Baby recently. I hope you found what you were looking for and that you were satisfied with the quality and the variety of baby products in our store.

Please help us by completing and returning this survey about our salespeople so that we can continue to improve the quality of our service. It is very short and will only take a few minutes of your time. Thank you very much for your help.

Sincerely yours,

Did a salesperson wait on you within a reasonable amount of time?
   [ ] Yes   [ ] No

Was the salesperson knowledgeable about the merchandise?
   [ ] Very [ ] Somewhat [ ] Not at all

Were you treated with courtesy?
   [ ] Yes   [ ] No

Did the salesperson mention:
   Our Free Special Order Service? [ ] Yes [ ] No
   Our Shower Planning Service? [ ] Yes [ ] No

Overall, how would you rate your salesperson at The Stork's Baby?
   [ ] Excellent [ ] Good [ ] Average [ ] Poor

Any suggestions or comments regarding our salespeople?
_____
_____

If anyone was particularly helpful, please let us know.
_____
_____

- Explain how the feedback you receive will help you improve the quality of the salesforce.
- Mention any special services which may have been overlooked.
- Thank the customer for his or her time and assistance.

Questionnaire to Inactive Client (1-35)

Dear Mr. Kerlinsky:

In reviewing our accounts we noticed that we have not received any orders from your store for our Maxi-Pipes Chrome Exhaust kit during the last six months. In the preceding year, you had ordered an average of 10 kits per month. Naturally, we hate to lose a steady customer.

It's important to us that we keep informed of our customers' degree of satisfaction with our products and service so we can continue to serve them well. It's particularly important that we learn why old customers no longer order from us.

Won't you please help us by completing the following questionnaire and returning it to us in the enclosed stamped envelope? It will only take a minute and your answers will help us provide better services in the future.

Thank you for your time, and we hope you'll be placing an order with us soon.

Sincerely,

Why did you stop ordering Maxi-Pipes Chrome Exhausts? (Check all that apply.)
    [ ] Dissatisfied with quality of product
    [ ] Dissatisfied with promptness of delivery
    [ ] Dissatisfied with payment terms
    [ ] Experienced customer service problems
    [ ] Other (Please explain.)

_____

_____

What will it take to get your business back?

_____

_____

- Ask direct questions—you'd be surprised at what people will tell you. Besides, you have nothing to lose.
- Express interest in getting the business back.

Consumer Expo Questionnaire (1-36)

Thank you for stopping by our booth at the Cleveland Outdoor Expo. Would you please help us by completing the following survey? As you'll see, it's a brief one and will only take a minute or two to complete. Then, either hand it to one of our sales representatives in our booth or place it in the attached return envelope and drop it in the mail. No postage is required.

Your answers are important because we analyze the information to help us learn more about our customers and their desires and to provide better products in the future.

Again, thank you for your time and your interest.

SPIFFY CYCLES CUSTOMER SURVEY

1. Name: _____
    Address: _____

2. Date: _____

3. Why did you stop by our booth?
    [ ] Looking to buy a bicycle [ ] Attracted by display
    [ ] Spiffy's reputation   [ ] Other (please specify)

4. Have you ever heard of Spiffy before? [ ] Yes   [ ] No

5. If so, where?
    [ ] Owned one before   [ ] Friend/relative
    [ ] TV/magazine ad   [ ] Saw in store
    [ ] Other (please specify)

6. Based on what you have seen and heard, would you buy a Spiffy cycle?
    [ ] Yes   [ ] No

7. Are you interested in a bicycle for yourself or for someone else?
    [ ] Self   [ ] Other adult   [ ] Child

8. Have you ever owned a bicycle?
    [ ] Yes   [ ] No

9. Birthdate: _____

10. Marital status: [ ] Married   [ ] Single

11. Occupation: _____

12. Age of each child living at home: _____, _____, _____, _____

13. Which group describes your family income?
    [ ] Under $15,000   [ ] $35,001-$45,000
    [ ] $15,000-$25,000   [ ] $45,001-$55,000
    [ ] $25,001-$35,000   [ ] Over $55,000

14. Which of the following credit cards do you use regularly?
    [ ] Bank (Visa, MC)   [ ] American Express, Diners Club
    [ ] Gas, department store [ ] None of these

- Express appreciation for filling out the questionnaire and let them know why the information is valuable.

- Indicate how easy it is to complete the questionnaire and to return it.

- Make sure the questionnaire *is* easy to fill out.

Order Received, Being Processed (1-37)

Dear Mr. Sullivan:

Thank you for your recent order (PO #437-B) of stationery from The Inky Printing Company. We are currently processing your order for 2,000 letterheads, 1,000 second sheets, and 1,000 envelopes. I expect your order to be ready within the next two weeks; we will notify you when it is ready for pick-up.

Again, thank you for doing business with us.

Sincerely,

- Express your appreciation for the order.

- State each item of the order and, if possible, the expected date when it will be ready.

- Make sure you follow up as promised.

Order Received, Being Shipped (1-38)

Dear Mr. Jackson:

Thank you for ordering 10 cases of Cajun Cooking Magic spices. Your order (PO #S-43CC) is being shipped via the Package Express Company (Bill of Lading #IG46P00L) and should arrive in 7-10 days (their estimate). I've enclosed an invoice for the spices. I hope I can be of further service to you.

Sincerely,

- Express appreciation for the order.

- Detail what was ordered, who is shipping it, and when it is expected to arrive (if possible). Include all relevant purchase order and shipping numbers in case there are problems later.

Order Received, Delivery Delayed (1-39)

Dear Mrs. Rowland:

Thank you for your recent order of a "Christine" doll from Dreamgirls. As you know, our dolls are handmade in West Germany. Unfortunately, orders for "Christine" dolls this Christmas season have surpassed our expectations, and the doll is out of stock at the moment. We expect another shipment of dolls in two weeks, and as soon as it arrives, we will ship the doll to you via express mail, at our expense, so that your little girl will not be disappointed on Christmas morning.

I'm sorry for the inconvenience, and I thank you for your understanding.

Sincerely yours,

- Apologize, give the reason for the delay and, if possible, let the customer know when to expect delivery.
- Show the customer you care about the order by going out of your way—in this case, Express Mail—to expedite delivery.

Order Received, Merchandise Not Available (1-40)

Dear Mr. Somes:

I am returning your check for $153.00 because we no longer make the foul-weather gear (item G357) you ordered. I'm sorry to disappoint you, but that item has not been available for over six months now. We do make several other styles of foul-weather gear, and I hope you'll find one of these new styles, pictured in our new catalog that I've enclosed, to your liking.

I hope we can be of further service to you.

Very truly yours,

- Express empathy that the merchandise ordered is not available.
- If payment has been made, explain how you've dealt with it (returning their check, crediting their account, etc.).
- Offer comparable alternative merchandise if available.

Order Received, Unable to Process (1-41)

Dear Mr. Skillins:

Thank you for ordering the ski mask (item no. 69M) from our catalog. However, we are unable to process your order because you didn't indicate your color choice. The ski mask comes in red, navy blue, and black.

Please call me at (800) 555-5000 with your preference, so I can send you your ski mask as soon as possible.

Sincerely yours,

- Explain why you're unable to process the order.
- If a corrective measure needs to be taken before the order can be processed, detail what needs to be done and who is to do it.

Merchandise Being Shipped (1-42)

Dear Mr. Santos:

The 15 beige grass skirts, silver tops, and headdresses that you asked us to make for you are finished, and I've shipped them to you by UPS, insured. You should be receiving them around July 28.

I'm enclosing our invoice #4219 for the order, which totals $672.50, including shipping costs. Thank you again for your order; I look forward to providing you with other costumes in the future.

Best wishes,

- Indicate what is being shipped and when delivery is expected.
- Include the invoice number and amount, plus any other relevant information.
- Solicit future business.

Backorder Arrived, Being Shipped (1-43)

Dear Dr. Friedman:

We've received the 25 boxes of No. 2 rubber gloves (Purchase Order #12-8945J) that were backordered, and I am sending them to you by Jetline Air Freight (shipment #22-B-6732). They should arrive within a week.

I'm sorry for the problems this delay may have caused you. We look forward to serving you again soon.

Sincerely,

- Indicate what is being shipped and when and how the shipment should arrive.
- Express regret for the delay.
- Put in a plug for future business.

Merchandise Ready for Customer Pick-up (1-44)

Dear Mr. Downing:

The BMW 1225e you purchased through our European Delivery Program has arrived and is ready for pick-up. Please give me a call at 397-6622 so we can arrange a convenient time for you to come in; we are open from 9 a.m. to 6 p.m. Monday through Saturday. When you come, please bring with you a photo i.d. (driver's license) and the packet that you received from the BMW factory in Munich when you purchased the car.

I look forward to hearing from you.

Sincerely,

- Let the customer know what your business hours are and what he or she needs to do in order to pick up the merchandise.

Statement for Services (1-45)

Statement for Services

March 1 - March 15

March 1

| General Housecleaning | 4 hrs. @ $15.00 per hr. | $60.00 |

March 8

| General Housecleaning | 4 hrs. @ $15.00 per hr. | $60.00 |

March 15

| General Housecleaning | 2 hrs. @ $15.00 per hr. | $30.00 |
| Yard Maintenance | 2 hrs. @ $20.00 per hr. | $40.00 |

Total: $190.00

Payment is due upon receipt

- Give exact dates and hours of service.
- Specify hourly rates and total charges.
- Mention when the bill is to be paid.

Statement for Goods Delivered (1-46)

Statement for goods delivered   April 12, 1997

Qty. 4   "Jiminy Cricket" dwarf shrubs @ $150.00 ea.

| subtotal | $ 600.00 |
| delivery charge | $ 35.00 |

total	$ 635.00
less deposit	$ 100.00
amount due	$ 535.00

Payment is due upon receipt.

- Note date of delivery.
- Specify, exactly, goods and quantities delivered.
- Account for all charges exactly, crediting deposits.
- Note when bill is to be paid.

Request for Opportunity to Quote (1-47)

Dear Mr. Rossbach:

I would like to request the opportunity to quote for this year's ice skating show costumes. The Creative Costume Company has been making costumes for ice skating, ballet, dance, and theater productions for over fifteen years. We are known for our fast, reliable, high-quality work and reasonable prices. Our list of satisfied customers in your area includes the Cherry Hill Recreation Board Ice Show, the Doylestown Dance Troupe, and the Quakertown Thespians Company. I have enclosed pictures of some of the costumes we have made.

I would very much like to meet with you to get more information on your ice show costume requirements (approximate quantities, material, styles, etc.) so that we may submit a quote. May I see you next Thursday morning? I will call on Monday to check if this is convenient for you.

I look forward to meeting you and having the opportunity of doing business with you.

Sincerely,

- State what you would like to quote on and why you think the customer would be interested in a quote from your company (include information about your company if the customer does not know you: brochures, samples, a client list, and testimonials are all helpful).
- Ask for the information you need to submit the quote if you don't already have it.

Thank You for Opportunity to Quote, Proposal Enclosed (1-48)

Dear Mr. Hamilton:

It was a pleasure meeting with you last week. Thank you for your time and for giving us the opportunity to quote on our home, automobile, yacht, life, and disability insurance rates.

By analyzing your personal needs and financial goals, I believe we have come up with a coverage plan that will provide you with more than adequate protection for yourself and your family but will save you money over your present coverage policy. I have enclosed copies of the various proposed plans and rates.

I will call at the end of next week to see if you have any questions.

Sincerely,

- Express appreciation for their time and the opportunity to present your quote.
- State what you have enclosed and highlight special features.
- Establish a time to follow up.

Quotation Cover Letter (1-49)

Dear Mr. Plunkett:

In response to your recent inquiry, we are pleased to submit the attached quotation for Stargazer baseball shirts, as outlined in the attached specifications. We can ship these within six weeks after we receive your order.

We sincerely appreciate your inquiry. If you need additional information, please feel free to call me at 555-3343.

Very truly yours,

- Remind the reader of his interest in your product.
- Highlight any information you may want the customer to take special notice of—for example, the delivery schedule.
- Offer to provide additional information if the customer requires it.

Proposal (1-50)

Dear Mr. Beech:

Thank you for giving Foliage Factory this opportunity to inspect your landscape plants and recommend a comprehensive treatment program. During my March 3 inspection of your property, I found black vine weevils infesting your rhododendrons. These insects are the cause of the notches on the leaves. They are a serious problem and need to be controlled as soon as possible. In addition, your maple trees have leaf spot and powdery mildew diseases, and the arborvitae have tipblight.

I recommend five treatments for your trees and shrubs annually— an application of dormant oil in the late winter in order to destroy insect eggs, followed by three treatments (one each in early spring, late spring, and summer) for continuing insect and disease control; and a late fall application of fertilizer to encourage root growth and keep the plants strong through the winter. Foliage Factory uses only the finest materials and state certified horticulturists.

Each treatment costs $33.00. There is a 10% discount if you pay for the year's five visits in advance. For your convenience, we will return each spring to continue the service unless we hear from you. You may discontinue the service at any time. If you are not pleased with the results of any treatment, let me know and I will re-treat your trees and shrubs at no extra cost. You have nothing to lose and a better landscape to gain.

If you have any questions, please call me; otherwise I will call you on Monday to set up a schedule for the treatments.

Sincerely,

- Express appreciation for the opportunity to present your proposal.
- Say exactly what you will provide and what the customer will gain from your proposal (benefits).
- Set up a time when you will call to discuss the proposal. Don't wait for the prospect to get back to you.

Follow-up to Proposal (1-51)

Dear John:

I'm writing to make sure that you received our proposal for your office computer system and that everything was as we had discussed over the telephone.

Do you have any questions? We have two of the units in which you were interested in stock; shall we hold them for you? I will call Monday to discuss how we might proceed.

Sincerely yours,

- Request confirmation of the proposal's receipt and offer to clarify any questions.
- Ask for a decision on the order.
- State any additional actions you have taken or intend to take.

Revised Proposal Cover Letter (1-52)

Dear Ms. Bessemer:

I'm enclosing our revised proposal for the printing of your admission forms (RFQ 18-9910). By changing from a four-part form to a three-part form, we can reduce the cost by $1,230.00. I have also included the second color on the first form at no additional charge.

I hope this new proposal meets your needs and your budget. We look forward to receiving your business.

Sincerely,

Response to Request for Bid, with Questions (1-53)

Dear Mr. Snyder:

Thank you for requesting a quote on the landscaping for the inn's renovation. We are most interested in submitting a proposal for your consideration.

Before we submit our proposal, we have a few questions that we would like you to clarify:

1. Will all the landscaping work need to be done in July, or can it be spread out over July and August?
2. Will you be supplying topsoil from elsewhere on the property, or will the contractor have to supply it?
3. Will you require all refuse trucked away, or is there a location on site that can be used as a landfill?

I will call you next Tuesday to discuss these details if I have not heard from you before then.

Sincerely,

- Express your interest.
- Make your questions as specific as possible; certainty on the details will help you make an intelligent bid.
- Set a time to follow up for the answers.

Request to Extend Decision Deadline (1-54)

Dear Mr. Cockerham:

As I told your assistant, we just received your request for quotation RFQ 1991 for the new runway lights. It must have been delayed in the mail. May we have an additional week to work on this specification? I have already faxed the specifications to the factory and am preparing a bid package for the contractors. We should be ready to review our bid with you by next Friday.

Unless I hear differently from you tomorrow, I will assume that the extension is acceptable. I will call you if the factory has any questions. Thank you for your patience and consideration.

Sincerely,

Confirmation of Deadline Extension (1-55)

Dear Mr. Fleming:

I'm confirming that we have extended the deadline for submitting bids in response to our RFQ 1993 (Parking lot paving) until 5 p.m., May 15, as we discussed on the phone this morning.

Thank you for your interest; we shall notify you of the results of the bid selection by June 10.

Sincerely,

- State the project to which you are referring, as well as the new deadline.

- It is helpful to provide the date by which you'll be notifying them of your decision—you can cut down on the calls you'll be receiving to inquire about the decision.

Confirmation Letter, Terms Accepted (1-56)

Dear Mr. Longobucco:

Thank you for your order (PO# 10-87-C). Greentree Printers agrees to accept the special terms of net 45 days on this order, rather than our usual net 30 days, because your company will display samples of the catalog at the trade show with an appropriate credit to Greentree Printers.

We look forward to working with you on your catalog.

Sincerely,

- Identify the order and the terms that have been accepted, as well as any special conditions.

- Thank them for the business.

Confirmation Letter, Terms Accepted, Invoice Enclosed (1-57)

Dear Mr. Bunnell:

I would like to confirm the price and terms of the paving of the lot for your Shell Station.

- Net price: $3,270.00
- Payment terms: 10% with order
  40% after completion of grading
  50% after completion of paving

I'm enclosing the invoice for the first 10%. Thank you for selecting AJ Paving. I'm sure you will be pleased with the results.

Sincerely,

- State the terms clearly.

- Indicate what you've enclosed.

- Express appreciation for the business.

Confirmation Letter, Exception to Original Terms (1-58)

Dear Greg:

Thank you for your order (PO #12-81-77C, #2 Boiler rebuild). We have already begun the foundation design work and expect to have prints ready for approval to you in three weeks, as promised.

There is one item open on this order: the final payment. We would like the last 25% to be paid within 30 days of completion, rather than the 45 days your financial people suggested. If this is agreeable to you, we will proceed with the acknowledgment in this fashion.

Thank you again for your order. We are looking forward to a smooth start up.

Very truly yours,

- Express thanks for the order.

- State what the exception is.

- State what impact the resolution of the open item has on the progress of the order.

Confirmation Letter, Changes in Specifications (1-59)

Dear James:

Subject: PO #18-7711-B 100HP Motor

Thank you for your order. Before we start engineering on this order, I just want to clarify one point. Your specification states "Class B insulation." Our standard is "Class F," which is the next higher temperature rating. It is superior to B in every way and provides you with more thermal "life" in your motor.

Unless you tell us otherwise within 10 days, we will design and build the motor with "Class F" insulation.

We very much appreciate your business.

Sincerely yours,

- Explain the changes in specification and their consequences.
- Thank the customer for his business.

Confirmation Letter, Acceptance of Changes in Terms/Specifications (1-60)

Dear Mr. Burdette:

We would like to confirm the changes to the contract on Order #GMT-001762.

1. You will require the heavy-duty suspension.

2. You request the 306 V-8 engine.

3. You will pay cash and will not use our financing program.

The above changes should not affect the delivery schedule of your pickup truck. However, they will add $402.86 to the price. Your truck should be delivered in 10-12 weeks.

Thank you for choosing Athens Motors.

Sincerely,

- Detail the changes.
- Explain the consequences of the changes.
- Thank the customer for his business.

Consignment Terms (1-61)

Dear Ron:

We would like to confirm the terms of the consignment stock of motors that we have agreed to place in your building.

1. When you draw on the consigned stock, your purchase order will trigger us to replenish the stock and invoice for the motors taken.

2. At the end of the year, a physical inventory will be taken and any adjustments will be made.

3. Either party can discontinue this agreement on two month's notice.

This program has worked very well at other companies like yours. We are looking forward to working more closely with you.

Very truly yours,

- Describe the ordering and billing mechanism.
- State the length of the deal.
- Thank them for their business and express optimism in the program.

Contract Enclosed for Signature (1-62)

Dear Roger and Kitty:

It was so nice to see you again. I'm glad you liked the plans I proposed for the library. The soft rose color you chose for the carpet will look wonderful with the chestnut paneling and will tie in very nicely with the rest of the downstairs.

As usual, I've enclosed two copies of the contract detailing the cost of the materials (carpeting, window treatments, wallpaper, paint, and furnishings) and projected costs for the labor involved. Please sign and return one copy to me along with a check for the indicated deposit so that I may start ordering the materials as soon as possible. The other copy is for your records.

Thanks again for your business. I enjoy working with both of you very much.

Very truly yours,

- Indicate what is to be signed, why, and what else the client should do (e.g., return contract, send deposit).
- Express appreciation for the business.

Approval of Drawings (1-63)

Dear Ed:

Our Sales Order #GA-39482 for Universal Electric Co. (purchase order #PEC-409) requests that we transmit revised drawings for approval. The prints are enclosed with this letter; please return them by February 21. Should the prints not be returned by that date, we will have to extend the Sales Order Ship Date according to our published cycle times after the prints are returned to Athens.

Please let us know your best estimate as to when we should be receiving the approved drawings.

Thank you.

Sincerely,

- Specify when the deadline is for returning the approved drawings.

- Make certain to outline the consequences of not returning the drawings on time.

Request for Verification of EEOC Compliance (1-64)

Dear Mr. Wickersham:

Because Kingsley Building Company is a prime contractor for the State of California, we are required to verify that all our subcontractors comply with the EEOC standards. Please send me a letter by April 20 stating your compliance with these standards so that we may proceed with our pending order for your supplies.

If you do not have the statement of EEOC criteria at hand, the state's regional EEOC office can send it to you.

Thank you for your cooperation.

Sincerely,

- State why you need to have verification of compliance and by what date you need the letter.

- If you are dealing with a business that may not have experience in this area, be helpful and guide it in the necessary direction.

Advertising and Public Relations 2

Advertising and public relations, though related in their objective of increasing acceptance of a product, service or idea, use very different approaches to reach those objectives. While public relations is frequently described as free advertising, its primary goal is to make potential buyers and clients aware of the company and products—to keep its name before the public. The primary objective of advertising is to move the buyer from awareness to purchase. In both cases, the idea is to create positive images that will attract potential customers. Both advertising and public relations must be consistent with the objectives of the business and its approach to the market in order to succeed.

Advertising. When requesting rates from print and broadcast media, be specific as to what you want and why you want it. After receiving rate information, it's always a good idea to meet with the sales person to discuss the advertising schedule and negotiate the best rates. Working with an advertising agency can sometimes be a rocky road. The letters in this section help in dealing with some of the more difficult situations.

Announcements of new businesses, branch offices, employees and such should, as a rule, be short and to the point. The challenge is to get the reader's attention, and then give him the single message you want to communicate. Brevity and focus are the keys here.

Public relations. To understand how to put together a press release, it's helpful to see what route the press release takes when it leaves your office. First, it finds its way to an editor's desk at a newspaper, magazine or broadcasting station. The editor weeds through a pile of press releases and finds a few that look as if they would be of interest to his audience. A staff writer uses the press release as background material or rewrites the release into a story, sometimes barely changing it for the final version.

To have the best chance for publication, a press release must, therefore, be in a form that makes sense to a journalist. *Who, what, when, where, why* and *how* are the basic questions a journalist asks. Incorporate the answers to these questions in your press releases. What makes the event you are describing "newsworthy" must be clear and prominent. Be concise and accurate. And don't try to oversell your release. Journalists have a built-in baloney detector.

Hiring Advertising Agency (2-01)

Dear Regina:

The display ads are great. The print campaign you outlined is the best thing we've ever seen proposed. I guess we have no choice but to give you the account!

We were so excited about our meeting that we want to get this show on the road immediately. Let's get together and discuss a printer.

Next week we'll sign contracts over lunch. Call us soon to arrange the details.

So, congratulations! And thanks.

Sincerely,

- Simple is best. Say congratulations and tell them what happens next, and that's about it. Be upbeat and get things off on the right foot.

Request for Meeting on Agency Fees (2-02)

Dear Mr. Waring:

The Wheelhouse Discount Auto Dealership is planning a big promotion to announce the new model year, and we are interested in your agency. Please contact our Advertising Manager, Fred Tracy, to set up a meeting to discuss your fees and how you would propose to handle our account.

We want to produce two 30-second television spots and five radio spots to be aired on local stations and cable systems. We have seen some of your locally-produced commercials and were impressed with their quality and directness.

Please contact Fred as soon as possible. We want to get going with this immediately.

Sincerely,

- Tell the prospective agency what you plan to do (in general terms) and what you expect the agency to do. Your clarity will speed the process.
- Be specific about who should be contacted and when.

Notification to Advertising Agency of Impending Review (2-03)

Dear Janet:

At our annual review last Friday, the Board of Directors was quite disappointed at the soft sales growth for the last year. We have decided to review our entire promotional effort, including our advertising relationship with The Alpha Agency.

I'm sure you will want to be part of this review. This letter is meant to give you an opportunity to gather some information to present your side of the story. Please contact my office to set up a meeting.

I expect to hear from you soon.

Sincerely,

- This is not a pleasant task, so don't try to be too chummy. Just get to the point.

- Give them an opportunity to respond, at their initiative—but be sure they know it should be done ASAP.

Termination of Relationship with Advertising Agency (2-04)

Dear Arthur:

As you know, MicroData was recently acquired by General Systems, Inc. We have found it necessary to streamline many of our operations, and all of our promotions will now be handled by the Marketing Department of the parent company in New York. We regret to inform you that MicroData will no longer be needing the services of The Creative Partnership.

We are sorry that we must end what has been a mutually beneficial relationship. Thank you again for all the work you have done for us.

Very truly yours,

- Although not all terminations will be as friendly as this, it is preferable to avoid being too negative. Try to be upbeat without being false—no need to kick them when they're down.

- If possible, conclude on a cordial note; priorities may change again in the future.

Request for Newspaper Advertising Rates (2-05)

Dear Ms. Cavanaugh:

The Quilt Barn is planning a Spring Sale, and we would like to advertise in The Register. Please send us your rate sheet, along with information about the amount of lead time The Register requires for advertisements.

If you have any special requirements for the artwork and copy to be printed, please enclose these specifications with the rate sheet.

Sincerely,

- Short and sweet. All you want is their rates and lead time (how soon before publication the ad needs to be submitted), and that's all you need to ask for.

- Cover your bases by asking if they need anything special. The chances are they don't, but you don't want to find that out too late.

Request for Magazine Advertising Rates (2-06)

Dear Mr. Bloska:

We are interested in placing several advertisements in your magazine and would like to know what your rates are. Please call me or send us a rate card as soon as possible.

Our plans are to place a two-page ad in your June issue and subsequently to place a full-page ad in the next five issues. We are having the artwork done right now. If you have any special requirements for the printing of artwork, please forward those with your rate card.

We also need to know what the lead time is for the submission of ads.

If you have any questions, call me immediately.

Sincerely,

- Perhaps even more important than rates is the lead time. Magazines have a huge lead time, six months or more in some cases, so plan ahead.

- Don't forget to cover yourself by asking for their printing requirements.

Request for Broadcast/Television Advertising Rates (2-07)

Dear Ms. Wise:

Our company will be buying television time in August for a back-to-school shoe promotion, and we are making inquiries now to lay the groundwork. Please have a sales representative call me at 645-2300 to discuss advertising on your station.

Our preliminary plan is to run 30-second spots during the last two weeks of August. We want airtime every day during the late afternoon movie for those two weeks, and possibly during the late night movie as well, depending on how far our budget will take us.

I realize that you book these spots well in advance, and I would appreciate your immediate attention in this matter.

Sincerely,

- Broadcast advertising rates (despite rate sheets) are extremely variable, and you will probably want to negotiate them face-to-face.

- Most spots are booked months in advance, so the first thing you should do is inquire about availability and set up a meeting.

Work Agreement with Freelancer (2-08)

To: _____   Date: _____

Guilford Associates, Inc. (Guilford) hereby requests you to prepare for and on behalf of Guilford, the following:

Description of Work	Date Due

Guilford agrees to pay you $ on receipt and acceptance of the work. You understand that the labor performed is a "work made for hire" and that Guilford shall own all the rights to the work in the name of Guilford or otherwise. You hereby warrant that the work will be an original work that has not been in the public domain or previously created, and that the work will be free of any unauthorized extractions from other sources. You further understand that Guilford shall have the privilege of referring to you in promotional and advertising material.

Please signify your acceptance of this agreement by completing the form below and return one copy to us at your earliest convenience.

_____
For Guilford Associates, Inc.

To: Guilford Associates, Inc.

I agree to perform the work listed above, and I accept the terms of this agreement as stated above.

_____
Signature

_____
Social Security Number
(Required by Internal Revenue Regulations)

- Your agreement should be crystal-clear as to ownership of materials produced, such as articles, artwork, or anything else created by the freelancer, and that these materials shall be original.

- Insist that freelancers sign agreements (thereby protecting you) and provide social security numbers (saving you time later).

Announcement of Change of Address (2-09)

Dear Sol:

Well, it finally happened. Nuevo Promos just got too big for its britches, and we had to move to a bigger office. So from now on, if you're looking for the best advertising agency since the dawn of mankind, you'll just have to go to:

Nuevo Promos
112 Atlantic Street
Stamford, CT 06906
(203) 555-4141

Call us, and we'll have Jim Prior, the account executive for your area, stop by your office to discuss your promotional needs. We will continue to offer maximum creativity at very reasonable rates.

Hope to hear from you soon.

Sincerely,

> - This letter is a fairly routine one, but do what you can to keep it from being too boring. Have fun with it and give them a reason for following up.
>
> - Be sure the new address stands out clearly, and always include the phone number, even if it *hasn't* changed.

Announcement of New Subsidiary (2-10)

Dear Ms. Deale:

Video Eyes—a new division of Prince Marketing—combines the creative expertise that is Prince's hallmark with a new, state-of-the-art video production facility.

The core of Video Eyes is a creative service team of independent professionals who work on projects as needed. Production managers, directors, screenwriters, computer-graphics artists and post-production specialists are all on call at the new facility.

The heart of the new subsidiary—the apple of Video Eyes—is the new post production facility. Built around a CMX edit controller, it offers full featured edit capability with list management, frame accuracy, and digital effects from a FOR A 440 TBC. Add to this full-frame graphics capability and eight-track audio mixing, and it all spells sophistication.

Sophistication is great, but more important to the video producer is configuration. All of Video Eyes capabilities are available for one remarkably reasonable rate. No add-ons, and no surprises when the bill comes. It's all right there, to be used as the production requires.

Video Eyes is located at 15 East Street, Cambridge, MA 02138. Rate sheets are available upon request.

Sincerely,

> - Treat the new subsidiary as a separate company and make sure the reader knows where to find you. Don't belabor the fact that it has been spun off from the parent. Your reader is more likely to be interested in what the subsidiary does.
>
> - A simple mention of the parent company suggests its expertise is available to the subsidiary.
>
> - Do some selling. Tell the reader what makes you better than everybody else.

HARVEY H. PITNEY, STEVEN P. SUPER

AND

PAUL W. GORDON

TAKE PLEASURE IN ANNOUNCING

THE FORMATION OF

PITNEY, SUPER AND GORDON

A PROFESSIONAL CORPORATION

ENGAGED IN THE GENERAL PRACTICE OF LAW

3042 CENTURY PARK   (213) 554-3211
LOS ANGELES, CA 90041

- This is a formal announcement—appropriate to professional service firms. It would not be appropriate to such businesses as a plumbing contractor or a beauty parlor.

Regional Health Care, Inc.

is pleased to announce that

Barbara Chappell, M.S.W., C.I.S.W.

has joined the firm's Santa Fe Office

as a Psychiatric Social Worker

14 Elmont Ave.
Santa Fe
638-4218

- An announcement of a new employee gets the company's name before the public and implies that your company is growing and prosperous.

From Here to Maternity

is pleased to announce

that we now offer

A COMPLETE LINE OF CHILDREN'S WEAR

INCLUDING INFANTS' SIZE 0 TO CHILDREN'S 6X

SERENDIPITY SQUARE PLAZA

6 HIGH SCHOOL AVENUE

PROVIDENCE RI

(401) 654-0234

HOURS:

MONDAY - SATURDAY 10-9
SUNDAY 12-5

Ask for Joan or Thomasina!

- Focus on your unique capabilities (here, combining two related product lines in one store).
- Give the state name and area code if you operate in an area close to the state line.

Announcement of New Business Name (2-14)

Tina's Florists

has changed its name to

BUDS, BANGLES, AND BEADS

to reflect the addition of crafts supplies...

We'll continue to serve you with all kinds of floral designs,

and, as always, we're happy to sell a single orchid

or the full arrangements for a formal wedding.

Come see us.

We're at the same address:

340 Alderman Way (Across from the Shopper's Market)
Westfield

Or give us a call at 623-0999

- Although many people suggest ads with lots of long copy, a relatively concise one like this will be less likely to dilute your points.
- If you're not sure about the design the ad should take, consult with your local paper.

Announcement of Branch Office/Store (2-15)

WILD STEVE HAS OPENED A NEW STORE IN SCOTTSDALE!

Dear Neighbor:

Central Arizona has gotten Wilder since Wild Steve opened an all new store at the Apache Mall in Scottsdale! And this store is the Wildest one yet, with 25,000 square feet of the hottest fashions at the coolest prices!

To celebrate the Grand Opening, Wild Steve is giving away free tote bags to the first 1,000 customers. So come on down and check out Wild Steve's incredible selection of women's fashion jeans for under $30, our full range of colorful tops, and Arizona's biggest collection of exercise wear!

And when you're in Phoenix or Tempe, check out our other fantastic stores.

Wild Steve's will really drive you Wild!

- Give people an incentive to use your new branch—convenience, service, selection, pricing, etc.
- Assume nothing. Pretend they've never heard of you before and remind them of what your business is all about.
- Mention your other established locations.

Hiring Public Relations Firm (2-16)

Dear Bob:

After long consideration, Vulcan Products has decided that our public relations needs will be handled by McClatchey and Varnum. Congratulations!

We based our decision on your firm's excellent track record of dealing with mid-sized manufacturing companies. Your extensive client list, as well as the satisfaction expressed by those companies, made you the obvious choice.

As we have discussed in our preliminary meetings, Vulcan Products requires a full-service public relations approach. All inquiries not of a sales nature will be referred to McClatchey and Varnum, all of our press releases will be handled by your firm, and we will meet soon to discuss the updating and revamping of our other printed materials.

We would like to get a one-year contract signed and financial arrangements finalized as soon as possible. Please contact our legal department to work out the details and set up an appointment.

McClatchey and Varnum is an excellent firm, and we are excited about working with you. Let's hope this is the beginning of a long and profitable relationship for everyone involved.

Sincerely,

> • This is a formal communication in what is probably already a dynamic relationship. Give them the good news, be sure everyone knows what's expected of them, what the next step is, and sign off.

Request for Meeting on Public Relations Firm's Services (2-17)

Dear Mr. Gelso:

Cableview has decided to hire a firm to handle the public relations for our Tampa system. We are interested in your firm and would to discuss your services and fees.

Specifically, we need a firm to handle our brochures, releases, the annual report, and other written communications. Telephone inquiries and letters will be handled by our Public Affairs department, which will also coordinate our relationship with the outside public relations firm.

Please call to set up an appointment to discuss your services.

I look forward to hearing from you.

Sincerely,

> • Simple is best—tell them what you want and ask for the price. That's it.

Acceptance of Request for TV Interview (2-18)

Dear Mr. Applebaum:

Thank you for your invitation to be a guest on your program "Movers and Shakers." I will be at your studios at 11:00 a.m. on Tuesday, August 3 for the taping of the show.

My understanding is that the topic to be discussed is the recent acquisition of Affiliated Systems, Inc. by the Honeyman Corporation. I will represent Affiliated, Mr. James Knox will be there to give Honeyman's side of the acquisition process, and we will both be asked questions by members of the local business press who have not yet been chosen.

I have been informed that it is best not to wear a white shirt on television. If there are any other "tricks of the trade" I should know about, please contact my office. Also, if you could let me know who the interviewers will be when they are selected, I would appreciate it.

I look forward to it. See you then.

Sincerely,

> - State your acceptance, then give the time, date, and place for the interview in the first paragraph. Put any other details to be sorted out in the first paragraph.
>
> - Be certain the topic is mutually agreed upon in writing. There is no such thing as an open-ended interview. The last thing you want is any surprises when the tape rolls.

Announcement of New Product (2-19)

FOR IMMEDIATE RELEASE

Faust FX Expansion Card Adds 80986 Power to 80786 PCs

The Faust EX Expansion Card is the latest addition to the Cinque Computer Products line. Built around the sophisticated 80986 microprocessor, the Faust EX combines power and speed to put any 80786 IBM-compatible computer on the cutting edge of the latest technology.

The Faust EX requires only a single expansion slot and 20 watts additional power. It can be easily installed using ordinary tools. The 80986 microprocessor can handle twice the load of a conventional 80786 microprocessor in one-quarter the time. The Faust EX comes complete with an external communications port that makes networking convenient and easy.

For more information, contact Cinque Computer Products, 207 Tarry Way, San Luis Obispo, CA 93401 (1-800-555-4567).

> - *What* and *why* goes in the first paragraph as succinctly as possible. You are announcing a new product, not trying to sell it—your goal is to get the reader to remember the product name.
>
> - *How* gets detailed in the second paragraph, along with significant features. The source of the information goes at the end.

Announcement of New Product Line (2-20)

FOR IMMEDIATE RELEASE

Basta Pasta Incorporated is opening its new pasta factory in Brooklyn on June 15. Soon all America will be able to savor the fresh buttery noodles and other pasta varieties from Basta Pasta.

Twenty years ago, Sal and Doris DeCiccio opened a family-style Italian restaurant in Bayside, Queens. They served the same delicious pasta that they had served to their family. It was so tasty that soon people were coming from all over the New York and New Jersey area to sample the authentic Italian taste. The DeCiccios thought "Why not make the pasta available to everyone, not just the customers at our restaurant?"

And so Basta Pasta Incorporated was born. Local residents can still get authentic Italian spaghetti, tortellini, and stuffed shells at the restaurant in Bayside. And now shoppers across the country will be able to get the pastas at their supermarkets, too!

Basta Pastas are made from only the finest ingredients—pure, golden semolina and country fresh eggs. Aside from the traditional family favorites, like manicotti and linguine, Basta Pasta also makes specialty pasta—red pepper pasta, cheese and basil pasta, even pumpkin pasta! And every box of Basta Pasta comes with a recipe for one of Doris DeCiccio's favorite pasta sauces. Now consumers can learn the secrets behind the spicy red clam sauce, or the sophisticated lemon and chicken linguine sauce.

Once your customers have tried these pastas, they'll keep coming back for more.

For wholesale orders, call our toll-free Pasta Hotline: 1-800-YO-BASTA

- Because people remember stories, it's useful to construct a narrative. Talk about why and how the business was created, and why your product or service is really necessary and/or unique.

- Be complete in discussing your product line or service. Target your audience and give them an easy way to reach you.

Announcement of New Employee (2-21)

Dear Mr. McGaffigan:

Acoustic Engineering is pleased to announce that John W. Hill will be joining the company as Special Assistant to the President. Mr. Hill will oversee new product development, as well as report directly to the President on staffing and corporate development.

Mr. Hill comes to Acoustic Engineering from the Douge Corporation, where he was Chief Engineer as well as Operations Manager of the loudspeaker division. Previously, he designed public address systems for Theatre Sounds, Inc.

Mr. Hill is a graduate of Princeton University. He lives in Manhattan with his wife, Frances, and daughter, Melanie.

Sincerely,

- Begin with new position and responsibilities.
- Professional history, in the second paragraph, should include relevant items in reverse (most recent to earliest) order.
- Keep listing of personal items to a minimum.

Announcement of Employee Promotion (2-22)

FOR IMMEDIATE RELEASE

Dixie Advertising is pleased to announce that Laura Kiner has been named Vice-President, Account Supervisor. Ms. Kiner has been an Account Executive with Dixie for over five years. Her new responsibilities will include overseeing eight Account Executives as well as guiding the continued growth of Dixie Advertising. Ms. Kiner has generated accounts worth over $2.5 million in business for Dixie and has been the prime mover in the firm's recent successful campaigns for Southern Air Transport and Frontierland Amusement Park. She lives in Atlanta with her husband, Tad, and son, Tim.

- Talk about new job responsibilities first, then the previous position.
- Don't get bogged down in the specifics of the new position.
- Keep personal details to a minimum.

Announcement of Award/Achievement by Employee/Principal (2-23)

FOR IMMEDIATE RELEASE

The First Hartford Bank is proud to announce that Chief Executive Warren Hardman has been named to the Board of Directors of the United Way.

Mr. Hardman recently celebrated his twenty-third year as an employee of First Hartford. Long active in community affairs, he also sits on the board of Saint Stanislaw's Hospital and is past President of the Rotary Club of Middlesex County. Mr. Hardman feels it is a privilege to respresent the Bank in such an important capacity. "I can't think of an organization that makes more of an actual difference in the community. I hope I can help them maintain that tradition."

The United Way raises money for a number of well-established charities, including the American Red Cross and The Cancer Society, through a partnership with business and community leaders.

- Keep biographical details brief and relevant to the award/achievement.
- Blow your horn, but softly.
- Include a brief explanation of the award/achievement at the end.

Announcement of Merger (2-24)

FOR IMMEDIATE RELEASE

Robert McDonald, President of McDonald Financial, Inc., and Christopher T. Martin, President of Plan-Financial, Inc., announce that their two firms will merge on November 20.

The new firm, which will be callled Lifetime Financial Planning, Inc., will be located at 54 State Street, New Haven, Connecticut 06511. The telephone number is (203) 787-2982. Mr. McDonald and Mr. Martin are well-versed in financial planning, each having more than ten years of experience in the field. Mr. McDonald is a lifetime resident of the New Haven area; Mr. Martin has lived in the area since attending Yale University.

Lifetime Financial Planning is prepared to help individuals develop a financial plan at any stage in their career. The firm will specialize in aiding small business owners and providing services to executives in local corporations.

The two firms have worked extensively with numerous local organizations and individuals. Current clients includ Seth Warner, Inc., Financial Management, Inc. and Managed Plans.

- This is a typical news release—relatively low key in view of the usual overblown approach.
- Be sure to ask your clients' permission to use their names in any publicity.

Announcement of a New Partner (2-25)

FOR IMMEDIATE RELEASE

Edward McVay Belding has been named a partner in the law firm of Anderson & Lakewood, 150 South Ninth Street, Minneapolis, Minnesota 55248. Mr. Belding was formerly a partner of Tilson, Johns, Zapata, and Thorpe of Minneapolis. Lewis Lakewood is the senior partner of Anderson & Lakewood.

Mr. Belding is a graduate of Carleton College and the University of Michigan Law School. He served in the Marine Corps in Lebanon.

- You can go into more detail—about academic honors and job history, for example—but it's well to keep it simple. Always review copy with the person concerned, and respect his or her wishes as to what's included or left out.

Company Press Release, Short Version (2-26)

FOR IMMEDIATEL RELEASE

<u>Martin Firearms Celebrates 70th Anniversary</u>

Martin Firearms, a world leader in manufacturing quality pistols and rifles since 1918, is celebrating its 70th anniversary. With its headquarters located in the original factory building in Schenectady, New York, Martin Firearms employs 161 people in both corporate and manufacturing capacities. Martin Firearms is an industry leader in sportsman's rifles and supplies handguns to many police departments in the United States and Canada. Last year, over 15,000 pieces were shipped around the world. No serious gun collection is complete without a custom-made Martin Firearms hunting rifle.

- Just the facts. Try to keep it under 100 words. Tell them what you do, where you do it, how many people it takes, and what your sales are.

- Include one or two salient features if you have the room. In this case, the reader is told that this is a company whose stock in trade is quality, not volume. Although this kind of piece is primarily informational, give readers something to remember you by.

Company Press Release, Long Version (2-27)

FOR IMMEDIATE RELEASE

<u>Martin Firearms Celebrates 70th Anniversary</u>

Martin Firearms, a world leader in manufacturing quality pistols and rifles, is celebrating its 70th anniversary. As part of its anniversary program, the company will conduct tours of the plant at 40 DeLong Drive in Schenectady, demonstrating all aspects of gun manufacturing, on Friday, July 11, from 10 am to 4 pm.

With its headquarters located in the original factory building in Schenectady, New York, Martin Firearms employs 161 people in both corporate and manufacturing capacities. President Preston Martin, a grandson of founder Joseph Martin, started his firearms career working summers in the tool and die shop, entered sales following his graduation from Union College in 1962, and became president in 1983.

Martin Firearms is an industry leader in sportsman's rifles and supplies handguns to many police departments in the United States and Canada. The .38 Patrol Officer's Special was adapted by the Dallas and Boulder, Colorado, police departments this year and is in use in more than 300 police departments nationwide. Last year, over 15,000 pieces were shipped around the world. No serious gun collection is complete without a custom-made Martin Firearms hunting rifle.

The company won the prestigious "Sam Houston" award six years in succession, 1981-1986, for its contribution to the sport of riflery. The award is presented each year to the rifle manufacturer who does the most to promote safety on the range.

Martin Firearms' most famous handgun was the one specially crafted and manufactured for General George Patton. The World War II officer's famed pearl-handled revolver was built to U.S. military specifications by Martin Firearms, by special order of the general. It now resides in the Smithsonian Institution in Washington.

- A longer version of a company press release is particularly well suited to local media, but can easily be edited by any publication. In it, the company can expand on the virtues of its products or services and its personnel.

- Stress recent accomplishments, sales achieved, honors won, etc.

Thank You for Printing Article (2-28)

Dear Mr. Mackie:

I was embarrassed to find the January copy of Finance News on my desk—since I haven't even thanked you for the great way you featured my article "CFO's Guide to the Newest Spread Sheets" in the December issue.

At least, being late gives me a chance to pass on the fact that I've had a lot of positive comments on the article.

I have two more ideas for articles, which I'll run by you as soon as they "jell."

Best wishes,

- Any time you get press exposure, be sure to thank those responsible.

- Prompt thank-you's are always better, but being late is no excuse for not expressing your appreciation.

Customer Relations 3

Customer relations letters are frequently referred to as "goodwill" letters since many of them are designed to engender positive feelings on the part of the reader. But there are also letters in this category which notify customers of changes to your business, deal with meetings, appointments and payments, and one of the most sensitive issues of all, handling customers whose checks have bounced. Because it is critical to maintain the best of relations with customers, the letters in this chapter are among some of the most important a business person will ever send.

Changes in business. When announcing changes in your business—from a price increase to a new salesperson in the territory—you should present those changes in the most positive way possible. Even seemingly negative situations can provide an opportunity to stress the professionalism of your company, both in the way you handle the news and in the sensitivity shown for the customer.

Complimentary letters. While these may be among the easiest to write, beware of complimenting someone on a trivial matter. It only serves to undermine your credibility. When complimenting an individual, choose a situation that truly warrants the attention.

The fact that you've taken the time to write a personal note indicates that you're interested in the customer and puts you and your company in a good light. Do not use this type of letter to make a direct solicitation for business.

Meetings and appointments. In addition to the obvious need for covering the specific arrangements, these letters should sell you and your company. After all, the purpose of a meeting is to generate business.

Payments and returns. Letters concerning payments range from the easy "Thank you for the prompt payment" to the more difficult clarifications regarding incorrect payments, and credit/exchange policies, to no-nonsense communications regarding payment problems such as returned checks. Clarity and a rational tone are essential, for these qualities will help you to resolve problems while keeping your existing customers. After all, they are the best source for future business and for referrals to potential new customers.

Announcement of New Product to Current Customer (3-01)

Dear Bill:

I was delighted to hear how popular our "English Manor" line of picture frames has been with your customers. We have just added a new line of Art Deco frames that appeal to customers with a similar eye for current trends. I have enclosed a brochure with color photographs of each of the ten sizes in the line, as well as measurement and component information and prices. I'm sure this line will be as big a winner for you as the "English Manor" line has been.

I'd like to be able to ship an introductory assortment of 100 frames as soon as I get a purchase order from you. Once you've looked at the photographs, you might find you prefer particular sizes. We'll be glad to put together a shipment that includes exactly the mix you want.

I'll call you early next week to discuss how you'd like to proceed.

Best regards,

- To get a current client interested in a new product, mention how much success they've been having with a product of yours they already carry.

- Be sure to include as much specific information on the new product as you can.

- Let the customer know exactly what you need to know to proceed with a first shipment and arrange to follow up on the order.

Notification of Price Increase (3-02)

Dear Chet:

Effective April 1, we're forced to increase the dealer's price of our "Handyman's Tool Kit" to $13.65 per unit (based on lots of 24).

For the past year we have had to pay increasingly higher prices for top-grade steel and are no longer able to absorb all of this increase ourselves. Since our goal is to continue to provide high quality tools for the avid do-it-yourselfer, we believe that the best course is to continue using this supplier. We hope you'll agree that even with the new price, the "Handyman's Tool Kit" remains an excellent value.

Best regards,

- Express regret that you have to increase prices.
- State specifically:

    - what the product now costs
    - when the increase is effective
    - why it's necessary

Notification of Price Decrease (3-03)

Dear Chet:

I'm pleased to report that effective April 1, we'll be decreasing the dealer's price of our "Handyman's Tool Kit" to $11.75 per unit (based on lots of 24). We have signed a more favorable price contract with our high quality steel supplier and are happy to be able to pass this savings on to you.

We hope this price decrease will contribute to your continued success with the "Handyman's Tool Kit" line.

Sincerely,

- Since everyone loves to save money, be sure to bring it to the customer's attention whenever you can pass on a cost savings.
- Let them know that quality hasn't suffered even though the price is lower.

Notification of Change in Services (3-04)

Dear Ms. Loomis:

We have extended the hours for our copying and printing service in order to accommodate our customers' needs. We are now open from 8:00 a.m. to 9:00 p.m. Monday to Friday, 9:00 a.m. to 6:00 p.m. on Saturday, and 9:00 a.m. to 1:00 p.m. on Sunday.

We hope that you will take advantage of our longer hours soon.

Sincerely,

- Tell them what is new or different and why you've done it-to help them.
- Ask for their business.

Notification of Change in Policy (3-05)

Dear RMG & Associates:

We regret we will no longer be able to accept returns for cash at Lesher Supplies. However, we will be happy to exchange your returned goods, with receipt attached, for credit towards any other purchase in our store.

Thank you for your understanding and for your business.

Sincerely,

- Clearly outline your new policy; explain how it differs from the old policy.
- Express appreciation for their understanding/cooperation.

Notification of New Salesperson in Territory (3-06)

Dear Mr. Hanson:

As you know, Jim Tynan has left our sales office to become an applications engineer at our head office in Chicago. Kevin Smith will be your new account manager. Kevin has worked for us for five years in our order administration department. We are pleased to have him in our office, and I'm sure he'll do an excellent job in servicing your account. To assure that the transition is smooth, I will be working with Kevin for the next two months.

I will introduce him to you on our next sales call on Thursday.

Sincerely,

- Give the qualifications of the new salesperson and sell him or her to your customer.
- Confirm the next meeting and assure the customer that you will help make the transition from one salesperson to another as painless as possible.

Notification of Change in Administrative Arrangements (3-07)

Dear Client:

We are pleased to advise you that we have entered into an agreement with the clearing house of Little, Ursine & Co., Inc., a long established and prestigious member of the New York Stock Exchange, to clear our customer accounts. The direct effect of this action will be that on or about May 2, your account will be carried by Little, Ursine & Co., Inc. rather than our present clearing firm, Nugent, Golden & Co.

As our clearing firm, Little, Ursine & Co., Inc. will be responsible for holding securities and cash, settling transactions, collecting dividends, issuing confirmations, and looking after the various details incidental to the clearing of accounts. In conjunction with the foregoing, the securities in your account will be insured for $2,500,000. The first $500,000 of protection, which includes up to $100,000 of protection for cash, is provided by SIPC, and the balance is provided by an insurance policy purchased by Little, Ursine & Co., Inc. from the Lolander Casualty Company.

Unless we hear from you to the contrary, your account will be delivered to Little, Ursine & Co., Inc. on or about May 2. Please call us with any questions you may have.

Very truly yours,

- Customers need to be informed of any change in administrative arrangements. Give them enough information so that they feel comfortable that everything is under control.
- Offer to answer any queries they may have—this increases the comfort level.

Congratulations on Promotion (3-08)

Dear Stuart:

Congratulations on becoming Director, National Accounts. It came as no surprise to any of us here—Loomis/Jones has a widely recognized eye for sharp talent. I am sure you'll meet with the same success in New York as you did in Houston and hope that you take with you pleasant memories of your two years here in Texas.

Best regards,

- Everyone appreciates recognition when they move up the corporate ladder. Brief, sincere congratulatory notes when customers enjoy success are important to maintaining a good client relationship.
- To avoid sounding insincere, avoid excessive detail in wishing the person success.

Congratulations on New Job (3-09)

Dear Charlie:

Congratulations on your new position at Omni International. I was delighted to hear you'd moved into management and know Omni International will be glad they found you. I'm sure this is just the first in a long series of moves up the professional ladder.

Best of luck to you—I hope we continue to see one another at the monthly DCG luncheon.

Sincerely,

- Take every opportunity to keep in contact with current clients. Congratulating someone on a promotion provides an ideal opportunity—it's a happy occasion, and your taking note of it shows you're alert.
- Don't be unnecessarily effusive. It's easy to step over the line between applause and flattery. For example, saying "I know you'll be President someday" exceeds the bounds of reality.

Congratulations on Being Quoted (3-10)

Dear Ken:

I've just finished reading the article in today's issue of *The Washington Post* in which you were quoted regarding calcium deficiency in teenage girls. I've always considered you to be one of the world's experts on calcium deficiency, and I'm glad that a respected newspaper such as *The Washington Post* agrees with me.

I hope you are well. I expect to be going to Ithaca later this spring; if so, I'll be sure to call you so we can get together. I'm currently working on marketing orange juice with added calcium for my company, and I'd like to discuss a couple of ideas with you.

Congratulations again on being quoted in such a prestigious source.

Best wishes,

- Indicate where you read or heard the quote.
- Tie the event or issue in with your own business affairs if feasible—don't force it.

Congratulations on New Office (3-11)

Dear Horace:

Thank you for inviting me to your open house. It was a wonderful party, and I enjoyed meeting your associates very much.

Congratulations on your beautiful new office. The view you have of the river is spectacular, and I like the way you've redesigned the interior, especially how you've opened up the roof to let in more light. It's hard to believe that place was once a hat factory!

I wish you all the best in your new location.

Sincerely,

- Include your wish for their business success in the new office.
- Be as specific as possible, especially with customized designs that the tenant will be particularly proud of.

Congratulations on Expansion of Business (3-12)

Dear Larry:

On my sales call to your restaurant last week, I noticed that you were breaking ground for an addition. Congratulations on the expansion of your business.

Please let me know if I can be of any help in meeting your increasing needs for Tres Equis Beer. I look forward to working with you in serving your additional customers.

Sincerely,

- Compliment the owner or manager on the obvious success of the business.
- Express an interest in serving the additional business, if appropriate.

Enjoyed Your Article/Speech (3-13)

Dear Dr. Rowe:

I very much enjoyed your article about the value of "orphan drugs" in the Sunday, March 15 edition of *The Plain Dealer*. I completely agree with you that our society will be in trouble unless something is done to stimulate the continued production of these drugs.

I am a distributor of one of these drugs, TRX-94, and I would like very much to speak with you about some of the points you discussed. I'll call you next week to see if we can arrange a convenient time to meet.

Sincerely,

- State where you read the article and what you enjoyed about it.
- Make clear your connection with the topic, especially if you anticipate further contact. You want the letter's recipient to think about your interests before such contact.

Appreciation of Business Suggestion (3-14)

Dear Mr. Unger:

Thank you for your letter suggesting that we have a pick-up and delivery service for our dry cleaning stores. I think it's a good idea, and my partners and I will be looking into the feasibility of having such a service.

We at Hawley Dry Cleaning are always looking for ways to improve our services to our customers.

We appreciate your taking the time to write us. Thank you for your continued patronage of our stores.

Sincerely,

- Express appreciation for any suggestion that a customer thinks will improve your business.
- If you have taken action due to the suggestion, state what you've done.
- Express thanks for their being a customer.

Acknowledgment of Compliment to Company/Employee (3-15)

Dear Mr. Farmer:

Thank you for writing and letting us know how much you enjoyed staying at Cypress House during your recent visit to Charleston. My wife, Betty, and I both take great pride in the restorations we have made to Cypress House; we are happy that our guests enjoy what we have done.

I'm enclosing the recipe for She-Crab Soup that you requested. Jim Tate, our chef, was delighted when I relayed to him how much you enjoyed the soup.

It was a pleasure having you here with us, and all of us at Cypress House hope that you'll visit us again in the near future.

Best wishes,

- Express appreciation for the business, as well as the compliment, and ask for continued patronage.

- Make the reply as personal as possible and show that you have valued the compliment enough to relay it to those responsible in your business.

Setting Up Meeting (3-16)

Dear George:

It was a pleasure catching up with you on Thursday and hearing that Robomatix wants to proceed with training for mid-level managers. I'm sure we can put together a program that is every bit as successful as the one we did for your support staff last year.

I believe we could proceed most quickly and productively if you, Marty, Gene, and I got together for a few hours one day next week to discuss program development, scheduling, and costs. By then I'll have developed a few possible program formats that can serve as the basis for our discussion about just what type of program best meets the company's objectives.

Either Tuesday, Wednesday, or Thursday of next week is fine for me—I'll leave it up to you, Gene, and Marty to choose a date and time that is most convenient for you. I'll call you on Friday after you've had a chance to check your schedules.

I look forward to seeing you again soon.

Best regards,

- Be sure to mention what you hope to accomplish at the meeting (informal agenda) as well as who should be there.

- Show willingness and flexibility to work within others' schedules.

- Set a time to confirm plans.

Confirmation of Meeting (3-17)

Dear George:

I'm glad you, Gene, and Marty all have time available next Tuesday morning, May 8, to discuss the program for mid-level managers. I'll be at your office at 10 so we'll have a few minutes to review the formats I've developed before we all meet at 10:30.

I'm planning to bring a few overheads with me to give you all an idea of the teaching materials I've found particularly effective with groups like yours. Can we arrange for a small conference room with an overhead projector?

I look forward to seeing you again and to moving ahead with plans when we meet next week. Thanks for making it all happen.

Best regards,

- State the date, time, and location of your meeting.
- Mention any equipment you need and why you need it.
- Express appreciation to the person who set up the meeting.

Request for Associate to Attend Meeting (3-18)

Dear Mr. Gates:

Thank you for choosing NC Advertising for your expansion campaign. We look forward to working with you in making the next year the best in HiTech's history.

May I bring along my associate, Pauline Green, when we meet on Wednesday, April 25? Pauline is our expert on promoting service businesses, and she'll be able to highlight the areas your company should emphasize in your promotions.

Sincerely,

- Give a reason why your associate will be an asset at the meeting.
- Touting an associate's or subordinate's expertise enhances the image you project, demonstrating your security and self-confidence in your own position.

Setting Up Appointment (3-19)

Dear Miss Waite:

It was a pleasure speaking with you on the phone last week. Thank you for your interest in Daisy Diaper Covers. It's always cheering to find people who care about the ecology and want to avoid disposable diapers. We are the revolutionary alternative to diaper pins and rubber pants. As our enclosed brochure explains, our patented design allows air to circulate but won't let wetness pass through, so clothes are kept dry while heat does not build up in the diapers, reducing the chance of diaper rash. Our velcro fasteners make changes easy and eliminate sharp pins.

I will be in your area the week of April 15. May I stop by at 2:30 p.m. on Wednesday, April 17, to show you some of our samples and answer any questions you may have about our diaper covers? I will call next week to confirm with you that this time is convenient for you. I look forward to meeting you.

Sincerely,

- Be specific as to the time, date, place, and purpose of the appointment.
- Set up a time to confirm the appointment.

Confirmation of Appointment (3-20)

Dear Cynthia and John:

Thank you for calling and letting me know that you're interested in putting your condominium on the market. I would be very pleased to represent you in this sale. I look forward to coming over to appraise your place and to providing you with a comparative market analysis. I'll also discuss with you how I can help you get the best possible exposure and the best possible price for your property.

As we agreed over the phone, I'll be at your condominium next Thursday at 2:00 p.m.

Very truly yours,

- State the date, time, and place of the appointment, as well as what you hope to achieve.

Thank You for Meeting (3-21)

Dear Mike:

It was a pleasure meeting with you last Friday. Thank you for letting me show you how Coleman Productions can handle all your program needs and improve your video productions.

I'm enclosing the literature that you requested on our computer graphics and animation services along with a copy of our demo tape, which I thought you'd find interesting. I will call you next week to see whether you have any questions. I look forward to exploring the possibilities of our working together.

Sincerely yours,

- Follow up on what occurred during the meeting (e.g., request for more information) in order to get more contact if your aim is to solicit business.
- Be assertive but don't act, particularly early in a relationship, as if doing business is a certainty.

Thank You for Setting Up Sales Call (3-22)

Dear Mr. Stephens:

Thanks for all your help setting up my appearance at the regional business development meeting today. I feel that it went very well and that you deserve a great deal of the credit.

I have one favor to ask. Is it possible for someone to send me a list of the people who attended the meeting? I generally create a seating chart so I can link names and faces, but unfortunately I had no time to do that. If it's easier, just jot the names at the bottom of this letter and return it to me. Again, thank you very much.

Best wishes,

- Get the thank-you up front and reinforce it at the end.
- Since names are all important in sales (in life?), asking for a list of attendees is perfectly appropriate (and essential for follow-ups).
- Asking the reader to reply by writing on the letter itself makes a prompt response likely.

Apology to Customer for Missing Meeting (3-23)

Dear Kyle:

I'm sorry I missed our meeting last Tuesday. As I explained to your secretary over the phone, all flights out of Boston on Monday and Tuesday were canceled due to the snow storm we had. I'm glad my colleagues from Atlanta were there to present our proposal to you. I have already spoken with them, and they have briefed me on the concerns you expressed during the meeting about the scheduled delivery dates. I'm researching that right now, and I'll call you on Monday with some answers.

I would also like to schedule another meeting with you before the end of March. Is the morning of March 26 convenient for you?

Sincerely,

- Explain why you missed the meeting.
- If the meeting went on as scheduled without you, get information as to what went on and what your responsiblities, if any, are.
- Schedule another meeting if necessary.

Apology to Business Associate for Missing Appointment (3-24)

Dear Dwayne:

Please forgive me for missing our lunch Tuesday. My problem was an overturned tractor trailer on I-95. You may have heard about it on the news. Had I been near an exit, I might have had a shot at it, but as it was, I sat in my car for close to two hours.

Then, when I finally got to New York, I heard you had already left for your cruise. I hope that you'll forgive me and that we can try to meet again when you return.

Best wishes,

- Apologies are best delivered on the phone or in person. In this case, that obviously wasn't possible. Next best is a hand-written note on personal stationery. For a business associate, company letterhead is also an alternative.

Check Returned, Polite Request for Payment (3-25)

Dear Ms. Jackson:

I've enclosed your check for #325 for $532.23, which was returned by your bank because of "insufficient funds." Because I'm sure this problem is the result of an oversight or some mistake on the bank's part, please call me at 655-3241 and tell me how to proceed.

Sincerely,

- People are funny about having their honesty called into question. If you have a long-standing relationship with the customer and there is no history of previous problems, a polite letter like this one will get the results you want.

Check Returned, Firm Request for Payment (3-26)

Dear Ms. Jackson:

On April 4, we redeposited your check #325 for $532.23, as you requested in our April 3 phone conversation, and it has again been returned to us marked "insufficient funds." We are sure this is as embarrassing for you as it is frustrating for us, but we must insist that you call us immediately and make arrangements to pay your bill by money order or cashier's check so that we may keep your account current.

Sincerely,

- Switching from "I" to "We" (meaning the firm) makes this letter sound sterner.

- A check that has been returned a second time is a signal that your once-solid customer may be having financial difficulties. But if he or she pays up at this point you may want to forget the matter.

Check Returned, Warning of Collection Agency (3-27)

Dear Ms. Jackson:

We have not heard from you since your check (#325) for $532.23 was returned by your bank a second time. If we do not receive payment within seven days, we will have to place your account with a collection agency, with all the unpleasantness (and damage to your credit rating) that this implies.

Sincerely,

- Transferring an account to a collection agency will assure that you've lost your customer, so you should provide the customer with one more chance to pay before doing so.

Thank You for Prompt Payment (3-28)

Dear Ms. Pearl:

On May 10, we received your payment of $95.00 for April lawnmowing and weeding services. We have noticed that in the year you've been our customer, you have paid well in advance of the 15th every single month. We'd like to reward your promptness—this kind of payment schedule is an immeasurable help in running our business.

Starting with this month, we'll deduct 2% from your monthly bill each time you pay by the 15th.

Thank you again for your patronage.

Best wishes,

- Reliable, loyal customers should be rewarded. A simple "thank you" might have been enough in this case, but issuing a small discount packs more of a wallop.
- In small firms, the president should sign the letter.

Thank You for Payment, Other Products/Services of Interest (3-29)

Dear Ms. Ford:

Thank you for your payment of $73.95 for your recent order of swimming pool supplies. You might like to know more about our swimming pool maintenance contract, which spares you the task of carrying heavy containers of chlorine and algacide and ensures that your pool is at all times clean and safe. In your area, a pool maintenance contract usually includes a twice-monthly visit by one of our professional service people as well as all necessary supplies. The actual cost varies depending on the size and location of your pool, but it is usually about the same expense as performing the work yourself.

Mr. John Hardy, the professional responsible for your area, will be maintaining the pool of one of your neighbors next week, and he will call you to see if you would like a free estimate.

Sincerely,

- Try to interest the customer by filling a need—in this case, one implied by the need to carry heavy containers of pool cleaning supplies.

- If you promise someone will call, set up some system to ensure that they actually do so.

Discount for Early Payment (3-30)

Dear Ms. Tate:

Enclosed are the table linens you ordered on April 10 and our invoice #MFL-4X09 for $898.37. Please note that if we receive payment within 10 days, you may discount the invoice by 4%. This discount is double our usual 2% discount and is available only during this quarter, so I urge you to take advantage of it.

We hope you enjoy the linens and that you will call us with another order soon.

Yours very truly,

- Offer a special discount for early payment when cash flow is a concern.

- Let the customer know right away what he/she did to qualify for the discount—stating your time requirement exactly.

- Urge the customer to take advantage of the opportunity.

Payment Received, Pre-payment Required in the Future (3-31)

Dear Mr. Bloom:

Today we received your payment of $550.00 for catering services we performed at your Christmas party. Unfortunately, this is the third time you have paid for our catering services more than 60 days after the date of the invoice, despite our stated policy of payment within 10 days. As you can understand, a small business like ours must pay close attention to cash flow. Our suppliers demand cash up front, and we must have sufficient cash on hand to pay them.

In the future, we'll have to require that you pay for our catering services in advance. After a year, we'll be glad to reconsider our position since you have been a good customer in the past.

Sincerely,

Payment Incorrect, Will Credit Next Statement (3-32)

Dear Mr. Boone:

We have received your check #9749 for $1,610.24 in payment of our May statement. Although our statement showed shipping charges, Cape May was entitled to deduct this cost ($77.24) because the statement was paid within seven days. We have credited your account for these charges, and the credit will be reflected on your June statement.

If you have any questions, or if we can be of further service, please call us at the telephone number below.

Sincerely,

- Customers delight in being told that they're due money, and it reflects well on the supplier if you notice the error and credit the customer promptly.

- Avoid making the customer feel that he or she made a stupid mistake.

Payment Incorrect, Will Debit Account (3-33)

Dear Ms. Robertson:

We received your check #540 for $48.00 for our driveway plowing last month. I think you must have overlooked the usual surcharge of $12 for plowing after the second storm, when the snowfall exceeded 8 inches.

There's no need to pay us separately for the surcharge; we will add it to SnowBusters' next monthly statement.

Thank you for your patronage.

Sincerely,

- Even if an unpaid item was clearly stated on an invoice, assume an inadvertent oversight if dealing with a regular customer. (People sometimes don't read statements carefully.)

- Reminding a customer of your reasonable attitude reflects well on your company and will build good will.

Payment Incorrect, Send Balance (3-34)

Dear Accounts Payable Supervisor:

We have received your payment of $198.54 (check #2361) for our invoice #002189. Unfortunately, you have a balance due of $12.30 because you have overlooked the relevant tax and freight charges.

Please send your check as soon as possible so that we can stop the computer's collection letter sequence, which most people find extremely annoying.

Very truly yours,

- It's better to have a person's name, even for form letters, but this salutation is better than "Gentlemen."
- Be sure to include all relevant information: amount paid, check number, and invoice number.
- The ending sentence humanizes the "form" letter.

Overpayment, Check Enclosed (3-35)

Dear Mr. Hillhouse:

Enclosed is our check #2032 for $212.50. You apparently paid your June bill for computer services twice, resulting in an overpayment of that amount. Ordinarily, we would give you a credit, but since you have plans to close the office for the months of July and August, we believe you would prefer to have a check.

Have a good vacation.

Best wishes,

- Most customers do not object to receiving a credit. You must provide a check if the customer requests one, however.
- In this case, the writer knows the customer personally, so wishing him a good holiday is totally appropriate.

Duplicate Invoice Provided as Requested (3-36)

Dear Mrs. Stargis:

As requested, here is a copy of our invoice #2160543 for the merchandise we shipped to you on March 17. I've also enclosed a copy of our newest catalog; we welcome your next order and hope that you will call us whenever we can help you.

Yours very truly,

Acknowledgment of Return for Exchange (3-37)

Dear Mr. Walters:

We received your return of the model 42Z11 Zip-o-mat power saw (invoice #120211) and are happy to exchange it for model 51X12, which we hope is more suitable to your needs. Since model 51X12 is priced lower than model 42Z11 (at $89.95), we have credited your account $20.00.

I've enclosed a copy of our new spring catalog in which we feature a new line of small handheld power tools that appeals to home woodworking enthusiasts like yourself. Please call at 1-800-555-6660 or use the form in the catalog whenever you would like to place another order.

Sincerely,

Acknowledgment of Return for Credit (3-38)

Dear Mr. Jarvis:

We are sorry to hear the model 1240G Deluxe Router we shipped you on March 4 (invoice #22610) did not fulfill your expectations and are happy to credit your account $129.98 for its return.

I've enclosed a copy of our new spring catalog. We feature a complete line of power tools designed specifically for the home woodworker. Please use this catalog's order form or call us at 1-800-555-6660 whenever we can help you with another order.

Sincerely,

Acknowledgment of Refund for Damaged Goods (3-39)

Dear Mr. LaPointe:

We're sorry the model 182CZ handdrill you ordered (invoice #26675) did not arrive safely and are happy to refund your $62.95 (enclosed check #8669). Unfortunately, we have no more model 182CZ drills in stock, since we discontinued the line this spring.

Here is a copy of our new summer catalog, which features a complete line of tools for the home woodworker. Model 184CZ (p. 22) is closest in price and speed to the 182CZ. We hope you will consider ordering the 184CZ, which has two more drill bits than the older model.

We apologize for any inconvenience you suffered and hope we will have another opportunity to ship you one of our fine products.

Sincerely,

- Express sincere apologies for any customer dissatisfaction.

- Refer specifically to order, invoice, and check numbers and amounts.

- Show interest in continuing the customer relationship by suggesting other suitable products.

No Record of Returned Goods (3-40)

Dear Ms. Bovan:

I'm glad you called to check on the status of the 25 sweaters you sent back to us two weeks ago. After checking our records carefully, I find that we have not received your returned sweaters. Please contact your shipper to start tracing the shipment. I'm sorry, but we cannot be responsible for returned goods that are lost in transit. However, if you send me the details in writing (sales order number, shipping company name, shipment number, date it was shipped, etc.), I will gladly help you trace it from this end.

Please keep me posted. We value your business and look forward to assisting you whenever possible.

Sincerely,

- Be clear as to who will be responsible if the returned goods are not located.

- Express interest in resolving the matter and in helping when possible.

Handling Customer Complaints 4

There are no complaint-free businesses. In fact, dissatisfied customers who silently take business elsewhere are a far worse problem than those who complain. A customer who complains can usually be salvaged. Businesses should take the time to solicit feedback from their customers, especially unhappy ones.

Ideally, complaints should be handled on the phone. A customer's complaint can best be understood in a conversation. If the customer cannot be reached, or a discussion doesn't resolve the situation, a letter is required. In any case, a letter confirming the details of the conversation should be sent.

Whether the customer's complaint has any basis or not, the letter writer needs to acknowledge in some way that the company welcomes hearing from the customer for any reason. Even seemingly frivolous complaints can reveal significant needs for improvement in customer relations. The tone of the letter should reflect the fact that company people are approachable and ready to help if possible.

Justified complaints. If the complaint is justified, the company should respond immediately, offering to "make things right" if possible, or offering alternative solutions if that's not possible. The tone should not be defensive or cringing. After all, mistakes happen, even in the best run company. If the company has made an error, admit it promptly and make amends as best you can. Because customers are so accustomed to shabby treatment, promptness in satisfying them may even make them into public relations people for your firm. They may comment to others on the company's unusual responsiveness.

Partially justified complaints. The key here is in the approach you take. Focus on the fact that the customer is partially right. Ignore the fact that this also makes him or her partially wrong. It's far harder to get a new customer than to keep the good will of an old customer. If there's any element of truth in what the customer is saying, it is better to agree (and make things right, even if it costs money) than it is to get into a no-win argument. Similarly, in cases of misunderstanding, the thrust is for the company to take at least part of the responsibility (a miscommunication has two possible causes— a garbled message or an inattentive receiver.)

Unjustified complaints. If you believe the customer is unjustified, ask for clarification—it may be that he has not expressed himself well and the complaint is the result of a simple misunderstanding that can be easily cleared up. If you are unable to respond positively, an honest, straightforward "no," along with the reasons for the refusal, is best. If the company is not responsible, suggest the action the customer can take to get satisfaction elsewhere, without actually blaming someone else. It's unlikely the customer is trying to cheat the company, and accusing him of that will ensure undying enmity. This type of ill will can spread to other customers of your company.

To sum up, respond positively and promptly to all complaints—and consider even the most vituperative attack as providing valuable information about customer relations.

Clarification of Billing (4-01)

Dear Mr. Delaplaine:

Here's the breakdown that you requested of the billing on your sound system (PO #88177-B, Factory Order 96N-00182):

Suborder	Description	Amount
1GA	amplifier	$ 106.24
2GA	turntable	$ 261.89
3GA	speakers	$ 649.41
	Subtotal:	$ 1,017.54
	State tax (5%):	$ 50.88
	Freight:	$ 17.50
	Total:	$ 1,085.92

I hope this will allow you to pay the invoice. If you have any further questions, please call me at 889-6249.

Respectfully yours,

- Be clear—show all discounts, taxes, freight, etc.
- State your expectations—that the customer will either pay the invoice or call.

Apology for Billing Error (4-02)

Dear Mr. Feinstein:

I would like to apologize for the error we made on our invoice DCI-92J, dated June 15. I'm canceling that invoice and reinvoicing you as follows:

12	tables @ $11.48 each	$137.76
48	chairs @ $2.05 each	98.40
12	tablecloths @ $1.88 each	22.56
24	5-piece place settings @ $3.24 each	77.76
	Subtotal	$336.48
	Tax (4.5%)	15.14
	Total	$351.62

I hope this resolves the issue to your satisfaction. I look forward to doing more business with you in the future.

Sincerely,

- Explain what action you will take (reinvoice, credit, accept deduction, etc.)
- Solicit more business.

Apology for Computer Error (4-03)

Dear Mr. Hudak:

Thank you for calling last week regarding our error in your billing last month. Your check (#489) was credited to the wrong account due to an error in our computer records. I have corrected the situation, and I'm very sorry for the inconvenience that our error has caused.

Please take a moment to review our records and confirm that we now have your information correctly in our computer:

Cardholder:	Robert J. Hudak
Address:	45 Yankee Peddler Path
	Madison, CT 06443
Home phone:	(203) 555-4872
Work phone:	(203) 555-6079
Account number:	128-9771-553

Thank you for your understanding. We look forward to serving you in the future.

Sincerely,

- Apologize for the error.
- State the action you took or to be taken by another party (e.g., submit corrected information).
- Confirm the correctness of your present records.

Apology for Delay in Shipment (4-04)

Dear Mr. Kebebian:

I'm sorry that we have not been able to deliver as scheduled your shipment of rugs from India. Unfortunately, the dock workers' strike in New York has prevented the unloading of the ship. I expect that the strike will be over soon and that we can deliver your shipment within the next month.

I apologize for the delay and inconvenience this has caused you. I will notify you as soon the strike is over.

Very truly yours,

- Explain the reason for the delay.
- Give your best estimate of reschedule.
- Express empathy, whether the delay is caused by you or by others.

Apology for Error in Shipment (4-05)

Dear Mr. Walton:

I'm sorry we sent you the Mahogany Queen Anne Footstool Kit (No. 347A) instead of the Cherry Queen Anne Footstool Kit (No. 347B) that you ordered. I am sending you the correct kit today. Please return the mahogany kit to us by UPS with insurance; we will reimburse you for all shipping costs.

Again, I apologize for the inconvenience this has caused you. Thank you for your help and understanding. We truly appreciate your business and look forward to serving you again in the near future.

Sincerely,

- Acknowledge the error and express your apology.
- Say what you have done and/or what the customer should do to corrrect the error.

Apology for Damaged Shipment (4-06)

Dear Mr. Young:

I'm sorry to learn about the damage to the sofa that you purchased from us last month. Our driver has determined that the damage occurred in shipment (most likely from the manufacturer's warehouse to our store).

I've ordered an exact replacement from the factory, and I've been told that it will take four to six weeks to get here. I'll call you as soon as it arrives, and we will arrange a convenient time for delivery.

I am very sorry for the inconvenience this has caused you. I'll be in touch very soon.

Sincerely,

- Acknowledge the party responsible for the damage.
- Outline corrective action taken or to be taken.
- Make sure that you follow up as promised.

Apology for Employee Rudeness (4-07)

Dear Mrs. Jackson:

Please accept my sincerest apologies for the rudeness you experienced at our restaurant last night. There was no excuse for the way you were treated, and the person involved is no longer employed at PJ Willy's. PJ Willy's prides itself on being a family restaurant where good food and good service are always "on the menu."

I hope that you will try us again. Please call me at 459-3398, and I will be very happy to take your reservations for a dinner for two on the house. Thank you for your understanding and for bringing this matter to my attention.

Very truly yours,

- Acknowledge and apologize for the rudeness.
- Outline the corrective action to be taken.
- Ask the customer to try you again and offer an incentive (a free dinner) for doing so.

Apology for Missing Documentation (4-08)

Dear Mr. Blakely:

I am sorry that the instruction manual for operating your new Frostee-Lite ice cream maker was missing. I am sending you a new manual along with a booklet of recipes for some wonderful ice cream and sherbet delights that you might like to try.

Thank you for your understanding and for selecting Frostee-Lite. I'm sure you will be very pleased with your new ice cream maker.

Sincerely,

- Apologize for the missing documentation.
- Enclose the missing documentation.
- Express appreciation for the business.

Company Not at Fault (4-09)

Dear Mr. Marino:

We're sorry to learn of the damage to our latest solenoid shipment (PO# 77J-4P). You should file a damage claim with the trucking firm, as our standard terms and conditions of sale state "FOB factory." Our responsibility therefore ends when the trucker signs for the shipment. I have enclosed a copy of the trucker's pick-up slip, showing that the shipment was in good condition, in case this will help you in filing a claim.

We have enough stock on hand to reship your order. If you would like us to do so, please call us with a purchase order.

Sincerely,

- State clearly who is and who is not responsible.
- Be as helpful as possible to the customer.
- Express empathy.

Company Not Responsible for Delay in Shipment (4-10)

Dear Mr. Mallion:

Thank you for writing us about your irritation concerning the delay in CSC's receipt of four (4) MacDonald Customized Video Display Terminals (CSC PO# 3214; our invoice #80-1219-G).

The delay, however, was not caused at our end. As specified in your Purchase Order, we shipped via Transcontinental Truckers before July 14. The terminals were actually picked up on July 12, as you can see from the enclosed copy of the bill of lading (Transcontinental #55-MC-9906).

Unless I have misunderstood something, it appears that Transcontinental is responsible for the delay. Please let me know if I may help further in this matter.

Sincerely,

- Acknowledge the customer's complaint. Reference all purchase orders, invoices, etc.
- Be direct about where the fault (if any) lies.
- Appear flexible; there may be additional issues the customer will raise subsequently.

Company Not Responsible for Rudeness (4-11)

Dear Miss deWinter:

I'm sorry to hear about the rudeness you experienced while shopping at our store. I wish there was something we could do to prevent such unpleasant events from occurring but, unfortunately, we cannot always observe peculiar behavior in people who come through our store, or intercept them as an incident develops.

I hope this incident will not give you a bad impression of Fashion Fair stores. We value you as a customer, and I look forward to seeing you again.

Sincerely,

- Express understanding for the customer's feelings.
- Establish that there was nothing you could have done to prevent the rudeness from occurring.
- Express hope that the incident will not affect your customer's patronage and that he or she will try you again.

Customer Misunderstood Delivery Time (4-12)

Dear Mr. D'Attalo:

Thank you for calling to check on the status of the shirts you ordered from us (Item 53J, Order #29746) three weeks ago (July 28). I have looked into your order, and everything is on schedule. Perhaps you did not notice that on the bottom of the order form we have noted that any items that are monogrammed, such as your shirts, will require a delivery time of four to five weeks instead of the usual two to three weeks.

Your shirts should be arriving next week. I believe that you will be very satisfied with your Wellington Bay shirts. Please let me know if I can be of any further assistance.

Sincerely,

- Clarify what the delivery time is for the order.
- Refer to the item as specifically as possible (Sales# or PO#, etc.).
- Express goodwill and willingness to help out further.

Customer Misunderstood Terms of Sale (4-13)

Dear Mr. Rew:

I've tried to reach you by phone because I feel problems should be dealt with in person. However, I have been unable to catch you at home this last week, and I don't want our disagreement to go on much longer.

I understand from J. C. Gilbert, our stylist, that you were very unhappy with Radar's grooming last Monday. She said you felt we had "dandified" and "emasculated" Radar by putting him in a "business suit." As we discussed when you brought Radar in, Airedales cost $20 more to groom because their clip is very difficult. For example, they must retain "eyebrows," always difficult to achieve with such energetic dogs. During our conversation, I felt you were familiar with the way Airedales looked after they had been clipped. I'm very sorry for the misunderstanding.

Nevertheless, I must insist you pay your account in full. We spent considerable time removing burrs and snarls and gave Radar a flea bath as well as clipping him. I'm afraid the aesthetics of the cut have no bearing on the necessity to pay for work performed.

I look forward to receiving your check for $40.00 as soon as possible.

Sincerely,

- Acknowledge that the customer may have misunderstood, and detail clearly the work performed, but firmly insist on your right to payment.

Customer Misunderstood Terms of Sale, Special Order (4-14)

Dear Miss Steinkraus:

Along with this letter, I'm sending back the sheets (Sales #4503) that you returned to us. I'm sorry to hear that they were not the color you expected, especially since there were color swatches as well as color photographs of the sheets in the catalog. Unfortunately, as we have indicated in large type on the bottom of our order form, we cannot accept any items for return or exchange that have been monogrammed, unless there is a defect in either the material or workmanship.

I apologize for the inconvenience our policy has caused you. Thank you for your understanding.

Sincerely,

- Outline the terms of sale specifically and indicate where that information is located in the sales literature that the customer already has (e.g., the order form, the catalog).
- Clarify the misunderstanding.
- Express goodwill.

Customer Misunderstood Product Specifications, Features Explained (4-15)

Dear Mr. Stang:

I am sorry to hear you are dissatisfied with the capacity of your Patsy Ice Cream Maker, Model IC-BIG, which makes one quart. I cannot understand why you thought it would make a half-gallon since our ad, the box and the owner's manual clearly state the quantity that each operating cycle will produce is one quart.

I think that your using the Patsy Model IC-BIG you will find that the one quart capacity is quite convenient. Also, since the operating cycle is only 30 minutes, another batch can be prepared quickly.

Sincerely,

- Clarify the misunderstanding by stating the product specifications and where the information can be found in the sales literature.
- If possible, explain why the product specifications are positive features.

Customer Misunderstood Product Specifications, Return Authorized (4-16)

Dear Mrs. Yamamoto:

I have received your letter concerning the A-Pro 1900 hairdryer that you recently purchased. I'm sorry that you misunderstood the product specifications. As indicated in the sales literature, the hairdryer is designed to be used only on 115 volts, 60 hertz electrical current; it cannot be used on 220 volts, 50 hertz current.

Our policy is to accept authorized returns within 30 days of purchase if the product is returned in the original box. I have enclosed a shipping label for your convenience.

If you wish, we will send you a refund check for $28.95 upon receipt of the hairdryer. However, if you are interested in a hairdryer that runs on 220 volts, 50 hertz electrical current, I suggest the A-Pro 2400 model. It is very similar to the A-Pro 1900 and lists for the same price, $28.95. We also carry a model that can be used on both 115 volts and 220 volts, the A-Pro 3500. It is extremely popular and lists for $36.95. Please write me or call our toll-free, 24-hour number, (800) 555-6000, if you wish to make arrangements about either of these models. We can ship the 2400 model at no cost to you or the 3500 model upon receipt of an additional $8.00 (in both cases, upon receipt of the 1900 model you now have).

Sincerely,

- Acknowledge the customer's specific complaint and state the courses of action available.

- If you have other products that fit the customer's needs, steer the customer toward them. The customer will be more satisfied, and you'll have kept the sale.

Customer Misunderstood Product Specifications, Return Not Possible (4-17)

Dear Miss Hemeyer:

I'm sorry to hear of the damage to your A-Pro 1900 hairdryer during your trip to Italy. Unfortunately, we cannot be held responsible for this damage, which occurred because the hairdryer was plugged into a 220 volt, 50 hertz electrical outlet. As specifically indicated on the box, on the documentation inside the box, and on the actual product, the A-Pro 1900 is designed to be used only on 115 volt, 60 hertz electrical current. No return is therefore possible.

Sincerely yours,

- Clarify the product specifications and indicate where they can be found in the sales literature.

- Explain why no return is possible.

Customer Misunderstood Delivery Terms (4-18)

Dear Mr. Metz:

I'm glad to hear that you are pleased with the quality of sharpening that EdgeTech has provided. I hope that you will give us the opportunity to serve you again.

I'd like to clarify a misunderstanding we may have had regarding delivery terms and turn-around time. The rates that we quoted you for the sharpening of your surgical instruments is based on the normal Wednesday afternoon pickup from your office and delivery to your office on the following Monday morning by our representative. If you require a pickup other than on Wednesday afternoon, there is a special charge of $10.00 per order, but the sharpening price is still the same as quoted per surgical instrument. If you require an overnight turnaround, there is again a special pickup charge of $10.00 and, in addition, the sharpening rates are 15% above the regular quoted rates.

Please let me know if you have any questions. I look forward to your business.

Sincerely,

- Specifically state the delivery terms in question and clarify the misunderstanding.

- Express appreciation for the business.

Response to Customer Who Is Threatening Legal Action (4-19)

Dear Ms. Johnson:

Larry Crosby, our Credit and Collections Manager, has told me of your intense dissatisfaction with the way your father's recent auto repair was handled here in our shop.

I am terribly sorry that you and your family have had these difficulties. Please be sure that I will give the entire matter a very thorough review. Mr. Johnson's repairs were extremely complicated. It will take me some time to review this with the mechanics involved and the Shop Manager, but after I have completed my investigation, I would very much like to meet with you and your father to discuss the problem he experienced. Is there a possibility that you will be visiting your parents over the holidays? If so, perhaps we can arrange a mutually convenient time to meet.

I asked Mr. Crosby to hold up any further collection proceedings until I have discussed the matter with you and your father in person. I will be in touch as soon as I have completed my review. I would appreciate your speaking to your attorney as soon as possible to delay the legal action he contemplates—that would serve no one's best interests.

Sincerely yours,

- No one really wants legal action. Try to forestall it by offering to establish the facts and have a face-to-face discussion.

- The tone should be reasonable but not apologetic. You do not know if your company is at fault or what action you wish to take if it is. Do not make specific reference to the "facts." If they disagree with the customer's version, you'll engender hostility.

Credit and Collections 5

Strangely enough, when matters of credit and collection come up, businesspeople often forget that they are writing to other human beings. More than that, they forget that they are writing to *customers*, people whose business they value. It is absolutely essential that you treat everyone with courtesy and understanding, and that includes customers who have not paid their bills or customers to whom you cannot yet extend credit for one reason or another.

In fact, the collection process begins with the sale. Overselling—selling to someone who truly cannot afford an item or a service or to someone who doesn't need the item or service—often creates massive problems later on. Credit and collections are actually part of the selling process, since the sale is not really complete until the seller receives payment.

Credit letters. Many people have been offended or hurt by the way creditors have dealt with them in the past. As a result, refusing credit is a very ticklish issue, and the tone of any letter should be extremely sensitive. Offering to provide credit after the customer has established a track record is a good way to present the bad news positively. Remember, though, that you do no one a favor if you extend credit to someone who is truly not creditworthy.

Collection letters. To avoid having to write collection letters in the first place, make it as easy as possible for the customer to pay on time by offering discounts for timely payment, by providing self-addressed envelopes, or by making it an option to charge the payment to a major credit card. The easier you make it, the more likely you are to get what you want—first, attention to your bill among the plethora of pieces anyone receives in the course of the day and second, actual and prompt payment.

If your customer is late in paying, however, you need to establish an automatic sequence of collection letters. It has been documented that the longer the customer goes without paying, the less likely you are to see any payment, even if you turn the account over to a collection agency. Collection sequences follow a standard pattern—notification or reminder, inquiry, appeal, demand, ultimatum. It's correct to start any collection sequence with a notification that payment has not been received (a statement of fact) and an inquiry as to whether a problem exists.

Despite all the "the check is in the mail" jokes, someone may not have paid because of events beyond his or her control. The U. S. Postal Service may be at fault or the business or person may have moved or be on vacation. If a personal tragedy has occurred (a death in the family perhaps), sending a hostile letter will not only lose you a customer, but may blacken your reputation with other potential customers.

Of course, if you ask people whether there's a problem, they may actually respond by calling and telling you what it is. Although this is precisely what you want (you want to keep the communication going at almost any cost), you'll need to have someone available to talk with them and possibly to negotiate an extended payment schedule.

If your reminder and/or inquiry doesn't work (the two letters are frequently combined), then you'll need to have a letter that appeals to the customer's sense of fair play. You have provided a service or a product; the customer owes you something in return. You then proceed to demanding payment and to an ultimate threat to turn the account over to a collection agency. At each stage, though, whether you adopt the moderate tone of the first sequence of letters or the stern tone of the second sequence, keep your determination to treat the customer with sensitivity and honesty. Treating a slow payer with politeness is difficult, but the ability to do so may preserve that customer's goodwill in the future.

Request to Customer to Complete Credit Application (5-01)

Dear Mr. Maxham:

We're pleased to hear you'd like to establish a credit account with H. R. Stoneham Corporation and look forward to the opportunity to serve you on an ongoing basis.

We do require that credit applicants complete the enclosed application form before receiving formal credit approval. Once we've received your completed form we'll notify you within three weeks regarding its acceptance.

If you have any questions about the form or our approval requirements, please call me at 1-800-555-4269. I will be pleased to help you provide the information we need.

Yours truly,

- Use a cordial tone to maintain a good relationship with an existing or potential customer and let the customer know you appreciate the patronage.
- Specify when the applicant can expect a decision.
- Let the applicant know how to request assistance.

Request to Customer for Financial Information (5-02)

Dear Mr. Miller:

Thank you for your purchase order ST-1950. So that we may extend our normal terms of net 30 days, please furnish us with the following information:

1. your annual report

2. name of your bank, account number, and contact

3. names of two suppliers with whom you are presently doing business.

We look forward to serving you, and we feel that extending 30-day payment terms is part of that service. Thank you for your cooperation, and for your order.

Sincerely,

- Ask for the information (be specific) you need to make a good decision. Remember, it's your money that they are asking to use!
- Express appreciation for their cooperation and for their business.

Request for Credit Report on Individual (5-03)

Dear Ms. Johanneson:

Thomas Slate (Acct. #2276052) has named your company as a credit reference in his application for an account with our store. We are now reviewing Mr. Slate's application and would appreciate your providing the following information regarding your experience as one of Mr. Slate's creditors:

- length of credit relationship
- amounts billed monthly and annually
- promptness in payment/delinquency

As soon as we receive this information, we can complete processing Mr. Slate's account. We would appreciate your prompt reply.

Thank you.

Sincerely,

- Give the name and account number of applicant.

- Specify information you need.

- Ask for prompt action, noting the importance of the report in your decision.

Request for Credit Report on Company (5-04)

Dear Mr. McCormick:

One of our credit applicants, Perkins/Neville Associates of Grand Rapids, MI, has named your company as a credit reference. Before extending credit to an applicant, we require information on that applicant's experience with other creditors. Would you please furnish a credit report on Perkins/Neville, including length of relationship, amounts billed annually, and promptness of payment?

We would appreciate your response soon so that we can complete our review of Perkins/Neville's application within a month.

Thank you for your cooperation.

Sincerely,

- Identify the credit applicant about whom you seek information.

- Specify information you need.

- Note the time span in which you need a response.

Approval of Credit, Retail (5-05)

Dear Ms. Vosburgh:

We at Temple Department Stores are pleased to welcome you as a Temple Card holder. We think you'll find the Temple Card opens the door to enjoying many valuable services, including easy credit terms and advance notice of special sales.

Please validate the enclosed Temple Card by signing your name in ink in the space indicated on the back. You can then use it when you shop in any one of our four stores in the greater Richmond area. We have also enclosed a copy of our credit terms specifying how your account will be billed each month.

Again, welcome to our family of Temple Card Holders!

Sincerely,

- Cordially welcome the new credit customer.
- State what the customer needs to know/do before using the account.
- Include written notice of credit terms.

Refusal of Credit, Commercial (5-06)

Dear Mr. Martin:

Thank you for your recent order. We have a long history of serving new businesses. Your initiative in providing low-cost homes in an urban setting is bound to draw a large clientele.

Because a steady cash flow is important to us, however, we approve very few credit accounts. Although the credit reference you provided is favorable, you will need to establish two more credit references to charge orders exceeding $1,000.

We do, though, offer a 5% discount on cash orders. Please indicate on the enclosed copy of your order form whether you want to place a cash order now.

We will review your application in three months. If at that time you have established additional references, we will accept a credit order.

We wish you the best of luck in your new endeavor.

Sincerely,

- Credit is refused for a variety of reasons. A regular customer may have fallen behind in payment. A young credit candidate or new business may have no credit history. A customer may have a history of being delinquent on credit payments.
- Exercise good judgment in refusing a candidate for credit to avoid legal action.

Refusal of Credit, Retail (5-07)

Dear Ms. Woodley:

Thank you for showing your interest in becoming a Thomas Furniture Mart credit account holder. We're happy to know you appreciate the fine quality of our merchandise as well as our wide selection of contemporary and traditional home furnishings.

We've received your application and are sorry that we cannot extend you credit at this time. One of our requirements for credit is that applicants have lived in the area for at least one year. As a newcomer to Marietta, you do not meet that requirement.

We hope, though, that you will continue to shop at Thomas's and that you will resubmit your application after you have met our residency requirement.

Sincerely,

- Thank the customer for the application.
- Refuse the request graciously and regretfully.
- Specify *why* the application was refused.
- Invite the applicant to try again should circumstances change.

Collection Letter, Moderate Tone, Letter #1 (5-08)

Dear Mr. Randall:

As of March 31, we have not received your February payment. Have you forgotten? Please check your records.

If you have already sent your payment, please disregard this notice and accept our thanks for your payment.

Sincerely,

- A first reminder for payment reflects your understanding that some minor problem may have delayed payment. You assume that the customer has every intention of paying and needs only to be reminded.

Collection Letter, Moderate Tone, Letter #2 (5-09)

Dear Mr. Randall:

You have been a valued customer for many years, and you have always been conscientious about paying your bills within the 30-day payment period.

Your good credit rating has enabled you to purchase from us on convenient payment terms at a substantial discount. Because of your prompt payment record, we have been glad to serve as a reference when you have applied for credit with other suppliers.

To keep your good credit rating and to continue receiving a substantial discount, payment of your account is necessary. Are you having some problem that we can help you with?

By sending your check for $350.00 in the enclosed stamped envelope, you will bring your account up-to-date and protect your credit rating. If this is not feasible, please call or write me today.

Sincerely,

- As frustrating as it is to send out a reminder and still get no response, assume that the customer has overlooked your payment request, or that other circumstances are preventing payment.
- Be specific as to the payment required and make it easy for the customer to pay you (the return envelope).

Collection Letter, Moderate Tone, Letter #3 (5-10)

Dear Mr. Randall:

This morning I received your file with a big OVERDUE stamped on it. I receive customer files only when some serious problem has occurred.

Your order was shipped over four months ago, and we still have not received a payment from you. As you are in business, Mr. Randall, you must realize that we cannot afford to carry this debt on our books any longer.

To preserve your credit privileges, please do one of the following:

- Remit the full amount of $350.00 today.
- Send us $150.00 as partial payment, with the balance payable by June 30.
- Explain your situation, and let us know what you can do to meet your obligation.

Your immediate response is necessary.

Sincerely,

- Avoid overt threats, but convey your desire to collect the overdue payment immediately. Having a senior company official sign the letter will signal urgency.
- Allow the customer to make a payment without losing face.

Collection Letter, Moderate Tone, Final Notice (5-11)

Dear Mr. Randall:

We are sending this letter to you with regret that previous efforts to obtain payment of your account have been unsuccessful.

We sent a bill for $350.00 for payment by March 1. Over the past four months, we have tried to get you to fulfill your obligations to us. We assumed, since you had an excellent credit rating and have always been responsible in paying your bills before, that some small oversight was to blame.

Please send us your payment for the overdue bill within five days so that we do not have to turn your account over to a collection agency.

Sincerely,

- Do not send an ultimatum unless you are able to back it up. By sending this letter, you can encourage customers to reevaluate their priorities. If their finances are in disorder, you will not get results until this stage.
- You are no longer interested in excuses, but only want your payment.

Collection Letter, Stern Tone, Letter #1 (5-12)

Dear Mr. and Mrs. Sternin:

We're delighted you're enjoying your new living room furniture, including our popular Relax-a-lounger. However, it has been two months now since we delivered your furniture, and we have yet to receive your payment for $2,375.60 (Invoice #46237, copy enclosed). Have you already put a check in the mail to us?

If not, please give this matter your attention today, since we want to be able to extend you credit the next time you shop for quality home furnishings.

Sincerely,

- A polite, cordial reminder encourages the customer to settle the matter immediately. You want to be paid *and* keep the customer.

Collection Letter, Stern Tone, Letter #2 (5-13)

Dear Mrs. and Mrs. Sternin:

Unfortunately, we still haven't received your $2,375.60 payment for merchandise you purchased January 5 (Invoice #46237, dated January 12). Because your account is three months past due, we are now forced to add a late charge of $23.75 in accordance with our credit policy. The new balance is $2,399.35.

Please be sure to settle your account with us today. If you have difficulty paying the full amount now, please call me today to discuss arranging a payment schedule.

Yours truly,

- Note *how* and *why* late charges were assessed.
- Offer to adjust the payment schedule. It's better to get the money slowly than not at all.

Collection Letter, Stern Tone, Letter #3 (5-14)

Dear Mr. and Mrs. Sternin:

Your letter has been referred to me by Claire McManus of our Billing Department. Because you have failed to make any payment on Invoice #46237 for $2,399.35 (including late charges) or to contact us to arrange a payment schedule, we have been forced to initiate procedures to repossess the furniture you bought at our store.

We will be contacting you to arrange a date for repossession if we do not receive full payment from you within two weeks. Please make every effort to ensure that we are not forced to take this drastic action.

Sincerely,

- Have the collection letter written by someone high in the company and threaten action only after repeated attempts to secure payment have failed and the customer has shown no intention of cooperating.
- Note that you regret the severity of your action, which leaves the door open for the customer to settle.

Collection Letter, Stern Tone, Letter #4 (5-15)

Dear Mr. and Mrs. Sternin:

Regrettably, we are forced to repossess the five items of furniture we delivered to you on January 5, due to your failure to pay the $2,399.35 you owe for them.

On May 5, representatives of our company will arrive at your home at 10 a.m. to collect:

(1)	queen-size sleep sofa (model 206G)
(1)	"Corona" coffee table
(2)	"Corona" end tables
(1)	"Relax-a-lounger" (model 460L)

We had hoped to avoid this extreme action by offering you flexible credit options to lessen the difficulty you face making payments. However, your unwillingness to cooperate with our billing department has left us no choice.

Sincerely,

- When notifying a customer of intent to repossess, list the items involved and set a date for repossession.
- Send the letter via certified mail, return receipt, so you will have evidence that the customer was aware of your intentions.

Collection Letter, Stern Tone, Letter #5 (5-16)

Dear Mr. and Mrs. Sternin:

We were unhappy to find that we could not gain admittance (to take delivery of our merchandise) when our representatives arrived at your home on May 5. R. Lane Peterson, our chief financial officer, has turned over your file to me, and, as president of the company, I have decided that legal action is necessary.

Our decision to repossess our merchandise came only after several months of our repeated attempts to come to payment terms with you. Your continuing lack of cooperation leaves us no choice but to turn this matter over to the County Sheriff's office for resolution. All our future efforts to contact you will be through that office.

Sincerely,

- As a last resort, refer the matter to law enforcement authorities.

- Having the company president write the final letter underlines the gravity of the situation and demonstrates that everyone in authority has considered the matter carefully.

Response to Credit Report, Misleading Report (5-17)

Dear Mr. Bonnard:

Kindly include this letter in our company's credit file. Although in the main the material you summarized is correct, your summary does not provide a clear picture of the history of our business and therefore may be misinterpreted by lenders.

Our company, Simple Tools, has actually been in business since December 31, 1976. However, for the first five years, it was known as Thomas Canner, DBA Simple Tools. We incorporated as Simple Tools, Inc., on December 31, 1981, and that is the date you give for the inception of the business.

I look forward to receiving a revised summary including this additional information.

Sincerely,

- Credit bureaus must include pertinent information in their files if that information is verifiably correct. It's worthwhile to check occasionally to make sure that their files are complete and accurate.

- Always request written verification that a change has been made.

Response to Credit Report, False Report (5-18)

Dear Ms. Foxx:

As I stated on the phone, the information in your files relating to our mortgage payment history is erroneous. As you can see from the attached statements provided by Howland

Savings Bank, the holder of our mortgage, we have never been notified of foreclosure proceedings, as stipulated in your file. In fact, our company's payment record is exemplary, as you can clearly see.

I will look forward to seeing a new synopsis of our company, indicating that this grossly false statement has been corrected, and to seeing, as you promised on the phone, copies of letters detailing the correct information to all those who have made inquiries about our credit standing.

Sincerely,

- A good credit rating is vital in business. If you learn of a false statement, ensure that the credit bureau corrects it as soon as possible and that they send correction statements to anyone they have misinformed.

Dealing with Suppliers 6

The most important thing you can remember when writing letters to suppliers is to be clear. Tell your reader exactly what you need and when you expect it, or what you are going to provide and when. When making requests for information, as in inquiring about credit terms, you will help yourself by making the request as specific as possible. If you take the time to think through your needs and communicate them clearly to the supplier, you have a better chance of receiving a precise answer and, therefore, a better opportunity of making a sound business decision. Compliments and suggestions should be direct and unambiguous; don't get bogged down in flowery platitudes or general observations.

Are we speaking the same language? These days, people in business are constantly confronted with terminology and jargon. Refer to merchandise in the supplier's terms, use dates and numbers from invoices and bills of lading in your correspondence and, if necessary, look up the name of the part in the manual so that it is correctly identified in your communications. Be sure everyone knows what is going on.

Referring to invoice numbers, recalling dates and stating exact amounts is particularly important when your letter is expressing dissatisfaction. Command of these routine items demonstrates that you have looked into the matter carefully, have weighed the possibilities, and still find something unsatisfactory. A supplier who wants to keep your business will be more likely to see your side of a problem if you are precise, while remaining reasonable in tone.

I'm sorry, you're sorry. When you are inconvenienced by a supplier, remember that *your* company may inconvenience someone somewhere along the line. The best thing you can do is to assume that everyone wants to do a good job. Respect the professionalism of every supplier and insist that they respect your professionalism, too. This will create the best working environment for everyone.

Inquiry about Product (6-01)

Dear Samantha:

Both the "Garden Chintz" pillow line and your new specialty quilts are selling almost faster than we can keep them in stock. Since your products seem so popular with our customers, we are interested in carrying other items of a style and quality similar to that of the pillows and quilts—perhaps table accessories or throw rugs. Please send brochures and price information on any of these types of products you now have, and I will then call you to discuss an order.

Sincerely,

- If you're particularly happy with a certain product, let the supplier know.
- Be as specific as you can about the kinds of products about which you want more information.

Request for Credit (6-02)

Dear Mr. Kelton:

As we discussed on the phone, we look forward to your providing office-cleaning services every Tuesday and Friday evening (beginning May 17). To ensure you're paid regularly and promptly, we'd like to be billed on the last day of each month for the services you have provided that month. We will then pay each bill within 30 days of the date we receive it.

We hope this credit arrangement is satisfactory to you. If not, please call me to discuss alternatives.

Yours truly,

- State the circumstances of your agreement with the supplier.
- Specify the credit terms you would like to establish.
- Leave the door open for discussion if your suggestion does not satisfy the supplier.

Inquiry about Credit Terms (6-03)

Dear Mr. Harvey:

Good Earth and Lawn is expanding its services this year to include the northern half of the city. We have serviced residential and commercial accounts in the southern neighborhoods for the past nine years. I have enclosed a list of our larger accounts.

For our expansion, and to upgrade existing equipment, we will need three (3) 12 h.p. riding mowers (36" rotary), four (4) self-propelled mowers (20" rotary) and two (2) weed and brush cutters.

As I'm sure you can understand, there will be a time lag between our initial use of the equipment and our receipt of fees for work performed.

I would, therefore, appreciate receiving information regarding your firm's billing and credit terms.

Thank you.

Sincerely,

- Mention (for the supplier's benefit) your company's background; put yourself in as good a light as possible.
- Specify what type of goods or services you're considering buying. Explain why you want credit.

Inquiry about Discounts (6-04)

Dear Ms. Frost:

Several of our waiters at the Lucky Seven Restaurant, on Main Street in Billings, have told us of the superior drycleaning service you offer. We have now agreed to provide weekly uniform drycleaning to all of our staff members and are interested in contracting for these services. We would like to deliver approximately 25 uniforms (shirts and trousers) for cleaning each Tuesday morning and have them returned to us by noon the following day.

Before we decide on a particular service, we need to know what discount you are prepared to offer for this type of order and what the weekly charge per uniform would be. Would you please call me by Wednesday with this information?

Sincerely,

- Suppliers like to know where their business comes from—do mention any referrals from satisfied customers.
- Estimate as closely as possible the volume and regularity of the service or goods you require. This information is essential in figuring discounts.

Request for Bid (6-05)

Dear Sales Manager:

Our secretarial service company will be upgrading our computers. We would like you to quote the following for immediate delivery:

Quantity	Description
(2)	ProLine X computers
(2)	Ultraspeed modems
(1)	HiLiter printer
(1)	Varidot scanner

Your bid, including payment terms and/or credit options, should be submitted to me no later than Friday, July 28.

Sincerely,

> - Be specific about what you want them to bid on (including quantities and the projected delivery date), when they are to respond, and to whom they are to send the bid.
> - Ask about payment terms, as these may influence your purchasing decision.

Rejection of Bid (6-06)

Dear Mr. Lewis:

We're sorry to inform you that we did not choose your products for the PBX expansion for our Honolulu office. Your preferred delivery cycle of 18 weeks is too long, given our specified requirement of 12 weeks. Your quote for the 12-week delivery cycle was about 10% higher than the successful bidder.

Thank you, however, for the detailed bid you provided. We will be sure to call you when we have telecommunications needs in the future.

Sincerely,

> - Writing this type of letter is not pleasant, but should not be put off.
> - Tell a company why it was not selected, if it is constructive.
> - Be cordial and thank them for their effort (you want them to quote again).

Declining to Do Business at This Time (6-07)

Dear Mr. Costello:

Thank you for your letter and for your interest in supplying castings for our brake assemblies. Since yours is a new company and because our tolerances are so exact, we would have to see more of a track record before we consider you as a supplier. In addition, our turn-around times are quite demanding, so we would need more references than you can provide at this time.

We are, however, always looking for reliable new suppliers, and I would be interested in hearing from you again in about six months, when you've gotten through the start-up phase.

Sincerely,

> - Be specific about why you are refusing to do business.
> - If there's a possibility that you might do business with them in the future, let them know when to contact you again.

Rejection of Proposal (6-08)

Dear Mr. Cutting:

Thank you for coming to St. Louis to deliver your proposal for your "Time Management in the 21st century" seminar to our policy committee.

After reviewing all proposals with Mike Meyers, Marvin Quigley, and Hank Kramer, we have decided to use Jones & Vandendorpel, a local St. Louis firm.

We do appreciate your time and wish you continued success with your programs. Please keep us on your mailing list so we can stay current with your offerings.

Sincerely,

- Writing rejection letters is difficult, but essential. Proposals are time-consuming to write, and vendors deserve the courtesy of a response.

- To avoid "why didn't we get the contract?" phone calls, state the reason in the letter (second paragraph—presumably local firms are less costly).

Return of Item after Trial (6-09)

Dear Mr. Marra:

Under separate label, via United Parcel Service, we are returning the remaining 36 commercial grade staplers from our trial order of 50 (invoice #2306) for credit. Please apply the credit to our account.

Although this type of stapler is effective and does interest some of our customers, it has not been as successful for us as your other two grades—general office and industrial. I think that the commercial grade has too limited an application for our customer base, which is divided between professional offices and industrial manufacturers.

I'm sorry this new item didn't work out because we've had good results with your other products.

Sincerely,

- State what you are returning and how it is being shipped.

- Let the supplier know *why* you were dissatisfied (as objectively as possible), providing pertinent but not excessive details of the situation.

Request for Repair under Warranty (6-10)

Dear Mr. Wasserman:

I am returning for repair the enclosed "Splash Mate" AM/FM bath/shower radio, Model 560Z, which is covered under warranty #2094798 (copy enclosed). Since I bought it three weeks ago, the radio has inexplicably failed to work whenever I turn on the shower. If the radio cannot be repaired, I hope you will send me a replacement that is in good working order.

Thank you.

> • Be sure to note the model number and warranty number.
>
> • Give as much information *as you can* about the problem you're having and the circumstances under which the product does not work.

Request for Service under Warranty (6-11)

Dear Mr. Carabetta:

On March 25, you installed a Jet Splash 20 hot tub in our hotel. For two weeks, the tub functioned perfectly, giving our guests many hours of relaxing bathing. In the past week, however, we've had problems with the tub's water-heating mechanism. We have been unable to raise the tub's water temperature higher than 75 degrees Fahrenheit.

We would like our guests to be able to enjoy the tub as they did when it was functioning properly. I believe service and repair calls come under the terms of the tub's warranty and would like to have a service technician come to the hotel as soon as can be arranged. I will call on Friday to determine the first available date.

Thank you.

Yours very truly,

> • Give all the important details—what you bought, when you bought it.
>
> • Be as specific as possible about the type of problem you're having. Even if you don't know what caused it, describe the symptoms.
>
> • Be clear about how you would like the matter resolved.

Confirmation of Offer to Repair under Warranty (6-12)

Dear Mr. Carabetta:

Thank you for offering to send your repairman, Ted Evans, to service our hotel's hot tub. I will look forward to seeing him on Tuesday between 7 and 10 am.

If, as you suspect, the problem is with the temperature control mechanism, it is my understanding that both parts and labor are covered under the warranty. If the problem is with the hotel's hot water heater, we are responsible for repairs.

Thank you again for your prompt attention and courteous service.

Yours very truly,

- Express appreciation for the service to be provided.
- Outline any and all conditions that have been agreed upon. This will help ward off future misunderstandings.

Shipment Refused on Quality Grounds (6-13)

Dear Mr. Evans:

I am returning with this letter a recent shipment of 2,000 personalized ballpoint pens (order #21392943). Upon examination of the pens, we discovered that our company name had been misspelled. As your records will confirm, the order specified that each pen should read:

Lombardo Limousines

Coach of Kings

Please make the necessary correction and send another shipment of 2,000 pens as soon as possible.

Yours truly,

- Be sure to refer to your order by number.
- State exactly why you were dissatisfied with the quality of the product.
- State how you would like the matter remedied.

Payment to Be Made When Work Is Completed (6-14)

Dear Mr. Zale:

We've received your invoice (#2562) for carpentry work in our office. We'd very much like to pay you, but as we discussed on the phone on May 14, there are still several items that must be attended to before the job is finished. These include the countertop formica and the additional shelves in the supply closet. We cannot efficiently run the production side of our business until these tasks are done.

We will be delighted to send you a check when the work is completed.

Sincerely,

> • The name of this game is "leverage," and you have every right to withhold payment. Putting it in writing will forestall or delay legal action.

Invoice Cannot Be Processed, Shipment Incomplete (6-15)

Dear Mr. Hyman:

We are unable to process your invoice #8092 for disposable linens. This invoice represents only a portion of our purchase order #42658, and we cannot pay until the entire purchase order has been filled.

You are correct in thinking that we had a different policy in the past. Unfortunately, we have had problems with vendors who submitted invoices for part of a purchase order and later submitted invoices for the entire purchase order. The resulting confusion forced us to institute a new policy. Please submit a new invoice as soon as the entire order has been filled.

Sincerely,

> • Always state the main point first.
>
> • Although clearly you've changed the policy (because of dishonest vendors or ineptness on the part of your people), assigning blame is counterproductive. Referring to "confusion" is more politic.

Invoice Cannot Be Processed, Charges Incorrect (6-16)

Dear Len:

As you can see from the enclosed envelope and your invoice (#3429) for $695, your invoice of April 19 was delayed in reaching us because it was addressed to the wrong town. We did not receive it until today.

When I talked with you on the phone about a FAX, you said that the list price for the FAX 103 was $695, that Revere's usual price was $595, and that you would be able to sell one to us at $579. When I visited the store, no one was able to give me an exact price, but I was told that you'd call me when you returned. Since I did not hear from you, I assumed that the $579 price would be charged.

I would appreciate it if you would check your records and let me know whether there would be any problem in reissuing the invoice at $579. Please note that the invoice should be made out to Totoket Associates and that the mailing address is Box 298, Reading, MA 01867.

Sincerely,

- In something of this magnitude, "putting it in writing" is essential. Following up with a phone call is also a good idea.

- Decide before sending the letter how rigid or flexible your position is so you'll be prepared to react to the supplier's response.

Documentation Missing (6-17)

Dear Mr. Stuart:

Please send us the documentation for Micromouse Write 1.2 that we purchased from you on May 11. As you requested in our phone conversation earlier today, I am enclosing a copy of our receipt.

Yours truly,

- When possible, call the service department before writing in order to include in your letter whatever information the seller requires and to be certain you are writing to the appropriate person. If a call is not possible, include the full name of the product and enclose proof of purchase.

Cancellation of Order (6-18)

Dear Miss Randolf:

Please cancel our order (#1707-56) for 200 "Wooden Animal Puzzles for 2-4 Year Olds." We have just found a large number of these puzzles in our storeroom and do not have need for more at this time. We will place a new order when our present supply runs out.

Yours truly,

- Be certain to include the order number and full name of the product.

- If you believe there will be a question about why you are canceling the order, give the reason, particularly if the supplier is a regular one. Courtesy never hurts.

Performance Unsatisfactory, Temporary Employment Agency (6-19)

Dear Ms. Murphy:

We appreciate your efforts in sending us Tammy Renhouse on Monday in response to our request for a temporary secretary who could use UltraWord on a PC. Unfortunately, we have had to let Ms. Renhouse go after the first half-day. She had never worked with a PC. As a result, she was of no value to us, and she took up my valuable time asking questions.

You have provided us with good temporary help in the past, and I assume that Ms.

Renhouse was less than forthright with you about her abilities. We look forward to using your agency again.

Yours truly,

- Be sure that you make clear what services you required, how the individual failed, when the temporary began work, and when you let the temporary go.
- Let the agency know whether this event alters your relationship.

Performance Unsatisfactory, Service Company (6-20)

Dear Mr. Thompson:

During the past week, Forest Cable technicians have twice failed to keep appointments to install a surge protection system for our computer equipment. On both Tuesday, May 17, and Friday, May 20, I arranged for our data communications supervisor to be on site from 9:00 am to noon to accommodate the schedule of your service crew. On neither day did the installation technician arrive, nor did he call to explain why the appointment had not been kept. This lack of concern has caused us both serious inconvenience and valuable time.

I would like to believe that Forest Cable values our company as a customer, but quite honestly, the events of last week do not support that view. Can I depend on you to arrange dependable installation at our mutual convenience sometime next week? We have enjoyed the services your company has provided in the past and look forward to reestablishing our relationship on a more pleasant footing. I will call you on Friday to arrange the appointment.

Yours truly,

- State specifically why you are dissatisfied. Mention the dates and times when service was unsatisfactory (or non-existent).
- Make it clear how you would like to resolve your issues with the supplier and arrange to discuss the matter further.

Refusal to Accept Proposed Remedy (6-21)

Dear Mr. Weiss:

I am sorry to hear that you are unable to provide the six Junior Executive Desks (model EX-102) that we ordered. I'm surprised that such a popular model was discontinued. The alternative desk you suggested (Secretarial Desk, model EX-101) would not fit our needs as it is smaller than what we require.

We will have to search elsewhere for these desks but will look forward to dealing with you again in the future.

Sincerely,

- Reiterate your request and the remedy offered.
- State why you cannot accept.
- Even in refusals, be cordial and leave the door open for future dealings.

Thank You for Cooperation During Difficult Project (6-22)

Dear Ted:

Enclosed is a check for $4,508.52, covering the balance due on Purchase Order 788-10 for the recent printing of our catalog.

While I think we both developed a few gray hairs over the printing difficulties, I have to praise you and your company for being sensitive to my needs and responding quickly and professionally.

The catalogs look great and we will be needing a new printing in about two months.

Again, thanks for your cooperation during this difficult situation.

Kindest regards,

- When things go awry during a project, and the supplier gives his all, it makes sense to tell him you appreciated the help.
- If additional work will be coming his way shortly, tell him so.

Suggestion to Supplier (6-23)

Dear Ms. Murphy:

I believe I have a suggestion that will help you and us. If you could test word processing personnel before sending them out on a job, we could both be assured that they can do the work they say they can do.

I know you cannot test every individual on every kind of software, but you could test, and therefore validate their ability, on those packages that you have in your office. You might also ask for references if they say they had experience with certain brands of software at previous jobs.

I hope this idea will be useful to you.

Yours truly,

- Open the letter with a statement that is sufficiently compelling for the recipient to continue to read. People get free advice all the time; they continue reading only when they perceive some personal value.
- If you are writing to someone you deal with personally, show understanding of that person's problem.

Compliment to Supplier (6-24)

Dear Mr. Sarnoff:

Thank you for the wonderful help your entire staff provided in feeding the participants at our annual meeting on April 20. The room looked lovely, the flowers were beautiful, the service was excellent and, most important, Chef Michael's food was exceptional. You more than kept your promise of being "the best in all ways."

You will hear from us again soon.

Yours truly,

- Keep it short and sweet but be sure to include, whenever possible, who should be complimented, what that person or people did, and when it happened.

Compliment for Supplier's Employee (6-25)

Dear Mr. Sanderson:

You are indeed fortunate to have as dedicated an engineer as William Southwick. Bill worked with me for hours to ensure that our lighting design will now meet our needs. He was concerned that each area of the shop have lighting appropriate to the work that will be done in that area and that, should we alter the production flow, we will be able to alter the lighting as well.

I have told Bill how much I appreciate his attention to detail, but I wanted to tell you as well. If you feel it is appropriate, feel free to include this letter in his personnel file.

Yours truly,

- Be sure to include the name of the employee and a brief description of what the employee did that you found especially helpful.
- If you are writing to a large organization, you might ask that your letter be added to the individual's personnel file or send a copy to the person you are complimenting.

Payment Enclosed (6-26)

Dear Mr. Vreelander:

Enclosed is our check #3098 for $3,097.62, which covers the balance due on invoice #28602. I believe this will bring our account up to date until we receive the shipment of parts due next month.

Sincerely,

- Be sure to note your check number, the amount of the check, and the invoice your payment covers.
- Confirm that this payment brings your account up-to-date.

Authorization to Transfer Funds (6-27)

Dear Ms. Rollins:

Please transfer, immediately, two thousand dollars ($2,000.00) from Handerson Service Co.'s savings account #23456789 to Handerson Service Co.'s checking account #785624983.

Yours truly,

- Be sure to include the account number and the name in which the account is listed.

- The person who signs the letter should have the authority to make transactions in the account from which funds are being withdrawn.

Apology for Incorrect Payment (6-28)

Dear Ms. Whitley:

Enclosed is our check #694 for $247.82. We regret that we inadvertently underpaid the balance due on invoice #27706 last month and hope that you will accept our apology for the error.

Sincerely,

- When you're wrong, admit it promptly.

- Don't go into excessive detail. This letter skips any mention of the people involved and thus avoids assigning blame.

Apology for Late Payment (6-29)

Dear Mr. Carlson:

Enclosed is our check #6714 for $789.55, covering the extra charges for the off-site planning meeting that Apex held at the Long Pond Conference Center last month. We apologize for the lateness of this check, but we had to wait for Long Pond to send us the paperwork on our two extra attendees before we could process your invoice (#AP-4948).

I hope that the delay has not caused you any inconvenience.

Sincerely,

- Be sure to state the number and amount of the check enclosed.
- Apologize for the delay and explain it briefly.

Explanation of Late Payment (6-30)

Dear Mrs. Purcell:

All who attended the annual fund raising luncheon last Friday remarked on the exquisite buffet. Our thanks to you for providing such a memorable feast.

We received your bill for $4,672.00 (#266084) yesterday. Enclosed is a check for $2,500.00 toward the balance of our account. Because we are entirely dependent on membership contributions for meeting our expenses, we are forced to pay the remaining $2,172.00 next month, when our fund drive has ended.

I regret that we cannot pay the entire amount due today and hope you understand our situation and the reason for the delay.

Sincerely,

- Express appreciation for good service provided.
- Refer to the invoice by number and propose an alternate payment schedule, giving the reason why you need more time.
- Express regret for not paying more promptly.

Payment Stopped on Check (6-31)

Dear Mr. Fisher:

I'm sorry that the check I sent you on May 12 (#4409) never arrived. Enclosed is a second check for $545.00 (#4432), which should cover the balance of our account. I've stopped payment on #4409; if it arrives, please return it to me. I apologize for this delay and for any inconvenience that the missing check may have caused you.

Yours very truly,

- Note the number and date of the first check sent.
- Give the number of the replacement check enclosed and tell the reader what to do if the missing check arrives.
- Apologize for any inconvenience.

Check Has Been Sent (6-32)

Dear Mr. Fisher:

Today I received your second bill for the flowers you provided for the Osgood wedding on April 29. I assume that as of May 16 you had not yet received my check #4409 for $545.00 that I mailed you on May 12. If the check does not arrive by Monday, will you please let me know? I'll be happy to stop payment on the original check and send you another. We were quite pleased with the beautiful arrangements you made for the Osgood wedding and want to be sure you receive prompt payment.

Yours very truly,

- Be sure to note the date when you sent the check (and its number and amount).
- Arrange to send another if the original check does not arrive by a specific date.
- As always, be cordial...maintain a good relationship.

Return of Item for Credit (6-33)

Dear Mr. Flaherty:

I have enclosed our final payment of $310.76 (check #6490) for 29,750 of the cards you shipped to us last year. Please apply the payment against the balance on the original invoice #2308.

As we agreed last year, we are paying for the cards on an as-used basis, returning any unused cards for credit. There are 20,250 cards remaining from the 50,000 you shipped us last year. Please let me know how we should arrange to return them to you for credit.

Sincerely,

- Identify for your reader exactly what figures you are basing your payment on (if it's different from the balance on the invoice).
- Give invoice number and any other relevant information.
- Ask how to proceed with returns (next steps).

Request Permission to Return Item in Shipment, Damaged (6-34)

Dear Mr. Smythe:

When we examined 2 of the 36 sets of Animal Family Figurines that your carrier, Apex Trucking, delivered last Wednesday, May 4, we were dismayed to find several figurines in two sets had arrived broken. I would like to arrange to have the sets with broken figurines returned to you as proof of damage.

Please credit our account for the two sets that were broken. Apart from this problem, we were very pleased with this new addition to your line and hope to reorder in the near future.

Sincerely,

- Specify how many items arrived damaged and describe the damage.
- State how you'd like the matter handled.
- Call attention to any possible billing situation.

Request Permission to Return Item in Shipment, Not Ordered (6-35)

Dear Mr. Robinson:

I would like to arrange to have 8 Home/Office Tool Kits returned to your warehouse on Friday, June 8. These kits were mistakenly included in the order you delivered to our store on May 26. Perhaps they were destined for another customer—our delivery was not short any of the items I ordered (PO# 155062).

Please let me know if June 8 is acceptable and credit our account accordingly if the tool kits were charged to it.

Regards,

- State exactly what you wish to return and why.
- Give all necessary details, including dates and number of merchandise items involved.
- Call attention to any possible billing error.

Request Permission to Return Shipment, Not Ordered (6-36)

Dear Ms. Chasen:

Enclosed are 24 pads of Strathmore Parchment Calligraphy Writing Paper that were mistakenly shipped to us on April 2 (invoice #578657). Ordering by phone from Lisa Roberts on March 30, we asked for 24 pads of white calligraphy paper. Please accept the parchment paper for return and send us 24 pads of the white as soon as possible.

Thank you for rectifying this matter promptly.

Sincerely,

- Specify what you were sent as well as what should have been sent.
- Include all necessary information: dates, invoice numbers, the name of the person with whom you placed the order.
- Be sure to state how you'd like the matter handled.

Request Permission to Return Shipment, Arrived Too Late (6-37)

Dear Mr. Blunt:

We received today the Adobe Project Billing System you shipped to us on May 4 (invoice #2934837). When we ordered this software package by phone on February 11, Doug Tanchum assured us that it would be shipped within two weeks. With that expectation, we looked forward to receiving the system by March 1 to fill an urgent need. When it had not arrived by April 1 and Doug could not guarantee that it would arrive promptly, we ordered a similar system through another vendor.

Please let me know how you would like this merchandise returned and credit our account for $675.00. We value your products and would like to order them again, providing you understand merchandise availability is a priority with us.

Sincerely,

- Specify the items received and when delivery was promised.
- Include all necessary information: dates, invoice numbers, the name of the person with whom you placed the order.
- Be sure to state how you'd like the matter handled and mention that delivery time is an important issue with you.

Request Permission to Return Shipment, Damaged (6-38)

Dear Ms. Trocfel:

When the Data Defender Diskette File (our PO #698) you shipped to us on March 12 (invoice #2049037) arrived, we were dismayed to find that it had been damaged in transit. The plastic cover was cracked. Please let me know how you would like it returned and send us a replacement as soon as possible.

Thank you for handling this matter promptly.

Sincerely,

- Specify what item(s) you were sent and exactly how it was damaged.
- Include all necessary information: dates, purchase order and invoice numbers.
- Be sure to state how you'd like the matter handled.

Request Permission to Return Shipment, No Longer Needed (6-39)

Dear Mr. Brownlee:

I would like to return the Rapidoprint DD3700 Processor (invoice #59302483) that was delivered last week. Fire destroyed our office on May 24. We are in the process of rebuilding our facility and cannot use the processor at this time. I am shipping the unit back to your warehouse. Please credit my account accordingly.

Thank you for your understanding.

Sincerely,

- Specify what item you were sent and when it was ordered.
- Explain why you no longer need the merchandise.
- Be sure to state how you'd like the matter handled.

Personnel Relations 7

Many people have become so fearful of employer-employee relations that they avoid putting anything in writing because they feel it may come back to haunt them. But all the same reasons for putting things in writing discussed in the introduction to this book apply equally to writing in the personnel area. Acrimonious disputes can be avoided if everyone understands hiring practices, job evaluation practices, and other policies and procedures that the company follows. Avoiding these disputes saves immense amounts of time and emotional capital.

The trade-off, of course, is that written practices do constrain employers, even though any policy can be changed at any time with appropriate notice. In practice, changing a "perk" is difficult to do. One entrepreneur cites the story of giving everyone a turkey for the holidays in his first year of business and the nightmare it grew into some years down the road when he found himself with several hundred employees, each waiting for his or her turkey. The moral here is to try to envision your company as it will be in a few years when you think about appropriate policies and procedures.

Hiring and references. From posting a job opening to writing a job confirmation letter, writing is part of the hiring process. Your first step is to think through what the job entails in terms of responsibilities and duties and then to develop a list of the skills necessary to do that job. Many people list very high qualifications (typing speed, college degree) as a way of screening people. One office manager says, "If a person has the discipline to learn to type 75 words per minute, I can teach him or her to do anything else required on the job." A good way to appraise realistically what the job involves is to talk with the person who currently holds the job, or to others in firms similar to yours if the position is new. Doing this preliminary spadework will allow you to write an announcement of a job opening or a job description. If you don't want to get the protest "but that's not in my job description," you may want to add "and other duties as assigned" to cover yourself.

Most managers hate the interviewing process. An interview outline can help immensely because it provides structure to the conversation and helps keep the interviewer in control.

A letter confirming or revising a job offer has contractual implications and should be looked over by an attorney. Be careful not to stipulate anything more than the salary and the starting date. If you have discussed a probationary period, you may also wish to include that in the letter. However, put nothing in the letter that has not been discussed in person. If you do, you're likely to poison the atmosphere of trust you have presumably tried to establish.

References should be handled with finesse. Sound too glowing and you're likely to be disbelieved, too negative and you might seem bitter or personally involved. Keep a reference factual, but if an employee was less than satisfactory, what you don't say can take on as much meaning as what you do say.

Problems. If you have a problem employee, your first step is to talk with the person. Discuss how performance has been falling short of expectations and agreed-upon goals. You may want to refer to the employee's latest performance appraisal. If the employee has personal problems, these can be dealt with on a case-by-case basis.

After each conversation, dictate a letter to the files giving the gist of the conversation. You may want to have the employee initial it so you have a record that the employee understands that he or she is not performing up to standards. If conversations do not achieve the desired result, you may want to write a warning memo.

There are several key things to remember in writing letters and memos that deal with personnel matters. Deal with facts (rather than opinions) as much as possible. Have an attorney check anything that has contractual implications—a statement of benefits, for example. And always adopt an objective rather than adversarial tone—people will simply respond better.

Announcement of Job Opening (7-01)

Subject: Opening for Secretary/Sales Assistant

As you know, Nina Kamchatka will be leaving us in two months to relocate to San Diego. Her position as Secretary/Sales Assistant will therefore be open. We always prefer to promote from within, and we welcome applications from anyone interested.

Duties include (but are not limited to):

- Providing secretarial support for Vice-President of Sales
- Typing all correspondence
- Managing extensive phone contact with clients
- Maintaining sales and records
- Making travel arrangements.

Skills required are:

- Typing at 65 wpm
- Six-months' familiarity with PC and spreadsheet programs

Nina has offered to discuss her duties and the nature of her job with anyone who has an interest in succeeding her. Please call Joe Doddsworth in Personnel if you would like additional information.

- Announcing a job opening should be done in memo format.
- Use a positive tone and be very specific about the skills required.
- Saying that the list of duties is not complete covers you later on and avoids having the new hire saying "that's not my job."

Request for Help in Recruiting New Employees (7-02)

Subject: Recruiting New Employees

The unemployment rate in our area is now 3% and dropping. As a result, we're having difficulty finding and recruiting new telemarketing hires, despite the fact that our wages are above average and we offer flexible hours for students and mothers.

Because we want the very best people available, we want to enlist your help in finding people who are as qualified as you. We'll give you $100 for each person you recommend that we ultimately hire, and we'll give you an additional $500 if that person stays with us for three months. Remember that the people we want must have superb telephone skills and an extremely responsible approach to working.

Please call me directly for further information (and please be sure anyone you refer to us mentions your name as a referral).

> • Your own employees are a valuable source of leads. Businesses live and die on the quality of their people, and it's worthwhile to reward referrals.

Response to Resume, Unsolicited (7-03)

Dear Mr. Stern:

Thank you for sending your resume.

At this time, we do not foresee any branch manager openings with our firm during the next six months to one year. Generally, these positions are filled internally. No one can anticipate the future, though, and we'll gladly call you if we expand even more rapidly than anticipated.

Thank you for your interest in New Age. Please keep us in mind as you progress in your career.

Yours truly,

> • Don't ignore an unsolicited resume even if you have no instant need for the person. There's always the future to consider.
>
> • Consider your letter another opportunity to "sell" your firm and indicate that your firm is a good place at which to work.

Response to Resume, with Referral (7-04)

Dear Mr. Canter:

I enjoyed talking with you on the phone Tuesday. We appreciate your promptness in sending along your resume, and, naturally, we give a great deal of weight to Phil Beckwith's recommendation.

As I mentioned on the phone, we expect to have openings for sales representatives in the spring. We will keep your resume on file and call you for an interview at that time.

If you do not hear from me by April 30, please call and check on the status of our hiring process.

Best,

> • Always respond immediately to job inquiries, even if you do not have an immediate opening. A job applicant is a potential member of your team and should be treated with courtesy.
>
> • Provide an opportunity for the job seeker to re-establish contact, if appropriate. Leaving the ball in the job seeker's court will ensure that you aren't viewed as neglectful in the future.

Thank You for Application, Will Keep on File (7-05)

Dear Mr. Fitzgibbons:

Thank you for taking the time to come in and fill out an application for the position of night store manager. Although we were certainly impressed with your qualifications, and the hours you were available were consistent with our requirements, I'm sorry to tell you that we'll have to put you on our waiting list.

While we currently do have a full roster of night managers, openings do occur from time to time. Please let us know if you change your address so that we may locate you if an opening does occur.

Sincerely,

- This letter is a bit more encouraging than a "we'll keep you on file" letter because it asks for notification of an address change, which is outside normal "form-letterese." It's always better to offer job seekers some hope (if it exists). It doesn't cost anything, and it leaves a very positive impression of your company.

Invitation to Interview (7-06)

Dear Mr. Plowright:

Mike Stamp tells me that you are interested in talking with financial planning firms like ours about the possibility of working as an associate with the expectation of ultimately being made partner. Mike speaks very highly of you, both as a solid person to work with and as a high producer with a substantial client base. We're very interested in both aspects of your experience.

Our firm has expanded rapidly in the past five years—we now have four partners and ten associates—and we have every expectation of continued growth as financial planning becomes more important to individuals and as our Long Island community grows.

We'd very much like to talk. Please call me at your earliest convenience.

Sincerely,

- A letter to the person's home is a good way to approach someone who can't be or shouldn't be reached on the job. (Calling at home may be viewed as intrusive.)
- "Sell" your firm in the letter.

Interview Outline (7-07)

1. Tell me about your present job.
2. Tell me how your boss and/or co-workers would describe you.
3. Describe your greatest work-related accomplishment within the last five years.
4. Describe your most frustrating work-related experience in the past five years and why it was so.

5. When given a new assignment or project, how do you approach it?
6. In what type of position are you most interested?
7. Do you prefer working with others or by yourself?
8. What led to your interest in our company?

- These questions should yield useful information about the applicant's strengths, weaknesses, working style, and self-perception. Good interviewers allow the applicant's own questions and responses to drive the interview.

- Do not ask questions that are either illegal (discrimination by race, creed, or sex) or highly personal.

Confirmation of Job Offer, with Terms (7-08)

Dear Brian:

We were quite impressed with your qualifications, and after some consideration, we have decided that you are the ideal choice for the position of Unit Manager at Wesley Video Productions. Congratulations, and welcome aboard!

The terms are as we discussed in the interview. The salary is $30,000 a year. You'll have three weeks vacation per year and Blue Cross/Blue Shield health insurance. All employees at Wesley Video get five personal days and 10 sick days per year. We have a pension plan that you can sign up for after working at Wesley Video for one year.

We would like you to start on Monday, April 23. If you have any questions, please call us. If not, we'll see you on the 23rd!

Very truly yours,

- Don't get into the specific responsibilities of the job. The point of this letter is to have a written record of the terms of employment. It's really a confirmation of previous discussions, so keep it simple and to the point.

Revised Job Offer (7-09)

Dear Mr. Pearle:

Thank you for responding to our job offer so promptly. We understand that there are some details to be worked out, but none of them appear to be insurmountable.

I spoke with the President of Kidsworks, Alan Weiss, and we both feel that we cannot increase the base salary we offered beyond $52,000 per annum. However, we can include a performance bonus of 15%, subject to review of both Mr. Weiss and myself. We will also include $5,000 to cover your relocation expenses.

If you have any further questions or comments, please call my office.

Sincerely,

- Pretty self-explanatory. Keep things congenial because everybody will soon be working together, and you should therefore reduce the potential for bad blood developing.
- Make your offer and be sure to keep the lines of communication open.

Follow-up to Interview, Rejection (7-10)

Dear Mr. Clarides:

It was a pleasure to meet with you last week in our offices at Senior Care, Inc. Your training in social work and business administration gives you a combination of skills that will be useful in any gerontology-related field.

As we discussed during the interview, Senior Care is looking for a person with at least five years of management experience in a residential facility for senior citizens. Because of your limited managerial experience, we are unable to offer you the position.

I wish you all the best for a successful career working on behalf of senior citizens.

Sincerely,

- Begin your letter by acknowledging one of the interviewee's areas of strength that you learned about during the interview.
- Let the applicant know why he or she doesn't meet your requirement by stating your unmet need.
- Close your letter with cordial good wishes for the future.

Termination of Job Offer (7-11)

Dear Mr. Hartland:

I am sorry to tell you that, since we did not hear from you in response to our job offer, the offer expired as of last Friday.

I understood, when we spoke three weeks ago, that you were considering other opportunities, and we agreed that our job offer would be time-limited. I am, as you can imagine, personally disappointed that you won't be joining us as my Executive Assistant, but I hope that you will remember our conversations and consider Thomlinson Antique Auction Gallery if you decide to reevaluate your career in the future.

Best of luck in your new job.

Sincerely,

> - Even if someone has been impolite (letting a job offer expire, rather than calling or writing, is quite rude), do not let your impatience be reflected in your tone. Something tragic may have happened, or the mail may have gone astray.
>
> - Always keep the door open for future contacts.

Warning about Excessive Lateness (7-12)

Subject: Hours of Work

As we discussed in our meeting on October 10, it's important for you to reach the office on time. No one objects to an occasional slip. In fact, with the difficulties of commuting these days, being late once in a while is quite understandable.

Here's the problem, though. In the last month, even though we had already discussed the company's expectations at our October 10 meeting, you have been from 30-45 minutes late on seven (7) days, specifically October 14, 17, 18, 20, 26, 27, and November 1. This kind of performance is unacceptable—it sends me the message that you don't care about the job, and it certainly sets a bad example for your secretary, who is always here on time, even early most days.

There may be something that prevents you from getting to work on time. If there's anything I need to know, let's talk. However, you must improve your on-time performance to no more than one day late during the next month or I'll have to send you a formal warning which will be placed in your personnel file.

> - It's only fair to tell employees when their performance is inadequate. Usually, you tell them first face-to-face. Then, if they don't improve, you should notify them in writing.
>
> - Be specific about what you want improved and state a deadline. In serious cases, this becomes part of a written record to justify termination.

Warning about Excessive Sick Days (7-13)

Subject: Excessive Sick Days

In my memo of March 3, I stated that you had already used 10 sick days this year—the number of sick days allowable for the entire year. During March, you called in sick an additional three days—March 17, 18, and 21.

We value all our staff members, but we must warn you formally that any additional sick leave this year will be unpaid. Please schedule a meeting with me to discuss this problem as soon as you can.

- This memo reflects a personnel situation that has already deteriorated and may be unsalvageable. It represents a formal warning. The plea for a meeting is a last-ditch attempt to save the situation.
- Be specific as to the action expected and the time period involved.

Termination of Employee (7-14)

Dear Joe:

As we discussed on Monday, the downturn in the market for industrial fans in the Washington region has led the company to close the regional office. As a consequence, your position has been eliminated.

To confirm our conversation, you will terminate your employment on June 22 and receive severance pay equal to three months' salary. The company will pay your medical insurance for the remainder of the year. In lieu of profit sharing for this year, you have agreed to accept a one-time payment of $5,000. Your retirement benefits will be retained by the company until we receive instructions from you.

Sincerely,

- Terminating an employee, for whatever reason, is a delicate subject and should be discussed first in person, then followed-up with a confirming letter like this one.

Reference for Departing Employee, Good Employee (7-15)

Dear Mr. Jobs:

I'm delighted to respond to your request for a reference for Bonnie Bronson, who was our office manager for the past two years.

We were extremely disappointed to lose Ms. Bronson because of her relocation to Maine. She took us from an office in which we were constantly on a catch-up basis to one in which our systems for billing, collections, and personnel were sensible and controllable. Furthermore, her management skills were evident through her relations with our part-time clerical staff. She was totally responsible for hiring and training these three individuals, and a conversation with any of them reveals that she dealt with them fairly and professionally.

If you need an office manager who is responsible, is skilled, and has potential for advancement, you should hire Ms. Bronson.

Sincerely,

- This is an easy letter to write—it's a rave review, and you can send a blind carbon copy to Ms. Bronson herself.
- Note, though, that the good reference is backed up with specific details.

Reference for Departing Employee, Unsolicited (7-16)

To Whom It May Concern:

During the past two years, I have had the distinct pleasure of having Caryl Adams work for me at Bilcott Industries. As she leaves to accept new challenges, I welcome this opportunity to provide a recommendation on her behalf.

In my association with Caryl, she has been an integral part of the Operations Research Department as an Operations Analyst. Her work has been exemplary. She has provided timely, accurate, and insightful analyses to our clients across all industries.

Her writing and analytical skills are sharply honed. She is industrious and dedicated. Caryl's approach to her job can be characterized as truly professional. I wish her my very best as she seeks new frontiers.

Sincerely,

- When a good employee leaves for "greener pastures," it's not uncommon to be asked to write such a letter.

- To provide context, mention where, in what relationship, and for how long you knew the candidate.

- Stress the person's strong points, and how they might fit in with the individual's career objectives.

Reference for Former Employee, Average Employee (7-17)

Dear Ms. Toth:

We received your letter asking for a reference for Jane Howell. I have reviewed our personnel records.

Ms. Howell worked for Atlee Industries for just under two years. She started out as a receptionist and became a secretary for our Marketing division after one year. Her salary when she left was $19,200. She left Atlee because her husband had been relocated. Ms. Howell was well liked by her co-workers.

If you have any further questions, please call my office.

Sincerely,

- Comments should be restricted to work-related matters. Personal criticisms should be avoided. You are being asked what kind of worker this person is, not whether you like him or her.

Request for Reference, to Company (7-18)

Dear Mr. Montgomery:

Edward Potts has given your name as a reference for an associate's position with Toombs, Hardy and Foulkes. Would you provide for us your impression of Mr. Potts' talents and strengths as a professional and as a team player, as well as any other thoughts that you feel would aid us in making a decision.

Thank you.

Sincerely,

- Give the name of the person and the position for which he or she is being considered.
- Give an idea of the kind of information you want, while also soliciting any additional facts that might prove helpful.

Request for Verification of Employment (7-19)

Dear Mr. Ramones:

We wish to verify that Bryan Constantine (SS #021-36-8080) was employed by your company as a driver from December 2, 1998, to April 4, 1999. We are considering Bryan for a position as a driver and would like this and any other information you have regarding his value as an employee.

Thank you.

Sincerely,

- Give the candidate's full name (and social security number if you have it) as well as the period of employment on which you're checking.
- Take advantage of the opportunity to ask for additional information you might need.

Response to Request for Employment Verification (7-20)

Dear Mr. Goodwin:

You asked us to confirm certain information from Harley Stone's employment application in writing.

Harley Stone worked for Catering Around, a division of our firm, from June 1997 to July 1999. He began as a driver, a position he held for 6 months. For the rest of his employment period, he was a bartender and waiter. He left our company to move to Atlanta, where his wife had taken a new job. This information agrees with that given on Mr. Stone's application.

If we can help you in any other way, please call or write.

Sincerely,

- If you're asked to verify facts of employment, do just that and no more. Launching into unsolicited opinions may get you into trouble.

Description of Employee Benefits (7-21)

Subject: Description of Expanded Health Insurance Coverage

Our department is constantly reviewing employee benefits to provide improvements. Most recently, we focused on our psychological benefits package in response to requests from employees and with a view to general trends among other major regional employers.

As a result of our evaluation, we are pleased to announce that as of June 30, the lifetime limit on reimbursements for in-patient psychiatric treatment has been increased to $50,000. In addition, GHCP will now reimburse out-patient psychological counseling at $40 per visit; annual limits on out-patient visits have been increased to $1,000 per year. The lifetime limit for out-patient psychological counseling has been increased to $10,000.

These new benefits will be described in our annual benefits brochure, but you may wish to keep a copy of this memo on file for reference.

- Benefits are important to employees, but the specifics may be ignored until the benefit is actually necessary. If you've made a major advance in benefit coverage, announcing it in a separate memo will encourage those concerned to pay attention and will give the personnel folks some welcome public relations help.

Job Description, Entry Level (7-22)

RESPONSIBILITIES OF A RETAIL CLERK

Retail Clerks in an Apple Pie Video Rental Store are primarily responsible for taking care of customers by receiving and renting films. Other duties may be assigned by the store manager.

Time Spent	Duties
75%	Handles customer requests in person and by telephone. Rents videos, receives returned videos. Completes paperwork for new memberships. Operates the store computer. Receives payment, makes change.

15%   Files returned videos. Returns display boxes to shelves. Keeps shelves orderly.

10%   Puts labels on promotional mailers. Dusts shelves. Receives shipments. Logs special requests. Checks drop box. Performs other duties as requested.

Skills Required

1. Must have good public relations skills.

2. Must be able to maintain the store's filing and shelving systems.

3. Must be able to learn and effectively operate the store computer.

4. Must be able to make change accurately.

5. Must be willing to perform other assigned duties.

6. Must be available and dependable for flexible scheduling of work hours, including holidays.

7. Must be able to work independently and without regular supervision.

Apple Pie Video Rental Stores, 2 Celluloid Square, Americus, GA 35291

- Time allotments help to explain both the nature of the work and the employer's priorities.

- Be sure to include special expectations in the job description, such as availability to work on holidays. This can deter the "but that's not in my job description!" blues for both employer and employee.

Job Description, Middle Level (7-23)

JOB DESCRIPTION

TITLE: Office Manager

GENERAL DESCRIPTION: This is a full-time position in which the person has responsibility for managing the office, handling assigned duties, supervising employees, and assisting the company president as needed. Because Summertime Concessions, Inc. is a small, family-owned business, the Office Manager has a broad range of duties. These vary from standard secretarial tasks to making sound judgment calls in the occasional absence of the president. The position answers to the company president.

SKILLS AND QUALIFICATIONS:

- Minimum of two-years experience as an office secretary with experience in supervising employees.

- Competence in use of the Macintosh computer for wordprocessing.

- Knowledge of food services and concessions management is highly desirable.

- Ability to work effectively with minimal supervision and to take initiative in problem-solving.

- Willingness to assist other office employees when needed and to perform other duties as required.

- Availability to work overtime to assist with inventory (usually one week per year).

- Ability to complete assigned workload satisfactorily.

- Ability to supervise and motivate employees effectively.

- A good job description is specific without being compulsively detailed. It should give the reader a clear idea of what the job entails and what is necessary to be successful at it.

- When writing a job description, think in terms of the qualities you desire in an employee (e.g., willingness to pitch in) as well as the skills required to get the job done.

Performance Appraisal, Written Evaluation (7-24)

PERFORMANCE APPRAISAL FORM

Use the reverse side if necessary

Date _____

Employee _____   Position _____

Evaluator _____   Position _____

COMPETENCIES/AREAS OF STRENGTH:

Brad, your skills as a training specialist and consultant are excellent. You are a very strong teacher and group facilitator. Your recent workshop for agoraphobics is a fine example of your abilities in this area, especially your ability to be sensitive to both individual and group needs.

I am pleased by your ability to research and design workshops and seminars. Your designs are practical, thorough, and suited to the knowledge level of the participants.

You have also been an asset to Pygmalion Consultants in your ability to network and generate referrals for the company. The increased business (and bonuses!) have made everyone happy.

CONCERNS/AREAS FOR IMPROVEMENT:

As we have discussed before, your tendency to produce results at the eleventh hour has been problematic. An example is the way several of the staff were forced to work overtime to finish the Golden Valley Public School Teachers project. Your expectation that the support staff can and will set aside their work at the last minute is unreasonable. As you know, good working relations between the staff and the consultants are a necessity. How can we work together to solve this problem?

Although you always dress neatly, your preference for casual dress in the office has become inappropriate. The company considers its image to be important both "at home" because of visiting clients and in public because of general professionalism. We expect you to wear business suits in and out of the office and to keep the tie tied and the sleeves buttoned.

- Make your evaluations specific. Back them up with examples.

- When evaluating undesirable performance, state clearly what you find unacceptable, why it is problematic, and what changes you expect the employee to make.

Performance Appraisal, Rating Form (7-25)

PERFORMANCE APPRAISAL FOR _____

This appraisal is based on the list of responsibilities, skills, and qualifications listed in the job description for an Office Manager. The evaluator should rate the employee in each category and use the adjacent space for explanatory comments.

Rating System
       1 = Needs improvement/Not adequate
       2 = Fair/Minimally adequate
       3 = Good/Adequate
       4 = Excellent/More than adequate

1. Competence in use of computer/word processor: 1 2 _3_ 4
   Your skills have been steadily improving.

2. Knowledge of food service and concessions management: 1 2 3 _4_
   What you didn't know when you started you've learned quickly!

3. Ability to work effectively with minimal supervision: 1 2 _3_ 4
   Although you still need some coaching on the Macintosh, you do fine otherwise.

4. Ability to take initiative in problem-solving: 1 2 _3_ 4
   I expect this will increase as you learn the business more thoroughly.

5. Willingness to assist other employees: 1 _2_ 3 4
   Could use improvement here, especially when facing deadlines.

6. Willingness to perform other duties as required: 1 2 3 _4_
   It's good to know we can count on you to get the job done—whatever it is!

7. Ability to complete assigned workload satisfactorily: 1 2 <u>3</u> 4

Your work is high quality but is sometimes completed late (usually because you are a perfectionist!), so time management is an issue here.

8. Ability to supervise and motivate employees effectively: 1 2 <u>3</u> 4

My concern here relates to #5. Your supervision is generally good, but it's hard for you to stop what you're doing to help others during a crunch.

<u>Additional Categories and Comments</u>

Overall, we're very pleased with your work. You are dependable, a hard worker, and able to manage efficiently several demanding tasks at once.

Your work could be improved by better monitoring of office expenditures to keep from going over budget again.

Another area of concern is your occasional tardiness. Although you make up your time, it is important that you arrive promptly at 8:30.

Signature of Evaluator	Position	Date

I have read and discussed this performance appraisal with the evaluator. My comments, if any, are on the reverse side.

Signature of Employee	Date

- A standardized form helps you to evaluate performance based on the actual job description. This style enables you to elaborate on your ratings.

- Leaving space for additional feedback allows you to include other points of praise or criticism and serves as an opener for discussion.

Notification of Promotion (7-26)

Dear Grant:

I'm delighted to confirm your promotion to Director of Parts & Service. When we interviewed internal and external candidates for the position, your five years of loyal service and progressively more responsible positions with the company weighed heavily.

I understand you're planning to take two weeks vacation and assume your new position April 18. At that time, your salary will be $30,000 a year. Your benefits, which we discussed earlier, are described in the attached customized printout.

Since Parts & Service is a major profit center for our dealership, we're very pleased to have you in charge.

Sincerely,

- Promotion letters are easy to write, especially since the promotion has already been discussed in person. Strive for a warm but not effusive tone.
- Make sure all details—salary, starting date—are clear.

Notification of Salary Increase (7-27)

Dear Linda:

I'm pleased to tell you that your salary for next year, starting on the anniversary day of your employment, will be increased 3% to reflect the cost-of-living increase, plus an additional 6% merit increase based on the achievements and increased skills we discussed at your appraisal meeting. This brings your salary to $37,500 next year.

We're delighted to have you with us and look forward to another productive year.

Best wishes,

- Because salary issues are sensitive, these letters are usually sent home.
- Be very specific about the salary figures. Don't let the reader puzzle over the impact of the percentages.

Motivation of Employee (7-28)

Dear Frank,

Thought I'd drop you a note to let you know how well you handled the presentation to Datastar yesterday. I tried to get to you afterward, but you were in deep conversation with John Truman and I had to dash for the plane.

The presentation was great. You really zeroed in on their main issues-turnaround time and capabilities. Even more impressive was the way you handled the question and answer session. You were brief and to the point. You refused to argue with our always contentious client, Mr. Ackerman, and you brought everything to closure after you wrapped up the question and answer session. Keep this up and we'll be giving you more of these kinds of assignments.

Best,

- This should be a very informal, handwritten note—sent to an employee you don't see daily.
- People are far more motivated by sincere praise than by blame, and the remarks are most effective when they are very specific.

Managing Your Business 8

Despite the fact that most of us would prefer to spend all our time on the creative or income producing aspects of our businesses, the reality is that no business can run itself—that is, operate efficiently without coming to grips with the day-to-day logistics of carrying on operations.

Inquiry letters are vitally important because even though you may have adequate financial backing or a large departmental budget, even if you are noted for your technical competence, you still need information on *how to run your business*. Given the complexity of the modern business environment, you have a much better chance of getting the information you need if you put your request on paper and you ask the reader to reply in writing. People may give you a glib answer over the phone, but they'll think twice about misinforming you in writing. In addition, because it takes time to write, you can use these letters to separate those who truly want your business (and therefore are likely to give you good service) from those who take a lackadaisical approach to their customers.

To get the maximum benefit from inquiry letters, be very specific about the result you want from the interchange. Even when your intent is to buy something, don't waste the reader's time and your own by making a vague request. Think about what your needs are before you write. If you can, lay out the precise criteria you intend to use to make the purchase. If you simply cannot pay more than a certain amount of money, for example, telling the vendor what your limits are may forestall his all-too-human tendency to suggest more elaborate and pricier products or services than you can afford.

Inquiries and confirmations concerning travel arrangements and meetings must be very exact. Anyone who has ever found himself in an inadequately curtained meeting room at high noon with the wrong slide carousel for a 35-mm slide presentation can attest to this. Getting all logistical arrangements in writing can save endless time and aggravation. It is also only fair to hotel or rental service personnel, who may be juggling numerous requests and demands for the same facilities on the same day.

If asking for exactly what you want is half the battle, using the appropriate tone is the other half. People can be better judged by the way they treat subordinates and service people than by the way they treat their bosses. If you have any question about the way you come across when you communicate with others, have someone else read your correspondence and give you some feedback.

Inquiry about Office Lease (8-01)

Dear Mr. Stimson:

We would like to renew our office lease for an additional two years. We are very pleased with the office and the maintenance of the building itself.

When we re-read our lease, we noted that there was no automatic renewal clause. We would be willing to increase the rent by 5%.

Please call and let us know if this is acceptable.

Best regards,

- Usually, you can initiate a matter like this with a phone call. Landlords are notoriously difficult to reach, however, so a letter is justified, particularly if the relationship has been relatively good in the past. More importantly, a written record will help avoid future misunderstandings about financial arrangements. You do *not* want to write if you are in a hostile, confrontational mood.

Inquiry to Bank about Outstanding Credit Application (8-02)

Dear Mr. Webster:

I need to know the fate of our application for a $50,000 line of credit which, according to McGregor Carlton, your assistant, has been given file number 20-4326112.

When we first discussed this matter, I stressed the need for access to this credit because of our seasonal cash requirements. We are now ordering for the Christmas season, and many of our overseas suppliers require cash deposits before making production commitments.

According to Mr. Carlton, all problems in granting our request were trivial, yet we have not yet received approval. We have had an account with Nornova for three years, and we feel we are not being treated with the consideration we deserve. Please call me as soon as you receive this letter. My phone number is 663-4499.

Sincerely,

- Banks, like all bureaucracies, are sometimes frustrating to deal with. If you can't get satisfaction with a phone call, write a letter. (To ensure the letter gets prompt attention, you may have to send it by messenger or overnight delivery service.)
- Say *why* your request is urgent in very specific terms. (Everyone says they needed it yesterday—give proof.)

Inquiry about Business Credit Card (8-03)

Dear New Accounts Manager:

Please send us an application for business credit cards. In addition, please write us with the answers to these questions:

- What are your annual fees?
- How is the interest rate calculated?
- Do you provide a computerized end-of-the-year statement broken down by individual user?
- Can we impose different charge limits for different users (specifically, $5,000 for partners; $1,200 for associates)?

We look forward to hearing from you soon.

Sincerely,

- Don't be intimidated by the size of the firm you're dealing with. If you're comparison shopping, and you should, get answers to the same questions from each firm so you can make an informed decision.

Inquiry about Insurance Coverage (8-04)

Dear Mr. Jagoe:

As I mentioned in our phone conversation, Kirk Specialty Products has expanded rapidly in the last year and now has 20 employees. We want to put together a comprehensive insurance plan for our employees and for the business. Three local firms have been asked to submit proposals.

Please consider the following possible types of coverage when structuring your proposal:

- Health insurance, including hospitalization and major medical.
- A SMP (Special Multi-Peril Policy) for on-premises liability.
- Surety bond that will cover both general employee honesty and our payroll people.
- An OLT (Owners, Landlords, and Tenants) policy for ourmachinery and other equipment.
- A Business Automobile policy for the company-owned cars driven by myself and our three sales representatives.

Please submit your proposal and quote as soon as possible. We want to make our decision on insurance coverage by the end of the month.

Sincerely,

Inquiry about Accounting Services (8-05)

Dear John:

Since you've done our partnership tax return for four years now, you're the obvious one to advise us on accounting services. Now that we're expanding, we can no longer take the time to keep the books. I assume Dunning, Hawkes, and Benisch will take these tasks off our hands for a fee. Please let us know what you would charge under the following conditions:

- You would provide the software consultation and training necessary to automate the process with additional help as needed.

- You would provide one of your bookkeeper's services on a monthly basis (no automation).

Please call if you have any questions.

Sincerely,

Inquiry about Office Equipment (8-06)

Dear Faxright:

Our firm, with 20 professional consultants, is interested in purchasing a facsimile machine to communicate more quickly with our clients.

Our criteria are:

- lowest possible price
- ability to delay transmissions until lowest phone rate periods
- good resolution of both text and photographs
- minimum service problems, preferably with self-diagnostics system

Please send me written information on how well your line of fax machines meets these criteria. (We will not respond to phone calls unless we have written information.)

Sincerely,

> - If you're seeking information, help the salespeople out by stating your criteria.
>
> - Insisting on written information helps you screen vendors. Those who don't bother to respond in writing don't care enough to deserve your business.

Inquiry about Car Leasing (8-07)

Dear Manager:

Our company is considering leasing 12 automobiles rather than buying them outright. Because it is important for us to present a favorable (and prosperous) image to our clients, we are interested in luxury cars only.

We have been talking with those of our colleagues who run similar businesses, so we have a rather specific view of what we need. We are interested in an open end, 36-month lease with a 20% down payment. Please let us know what our costs would be for a current-year model Mercedes, and provide a detailed explanation of the other terms of the lease, including our obligation and/or right to buy at the end of the lease term and the price we would pay for each vehicle.

We look forward to hearing from you soon.

Sincerely,

> - You'll naturally consult your tax advisor on any decision of this magnitude.
>
> - The more specific your request for information, the more knowledgeable you appear, the better the facts you will receive, and the better bargaining position you will have.

Inquiry about Consulting Services (8-08)

Dear Mr. Puhl:

We recently noted in the *Mill Valley News* "Business Talks" column that you offer consulting services to small businesses. We have a public relations firm, and we need help interconnecting our current systems. We have three new PC's and a laser printer, plus two very old PC's and a daisy wheel printer.

We would like consulting help to decide whether we should (or could) network our various systems, whether we need to purchase some software to port data between the two systems, and what kind of software we need to support our substantial business in presentation visuals.

Please call us and let us know your background and hourly rates.

Sincerely,

- It's helpful to tell people where you heard of them.
- Make sure you tell the reader what you want help with in the first paragraph.
- Don't overlook asking for background information.

Inquiry to Franchisor (8-09)

Dear Ms. Calhoun:

I am interested in buying a Picture Perfect franchise in Warwick, Rhode Island, and would like to know if you offer your franchisees:

- location analysis
- help in constructing facilities
- ongoing staff training
- discount on supplies
- national advertising

I would also like to know your requirements of franchisees regarding:

- start-up costs and fees
- royalties
- advertising and promotion contributions

Please send me whatever information you have for franchisees as well as details about each of these specific areas. I look forward to learning more about owning a Picture Perfect franchise.

Yours truly,

- It's important to understand each party's (yours and the franchisor's) obligations before you contract to buy a franchise.
- Know what the franchise will provide you in support (critical to your success) as well as what the start-up and operating costs will be.

Inquiry about Phone Equipment (8-10)

Dear Pete:

We are interested in purchasing six telephones for our new office, five to be used on desks and one that will be on the wall. We need a total of seven jacks. As you may remember, we have four lines coming in, three that roll over and one individual line that services our facsimile machine.

We'll be moving January 2, and we must have the phones installed and operating by that date.

Please call me at 632-7777 (I'm most easily available between 8:30 and 9:30 a.m.) and let me know what you would charge me for the phones and jacks and what your terms are. As usual, we're trying to conserve cash.

Sincerely,

- Try to be explicit in your requirements—even if you are just starting the process.
- Always give the person the best time to call.

Inquiry about Utilities Service (8-11)

Dear Mr. Smith:

We are interested in locating a small manufacturing plant at 7 Locust Square. According to our current plans, the manufacturing process in this plant will use a maximum of 5,000 gallons of water per hour during peak periods. In order to get a construction loan, we need written confirmation from you, by the end of the month, that the sewer system in this light manufacturing zone can, in fact, handle that gallonage and that this quantity of water is available from the town's water system.

If you need further clarification of our needs, please write or call me at 652-4411.

Sincerely,

- Even town officials need to know why you're asking for information and when you need it.
- Resist the urge to be abrupt, even if you've become irritated by the slowness of the bureaucratic process.
- Show that you're flexible and cooperative.

Inquiry to Planning and Zoning Commission (8-12)

Dear Mr. Nixon:

We are contemplating a third-floor addition to our boat dealership, which will include 10 office suites. (I've attached the architect's initial sketches.) Before we invest additional money in blueprints, could you please confirm that our location at 23 Birch Road (please see attached plot plan) is indeed zoned for "any industrial use" or whether we will have to seek a variance.

Please call me at 431-9622 and let me know as soon as you can so I can tell the architect to proceed.

Sincerely,

- Frequently, a letter provides the best way to deal with technical issues. In this case, providing sketches and plot plans makes it easy to respond.

Inquiry about Event Planning Services (8-13)

Dear Ms. Baker:

I would like to have a holiday party on December 15 for 50-60 of our firm's most important clients and their guests. The atmosphere should be friendly and sociable, as this is our way of thanking the people who do business with us.

I understand that you have access to caterers, facilities, musicians, and florists that I could not duplicate if I worked at it for months. Please call me at 742-6699 to set up an appointment to discuss how you would handle organizing this event and what your fee schedule is. As you'll notice, time is getting short, so I hope to hear from you soon.

Sincerely,

- If you're unfamiliar with the involved logistics of setting up events or meetings, you may wish to consult a meeting or event planner. The details, after all, can make or break an event—such as failing to have non-alcoholic beverages available for a health-conscious crowd or lack of extra bulbs for overhead projectors, for example.

Inquiry about Supplies (8-14)

Dear Mr. Griswold:

As newcomers to the Fort Lauderdale area, we are seeking a source of computer supplies. We have 11 PC's in house, plus 3 printers (2 laser printers and 1 daisy wheel printer). As you can imagine, we require a quantity of ribbons, disks, and cartridges.

In our old location we dealt with a store that gave us a 20% discount off list for all equipment. We are asking you and two of your competitors about their usual discount for regular customers. Please call me at the number listed below as soon as possible to discuss our opening an account with you.

Sincerely,

- If you want the best deal possible, indicate that you will be a loyal and substantial account—and that you are shopping around.
- Do the heavy negotiating by phone.

Inquiry about Medical Plans (8-15)

Dear Mr. Critelli:

As we discussed, we're interested in health care and possibly disability coverage for our four employees, all nonsmokers, including:

- office manager, female, married, one child (age 35)
- marketing representative, male, married, no children (age 26)
- marketing representative, male, single, no children (age 24)
- senior marketing associate, female, married, adult children who would not be covered by this policy (age 50)

You also offered to price a $10,000 life-insurance policy and a basic dental policy for these employees.

Please send me a letter with the detailed options. We can set up a meeting after I receive it.

Sincerely,

- Dealing with insurance complexities is tiring. Give the insurance representative enough information to provide a quote. Insist on a letter. It preserves your time, and the length of time it takes the person to respond is an indication of how well you'll be served in the future.

Inquiry about Banking Services (8-16)

Dear Optistar Bank:

We are a local gourmet pet food store with $1.1 million in annual sales. We have become dissatisfied with our current bank's service and feel its charges are excessive. We are therefore writing to other area banks to see what services they provide to retail businesses of our size.

Please reply in writing with a complete description of your services and include a schedule of fees. You are welcome to call me if you need further information. After I have researched this issue, I will call to set up an account with the bank we select.

Sincerely,

- If you don't know anyone who can provide a personal recommendation of a good bank (and an introduction to a responsive banker), you'll have to write.

- Try to get banks to respond first in writing. Whether they do so, and how soon, provides some indication of how badly they want your business.

Inquiry about Legal Services (8-17)

Dear Mr. Trotter:

Sarah Cahill has suggested that your firm has the expertise in intellectual properties law to assist me with a software copyright problem. Could you send me resumes of your firm's software copyright law experts, as well as a fee schedule? Because of the frequency with which these issues have arisen in the last two years, I might also be interested in a retainer agreement.

I will call you after I have had a chance to look at your materials.

Sincerely,

- Be specific about what kind of legal services you're interested in.
- Use the name of the person who referred you to get the reader's attention.

Inquiry to Business Association (8-18)

Dear Membership Chairman:

My good friend Bret McCumber tells me that your association has provided him with an "instant network" of like-minded people to share the pleasures and problems of sole proprietorship. I am interested in joining your organization and would like to receive information and a membership application as soon as possible.

Sincerely,

- Indicate why you are interested in becoming a member.
- Ask for action by requesting an application.

Inquiry to Venture Capital Firm (8-19)

Dear Mr. Duke:

George Welles tells me that your firm provides financing for start-up ventures. Before I submit a formal application, I'd like to know in more detail what types of situations you prefer, what kind of participation you usually require, what time limits you generally stipulate, and your collateral requirements.

I will call you on September 10 to discuss these issues.

I look forward to our conversation.

Sincerely,

- In this kind of situation, writing should get you a bit further than a phone call since it's formal and shows serious intent.
- It's vital that you get the details requested. The more similar your financial request is to those that the firm has favored in the past, the more likely you are to get funding.

Inquiry to Federal Government, New Business (8-20)

Dear Mr. Holmes:

I am planning to open a restaurant in Guilford, Connecticut, within a few months and need information regarding regulatory requirements for new business owners (particularly new restaurant owners). Would you please send me whatever information you have on:

- tax regulations
- food service regulations
- regulations of any agency under whose purview restaurants fall

If necessary, please direct me also to any other federal agencies that you feel I should contact.

Sincerely,

- Specify the kind of business you're opening.
- State the information you need as specifically as possible, while leaving the door open for additional information.
- Be prepared to follow up; bureaucracies are often slow.

Inquiry to State Government, New Business (8-21)

Dear Ms. Fountain:

I am planning to open a beauty salon in a small shopping mall within the next few months and would like information regarding:

- state tax filing requirements
- liability insurance requirements
- state regulations affecting beauty salons

Please send me whatever information you have available on the above (or other regulations that will affect my business) and direct me to the state agencies that I should contact before I begin my venture.

Sincerely,

- Specify the kind of business you're opening.
- State what kind of information you need and ask whether there are any other regulations of which you should be aware.
- Follow up if you do not get a prompt response.

Request for Help from Elected Representative (8-22)

Dear Mr. Marcus:

I understand from Thomas Lexington that Senator North has forwarded our correspondence to you. As you have seen, it concerns our interest in having the Environmental Protection Agency grant us a waiver that will allow our factory to burn low sulfur fuel oil.

We understand from Mr. Lexington that the EPA may not act on our application for several months, even a year or more. If so, our factory, as well as the others in our area, will lose the savings that would accompany use of this much less expensive fuel oil. For our factory alone, the savings would be in the $62,000 range, and I'm sure that the all-around savings in the area might be up to $1 million or even more.

As I explained in my letter to Senator North, I have called Mr. Fred Downey, who is a member of the House Subcommittee on Health and the Environment, to ask his help in urging the EPA to act on this matter as quickly as possible. I have not yet heard from his office. I imagine, however, that he has heard from many other businesspeople in this area on this matter.

We would very much appreciate your help in this matter. Because of the relatively shaky condition of the economy in our area, I know that we have a mutual interest in getting the kind of savings that will allow businesses like ours to survive.

Sincerely yours,

- Putting these matters before elected representatives is an extremely important part of an executive's job. This letter provides the reader with a sense of the bases that have already been covered, as well as the reasons for doing what the writer suggests (because the consequences otherwise might include closing a plant, with a loss of jobs, in his district).

Request for Action to Local Town Government (8-23)

Dear Mr. Tompkins:

During the last four months, the Town has undertaken various improvements related to the sewer installations in the Rockland Park area. During the course of these improvements, a landfill dike was constructed across the inlet that runs from the Sound to our property line.

My primary concern is that the dike has created a large area of trapped brackish water and mud between the dike and our property. The resulting stagnant pools are a nuisance that is both unsightly and unhealthy. Sewage drainage from several businesses is now trapped. This problem will continue until the final extension of the sewer line. Inquiries at your office last week indicate that this project may not be funded for some years.

We request, then, that the area between the dike and our property be filled to a sufficient height to eliminate the water/swamp problem. The attached map indicates the area of concern.

I would be pleased to accompany you, or someone from your department, on a site visit. If you prefer, please review the situation and let me know as soon as possible if my proposed solution is workable.

Sincerely,

- Create a sense of government responsibility for the problem in the first paragraph.
- Offer a solution or alternate solutions.

Request to Employment Agency for Information (8-24)

Dear Personnel Resources Staff:

We've noted with interest the bulletins on secretarial and administrative help that you send us on a regular basis, and we would like to inquire about your method of operation and your fees. Specifically, we would like to know whether you charge a percentage of the person's salary or a flat fee. We would also be interested in your guarantee. If the person leaves after a month's employment, is the fee refundable?

We would very much appreciate receiving your brochure and a current client listing.

Sincerely,

- It's always helpful to tell people where you heard about their firm. It establishes a more personal relationship immediately.
- Ask for a representative client listing so you can do a check of their competence and the types of businesses served.

Request to Executive Search Firm for Information (8-25)

Dear Mr. Silva:

Your firm has been recommended to me by Howard Davies at Thompson, Thornberg and Reiss, who speaks very highly of the candidates you placed at his firm.

Newton and Marcus has recently reorganized, leaving us in need of three product managers. I'd like information regarding your firm's services, particularly:

- fee structure
- guarantees
- approach

I'd like to talk with you personally about the type of people we're looking for as well as how your firm can help us with our staffing needs. Please call so we can arrange a mutually convenient time to talk.

Sincerely,

- If the firm has been recommended, state by whom.
- State what your company's needs are and what information you want.
- Ask the consultant to speak with you personally (he'll be happy to).

Request to Temporary Agency for Information and Rates (8-26)

Dear Mr. Groton:

Gerry Hought of Hought, Layton, and Steele suggested that you were the best person in the area to talk to about accounting temporaries. Our firm is not quite as large as Gerry's, but it is similar in most other respects, including our need for temporary help in the traditional peak seasons.

Gerry has given me some information about the way you work, but I would appreciate a detailed description of your rates, your guarantees (for example, what happens if we are dissatisfied with a particular temp?), and the fees you charge if we decide to hire an individual on a full-time basis.

I look forward to hearing from you soon.

Sincerely,

- If you have talked to a client of the temporary agency, make that very plain in the letter. You will get better service.
- The more specific your request for information, the better. For example, asking about the policy if you decide to hire someone full time indicates that you've dealt with temporary agencies before and are therefore relatively knowledgeable.

Dealing with Local Government (8-27)

Dear Mr. Brien:

I have checked the record of the assessment of my property at 2033 Buckskin Trail, and I believe I have found two errors: the assessment is calculated on a square footage of 100,000. In fact, the dimensions of the lot are 150' by 100', or 15,000 square feet. In addition, the "single-family dwelling" referred to in the assessment is a storage shed. In order to stay on good terms with the neighbors, we added a false front and landscaping. I would be pleased to meet you or someone from your office to show you the interior of the shed.

I understand that such problems arise in any major reassessment. I do hope, however, to resolve the matter as soon as possible as taxes based on this assessment represent a real burden to my business.

I will call you next week to set up an appointment.

Sincerely,

> - Mistakes can happen. Recognizing this, and taking a reasonable tone, will get you farther than ranting and raving.
>
> - It's always wise to evaluate your assessment by comparing it with that of similar properties. If you believe it is high, check the assessment itself for errors.

Dealing with Tenants (8-28)

Dear Ms. Dornfield:

We've very much enjoyed having your firm as tenants for the past two years and hope to continue the relationship. As you know, your lease ends August 31, and you have an option to renew for an additional two years with a 10% escalation in rent, as before.

Please call or write and let us know what you intend to do. We hope for a positive answer.

Sincerely,

> - If it's hard to reach someone by phone, a note may get his or her attention. But sending a letter by itself isn't enough. Make a note to call within a week or so as the mails can be unreliable.

Dealing with Your Landlord (8-29)

Dear George:

I'm happy that we've cleared up the misunderstanding about our renovations to our office space at 60 Ferry Street.

To recap, we are not making any changes to the building that will affect the load bearing capabilities of the existing structure. As you can see from the attached plan provided by our contractor, all new walls are non-load-bearing, and we plan no demolition of existing partitions or walls.

As we discussed yesterday, these changes are within the provisions of our lease. I'm glad you agree that these renovations will significantly improve the space.

Sincerely,

> - If there's any possibility of misunderstanding, put it in writing. (If the details imply any contractual obligations, you'll probably want your attorney to look at the letter.)
>
> - Make sure your tone is reasonably informal and neutral. An adversarial tone almost never serves your needs.

Request to Excuse Employee from Jury Duty (8-30)

Dear Chief Clerk:

Ms. Jodie L. Forbes has been notified to appear in the state court on July 2 for jury duty. Ms. Forbes is the sole secretary/administrative assistant in Watley and Carling's three-person office, and she is essential to the operation of the business. This is our busiest season and we could not process our orders if Ms. Forbes were to serve at this time.

Please excuse her from jury duty.

Sincerely,

- Serving on a jury is a civic duty, and no one should be excused unless there is real hardship. If the person is an essential employee, providing evidence of the hardship may help.

- In some states, where the obligation for jury service involves "one day or one trial," it's probable that only a medical excuse from a physician will get the person excused.

Business Plan, Executive Summary (8-31)

Executive Summary

The Concept House, Inc., an innovative desk-top publishing company, seeks $500,000 in venture capital to fund initial start-up costs and to acquire a database of high-quality conceptual graphics for executive presentations.

The current desk-top publishing market has five relatively large firms, but none of them provides conceptual graphics by top artists. The major problem is the antiquated retrieval system, which makes turnaround time excessively long. As a result, most executives hire outside artists at very high rates. The Concept House will create a database using only top artists by paying them top prices on a per use basis.

The Concept House's management team, T. L. Williams and Joseph Frey, are both experienced. Williams has created the top-selling conceptual graphics computer program in the industry; Frey is an award-winning artist with extensive connections. Frey's task is to sign artists to exclusive contracts.

Sales and marketing forecasts project that investors will have a significant profit within the first two years. The partners, who have invested a very substantial percentage of their personal assets, project that they will buy out the venture capitalist interest in Year 4.

The Concept House provides a much needed service in a growing market.

Full information on this opportunity is available from Kyle Benson, President, Benson Associates, 1400 Manorhaven Boulevard, Port Washington, NY 11050, who is representing The Concept House.

- The executive summary should provide enough information to "sell" the venture capitalist on the need to talk further, without giving everything away.

- Naturally, if you are representing yourself, you will give your own name and address.

Business Plan, Executive Summary Cover Letter (8-32)

Dear Mr. Isaacson:

I've attached an executive summary of a business plan for The Concept House, Inc., an innovative presentation graphics development company whose principals are seeking $500,000 in venture capital for a start-up situation.

If the financing arrangements interest you, I would be happy to send you a complete business plan. Please write or call me. I look forward to talking with you soon.

Sincerely yours,

- To save everyone's time, it's better to get someone's attention by sending an executive summary with a cover letter rather than sending the entire business plan. With this method, you can determine who is interested in the concept and the general financial arrangements, without letting everyone know your competitive secrets.

Request for Help (8-33)

Dear Tom:

How are you? I hope you and your family are fine and that business is treating you well.

Since I last saw you at the reunion, I've developed a new line of tamper-proof packaging for bottles. Do you know of any distributors in the food machinery business who would be interested in representing me? I'd greatly appreciate any contacts you could pass along. Please call if you have any questions; otherwise, I'll call next week.

Thanks for your help.

Sincerely yours,

- Be specific as to the information you want.
- Take the responsibility of getting back to them for the answers rather than waiting for them to get back to you.
- Express appreciation for their anticipated help.

Thank You for Help (8-34)

Dear Norm:

Thanks for answering my question the other day. I understand that there may be more to the issue than meets the eye, but I appreciate your giving me some sense of my legal obligations. If my informal negotiations aren't successful, I'll call you immediately to set up an appointment.

Again, thank you for helping me out. You know you can always count on me to serve as your "tax hotline."

Best wishes

- Professionals are in the business of charging for their expertise. Don't abuse a friendship by asking for detailed (and free) advice. In this situation, there is clearly reciprocity—the writer and the reader trade information and advice freely.

SBA Loan Application Cover Letter (8-35)

Dear Mr. Hallogan:

We've attached an application for a $100,000 business loan. You will note that there are three attachments explaining our financials and credit history. We also have someone interested in buying any portion of the loan that the SBA chooses to guarantee.

We look forward to your response.

Sincerely,

Attachments

- If you need to explain anything and there's no room on the application, provide attachments.
- If you have someone interested in buying the guaranteed portion of the loan, say so. (You need not give a name.)

Announcement of Annual Meeting (8-36)

The Annual Meeting of stockholders in Lidditz Corporation will be held in the Grand Ballroom of the Inn at Big Mountain, 7777 South Big Mountain Parkway, Phoenix, Arizona, on June 15, at 10 a.m., for the following purposes:

- to elect six directors
- to act upon stockholder proposals

- to transact such other business as properly may come before the meeting

Your vote is important!

- It's always a good idea to list the topics to be subject of the meeting, as well as the time and place.

Announcement of Board Meeting (8-37)

Subject: Quarterly Board Meeting

The Executive Board of the Regis Corporation will hold its quarterly meeting on Monday, October 17, at 10 a.m. in the Executive Conference Room at Regis Corporation Headquarters, Denver, Colorado. The attached agenda outlines the issues we have scheduled for discussion. Please call Celeste Talbott at (303) 555-6431 x6209 to indicate whether or not you will attend and if you wish to add additional items to the agenda.

Attachment

- Give all important data: date, time, location.
- Attach agenda.
- Provide an easy way to RSVP (you'll get a better response).

Request for Hotel Rates (8-38)

Dear Reservations Director:

Please send us your room rates for long-term arrangements. We need

four single rooms for two months starting October 1 and ending November 30. I understand you have only suite-style rooms, which our employees prefer. They must also have non-smoking rooms.

We are asking two of your competitors to tell us their rates. We do have a preference for your hotel, since it comes highly recommended and is located only four blocks from our client's headquarters. Price, however, is a factor, especially considering the lengthy stay.

Please respond in writing at your earliest convenience.

Sincerely,

- Normally, hotel reservations are made on the phone. If you want to negotiate, ask the reservations people to respond in writing.
- "Dear Sir or Madam" is another possibility when you don't have a name to use in the salutation.

Reservation of Hotel/Meeting Facility (8-39)

Dear Mr. Wayne:

I enjoyed talking to you Tuesday. The Proxmire Inn does indeed have the facilities we require for our firm's quarterly planning meeting.

I'd like to confirm that we've agreed to book "the cottage," which includes a large meeting room for our entire department (25 people), as well as two smaller conference rooms for committee meetings (8-10 people each). The date we agreed on was June 25.

We need the following A/V equipment:

> In the large meeting room:
>
> > An overhead projector and screen
> > A VCR and monitor
>
> In each of the smaller rooms:
>
> > An overhead projector and screen
> > Two flip charts

The fee for the cottage will be $800, to include the A/V equipment and lunch. I will be calling June 5 to check on these arrangements. In the meantime, please send me a written confirmation.

Sincerely,

- It doesn't hurt to treat hotel personnel as if they were human beings. If you did enjoy talking to them, say so.
- Conferences can be scuttled by insufficient attention to logistics. Put it in writing and get a written response. Then follow up with a phone call.

Confirmation of Equipment Rental (8-40)

Dear Ms. Nistrom:

As we discussed on the phone yesterday, you have agreed to rent us the following equipment on July 12 from 8:00 a.m. to 1:00 p.m.:

- black and white monitor
- VCR
- camera
- overhead projector
- whiteboard

In addition, you have agreed to have one of your staff set up the equipment by 7:30 a.m., and to run the equipment for the duration of our interviewing workshop. We will be holding the workshop in our fourth floor conference room.

According to your quote yesterday, the cost for the rental of the equipment and the assistance of your staff person will be $255.00 inclusive.

As I mentioned to you yesterday, your firm came highly recommended, and we look forward to working with you.

Sincerely yours,

> • Even if you've detailed everything thoroughly in a phone conversation, putting it all down on paper will avoid difficulties later. Be sure to refer to the cost that the firm quoted you and be very specific about the equipment.

Appreciation to Hotel/Facility for Help/Good Service (8-41)

Dear Manager:

Our firm, Bowden, Inc., had an offsite meeting at your facility on May 11. We were greeted by Gus Menzies when we arrived, and we found his assistance invaluable for the rest of the day. He checked on our needs frequently but unobtrusively, handled our crisis with the overhead projector (which we had supplied) with good humor and swiftness, and, all in all, gave us an enormous amount of confidence that our every need would be met.

Please thank him for us.

Sincerely,

> • Good service should be noted, and writing to the manager shows your gratitude, provides tangible recognition of the person, and helps assure that your company will get good service in the future. (People complain of the decline in service while failing to recognize that the decline in customer courtesy has accelerated it.)

Complaint to Hotel/Facility about Poor Service (8-42)

Dear Mr. Rivers:

I have stayed at the Trail Drive Inn every September, December, and May for over 7 years. In every instance, I have been more than pleased with the facility and service.

Last week, however, I was horrified to return to my room to find that the maid had discarded (and, it ultimately transpired, incinerated) an entire carton of confidential papers that I had left on the credenza in my room. I spoke to the front desk clerk, who kindly tore up my bill. Nevertheless, I wish to make sure this costly and personally embarrassing episode is not repeated.

Please note in your records that on subsequent stays, my room is to be cleaned, but that nothing, including the contents of wastebaskets, is to be removed until I check out.

Sincerely,

- If you're a steady customer, say so up front; it makes a difference.
- If you want something to happen, you'll have to ask for it. Giving a facility an opportunity to make good on a loss allows them to keep a valued customer and gives you a greater feeling of security. Writing to the hotel manager is a good way of ensuring that you'll get what you want.

Special Travel Requirements for Company Employees (8-43)

Dear Mr. Sliney:

Until further notice, please make these arrangements when booking airline reservations for the following employees:

Paul Gordon: aisle seat, vegetarian meal
Tonya Marinelli: bulkhead seat, low-calorie meal
Lindley Chitters: aisle seat, low-calorie meal

As you have already noted in your file, all these employees are non-smokers.

Thanks for your help.

Sincerely,

- Travel agents are among the most harried people on earth. Make it easy for them to serve you by putting special requirements in writing.

Internal Communications 9

Written communications were once the major method of communicating internally. As management styles became more participative and less directive, however, internal communication tended to be more in the form of a quick "huddle" in the hall, a short meeting, or a phone call rather than the standard memo. Now, with the advent of people operating in widely dispersed locations, the written word is once again assuming more importance.

A well run business or department demands writing. Take agendas, for example. Agendas have an action bias—they not only stipulate what actions are required, they also specify who is responsible for taking action. The person who writes them, therefore, has a much greater chance of getting decisions implemented than someone who runs a meeting by the "seat of his pants."

Recommendations and reports. A memo that makes a recommendation saves everyone time by highlighting the reasons for the recommendation. Many decision makers actually think better when they have something in writing (these are the people who say "send me a memo so I can react to it"), and creating a cogent, logical argument on paper may be all you need to do to convince the reader.

The report is a dying breed. It used to be considered a "product," an end in itself, but more and more the product is the decision, the action, or the plan rather than a tome gathering dust on the shelf. Whether or not reports are produced depends on the decision maker—some decision makers want reports to reassure them that all the bases have been covered; some only want a presentation that shows (rather than tells) them that the recommendation is based on tight reasoning and extensive research. In any case, the decision maker usually reads the executive summary. Perhaps he or she will read *only* the executive summary, especially if the writer has high credibility and a "good news" message. The executive summaries included in this section follow all the rules. They attract the reader's attention by telling him or her why it's important to read on, and then they tell the main point and summarize the organization of the report itself. To write a lucid executive summary, you must have good organization. Otherwise, you'll find yourself writing things like this: "This report begins with an introduction (what else

would it begin with?) and continues with an analysis of the problem...I then discuss..."
That approach, which may sound frighteningly familiar, is deadly dull.

Policies and procedures. Great care should be taken with any written explanation—whether it is a new policy or procedure or a clarification of an existing policy—because staff members often feel threatened by change. Take the time to detail why a change has been made or why a clarification is required. This will reduce needless speculation (often erroneous) by employees, and will help them understand the reasoning behind company decisions.

Announcements. Managers tend to speed through the writing of announcements, but that's a mistake. Even if a decision has already been made, and a change is already in the works, treating the staff as if they were uninvolved is insulting. Most efficient managers consult the people affected before making any major change, to get their comments and suggestions, so announcements of new procedures are surprise-free; that is, they merely confirm what has already been agreed upon. Similarly, promotions and resignations should be announced first in staff meetings, with memos following in case people haven't heard the news directly. Once again, the purpose of writing it down in these cases is to solidify and make real to people news that is already "old."

If an executive or manager must impart bad news to the entire company, a written communication is essential. A memo dealing with difficult conditions should be direct and should say clearly what problems must be faced. If there are potential solutions, of if employee cooperation can help in specific ways, the details should be spelled out.

Notification of Meeting (9-01)

Subject: Quarterly Meeting

In response to the feedback session at the last quarterly meeting, our fourth quarter meeting will be held offsite—at the Huckleberry River Inn in Blackthorn on January 30. I've enclosed a simplified map and an agenda. As usual, the meeting will start at 9 a.m. and end at 4 p.m. I look forward to seeing you there.

- Meeting notices should be complete, including references to who, what, when, and where. Enclosing a map is essential for offsite meetings, and an agenda is also vital.

- If you have responded to staff suggestions, make sure you point it out.

Agenda (9-02)

Objective: Revise vacation policy

Attendees: Lon Beardsley
Tony Marinelli
Sam Skryzak

Agenda Item	Purpose	Time	Presenter
Review vacation policies of competitors	Background	5 mins.	L.B.
Discuss feedback from staff	Establish criteria for change	10 mins.	L.B.
Review cost considerations	Establish cost criteria	10 mins.	L.B.
Brainstorm solutions	Generate alternatives	10 mins.	T.M.
Make decision		10-15 mins.	T.M.

- For major decisions, make sure you allow time to set criteria *and* brainstorm solutions.
- If you say you'll decide, you *will* decide.

Agenda, Background Meeting (9-03)

Objective: Decide whether to increase in-house production capacity in printing

Attendees: Christopher Covale
Michael Endolf
Simone Martens
Jud Powers
Jillian Stabley
Heather White

Agenda Item	Purpose	Time	Presenter	Material To Be Read in Advance
Establish criteria for making decision	Consensus	15 mins.	– –	– –
Review 5-year production figures	Information	10 mins.	J.S.	Figures
Estimate long and short-term demands	Decision	20 mins.	S.M.	– –
Review cost estimate	Information	15 mins.	J.P.	Estimates
Consider potential short-term use of excess capacity	Decision	20 mins.	C.C.	Estimates

- Always indicate your objective and plan of action to give participants a sense of comfort that their time won't be wasted.

- Assign tasks to people to make sure they are involved and prepared.

Follow-up to Meeting, Assignments (9-04)

Subject: Assignments for Facility Addition Presentation

Action	Person Responsible	Completion Date
Develop new exhibits showing demand by sector.	J.P.	July 18
Create chart for senior management, showing best, worst, and most	H.W.	July 16

likely printing demand
trends; support with text
attachments.

Gather cost estimate for 2,000 and 4,000 square foot print shop additions.	C.C.	July 16

Next meeting scheduled for July 21.

- When you reach agreement on an item requiring action, write out the action and identify the person responsible.

- Distribute assignments as soon as possible after the meeting so those concerned can be aware of everyone's tasks and will know where to direct their own input.

Planning Memo (9-05)

Subject: Sale of FORMATS

Microware, Inc., a commercial software firm, has expressed interest in purchasing a license to market FORMATS, an interactive computer program we've developed in-house. It is essential that we act promptly because one of the two programmers who developed FORMATS has already left us and the other will be leaving in two months. No one else in the firm can develop the program for the commercial market. As a result, we may both lose a useful tool and miss the opportunity to sell the program, since Microware has indicated it will not purchase the program unless we provide training.

There are two ways to sell FORMATS to Microware: The company can either agree to let Microware market FORMATS in exchange for royalties, or it can sell the rights to Microware for a one-time fee. I recommend the second option because the paperwork will be completed and tax problems resolved all at one time.

Microware and our remaining programmers have tentatively agreed both on the training schedule and on the one-time licensing fee. I will call you to set up an appointment to make final arrangements.

- If it is urgent to act, say so.
- If the decision-maker wants both options, give them to him, but also say what you want to have happen and why.
- Move towards action by asking for an appointment.

Recap of Meeting (9-06)

Subject: Media Strategy for Sunday Openings

At our February 20 meeting, we decided to open all suburban branches of the bank on

Sundays in order to serve our existing customers better and to attract new accounts. I've met with Stiller and Orlando, our advertising agency, and they suggest a 12-week advertising campaign, using newspapers as the umbrella media.

In brief, they recommend the following:

Newspapers. Place one full-page ad each week in the four regional weekly newspapers for the first four weeks of the campaign. Run a half page each week in the two urban newspapers during the same period. To sustain awareness of the Sunday opening, a third, smaller ad should run in all newspapers for the remaining eight weeks.

Statement Stuffers. Supplement the newspaper ads with 70,000 statement stuffers to reach existing bank customers. The stuffers will use the same creative theme as the newspaper ads and will also be available as "take ones" in each branch office.

Drive-In Window and Lobby Posters. Place color posters at drive-in windows and lobby entrances at each of the branches.

Outdoor Advertising. Change the copy on our 24 billboards and put up a new billboard sign advertising the Sunday opening on 16 additional billboards. (See attached example.)

So far, S & O has not provided the specific reasoning behind their strategy. I feel strongly that we should not go ahead with this plan until they provide the back-up. Neither you nor I have enough expertise to evaluate their recommendations without it. In addition, I have told them that they must provide a budget as soon as possible.

- Remind the reader of the reason for the memo-always a good idea.

- Highlight the main points with headings.

- Outline clearly the next steps to be taken.

Thank You for Employee Suggestion, Accepted (9-07)

Subject: Word Processing Work-flow

Thank you again for your recent suggestion about reorganizing the work flow in the word-processing department. We had a meeting with the people concerned last week, and they enthusiastically accepted your idea for assigning individual word processing operators to specific departments so that the operators can become familiar with the dictating styles of the individual managers and the technical subject matter. Naturally, we'll reassess the new system after a month or so to see how it's working, but we expect that it will be a great improvement over our current system, which has been the source of endless complaints.

John Harvey and I discussed this improvement in a recent meeting, and he wanted to make sure I thanked you for him as well.

- A steady flow of suggestions and recommendations is vital to a well-run business.

- Encourage communication by responding promptly, telling the specifics of the implementation, and making sure the word gets to higher-ups in the firm.

Thank You for Employee Suggestion, Cannot Use (9-08)

Subject: Quota Club Meeting

Thank you for suggesting that we hold this year's Quota Club meeting at Marco Island, Florida. I've visited there myself, and the spot certainly is idyllic. We are already committed to holding this year's meeting at Sea Island, Georgia, however, and cannot change at this late date. I will keep Marco in mind when I schedule next year's event, though, and will seriously explore finding a suitable facility there.

- Make your thanks sincere.

- Give a reasonable (and truthful) reason why you can't act on the suggestion and offer hope for future consideration, if it exists.

Request for Change in Project (9-09)

Subject: Change in Soldering Iron Design

It was great to hear in the Tuesday meeting that the design of the new soldering iron is almost complete. Unfortunately, something came up yesterday that will cause us a bit of a problem. As you know, Don Getman returned this week from India, and he's just now had an opportunity to look at the specs. His major issue is the placement of the logo. He wants the soldering iron to "fit in with the appearance of the entire product line," which essentially means that he wants the company logo to be displayed more prominently.

Since we had early discussions on the placement of the logo, I know that we anticipated this objection and that you have a series of alternatives in hand. Let's meet tomorrow and agree on the best alternative for giving Don what he wants. If you're available at 8:00 a.m., that's a good time for me. It also allows us time to schedule a meeting with Don later in the day.

I believe we can resolve this issue to everyone's satisfaction and still meet our deadline.

- Managers have to deal with last-minute changes, and explaining them to staff is difficult.

- Make your point directly and clearly.

Request for Employee Participation in Charity Drive (9-10)

Subject: Community Campaign

We have always had a proud tradition of supporting the Community Campaign, that excellent organization that helps us to extend a helping hand to the needy in our community.

Soon, you will have the opportunity to share in this fine tradition, once again, through your support of our annual Community Campaign.

By giving just one hour's pay each month, through payroll deduction, you ensure that the health and human care needs of our communities are met the whole year.

I urge you to join me in contributing to the Community Campaign so that together we may help improve the quality of life for everyone.

- Usually, the organizing institution provides boilerplate letters. Try to personalize them if possible.
- Make it easy by offering payroll deductions.

Progress Report, Executive Summary (9-11)

Subject: Mid-point Progress Report—Marmot River Plant

As I reported last month, changing the coating of the steam lines to a zinc base, while worthwhile in terms of reduced cost, has caused us to slip the schedule by two months. We have had additional problems in the last month. Because of an early freeze, we were not able to break ground for the laboratory addition. We estimate that this setback will cost us six months for that part of the project. Because of the increased time involved, we will incur additional labor costs. We will therefore be over budget by approximately $56,000.

Impact of the early freeze confined to laboratory addition. No one could have anticipated the severity of the October 20 freeze, the worst in 25 years. The schedule, as outlined in our original proposal and as revised last month, was predicated on more normal temperatures. Naturally, this affects only the laboratory addition. Renovations to the main plant itself, where we have already "closed the envelope," or made the building weather-tight, will progress on the schedule we set forth last month.

Renovations to main plant close to revised schedule. We have completed the new flooring and all major rewiring. We have also replaced all light fixtures. This month we will be testing the flooring's ability to bear the new equipment. (All equipment was delivered on schedule. It has been stored in the yard for the past month under weather-proof sheathing.)

- Executive summaries for progress reports may be in the form of transmittal letters, memos (like this one), or individual pages after the title page.

- Use action headings (statements of significance) rather than generic headings (work completed, cost, conclusion) to make your points. If you're not on schedule, say so, and say why, without assigning blame or whining.

Final Report, Executive Summary (9-12)

Executive Summary

J. M. Finnerty Corporation has had a contractual agreement with the Leveland County Commission on Human Rights since 1986. This year's goal under the agreement was to fill 15% of the Corporation's middle-management positions with minorities and 35% with females, through either promotion or external search. Unfortunately, we have been unsuccessful thus far. Only 7% of our middle-management positions are held by minorities, 16% by women. If the corporation fails to meet these goals in the next 10-month period, the ensuing litigation could represent a cost of a minimum of $95,000, even if arbitration is possible in some instances.

We have contacted Herman K. Fanton, a consultant skilled in training management in minority recruiting practices, and he is willing to help us institute a new program that will:

- provide intensive training for each manager with hiring responsibility
- institute new skills training programs to encourage promotion from within
- evaluate progress at each step

Rationale and technical back-up (including consultant's proposal, graph detailing minority and female recruitment, and table of median legal costs in similar cases) are attached.

- Executive summaries for final reports come after the title page of the report and so require no heading but the title.

- State why the report is important and highlight its organization through the use of bullets. If the writer has high credibility, and if the reader finds the message convincing, agreement could be reached on the basis of the summary.

Explanation for Lateness of Work/Report (9-13)

Subject: Lateness of Promotional Materials for Schweitzer's Soda

We've had a terrible time getting the printer to stick to the delivery schedule on the Schweitzer's Soda posters. I believe it is still possible to meet the deadline for delivery to the distributors, but it's going to be close.

There are two reasons for the delay. We were set back almost a full week when we discovered errors in the artwork. These mistakes should have been caught by my staff. We are going to change some procedures to prevent this from happening in the future.

The second problem is that we increased the printing order by over 50% at the client's request. The printer couldn't handle it, and it was too late to find another. We found another shop to augment the first, but we were already behind.

As I said, I think we will still make the deadline of June 5, but it's going to take some serious babysitting.

- Admit any errors or misjudgments on your part, but don't grovel. Take responsibility, and use straightforward, non-evasive language.

- Give the whole story. Often your boss must report to his boss, and he/she needs all the facts.

Recommendation to Purchase Equipment (9-14)

Subject: System 10 Upgrade

I recommend we purchase an IBM 4420-H12 disk drive to address the storage capacity problem we now have with System 10.

Purchasing this unit will allow us to:

- add the storage capacity we need to complete projects now underway
- upgrade System 10 cost-effectively

Add Storage Capacity

The IBM 4420-H12 will provide 700 megabytes of auxiliary storage to System 10. It will eliminate our current critical capacity problem and allow us to move forward with our plan to provide additional system functions.

Upgrade Cost-effectively

The IBM 4420-H12, at $13,000, is the least expensive option for meeting our needs and avoids having to upgrade the entire system now. The two other units we have considered, the 3840-A12 and the 4420-H13, cost $41,000 and $26,000, respectively. Upgrading the entire System 10 now would cost over $50,000. Although the entire system will have to be upgraded eventually, I do not see sufficient reason to do so now.

The IBM 4420-H12 clearly suits our needs best. With your authorization, we can move ahead on purchasing and installing this unit.

- Lay out your specific recommendation up front and let the reader know why it's important.

- Clearly state the benefits of your recommendation.

- Be sure to end by restating your recommendation and telling the reader what needs to be done next.

Recommendation to Adopt a Course of Action (9-15)

Subject: Budget Finance Loan

At its next meeting, the Committee must decide whether to approve the purchase of $1.2 million of convertible debentures in Budget Finance Corporation, a financial services company, headed by George Ephram, that buys commercial paper from retailers in low-income neighborhoods. I recommend that we approve this purchase: It both meets our financial criteria and advances us toward our advertised goal of participating in the revitalization of low-income areas.

Financial Criteria

- Budget Finance should be able to make payments on schedule. The anticipated increase in business seems reasonable, given Budget's strong management and projected market growth.

  1. Budget's program should attract retailers and overcome the industry's traditional problems—shoddy merchandise, inadequate follow-up on defaults, and poor selection of potential customers.

  2. In addition, the bilingual partner and employees should attract new business in the Spanish-speaking community.

  3. Budget's experienced management, innovative systems, and training and computer programs, combined with a growing economy, should easily provide Budget with the cash flow necessary to repay its debt to the bank.

Minority Community

- This loan will be a visible symbol of the bank's commitment to helping low-income areas.

  1. Budget is involved in almost every neighborhood in which we have a branch (see Exhibit 1).

  2. Joint advertising, both print and TV, will reinforce this tie.

  3. Acquisition of convertible debentures will demonstrate the bank's interest in participating in the ownership of local business.

  4. Budget's training programs and the loan will have a ripple effect: Budget will channel the bank's funds to retailers, indirectly contributing to their increased sales.

- Memos recommending a course of action should have a very tight argument. Here the investment committee clearly cares about the financial issue—and about aiding the minority community.

- Use of bullets and numbered points help readers to absorb the major points quickly.

Recommendation to Adopt a Strategy (9-16)

Subject: Increasing Support for Work Art Programs

Attendance at the city-funded "Work Art" project at the South plant has been light. As we discussed last week, city involvement at the plant is an important and visible example of business and government cooperation that should receive strong support. My informal analysis suggests that poor scheduling is the primary reason for low attendance, and I have developed a strategy to solve that problem.

Low Attendance Follows Poor Scheduling. Poor scheduling has adversely influenced the possibility of getting a good turnout. For example, "art-break" activities have been planned for the cafeteria during the noon hour. Because the previous plant manager declared the cafeteria off-limits to production line workers during lunchtime, these workers are still reluctant to attend events there, even though the new manager has rescinded that rule. In addition, several events have been scheduled during the 10-minute morning breaks. Workers stationed at any distance from the sites of these events cannot possibly get to them.

New Scheduling Strategy Will Improve Chances of Success. Scheduling changes can directly improve worker participation. Future events should be located in "neutral" areas, preferably outside the plant. Programs should be scheduled during shift changes rather than during working hours, and all programs should be scheduled during daylight hours to allay fears of workers who do not live in the area.

Next Steps. I suggest we meet next week to discuss how to implement this strategy and to consider other informal ways to encourage attendance at art events.

- This memo provides a cogent strategy and the support for it.
- Headings highlight the main points.

Procedure for Dealing with the Media (9-17)

Subject: Media Policy

Our policy for dealing with the media is to respond quickly and politely. Do not refuse to speak to media representatives or fail to return their phone calls. News is only news for a very short time, and the media must print or broadcast something. It's better if that something comes directly from a spokesperson for our company.

In general, it is best to refer media calls to me. I'm trained to deal with the media, and individual reporters are likely to prefer dealing with me in any case. If I am not available, Nancy Anne Hart, my administrative assistant, will know whom to call.

If no one is available and you must talk with a media representative, be sure that you do not give him or her misleading or incomplete information. Do not provide any information that could be construed as proprietary or personal. Do not give opinions—only factual information. If you do not know the answer to a question, say so. Never speculate. Your speculation is likely to be printed as a fact.

Clarification of Existing Policy (9-18)

Subject: Long-Term Salary Continuance Insurance Policy

Because we're a new firm, we've only recently started to provide formal, written notices of our policies and procedures. As some of you know, Joe Drabnik and I are working on a booklet describing these policies. We hope to have it ready by January 1.

In the meantime, though, many of you have asked about the long-term salary continuance plan. An employee becomes eligible after completing two years of continuous employment with the company, provided the employee works at least an average of 30 hours a week.

Once you are eligible, you are automatically enrolled in the plan. The plan pays you monthly benefits if you become totally disabled. The payments start 90 days after the disability, and continue until age 65. Payments are 60% of your base monthly salary up to a maximum benefit of $3,000 a month. "Base monthly salary" means your monthly rate of earnings immediately prior to becoming disabled. It does not include overtime or bonuses. Benefits will be reduced by any income you are entitled to receive from Workers' Compensation, Social Security or any retirement plan sponsored by the company.

If you have any questions before we issue the policy booklet, please don't hesitate to call me.

- When you're clarifying an existing policy, be sure to include all the relevant points.
- When dealing with employee benefits, keep an open door policy. Issues can be confusing and employees may need help in understanding the details.

Recommendation to Change a Policy (9-19)

Subject: Changing Holiday Policy

We recommend changing the firm's holiday policy from 10 fixed holidays to 7 fixed holidays (those indicated with an asterisk) and 3 "floaters":

> Day before New Year's
> New Year's*
> Good Friday
> Memorial Day*
> July Fourth*

Labor Day*
Thanksgiving*
Day after Thanksgiving*
Day before Christmas
Christmas*

Our employees have asked for this change because the days before New Year's and Christmas sometimes fall on a Saturday or Sunday and because Good Friday has no significance for some of them.

We feel we should respond positively to their request as long as there is adequate coverage assured in the office on "floating holidays." If you agree with this change, please initial on the bottom and return this memo to me. I'll take care of the rest.

- Make the nature of the change clear by stating what exists as well as what you recommend.

- Make it easy for the decision-maker to respond by giving your reasons and saying "initial this." The easier you make it, the more likely you'll be to get what you want.

Announcement of New Procedures, Developed within Company (9-20)

Subject: New File Back-up Procedures

For several years, we've survived quite nicely with a rather haphazard procedure for backing up our file disks. As the company has grown, however, we have been having problems. For example, people take the disks home to work on them, and other members of the staff cannot find copies. Furthermore, our insurance representative has pointed out that should we have a fire, our mailing lists and other proprietary data disks would be lost, and we would find it extremely difficult to reconstruct them.

As a result, we have instituted a new policy:

- Anyone using a disk must make a back-up copy. Back-up copies should be updated every Friday afternoon.
- Anyone who takes a data disk home must leave a copy in the office.
- Every two weeks, Hilary Newsome will take the essential data disks to the company's safe-deposit box. At that time, she will retrieve the old copies of the data disks for reuse. Program disks are already in the safe-deposit box. If any new programs are purchased, they must be taken to the safe deposit box on the next trip. If there should be any problem with initiating this policy, please contact me.

- Make sure everyone knows why the procedures are being implemented.

- Be very specific about *who, what, where,* and *when.* Assigning tasks and responsibilities by name is very helpful.

Announcement of New Procedures, Imposed from Outside (9-21)

Subject: Expense Account Procedures

Our accountant has told us that we must be very stringent about our records for expense account reimbursements. According to IRS rules, we must have written documentation (in the form of a bill or receipt) for any expense over $25.00. I understand how hard it is to remember to keep documentation, especially when you've been on the road for an extended period, but we (and you) do not want to violate any IRS dictates. As a result, we'll have to insist on written documentation (copies are fine) before we can reimburse you.

- Anything that constrains people, especially people who travel, will be greeted with a distinct lack of enthusiasm. Point out the reasons for the action and the consequences if they don't comply.

- Be understanding about the burdens of a policy, but never indicate that policy exceptions are possible.

Announcement of Promotion (9-22)

Subject: Lloyd Reed

I'm pleased to announce that Lloyd Reed has been made a principal in our firm. Lloyd has been with Robards, Robards, and Tolsory for five years. Previously he was Director, Human Resources, for Weaver Industries, with responsibilities encompassing diverse manufacturing operations, including international operations in the Far East.

A broadly experienced personnel executive, Lloyd spent ten years with Wellfleet, Inc. in a variety of personnel positions with emphasis in organization planning, executive selection, management development, and labor relations.

Lloyd is currently President of the Arthritis Foundation of Whittier, and a member of the Executive Committee of the Human Resources Research Association. Previously he served as a Director for the Whittier United Way.

- Business career information, both in the company and elsewhere, reinforces the individual's professional expertise.

- Non-business background information on the individual provides the human touch.

Announcement of New Company Policy, Travel Expenses (9-23)

Subject: New Travel Expense Policy

With the growth of our firm, expenses for business related travel have increased significantly. As a result, we've worked out a new travel policy based on a very favorable agreement we've reached with Thompson Travel. This policy should ensure we keep our costs in line with the competition's.

All travel arrangements will be made through Thompson to ensure that we obtain the most advantageous rates for airline tickets, hotel bookings, car rentals, and transportation to and from the airport. Please follow these guidelines:

- Book accommodations only in mid-range hotels (for example, Ramada Inns, Best Western).
- Choose the least expensive transportation option available,(i.e., taxis and hotel and airport courtesy cars rather than rental cars).
- Rent cars only from carriers with whom we have a corporate discount.
- Please make every effort to keep meal expenses under $35 per day. The company will not reimburse for bar bills.

We'll discuss this new policy at the regular Monday staff meeting, but if you have questions in the meantime, please call me.

- When dealing with something that could conceivably inconvenience people (in this case, limit their travel options), always say why. Make sure there is always some forum for discussing a new policy.

- Bullet format helps readability—and you do want this read and absorbed.

Announcement of New Company Policy, No Smoking (9-24)

Subject: Smoking in the Office

As of March 1, employees are not allowed to smoke anywhere in the office, including the restrooms. This policy is mandated by state law, and there can be absolutely no exceptions.

We understand this represents a serious inconvenience for the smokers in the office, so we have expanded the morning and afternoon coffee break period from 10 minutes to 15 minutes to allow time to go outside or to the nearby coffee shop.

- Writing a memo like this is called for only if you are truly creating a new policy. Even then, you may well have to speak to people individually.

- Accommodating employees in some way (here, by extending breaks) is a conciliatory gesture, encouraging cooperation.

Announcement of Motivational Award (9-25)

Subject: Fiona Maxwell Wins Annual Super Saver Award

We are very pleased to announce that Fiona Maxwell, our office manager, is the winner of the annual Super Saver Award for her suggestion to reuse and refurbish laser printer cartridges rather than buying new ones. Ms. Maxwell's suggestion has saved the company over $2,000 during the past six months.

Keep those suggestions coming. Send a short description of your suggestion to John Theodore, our Personnel Manager. A brief (four to six sentence) rationale may also be included.

- To be effective, motivational awards should be meaningful (as this one is), and employees should believe that they are capable of achieving them.

- Giving public recognition to the winner of the award and describing the suggestion itself gives employees confidence that they, too, can be rewarded for making a difference.

Announcement of Resignation of Employee (9-26)

Subject: Sam Griffith's Departure

Sam Griffith, Vice-President of Product Marketing, has resigned to start his own marketing consulting firm, Griffith & Associates, in Phoenix. We are sorry to see Sam leave and will miss his sharp, incisive wit, but wish him the best in his new venture.

Those who wish to give Sam a proper send-off are invited for wine and cheese in the 3rd floor conference room on Friday the 23rd at 4 p.m.

- Say what the departing employee will be doing (if he's joining a competitor, you can merely say he's "leaving to join another firm").
- Mention some positive aspect of the person that you will miss.

Announcement of Bad News (9-27)

Subject: Loss of Business

I am very sorry to announce that Southeastern Telecommunications, Inc., our largest customer, has decided not to renew its contract with us to supply computer maintenance services. More than 30% of our business was with Southeastern, so the loss of the contract will substantially diminish our operating revenues.

We expect to know the full impact of the contract loss within 30 days. Within that period we will learn whether contract negotiations with several potential customers, which would replace half of the Southeastern revenues, have been successful. I will keep everyone informed as events develop.

Because of the problems we will experience over the next few months, the company has furloughed six service technicians and three home office personnel. Jack Wiggins, Marketing Vice President, has left the company. No further reductions in staff are anticipated.

Our company has grown fast and established an enviable record in its 12-year history. I know that everyone will pull together in the next few months to help us get back on track.

- Be direct about bad news and state plainly its impact—on the company and employees.
- Outline what the company is doing to solve the problems and appeal for cooperation.
- Promise to keep the staff informed—and do so.

Request for Cooperation in Difficult Times (9-28)

Subject: Office Move

As you all know, we recently lost the Hechlind Lawn Maintenance and Landscaping account. Hechlind represented over 28% of our annual business, and we're doing everything we can to replace their account by soliciting new clients. In the meantime, however, we'll need to cut overhead costs in every way possible.

Our move to 46 Quinnipiac Place has been postponed indefinitely, and we'll have to endure our overcrowded conditions for a longer period of time. We hope we can make this situation more bearable by adjusting sales representatives' schedules. Clearly, however, we need to discuss contingency plans. I've called a staff meeting for next Monday, to discuss everyone's concerns and answer questions. In the meantime, please call me if you have any questions.

- Make sure people learn the bad news (that you lost the contract) from a company representative, not outside suppliers.
- Set up a meeting to discuss the implications as soon as possible.
- Make any explanation straightforward. Skip convoluted phrasing. People will think they are being conned.

Procedures for Dealing with the Media, Company Problem (9-29)

Subject: Policy Regarding Contacts with News Media

Because of the recent gas leak and explosion at our plant in Marlborough, some of you have been approached by the local press to talk about working conditions. I felt it was a good time to reiterate our policy regarding such matters.

Our policy is simple. All contacts and queries will be referred either

to my office or to the office of the President. No one is to speak for the company, or speak as an employee of United Manufacturing, except for myself or Mr. Greenberg. This includes all "off the record" inquiries.

We want to emphasize that we do not wish to cover anything up. But it is important, especially when there is the threat of lawsuits, that the company speak with a single voice. We will continue to cooperate with the authorities on this matter, and we feel that it is important that we all do our jobs as effectively as we can. We believe that this policy makes everyone's life easier.

If you have any questions, you may reach me at ext. 500.

- The policy stated in this memo is pretty standard. While it is quite restrictive, it's important not to come on too strong. Be forceful and to the point. Avoid spelling out sanctions.

- Be sure to say that this policy is for everyone's benefit, state the reason for your concern, and give people an opportunity to ask you questions.

Community Service 10

Businesses and their managements play an important role in every community, large or small, that extends far beyond creating products, offering services, or providing employment. Business owners and leaders are frequently called upon to play key roles in community activities. These include local boards, service organizations, and community charities. Whether or not you participate, your responses to these types of requests will be a primary factor in shaping your community image. Therefore, your role (and that of your business) in your community should always be on your mind when writing letters in this area.

Requests, acceptances, and refusals. When writing a request for someone to serve on a board, head up an organization's program or join in a charitable venture, it is tempting to yank hard on the heartstrings. Certainly, stressing the value of an organization's goals, appealing to a sense of obligation, or using images of the downtrodden and unfortunate can be effective, but a little of this goes a long way. You want to write an appeal that gets a response, but sounding self-righteous or maudlin runs the risk of turning people off. The best tack is not to tell people how important, enormous or painful the situation is, but to impress upon them how much of a difference they can make by lending a hand.

Acceptances are the easiest letters to write. Remember to state clearly the amount of effort you are willing to contribute, or the subject of the speech or the content of the article you will write, so as to head off any future misunderstandings. Also, give some reasons why this activity is important to you.

Give reasons why you are refusing something, too. "I don't have enough time" isn't a reason, it's a given. Be more explicit about the demands on your time, leave things open for future contacts, and above all be human. A formal, curt refusal borders on rudeness. Keep in mind that the best reason of all is that you are donating your time to another community activity or service organization.

Fundraising letters. The guidelines set up for requests also apply to fundraising. Don't overdo it. More importantly, don't apologize because you're asking for a donation. Describe briefly the cause for which you are raising money, establishing why it is worthy of support. In asking for a donation of cash, give a range of contributions from a modest amount (relative to those you are soliciting) to a large amount, and let the contributors choose the amount with which they are comfortable.

Follow-up letters are particularly important in fundraising. Every donation must be acknowledged—just as you would send thanks for any gift, but also because people who feel appreciated are likely to give even more generously the next time. For large gifts, a handwritten, personal note is best.

Approach Letter (10-01)

Dear Mr. Jacobs:

Jack Cimarron has told me that you have been a staunch supporter of Great Lakes Museum for many years, and I should very much like to thank you in person. Do you still spend summers in Mackinac Island? If so, perhaps we could find a time to have lunch when you arrive for the season in July.

Alternately, you might like to come to the Museum for the opening of the <u>Voyageurs</u> exhibit in May. Joni and I would be pleased to have you for dinner first at 31 Glendale Avenue, and we could attend the opening together. Do let me know.

With best regards,

- This doesn't sound like an "approach" letter, but that's what it is—and everyone concerned knows it.
- Since most major donors are extremely busy, a letter is a polite way to get their attention.

Direct Solicitation, Cash Donation (10-02)

Dear Mr. and Mrs. Merrill,

Our school has been presented with an exciting opportunity. An anonymous donor has offered us a one for two matching grant, based on our ability to raise new dollars.

Since you were willing to stand behind the school when it was in crisis last year, we are turning to you now in hopes of enlisting your support. For every $20 you give, the donor will provide $10 from his grant.

With your help, we have brought the school to a solvent state, and we have greatly broadened our donor base so that we no longer depend on a few benefactors. But much remains to be done—teachers' salaries are still low, the library still needs to add to its collection, and the playing fields require renovation.

Won't you help us take advantage of the donor's challenge and send your check for $20, $50, or $100 today?

Sincerely,

- Form letters like these are sometimes unavoidable, but adding a handwritten postscript would personalize it and attract attention.

Direct Solicitation, Fund Raiser (10-03)

Dear Mr. Edmunds:

The Wickwire Tennis Tournament has benefited needy students in our community for the past 10 years, raising an average of $55,000 per year. This year, United Community Bank has once again agreed to be our primary sponsor.

Ronald F. Wickwire, our Superintendent of Schools, has again requested that I, along with Roy Thorpe from United Community Bank, co-chair the Tournament. Last year, as you probably recall, Pilots Unlimited gave the Tournament $500. At the time, you mentioned that you could probably do better than that this year, so we would like to ask you to consider a gift of $1,000. As we have done in previous years, we'll be happy to recognize your contribution in the program and to announce your participation during the Tournament itself.

We hope you will once again help us help our deserving high school graduates. Please make your check payable to the Wickwire Tennis Tournament and send it to the address at the top of this letter.

We look forward to seeing you in May at the Tournament.

Sincerely,

- If there are co-chairpersons, both should sign the letter.
- Remind the donor what he/she gave last year. Mention an increased amount. You (almost) never get more than you ask for.

Thank You for Cash Pledge (10-04)

Dear Jim:

Thank you for taking the time to meet with Rick Stoddard and me Tuesday in Detroit. I enjoyed meeting you and want you to know how much we appreciate your information about alumni and others who might have an interest in supporting Boulder College.

We greatly appreciate your pledge of $1,000. In addition, your advice and suggestions about potential supporters are very helpful, and I hope you'll continue to keep us informed about others you may discover.

Many thanks again for your support.

Best wishes,

- Naturally, you'll turn all this information over to the professional staff (who may have actually written this letter for you).
- Since you're acting as a volunteer, use a personal letterhead.

Thank You for Item Pledge (10-05)

Dear Beth:

Thank you so much for pledging the two framed Calder posters for our silent auction on May 2. We'll price them to start at $200 each, with the hope that they'll generate so much interest that they'll ultimately go to $500-600.

As we discussed, if you don't find it convenient to bring the prints in by April 15, we'll be glad to pick them up. Let us know.

Again, thank you for supporting the Wolf's Head Day School.

Best wishes,

- Make it easy for the donor to make good on his or her pledge.
- Express gratitude directly.

Thank You for Cash Donation (10-06)

Dear Ms. Baird:

As Chairman of the Board of the School Volunteers of San Bernardino, I'd like to thank you for your generous gift of $125 toward our summer reading program fund-raising efforts.

Your gift will help make training possible for elementary school aides in the fourth and fifth grades. We appreciate your continued support, and we'll keep you updated on our progress.

Sincerely,

- It's important to keep people up-to-date on an organization they have helped. Doing so is an essential part of continuing the relationship. If possible, be specific about how the gift will be used.
- Even if your organization provides a form letter, try to customize it by changing the body or by adding a postscript.

Thank You for Item Donation (10-07)

Dear Mr. Reynolds:

As chairman of the Frontier Church Lawn Sale, I'd like to thank you personally for your donation of the antique squirrel gun. We understand that the weapon dates back to 1867 and according to Milt Stone, our local appraiser, it is museum-quality. We have every hope that it will fetch close to the $450 appraisal at the sale. As you know, this money will be applied to the restoration of the steeple, which was damaged in the recent tornado.

Thanks so much for your help.

Sincerely,

- Be very explicit in your thanks. Form letters put donors off and may adversely affect future donations.
- The organization will likely thank Mr. Reynolds as well.

Understanding of Inability to Give (10-08)

Dear Al:

I certainly understand that circumstances don't permit your supporting the Bootstrap Halfway House at this time. We all get solicited for a great many worthy causes, and everyone must set his own priorities.

When we talked Wednesday, though, I thought I detected some feeling that you might consider helping us out in six months or so, or at least that you'd take another look at your circumstances in December. I'll put it on my calendar and call you then.

Best to Millie,

- Be persistent, but not obnoxious. People have legitimate reasons for refusing to give—it serves no purpose to lay on the guilt.
- If you say you're going to follow up, make sure you do it, just as you do in business.

Acceptance to Donate (10-09)

Dear Mr. Baptista:

I've enclosed my check #107 for $1,000.00 to be applied toward the Dr. Hernando Rojas Memorial Center. As we discussed on the phone, Dr. Rojas was not only a superb physician, but also a great personal friend, and I am delighted to be able to help in the effort to memorialize his name.

Sincerely,

- When making contributions, always indicate the use to which you wish them put— unless you are supplying an unrestricted gift (which is always welcome from the organization's point of view).
- If this were a business contribution, you would naturally write this letter on a business letterhead.

Refusal to Donate (10-10)

Dear Mr. Rolfe:

I am very sorry that we will not be able to make our usual contribution to the Patrolmen's Assistance Organization Annual Ball this year. As you can see from our letterhead, we have moved our offices to an adjoining town and we are sure we will be called upon to support the policemen's association here. We wish you good luck with your fund-raising efforts.

Best wishes,

- If you're turning someone down, keep it simple. Convoluted explanations sound defensive.
- Writing a letter like this may forestall a series of increasingly persistent phone calls.

Asking Individual to Serve as Program Chairman (10-11)

Dear Gordy:

As you know from your long tenure as Recording Knight of the Knights of the Roundtable, one of the last tasks of the program manager is finding a replacement. I've had a great time organizing things this past year, and I'd like to ask you to be program manager next year. Naturally, I'll be glad to help you in any way possible. I have files galore—and a list of many people I have already approached who said they'd be glad to address our group but couldn't fit it into their schedule this year. They'd be ideal candidates for the coming year.

Please call me or drop me a note and let me know what you think.

Best,

- If you are asking someone to act as your replacement, always offer to help in any way possible. Make the offer attractive by being specific about how you can make the job easier.

Asking Individual to Serve as Development Chairperson (10-12)

Dear Milt:

I'm happy to hear from Howard Bussey that you're considering serving as development chairman for the 100th Anniversary celebration of the founding of our hometown. As chairman, I just want to make our invitation official.

As Howard mentioned to you, he had already gotten the campaign largely organized before his bank told him they were transferring him to New Orleans. Of the $230,000 we're aiming for, Howard tells me we already have firm commitments for $100,000, and, of course, the campaign has not even been announced yet.

I'm not saying there isn't a great deal of effort ahead, but I'm convinced that your energy and leadership will put us quickly over the top. I look forward to hearing you say "yes" at lunch next Wednesday.

Best to Sally,

- Development chairpersons are crucial to any endeavor, and this letter represents part of a long courtship. It's likely that the chairperson has tried to reach the reader by phone but has been frustrated by telephone tag.

Asking Individual to Serve as Board Member (10-13)

Dear Pat:

I truly enjoyed our lunch Wednesday, and I'm very excited by the prospect of your joining the board of the Mianus Toy Museum. As we discussed, I'm setting up a luncheon with Harry Klein, Ralph Delieto, and Jane Brainherd so you can meet some of the key members of the committees in which you're most interested. I'll call you in a week or so, after I've talked to them.

Again, I hope you decide to join us. The Museum board needs people like you.

Best wishes,

- You should issue invitations of this sort in person, following up with a letter confirming the items discussed and stating the next steps to be taken.

Welcome to the Board (10-14)

Dear Leb:

I'm absolutely delighted you'll be serving with me on the board of the Texas Ranger Collection. You'll find that the chairman, Joe Tewkes, runs productive meetings and that we really get things accomplished.

As I said when we met a month ago, we can really use someone with your legal background to guide us in some of the fine points of deferred giving.

Welcome,

- It's great to feel welcome in any new position. Don't forget to extend this rule to community service as well.
- Underscore the particular area in which the new member will be expected to contribute.

Refusal to Serve on Board (10-15)

Dear Hattie:

I'm honored that you've asked me to serve on the board of Walk Against Want. Unfortunately, I'm simply overcommitted this year. I'm sorry I misled you during our lunch last week. I greatly respect the work Walk Against Want does with the homeless. But I took a good look at my calendar, and decided that it simply wouldn't be fair to take on anything else.

I will be going off the Board of Deacons next year, and that will provide me with a block of time for other volunteer activities. I hope you'll think of me again.

Best wishes,

- If you must say no, do so gracefully. You don't have to list all the commitments that make it impossible for you to say yes—doing so sounds a bit too much like whining.

- If you do want to leave the door open, tell the reader when to ask you again.

Solicitation of Votes for Election to Board (10-16)

Dear Association Member:

Our association has always prided itself on the proportion of members who vote in board elections. Last year, for example, over 75% of you cast ballots for candidates for the board of directors, and we hope to better that percentage this year.

Some of you have expressed concern that you could not make an informed choice on the basis of the information we have provided in the past. As a result, we have expanded our biographical coverage of each candidate in the enclosed election kit. We hope that this additional information will enable you to cast your vote with more confidence.

The nominating committee selected the nine candidates from names recommended by the membership. Please vote for three (and only three) of the candidates by marking the attached ballot and returning it in the enclosed envelope.

Your vote can make a difference.

Sincerely,

- Make it easy for people to vote. Provide an envelope (with postage, if the association can afford it). Give people the assurance that even if they don't know the candidates, they can still make an informed choice.

- It doesn't hurt to appeal to people's competitive spirit or to indicate that you've responded to the members' comments by providing additional information.

Acceptance to Serve in Trade Association (10-17)

Dear Mr. Ortega:

I would be very proud to serve as a member of the Santa Cruz Board of Realtors. I understand that members serve for two-year terms and that my tenure begins in two weeks, on September 2.

I also understand that there will be a swearing-in ceremony on September 2. My office would like to send a photographer, if that would be allowed. If you could call my office to confirm the details, I would appreciate it.

I look forward to our first meeting. If you need anything from me, just call.

Sincerely,

- Put your acceptance and appreciation in the opening.
- Define the terms of your acceptance.
- Make sure that any requests on your part (the photographer) are clearly stated.

Declining to Join Organization (10-18)

Dear Pete:

I appreciate your thinking of me, but I won't be able to join the Local Industry Council this year. I understand all the advantages, especially the opportunity to talk with other business owners on a regular basis. That's something I've missed since leaving Mammoth Construction—the contact with peers.

So you've made a good pitch, but I'm heavily committed this year, as I believe I mentioned. Keep me in mind, though. I expect my schedule to free up considerably after the end of June.

Best wishes,

- Give a reason for turning down the offer.
- If you have an interest in being asked to join at a later date, indicate this.

Inability to Attend Function (10-19)

Dear Jill:

I regret that Tom and I will not be able to attend The Caring Society's Dinner Dance next month. We are planning a vacation and will be out of state.

We do, however, insist on purchasing two tickets for the dance. Enclosed is my check for $150.00.

We are sorry we won't be there. It's always such a wonderful evening, and for such a good cause.

Sincerely,

> - Keep it brief and to the point. You want to stay on the guest list for future events, but there's no need to write a novel about it.

Offer to Write Article (10-20)

Dear Mr. Cabrisi:

I would very much like to contribute to The Bulletin's upcoming special report on the housing crisis in Orange County. I understand from our phone conversation that the deadline for submissions is November 16.

As a real-estate professional, I feel I have an important perspective to explore. There is a lot that developers in Orange County can be doing to relieve the crunch in affordable housing, but first perceptions must be changed. Too many people hear the term "affordable housing" and have visions of poorly constructed apartment houses slowly turning to slums. But what "affordable housing" really means is being able to afford living in the town in which you work. Diversity is good for our towns. There is room for everyone.

These are the issues I want to write about. I will submit an article of approximately 1,500 words.

If there is anything else you expect from your contributors, please contact me at my office.

Sincerely,

> - Tell them in your letter what you intend to write about, even if you've discussed it already. Some things look a lot different on paper than in conversation, and you don't want to do all that work and not get published.
> - Always confirm the deadline and length of the article.

Request for Company/Organization to Provide Speaker (10-21)

Dear Mr. Feinstein:

Our bimonthly luncheon group, Businessperson's Nosh (BPN), would very much like to have someone from your company address our group on the use of alternative energy sources in the Bay Area. As you may be aware, BPN prides itself on its socially responsible approach to all business decisions. Our members are especially interested in the steps Mystic Utilities is taking to reduce dependence on fossil fuels and nuclear energy.

We are currently scheduling programs for the fall season, and we have meetings on the first and third Wednesday of every month. I'll call you in a week to see who from your company would be willing to speak to us. We appreciate your help.

Sincerely yours,

> - It's only fair to tell a potential speaker what kind of group you're asking him or her to address. In this case, that information will help the community relations director pick the right person.
> - Follow up with a phone call.

Acceptance of Invitation to Speak (10-22)

Dear Mr. Lithgow:

I gladly accept your invitation to speak at the upcoming Western Massachusetts Business Seminar. I understand my speech will be at 2:30 p.m. on June 14, to be followed by a reception.

My speech will be on the topic "State Sources for Small Business Financing." I will be prepared to talk for 45 minutes and answer questions from the audience. There will also be some printed materials to be distributed and a chart that I will refer to in my speech. If you could provide an easel for the chart, that would be helpful.

Thank you again for the invitation. See you on the 14th!

Very truly yours,

> - The acceptance, when, and where, go in the first paragraph.
> - Be sure the topic is established, as well as the length of the talk. Any special needs you have, such as a slide projector or blackboard, should be in the letter.

Confirmation of Individual's Agreement to Speak (10-23)

Dear Mr. Sorensen:

I'm delighted you'll be addressing the New Businesses in the 1990s Conference on May 25 at the Orange Roof Hotel in Norwalk. As we discussed, you'll talk about "Investments for Entrepreneurs" at the luncheon meeting. The luncheon starts at 12 noon, and you'll be speaking from 12:30 to 1:00, with an additional 15 minutes allocated for questions.

I am particularly interested in what equipment (for example, an overhead projector, 35-mm slide projector, or chart easels) you'll need. If you'll let me know your requirements by April 29, I'll have plenty of time to ensure that the hotel provides you with what you need. If you are providing your own equipment and will need help bringing it into the ballroom, please let me know and I'll arrange for assistance.

I will call you the second week in April to make sure everything is in order. Again, thank you for agreeing to speak. Everyone is looking forward to hearing your views.

Sincerely yours,

- Ask an individual to speak in person or on the phone-confirm the details in writing as soon as possible.

- Always stipulate a time limit for the speech and the Q-and-A session. Also, give a deadline for requesting equipment. Make the deadline at the month's end, not the beginning—people always assume they have the full month, whatever the actual date.

Declining Request to Speak (10-24)

Dear Ms. Loundsberry:

I enjoyed talking with you last week and very much appreciate your invitation to participate next month in Executive Communications' workshop as the speaker on "Utilizing Electronic Mail." As you know, I am a great believer, and user, of this form of telecommunications.

Unfortunately, I will be on my annual tour of the company's domestic offices during the seminar and cannot break away even for a day, so I will have to decline the invitation.

If you have other workshops in the future that will feature the same subject, I would be glad to speak, schedule permitting.

Sincerely,

- Whether declining or accepting, clearly identify the subject matter for the letter's recipient—who is probably trying to schedule many speakers.

- Leave the door open for future contact.

Acceptance to Attend Function by Award Recipient (10-25)

Dear Rand:

I am extremely honored to have been chosen Realtor of the Year by the Boulder Board of Realtors. As you are aware, I have lived and worked in Boulder all my life (not a mean feat in these days of mobility), and it's always especially gratifying to be recognized in one's home town.

I understand from your letter that the banquet is at the Boulderado Hotel at 7 p.m. on September 30. My husband and I would be pleased to attend. Do I need to prepare any remarks, or is a simple "thank you" all that's required?

As you requested, I've enclosed a biography and a 5x7 glossy photograph for you to use for publicity purposes. Please be sure to credit the photographer, Michael Snow, whose name and address are printed on the back.

Thank you again for the honor.

Best wishes,

- When accepting an honor, warm appreciation should shine through your letter.
- Make sure you help the person coordinating the event by providing photographs, bios, and other publicity materials.

Resignation from Organization (10-26)

Dear Henry:

I'm sorry to have to tell you that I will be resigning from the Board as of June 30, the last day of the spring semester. As you know, Samantha will be entering a pre-K program in the fall, and I feel I should be helping her new institution.

You know you can count on me for continued financial support and advice, and I will be pleased to counsel you about fund-raising matters as I have in the past. I have greatly enjoyed working with you and all the other members of the Board, and I gained a great deal from your wisdom and sane approach to problem-solving under difficult conditions.

All the best,

- Relationships are everything in business and community service. You may be leaving the Board, but you want to make sure that the relationship continues.
- If you have a legitimate excuse for leaving, mention it. If you have some other issue—a personality conflict, perhaps—this letter is definitely not the place to air it. If you want to get it off your chest, do so in person.

Invitation to Dinner/Luncheon (10-27)

The pleasure of your company
is cordially requested at the
TENTH ANNIVERSARY CELEBRATION
of the
Permanent Commission
on Small Business Advancement
Wednesday, May 25
7:00 p.m.
Statler Inn
56 Wildwoode Courtyard
Greenville, South Carolina

Donation: $35 per person   Dinner
R.S.V.P. before May 22nd to 562-3441

- This invitation provides all the necessary information, but it should be accompanied by a self-addressed stamped envelope and response card for maximum return.

Response Card (10-28)

Please make _____ reservation(s) at $35 per person for the 10th Anniversary Celebration of the Permanent Commission on Business Advancement, May 25 at the Statler Inn, Greenville.

NAME: _____

ADDRESS: _____

CITY:_____ STATE: _____ZIP:_____

PHONE:_____

Please find my check enclosed payable to the *Permanent Commission on Business Advancement* for the amount of $_____.
(Please list guests on reverse side)

Tickets will not be mailed to you.
Reservations will be held at the door.

> • Make it easy for people to let you know they'll attend by providing a response card like this one and a stamped reply envelope.

Thank You for Company Hospitality (10-29)

Dear Ms. Glickson:

Please thank everyone at Arrowhead Mechanical for the hospitality they extended to our high school physics teachers last Friday. We had a "debriefing" Monday, and our teachers had unanimous praise for the way your engineers explained the basic principles behind your newest designs. They felt, for example, that your main speakers, Drs. Kaplan, Williams, and York, geared their remarks precisely to the level of the teachers' experience and education.

They also expressed appreciation for the patience and enthusiasm of Mr. Andrews and Ms. Coburn, the technicians who led them through the laboratory.

Thank you again for all the help you've given us in our continuing education program. Once again, your people have surpassed themselves. The photograph we took will be featured in our April newsletter. I'll send you several copies to distribute and post.

Best wishes,

> • After showering the company with general gratitude, be specific about who deserves the thanks.
>
> • Since the company hopes for good PR from these outings, be sure to note that their help will be recognized in print, if you can.

Faxes 11

Facsimile machines have changed the pace of business forever. Managers and customers who were once satisfied with reading something the next day or next week now insist on seeing something within hours, if not minutes.

Because of the speed of the medium, some writers equate faxes with phone calls and wrongly assume that their readers will not object to incorrect grammar and usage, just as they would not object to sentence fragments or the occasional slip of the tongue during a phone conversation. This assumption is dangerous, as anyone who has ever received a sloppy fax knows.

Faxes should be prepared with the same care you would use in writing a letter. As with a letter—but even more so with a fax—be as brief as possible. A long, involved fax diminishes its sense of urgency and immediacy.

Faxes are excellent vehicles for placing, receiving and confirming orders, keeping customers informed about new products and services, preparing people for meetings and following up with assignments, and for keeping in touch with salespeople, customers, and divisions outside the home office, to name just a few uses.

When using the faxes in this section as models, be guided by the following rules.

Always send a cover sheet. There are two kinds of cover sheets required for faxing. The first, which we'll refer to as the *master* cover sheet, shows the name of the recipient, their fax and phone numbers, the number of pages being sent, and a phone number to call in the event that there is trouble receiving the fax. In addition, when faxing a price list or other sales material, a resume or other informational documents, include what we'll call an *explanatory* cover sheet. This brief document permits you to explain the attachments and as well as gives you an opportunity to interject a personal touch. The cover sheet for a resume and response to request for information in this chapter are examples.

Use appropriate design. Both kinds of cover sheets should be designed with an attractive logo that reproduces clearly on fax paper, giving you another opportunity to reinforce the identity of your company. Don't use your regular letterhead if it has embossing or metallic type because it won't reproduce effectively by fax. Instead, create one just for faxes that will look crisp and attractive. Make sure the margins are wide enough (at least three-quarters of an inch) so that words will not get cut off. Use a type size of at least 12 points and a sans serif typeface such as Helvetica (also known as Arial).

Confidentiality is a serious concern. Never fax anything you would not care to see on the front page of a newspaper. Many offices have their fax machines stationed in public locations where anyone passing by can read what is transmitted. If there is any sensitive material in your fax, call the recipient and tell them the fax is being sent so they can be there to receive it.

Proofreading is crucial. Faxes are legally binding documents. If you quote prices or send any other contractual information, make sure it is correct. Don't let the demand to "fax me something on that right away" hurry you into neglecting proofreading.

Don't handwrite your faxes. First, it's unprofessional. Second, documents are difficult enough to read when faxed. Faxing a handwritten note can make your message unreadable. Take the extra couple of minutes to type your fax.

Master Cover Sheet (11-01)

Company Name
Address
City, State Zip
Phone number
Fax number

Date:

To:

Fax #:

From:

Number of pages (including cover sheet):

In case of transmittal problems, please call _____ at
(212) 555-_____.

- The cover sheet should include all information necessary for the fax to get to the intended recipient and for the recipient to reply to the sender.
- Use your company logo if it reproduces crisply. Using the logo is the equivalent of a mini-advertisement.

Cover Sheet for Resume (11-02)

Subject: Financial Analyst Opening

Thank you for taking time to talk with me about the financial analyst position. As you requested, here is my resume. I believe my experience as a financial assistant with Air Limited has been excellent preparation for your position.

I am excited about the possibility of working with a growing, innovative company like Philbrick. I look forward to meeting you in person and will call your office on Tuesday to set up an appointment.

- Use the fax to sell yourself. Be brief, but show enthusiasm.
- Point out specific items you would like the recipient to notice. Tell why you are interested in their company.
- Say how you plan to follow up.

Response to Request for Information (11-03)

Subject: Catalog Request

At your request, I am faxing catalog sheets for our Carry Case #33-11 and Carry Case #33-15. Both are available for immediate shipment.

If you'd like to order, you can phone our sales line: (202) 555-6630 between 9 am and 6 pm eastern time. We accept all major credit cards.

- Mention availability of the product.
- Include ordering information.

Quotation (11-04)

Subject: Price Quotation: Carpenter Ant Control

Now that we have completed the inspection of your office and shop, we can confirm the price of the service you requested:

Type of Service: One-time service to control carpenter ants

Property to be Serviced: One-story commercial property with attic

Included in Service: Carpenter ants and other ants only

Application:	Power-spray exterior with Empire M.E.; spray cracks and crevices all rooms and attic; dust attic soffits

Cost:	Service	$130.00
	Tax	10.40
	TOTAL	$140.40	(payable at time of service)

As we discussed, we can schedule service for Sunday, August 20 (while you are closed), provided we make arrangements for access. We look forward to serving you.

- Make information clear and specific—even though it's a fax, you should include enough information to protect yourself. Since it is a written document, you can be held responsible for the information given, as with any contract.

- Don't miss an opportunity to include a human touch. People do business with people, not with organizations.

Correction of Pricing Information (11-05)

Subject: Correction of Price Information

We regret that the price information sent to you on June 23 contained an error. The correct price for the Roto Literature Display Rack is $356.75. This price went into effect on June 1. We are sending you a catalog with the new pricing, which should arrive by Thursday.

We hope our error will not cause you any inconvenience. If you wish to change your order, please phone Jennie Tomkins (collect) at (203) 555-3985, and she will make any adjustments immediately.

- Acknowledge your error.
- Take corrective action immediately, and give the name of a contact to talk to.

Confirmation of Order by Fax or Phone (11-06)

Subject: Confirmation of 8/13 Phone Order

Thank you for your August 13 order of :

Three (3) Ease-E hydroculators @ $29.95	$89.85
One case (12 bottles) of Ease-E muscle liniment	27.95
One box (10) Ace bandages	15.95
Sub Total	133.75

10% educational discount	(13.38)
State tax (6-1/2%)	7.82
Postage and handling	4.95
Total	$133.14

These items will be shipped on Monday, August 17, via UPS and should reach you by Friday, August 21. If your order has not arrived by Friday afternoon, please telephone Missy Curtis at (213) 555-2295.

- Itemize the order (include unit prices) as well as any other costs (shipping, tax).

- Include shipping details and the name and number of someone to contact if the order is not received on time.

Notification of Shipment (11-07)

Subject: Shipping Date of Thermocycling Oven
        Your Order #6667-552

We shipped your thermocycling oven (Model #345A) by air courier at 10:00 a.m. today. In the ten years we have been dealing with British customs, this method of transport has averted major delays in delivering products to our customers. If you do not receive your oven by 3 pm your time on Friday, December 6, please fax or call me and I will expedite its delivery.

- Letting customers know when to expect merchandise is especially important when dealing overseas. Giving them a contingency plan if the merchandise fails to arrive is equally crucial.

- Use the name of the item rather than model number in the Subject line. It's more meaningful than a bunch of numbers.

Apology for Shipment Error (11-08)

Subject: Replacement of Incorrect Shipment (Order #LL-52-4597)

When we received your fax this morning, we checked with our shipping department, and we did indeed send you the 42" space organizers instead of the 52" organizers. We are very sorry for this error.

We will ship the correct items to you today, via Federal Express, at our expense. You will receive them tomorrow. Please return the 42" organizers in the original box, and we will credit your account for the purchase price and all shipping and handling charges. Please send the box by Federal Express and charge the shipment to our account (#8005-5555-0).

If you need any additional information, please call Tom Binder (collect) at (815) 443-0077. Please refer to your order number: LL-52-4597.

- Apologize for the error, but keep it simple and matter of fact (errors can happen to anyone and don't require abject apologies).
- Be clear about exactly what the customer needs to do and about exactly what costs you will cover (or reimburse).

Request for Price Quotation (11-09)

Subject: Price Quotation

We wish to purchase a personal computer and need written price quotes for the following equipment. You may use this form to respond.

1. PC 10000X with $_____
   32 mb RAM
   6 gigabyte Internal hard drive

2. Quest 300 Super XXA $_____
   21" Monitor

3. Scope 96HX modem $_____

4. DataMost PS 90 printer $_____

Are there any price advantages if we order all of these items as a package at one time?

Please fax this information to me at the cover sheet number. (We will not respond to phone calls without a written quote.)

- Make it easy for the recipient to respond.
- It's easier to see items in a list than if you put the same information in paragraph form—and you're more likely to get all the information you want.

Order (11-10)

Subject: Costume Order—Urgent

Please send us the following by UPS 2nd Day or equivalent:

4 (four) child (#12M) frog costumes	@$22.00	$88.00
3 (three) child (#24M) reptile costumes	@$25.00	$75.00
Total		$163.00

Our tax-exempt number is: 4569078

Our address is:
> Whitfield Theater Company
> 23 High Street
> Alma, MI 07984

We have always been very pleased by the quality of your costumes and the service you provide. We need these costumes by April 3 for dress rehearsal. Please notify us immediately by fax or phone if there is any problem filling this order by that date. Thanks for your help.

- If you have an urgent deadline, let your supplier know, both in the Subject line and in the body of the fax.
- Treating suppliers as partners rather than adversaries can help in getting orders filled on time. Mentioning that you've been pleased with past service seems trivial, but this kind of positive feedback can be very helpful in getting what you want.

Request Permission to Return Shipment, Damaged (11-11)

Subject: Return of Damaged Shipment

Your September 4 shipment of vegetarian dog biscuits and cat croutons (Order #6754A) arrived damaged. It appears that water penetrated the packaging material at some time before we received it because mold is apparent on portions of the cartons.

I'm certain you'll want to examine the shipment to ensure that this sort of problem does not happen again. Please fax us how the shipment will be picked up and when you can reship. We need to receive a replacement no later than one week from today, since we have almost no inventory left.

- A fax gives a sense of urgency when a deadline is involved.
- Be sure to give your original order number and your expectation of how the damaged shipment will be resolved.

Cancellation of Order (11-12)

Subject: Cancellation of PO #1908832

Mort, this fax is to advise you of our cancellation of our Purchase Order #1908832 for 500 serial cables. As we've discussed, our sales have slowed down this summer and we won't need the cables until October. You can expect a Purchase Order for the original 500 plus another 250 at that time.

Sorry for any inconvenience. We value your company as a key supplier and look forward to a continuing relationship.

> • Canceling or changing orders by fax saves valuable time and is particularly critical if you need to get to the supplier before manufacturing begins.
>
> • When dealing with suppliers, particularly in situations like this, be sure to remind them that they are important to your company.

Complaint to Supplier, Cannot Reach by Phone (11-13)

Subject: Delay in Order

We have been trying to reach you by phone since Tuesday, but you have not been available and no one has returned our calls.

We are very concerned about the delay in our order for three Elite Display Adapters (EM 12-4668). We placed the order with you three weeks ago, on August 12, and were assured by Ted Simms that we would have the adapters by last Friday at the latest.

These delays have caused us to miss deadlines with our customers, which has put us in an awkward position. We have had a good working relationship with your company until now. But unless we hear from someone by tomorrow noon, we will be obliged to place our orders with another supplier. I certainly hope this will not be necessary.

> • Keep your language direct and firm, but leave an opening to resolve the problem amicably.
>
> • Give enough information so that someone can track the problem.
>
> • Be specific about any deadlines and what action you plan to take.

Communication of Urgent Data (11-14)

Subject: Clark Technical Financials for Steinman Meeting

Here are the numbers you need on Clark Technical for your meeting tomorrow afternoon:

Revenue	$130,114,000.00
Operating expenses	112,320,000.00
Operating income	17,794,000.00
Interest expense	463,000.00
Net income	17,331,000.00
Earnings per share	.64
No. of shares outstanding	27,079,687

I will send the full report on the company by overnight courier tonight; you should have it by 10:00 a.m. tomorrow. I will be in my office until 4:00 p.m. today (212-555-5672) if you need any additional information.

- Since this is urgent data, give the recipient a contact (in this case, the sender) who can answer questions or provide additional information.

Decision Required (11-15)

Subject: QualityCare, Inc. Presentation

As you know, we've been trying to land the QualityCare account for more than a year. I've just been advised that they have begun interviewing new agencies. I want your approval to call Ed Bascomb, president of QualityCare, to set up a presentation for one week from today. If we wait any longer, I'm afraid they will have already made their decision.

Please fax or phone me as soon as you arrive at your hotel so I can proceed.

- Faxing someone at their hotel is better than leaving a phone message at the desk, since you can be sure they'll get the entire message in a clear, ungarbled way.

- A fax to a guest who has not yet arrived at the hotel should be clearly marked on the cover sheet "Hold for Arriving Guest."

Request for Immediate Approval (11-16)

Subject: Immediate Approval Required

Ed, I've attached copy and layout for the new trade ad which has to be shipped to Hardware Buyer magazine by Friday. If it's okay, please initial the cover sheet and fax it back to me.

If you have changes, please call me right away so we can implement them in time to make the closing date.

Thanks for your quick response.

- Faxes are ideal for getting written approvals. Specify when the approval is needed and why it is urgent.

- Allow for the possibility of not getting the approval, and what steps will be necessary as a result.

Conveying Client Information to Colleague (11-17)

Subject: Alyce Carson, Potential Customer

Ted Cochran tells me that you will be in San Francisco on Monday and Tuesday to meet with the Dickson Company. While you are in San Francisco, I thought you might want to get in touch with a former colleague of mine, Alyce Carson, who has just been promoted to head buyer for Tigress Cosmetics: (415) 555-6800.

Tigress is developing a new line of all-natural cosmetics; they are looking for suppliers. I think they would be particularly interested in our aloe and collagen products.

Alyce is a graduate of Oberlin (art history) and spent three years in Albuquerque with Macon Department Stores (she was assistant buyer for ladies wear and cosmetics when I headed purchasing there). She joined Tigress in January of last year, transferred to the West Coast in April, and was promoted to her present position on October 1. She lives in Tiburon with her husband, Walt, and two children. Alyce enjoys sailing, antique toys, and Impressionist painters. You can reach her through Tigress or at her home: (415) 555-4825.

She is a very bright lady—I think you will enjoy each other's company. Relay my greetings, and tell her I'm still looking for the tin wind-up Scottie to add to her collection.

- Tell the person why he or she should meet the contact.
- Provide nonsensitive personal information, so your colleague will have something to talk about.

Confirmation of Phone Conversation (11-18)

Subject: Confirmation of Phone Conversation 9/22

I thought it would be helpful to confirm our phone conversation of this morning to be sure we cover all points.

You advised that payment for Invoice #667332 will be mailed by the end of the week. Your order #12234-5 will be shipped no later than January 22.

In addition, you asked me to provide you a quotation for the following items:
> 1,000 2" diameter x 3' poles
> 2,500 gold tassels, 2"
> 2,000 bronze wall mounts

As I said, you'll have my quote within 7 days. If you'd like to add to this request, please let me know by Monday and I will incorporate the additional items in the quote.

We appreciate your business.

- Confirming phone conversations avoids misunderstandings and gives you another opportunity to maintain a strong relationship with customers.
- Thanking a customer for business is always appreciated.

Setting Time for Telephone Conversation (11-19)

Subject: Final Arrangements for Convention Logistics

I have just spoken to Tom McCaw and Sarah Greenlee, who were able to answer all our questions about the convention logistics.

It is important that you and I talk to confirm the final arrangements before you leave Tokyo on Wednesday. I will call your office Monday about 10:00 a.m. your time; if that is not convenient, you may call me at (201) 555-6688 Monday, between 9:00 a.m. and 11:00 a.m. Tokyo time.

It will be a pleasure finally to meet you at the convention.

- Be clear about whose time zone you are referring to.
- Allow a second option—a way for the other party to reach you—since you cannot be sure of his or her availability.

Networking 12

The saying, "The best things in life are free" doesn't apply to most aspects of business, but when it comes to networking, nothing could be truer. By spending just a small amount of time investing in business relationships you can produce bountiful rewards. Work toward building positive relationships today with the knowledge that you'll be able to ask for assistance, if you should need it, tomorrow.

Be appreciative. Most people are flattered when you turn to them for their expertise or assistance and are eager to help (unless you become a nuisance). But if and when you do need help, remember to ask for it as a favor, rather than as something to which you're entitled. Take nothing for granted, and always express your gratitude. And if you can offer to return the favor, do so. Be gracious but don't grovel.

Be specific. Have a clear idea of what you're seeking and be as specific as possible. Generally, those people you want to network with are the most successful and busiest. Don't waste their time with broad, unfocused requests.

Be realistic. Recognize that access to other people is one of the most valuable assets a business person has. Don't expect, for example, that your network contact will call the CEO of his company to arrange an informational interview for you just because you ask. Give a reason why the CEO might find talking to you of interest—perhaps you can provide competitive intelligence based on recent research in the industry. If you make unreasonable requests, you may not get a second chance.

Be honest. If you are in the early stages of a job search, product development, or market research, be very open about your need to "pick someone's brain" so that the person will not expect too much structure in your request—and will understand your objective.

Don't be greedy. If you are describing a new product or service to members of your network, don't attempt to "sell" them at the same time. If you truly believe network members might have a need for your product or service, you can always pursue sales, on a very non-aggressive basis, a bit later on. Remember that maintaining your network is more important than making a sale.

Announcement of Start-Up Business (12-01)

Dear Lucy:

It's a pleasure to announce the formation of Global Prospects, Inc. I wanted you to be one of the first to know, since we were all in Taos together the night we first discussed the idea. We've gotten the backing we needed from a group of private investors who are extremely enthusiastic and supportive. I think you know Joseph Timm, who has been instrumental in putting the deal together.

We'll be sending you our promotional material as soon as we get it. In the meantime, thanks for all your support and good wishes and, most of all, for providing an example of success and quality in a challenging market. Your company is the best in your industry. I hope we can be half as successful in ours.

Sincerely,

- Providing news about your endeavors gives your network something to talk about, and the ability to spread the word about you at the same time.

- A flattering comment will be remembered and will cast a favorable light on you as well.

Request for Feedback on New Product (12-02)

Dear Diana:

You've always offered useful advice when I was pondering new markets for our training programs. What do you think about this idea? A Curriculum Advisor from Ames Secretarial School has come to us with a proposal to create and teach a program for administrative assistants tentatively titled, "Interpersonal Skills for Support Staff." (I've attached the preliminary schedule.)

I know that service has always been your watchword at Partners Insurance. Do you think that other major insurance companies like Partners would be interested in a program such as this? How much would you be willing to pay for such a program? Do you think your administrative assistants would be receptive to a program of this type?

I'll call you Tuesday to set up a lunch so I can hear your thoughts.

Best wishes,

- Provide a series of thought-provoking questions to start things going.

- You'll get the most helpful insights in person, so try to set up a face-to-face meeting. The offer of a meal is a good incentive to the party whose help you're seeking.

Thank You for Input, Request for Referrals (12-03)

Dear Diana:

Thanks for your encouragement concerning our "Interpersonal Skills for Administrative Assistants" workshop. As a direct result of your input, we've expanded the program from four hours to eight hours and have added a two-part exercise on "dealing with difficult people." As I mentioned, we field-tested the program in New Orleans a month ago, and participants in that workshop were so enthusiastic that we were able to book four programs at that company for next month.

Now that I feel confident the program is of the same high quality as our other offerings, I'd like to ask another favor. I know you have many associates in human resources within the insurance industry, and you did say that several of them had a need for this kind of workshop when we conducted our preliminary market research. Would you be willing to provide us with introductions to some of these people? I'd be more than happy to have one or two of our recent participants fill you in on their reactions to the program, if that would be helpful.

I'll call Thursday so we can talk further.

Yours truly,

- Anything regarding names and referrals is best discussed on the phone or in person, especially since you may be able to get additional marketing intelligence that way.

- Don't make members of your network guinea pigs for your untested ideas. Always field-test first. Maintaining the trust of the network is far more important than making the first sale.

Offer to Exchange Referrals (12-04)

Dear Kyle:

I just finished speaking with Charles Stein. Thanks for referring him to me. I'm confident I can be of help to him in both his business and personal accounting needs.

As I discussed with you after the Rotary Club dinner last Thursday, I'll be happy to direct any clients to you who are in need of your marketing expertise. In fact, I'm seeing someone next week who I suspect is a perfect candidate for your services. I'll give you a call after the meeting.

Kindest regards,

- One of the best uses of networking is exchanging referrals. Select business associates to refer to who you know are skilled in their professions as well as completely dependable. After all, your reputation is at stake.

- Keep in touch with those with whom you've agreed to exchange referrals, not only so they'll keep you in mind, but also to let them know *you* are thinking of *them*.

Request for Help with Employee Search (12-05)

Dear Andrea:

I know you've just gone through the horrors of hiring people for your new location, and lived to tell the tale. Now I face a similar fate. Graham McNamara, our computer guru, is leaving us to relocate to Fiji (really!)

You mentioned that several candidates you interviewed for your company impressed you, but didn't quite suit your needs. Would you be good enough to fax their resumes to me (after checking with them first, of course). That would be of tremendous assistance in my search for a qualified replacement for Graham.

Thanks for your help.

Sincerely yours,

- Personalize your request with a few details.
- Most people will respond positively to a request for help. Make it easy by stating exactly what you want.

Request for Names of Professionals (12-06)

Dear Edie:

As you may have read in the trades, Yorke, Pardee, and Choate, the law firm that has represented us for ten years, is no longer operating. The breakup of the partnership was extremely messy, and there is no way that I would continue the relationship with any of the partners on an individual basis.

I know that many of your clients have relationships with the top firms in L.A. Could you let me know whether there is anyone that they could recommend? Of course, I'm also going to call Judwin, Lawrence and Chasen, but I understand they have a tendency to assign associates to accounts as small as mine, and I prefer to deal with a partner.

My priorities are excellent service, extensive knowledge of international licensing, and then, and only then, price.

Hope to hear from you soon.

Yours truly,

- The best sources for recommendations of professionals are people in your industry.
- State why you are changing professionals without going into too much detail; then give your criteria so the reader can make useful recommendations.

Letter Formats and Forms 13

Business correspondence. How business documents look, particularly those sent outside the company, is as important to successful communications as their contents. This section provides styles for the major kinds of documents.

In addition to using the proper formatting, attention should be paid to the other physical aspects of business writing. You should use good quality paper and spelling should always be checked (particularly the name of the reader).

Forms should be readable and simple to follow. This can be accomplished through appropriate use of white space (margins, space between paragraphs) and headings. Using a readable type face and resisting the temptation to mix fonts or to overuse italics or bold face also help ensure readability.

Social correspondence. Social letters differ substantially in format from letters you write to companies and organizations. These days, many people find computer-printed or typewritten letters acceptable for almost every circumstance. But to make your social correspondence truly personal, and especially if highly personal matters are involved (as in condolence letters or love letters), they should be hand written. Choose either plain or personalized social stationary or note cards that reflect your personality and the occasion.

You do not need to use a letterhead, and an inside address is not only unnecessary, but inappropriate. The salutation (for example, Dear Jane) should be followed by a comma, rather than a colon, and there is wide latitude to vary from the style used in business letters. A typical personal letter style is included in this chapter.

Memo (13-01)

Company Name
Address
City, State Zip

quadruple space

To:
> *double space*

From:
> *double space*

Date:
> *double space*

Subject:
> *triple space*

First paragraph, body of the memo begins. (This is always single spaced with the paragraphs starting at the left margin.)
> *double space*

Next paragraph
> *double space*

Last paragraph
> *double space*

Writer's initials (uppercase): typist's initials (lowercase)

- The most important line in the memo format is the Subject line, which gives the reader a quick understanding of the content.

- Be sure that the major point is contained in the first paragraph so busy people will quickly understand the point you are making.

Report Format (13-02)

CHAPTER TITLES

Chapter titles are set in all caps and centered on the page.

Section Headings

Section headings are also centered. They are upper case and lower case and underlined. You should have at least two heads at every level of subdivision.

Section Subheadings

Underlined subheadings, flush left, head each subdivision.

- If you are going to divide a subsection further, you may do so by using bullets or some similar mark of distinction. These sections should be indented.
- This is a popular format. You should also include an Executive Summary, a one-page summary of the entire report.

Agenda for Meeting (13-03)

Company Name
Address
City, State Zip

Date:

Time:

Location:

Objective:

Attendees:

Agenda Item	Purpose	Time	Presenter	Material to Be Read in Advance

- A meeting's objectives should be clearly and precisely stated so participants will focus on the issues.
- Agenda items should start with broad topics and narrow toward the decision; stating the time for each item will force concentration.

Outline (13-04)

Title

triple space

    I.   FIRST ORDER DIVISION-ALL CAPITALS

double space

        A. Second Order Division—First Letter Of Each Word Is Capitalized

               1. Third order division—Only first letter is capitalized

               2. Note that each division and subdivision is indented 4 spaces from the heading superior to it

                    a. Fourth order division

                    b. If you have an a, you must have a b

double space

   II. IF YOU HAVE A 1, YOU MUST HAVE A 2

        A. _____

               1. _____

                    a. _____

                    b. _____

               2.

        B. _____

               1. _____

               2. _____

- Maintain a consistent numbering pattern or you'll confuse yourself and anyone else who reads it.

- A computer is the ideal tool on which to prepare an outline. Most word processing software automatically formats your outline in any of several numbering styles.

Performance Appraisal Form (13-05)

Company Name
Address
City, State Zip

Name of employee: _____ Department: _____

Performance Appraisal

Performance evaluation criteria

	Excellent	Very Good	Good	Satisfactory	Needs Improvement
Quality of work					
Production output (quantity)					
Reliability (attendance, consistency of effort)					
Attitude (acceptance of direction)					
Interpersonal skills (communication)					
Knowledge of job					
Office skills (if applicable)					
Initiative (ability to work without supervision)					

Comments:

_____

_____

_____

Action steps: _____

Overall rating   <u>Excellent</u> <u>Very Good</u> <u>Good</u> <u>Satisfactory</u> <u>Needs Improvement</u>

Evaluated by: _____

Employee signature: _____

Date: _____

- This form provides a place for free-form commentary as well as forcing "scoring." It should provide a starting point for discussion, not a substitute for it, and will help the evaluator to view the employee objectively.
- Fill out the action-steps section only after consultation with the employee.

Employment Application (13-06)

Company Name
Address
City, State Zip

Name: _____   Social Security #: _____

Address: _____   Phone Number: _____

EMPLOYMENT

List all periods of employment, starting with the most recent.

		From	To
Company:	_____	_____	_____
Address:	_____		
Supervisor:	_____		
Company:	_____	_____	_____
Address:	_____		
Supervisor:	_____		

(If you need more space, attach another sheet or your resume.)

EDUCATION		From	To	Degrees Obtained
High School:	_____	_____	_____	_____
College or University:	_____	_____	_____	_____

Other educational training, including trade, business, or military

_____

_____

REFERENCES

Please provide names of three people who are familiar with your qualifications. We will be calling or writing them so they must be those you want us to contact.

Name	Address and Phone No.	Position

1. _____
2. _____
3. _____

What else would you like to tell us? Please comment on anything about you—skills, work you have done, goals you have—anything we cannot tell from looking at your application (use the back of this sheet if necessary).

_____
_____
_____

I authorize the company to obtain information from any person named above, and I release all concerned from any liability in connection with obtaining and releasing such information.

_____
Applicant's Signature   Date

- Some firms ask everyone to fill out an application because it's easier to discern gaps or inconsistencies on an application than it is on a resume.

- This application is relatively simple, but it does allow for free-form comment. The tone of the questions is friendly rather than intimidating, a good reflection on your firm.

Balance Sheet, Service Company (13-07)

Company Name
Balance Sheet
December 31, Year

Assets

Cash and short term investments	$XXX
Accounts receivable, less allowance for bad debts of $XXX	XXX
Prepaid expenses	XXX
Furniture and fixtures, less accumulated depreciation of $XXX	XXX
Leasehold improvements, less accumulated amortization of $XXX	XXX
Other assets	XXX
Total assets	$XXX

Liabilities and Shareholders' Equity

Accounts payable	$XXX
Notes payable to banks	XXX
Income taxes payable	XXX
Other liabilities	XXX
Total liabilities	$XXX

Stockholders' equity:

Common stock, $XX par value	$XXX
Amount in excess of par value	XXX
Retained earnings	XXX
Stockholders' equity	$XXX
Total liabilities and stockholders' equity	$XXX

- A Balance Sheet is a "snapshot" of your company's assets and liabilities as of a specific point in time, usually at the end of your financial year.

Balance Sheet, Manufacturing Company (13-08)

Company Name
Balance Sheet
December 31, Year

Assets

Cash and short term investments	$XXX
Accounts receivable, less allowance for bad debts of $XXX	XXX
Inventories	XXX
Prepaid expenses	XXX
Property, plant and equipment, less accumulated depreciation and amortization of $XXX	XXX
Other assets	XXX
Total assets	$XXX

Liabilities and Shareholders' Equity

Accounts payable	$XXX
Notes payable to banks	XXX
Accrued expenses	XXX
Income taxes payable	XXX
Other liabilities	XXX
Total liabilities	$XXX
Stockholders' equity:	
Common stock, $XX par value	$XXX
Amount in excess of par value	XXX
Retained earnings	XXX
Stockholders' equity	$XXX
Total liabilities and stockholders' equity	$XXX

- A Balance Sheet is a "snapshot" of your company's assets and liabilities as of a specific point in time, usually at the end of your financial year.

Income Statement, Service Company (13-09)

Company Name
Income Statement
For the Year Ending December 31, Year

Revenue

Service income	$XXX	
Interest and other income	XXX	
Total revenues		$XXX

Expenses

Salaries and benefits	$XXX	
Rent	XXX	
Utilities	XXX	
Interest	XXX	
Depreciation and amortization	XXX	
Bad debts	XXX	
Other expenses	XXX	
Total expenses		XXX
Income before taxes		XXX
Provision for income taxes		(XXX)
Net income		$XXX

- An Income Statement, also called Statement of Profit and Loss, summarizes revenue and expenses for a given period, usually one year, and reports the profit and loss from operations.

Income Statement, Manufacturing Company (13-10)

Company Name
Income Statement
For the Year Ending December 31, Year

Gross sales	$XXX	
Less: Sales returns, allowances and discounts	XXX	
Net sales		$XXX
Cost of goods sold	$XXX	
Sales salaries	XXX	
Advertising	XXX	
Depreciation and amortization	XXX	
Office salaries	XXX	
Bad debts	XXX	
Other expenses	XXX	
Total expenses		XXX
Net operating income		XXX
Other revenue and expense items:		
Interest and dividend income		XXX
Net income before income taxes		XXX
Provision for income taxes		(XXX)
Net income		$XXX

- An Income Statement, also called Statement of Profit and Loss, summarizes revenue and expenses for a given period, usually one year, and reports the profit and loss from operations.

Business Letter, Full Block (13-11)

Company Name
Address
City, State Zip

1 to 12 blank lines depending on length of letter (for shorter letters leave more blank lines)

Date

1 to 12 blank lines depending on length of letter (for shorter letters leave more blank lines)

Person's name
Title
Company name
Street address
City, State Zip

double space

Dear (salutation):

double space

First paragraph, body of the letter begins. (This is always single spaced with the paragraphs starting at the left margin.)

double space

Next paragraph

double space

Last paragraph

double space

Sincerely yours,

quadruple space

Typed name
Title

double space

Writer's initials (uppercase): typist's initials (lowercase)

double space

Enclosure (if needed)

- This is one of the easiest styles to set up and use since everything is aligned on the left.

Business Letter, Full Block, 2nd Page (13-12)

6 blank lines from top of page
Name of person who is receiving letter
Page 2
Date
      triple space

This is how you set up the second page of a letter in Full Block Style. All paragraphs begin at the left.
      double space
Next paragraph
      double space
Last paragraph
      double space
Sincerely yours,
      quadruple space

Typed name
Title
      double space
Writer's initials (uppercase): typist's initials (lowercase)
      double space
Enclosure (if needed)

- This is one of the easiest styles to set up and use since everything is aligned on the left.

Business Letter, Modified Block (13-13)

Company Name
Address
City, State Zip

1 to 12 blank lines depending on length of letter (for shorter letters leave more blank lines)

Date

1 to 12 blank lines depending on length of letter (for shorter letters leave more blank lines)

Person's name
Title
Company name
Street address
City, State Zip
> *double space*

Dear (salutation):
> *double space*

First paragraph, body of the letter begins. (This is always single spaced with the paragraphs starting at the left margin or indented 5 spaces.)
> *double space*

Next paragraph
> *double space*

Last paragraph
> *double space*

Sincerely yours,
quadruple space

Typed name
Title

> *double space*

Writer's initials (uppercase): typist's initials (lowercase)
> *double space*

Enclosure (if needed)

- This format is similar to Full Block, except that the date and signature lines are aligned at the right of the sheet.

Business Letter, Modified Block, 2nd Page (13-14)

6 blank lines from top of page

Name of recipient   -2-   Date
                                        triple space

This is how you set up the second page of a letter in Modified Block Style. Remember that you can start paragraphs at the left margin or indent 5 spaces.

    double space   Sincerely yours,
                                                        quadruple space

                                                 Typed Name
                                                 Title

    double space

Writer's initials (uppercase): typist's initials (lowercase)

    double space

Enclosure (if needed)

- This format is similar to Full Block, except that the date and signature lines are aligned at the right of the sheet.

Personal Letter (13-15)

September 19, 19XX

Dear Joe,

I couldn't help noticing that you seemed particularly happy when I saw you last Thursday. It's possible that your new job has you elated, but my guess is that it's more likely your recent move to a new house is causing your positive attitude.

In any case, you have much to be thankful for. Enjoy all the good things that have come your way. Congratulations!

Love,

Betsy

- Condolence letters should always be handwritten, as should letters dealing with very personal matters. But most other personal letters, such as this congratulatory letter, can be either handwritten or prepared on a computer or typewriter.

- With personal letters, a comma follows the salutation (in this case, "Dear Joe") in place of the colon which is used in business correspondence.

Invoice for Services (13-16)

Company Name
Address
City, State Zip

Date

Company Name
Address
City, State Zip

INVOICE

Basic fee .... $

Other itemized expenses .... $

Total: $

Invoice is payable upon receipt.

Please make check payable to:

Company Name
Address
City, State Zip

- This form should satisfy accounting departments because it provides a description of the basic service and allows for extra expenses.
- There's no need to include the "Please make check payable to" unless it's different from the letterhead.
- Be sure to include when payment is due.

Invoice for Goods (13-17)

Company Name
Address
City, State Zip

INVOICE

Date   Number

Order #:
P.O. #:
Cust. #:
Terms:

SOLD TO: SHIP TO:

ITEM #	DESCRIPTION	QTY.	UNIT PRICE	EXT. PRICE

Sale Amount: $
Discount: $
Tax: $
Freight: $

Total Sale: $

- If the columns are too narrow to contain the required information, turn the page horizontally to take advantage of the full 11 inch width.

Invitation, Formal (13-18)

The Withey/Beatson Insurance Agency

cordially invites you to attend

their Christmas Open House

Tuesday, December 21, Year

6:00 - 8:00 p.m.

810 High Street

East Haven, Connecticut

R.S.V.P. by December 19
(203) 555-0728

- If you choose a formal typeface, the invitation will look even more impressive.
- Include all details on time and place and a map, if possible.

Change of Address (13-19)

Company Name
Address
City, State Zip

Date

Name
Company Name
Address
City, State Zip

Dear

Please note that we have moved to a new location:

Company Name
Address
City, State Zip

Our new telephone number is: (212) 555-6789

Our previous address was:

Company Name
Address
City, State Zip

Please change your files to reflect this move.

Sincerely,

Name
Title

- Be sure to include your telephone number, even if it isn't new.
- Always include the previous address for reference.

Apologies 14

It can be embarrassing to find yourself in a situation where a written apology seems necessary. But, by making the decision to send such a letter, you're taking a giant first step toward making amends. You're presenting yourself as someone who's mature enough to take responsibility for their own behavior.

Before beginning your letter, focus on what you want to accomplish. Are you apologizing because you're genuinely remorseful for something, or is it just a courtesy? There's a big difference between a polite apology to excuse your absence from a social event and an apology where the words will salvage a damaged relationship. Remember, in either case, your objective is to appease the reader—not to make a bad situation worse.

Keep the reader's feelings in mind as you write your apology, and express the degree of remorse or regret that matches the circumstances. If your beloved Great Dane relieved himself on a friend's priceless Persian carpet, it's appropriate for you to offer to pay to have the carpet cleaned. It isn't necessary for you to offer to put Rover to sleep.

On the other hand, if you've forgotten a loved one's birthday or anniversary, your letter had better put your heart on your sleeve. Leave no question in the reader's mind about just how devastated you feel about your blunder.

Apologies about events. When you're apologizing for events, keep the following objectives in mind:

1. Admit that you misbehaved, missed the event, or missed the point.
2. Express your regret.
3. Indicate that you plan to take action to make amends. (Offer to pay for damages, promise to change your behavior, etc.) Be sure to follow up, or you'll risk losing your credibility.

If there were extenuating circumstances, it's okay to mention them. But remember—the key ingredient in a sincere apology is *accepting* blame, not *dodging* it.

Apologies about feelings. So you've hurt someone's feelings. You've said something insensitive, or you've betrayed a confidence. Feelings are uniquely personal. What seems like an off-handed remark to you, may be an insult to someone else. That's why writing an apology about feelings requires a tactful approach.

Begin with the premise that the reader is entitled to their feelings, and that you respect those feelings. By doing so, you're avoiding conflict, and making the reader more receptive to your apology. Emphasize how much you value the relationship, ask for forgiveness, and promise not to repeat the offending behavior.

Sorry My Child Misbehaved (14-01)

Dear Polly,

I'm not sure which was worse: my lack of judgment in bringing Andy to your luncheon, or my inability to control him. He's at a stage where he can't be exposed to polite company... which, of course, you observed first-hand.

When my babysitter canceled at the last minute, I should have swallowed my disappointment, called, and told you I couldn't make it. But I wanted to see you and the rest of the gang so badly that I acted without thinking of anyone but myself.

Rather than recount everything Andy (and I) did to help ruin the afternoon, I'll offer a blanket apology. His behavior was more hyper than usual, and I wish I had shown more sense than to bring him.

I'm sorry, Polly. Take as long as you need to forgive me, but please forgive me.

Your repentant friend,

- Apologize in terms that show that you are sincerely sorry.
- Acknowledge the poor behavior, but don't irritate the reader further by listing all the misdeeds.

Sorry My Pet Caused Trouble (14-02)

Dear Rocco,

When I erected a fence between your property and mine, I assumed that it would end my dog's raids on your yard. I obviously underestimated his digging skills.

I've repaired the fence and added mesh that should end Lucky's unwelcome visits. And, of course I'll pay for replacing the shrubs he destroyed.

I really appreciate your not making a big issue of this. In a sense, you've gotten some revenge for this incident because the plants he ate didn't agree with Lucky. We had quite a clean-up last night!

Thanks for being such a great neighbor. I apologize for the inconvenience.

Cordially,

- Don't rationalize your pet's bad behavior; apologize for it.
- Describe what you're doing to correct the offensive behavior.

Sorry I Spoiled Your Party (14-03)

Dear Anne,

The more your guests laughed, the more I clowned around. It never occurred to me that

I was having more fun at your party than you were.

As you know, I've always loved having an audience. But my "performance" was at your expense. I was ungracious and totally out of order, and I apologize.

It was such a lovely party, except for my antics. I'm sorry I upset you. Please forgive me.

Regretfully,

- No matter how unintentional your poor behavior might have been, accept responsibility for your lack of judgement.

- Even if you said you were sorry in person, a follow-up letter shows you continued to feel remorse.

Sorry I Was Out of Town for Your Award (14-04)

Dear Lee,

I was really looking forward to attending your company's Wallace A. Buchanan Lifetime Achievement Award presentation—particularly since you were the recipient—but mother nature hissed at me.

I had to wrap up a trip in Indianapolis that day, and I thought if I left by 3:00 o'clock, I'd easily be back in time. As you probably know, a snow and ice storm hit the area, and that 180 mile drive might as well have been 1,800 miles. I didn't even reach the state line.

While I'm disappointed I wasn't able to attend, I'm very pleased that you invited me to share your special evening. Congratulations on a well-earned, richly-deserved award.

Cordially,

- Don't go too deeply into details about the circumstances of missing the event (the reader may find them less than compelling!).

- Show that you, too, are disappointed.

Sorry I Broke Your CD Player (14-05)

Dear Evelyn and Jon,

The enclosed check speaks for itself. It will cover the cost of purchasing the same kind of CD player that slipped through my fingers during your party. The apology requires some explaining.

I had never seen a unit quite like yours, and you know how I am about electronic gadgets. I can't resist an up-close-and-personal inspection. I don't know why it fell, but fall it did.

I'm <u>really</u> sorry. Will you give me a chance to be more careful next time? Please call to let me know I've been forgiven.

Your clumsy friend,

- If you break something of value, covering the cost of repair or replacement makes an apology palatable.

- You can be as innovative with your sign-off as the situation demands. "Sincerely," "Yours very truly," and the like are more formal and not mandatory among friends.

Sorry I Burned a Hole in Your Sofa (14-06)

Dear Rose,

If you noticed that I skulked out of your house Saturday night, it was because I was so embarrassed I couldn't look you in the eye. I'm the one who burned the hole in your new sofa. I was so mortified, my first reaction was to run.

Please allow me to pay for the repair. I'd be happy to make arrangements with an upholsterer I've worked with to have the sofa picked up at your convenience. I'll call in a few days to find out what's best for you.

Aside from my blunder, it was one great party! Thanks for inviting me. I hope you'll forgive me for the accident and the unconscionable way I dealt with it.

Sincerest regrets,

- Explain what happened, and how you feel about it. Don't trivialize the incident.

- Offer to take care of any expense, and be sure to follow up in good faith.

Sorry I Drank Too Much (14-07)

Dear Jim,

Even though I can't seem to remember how I acted last Saturday, enough people have made it a point to tell me, which somehow makes me feel doubly embarrassed.

I'm sorry for the verbal abuse I threw at you for taking my car keys away. You obviously did me a giant favor, and I repaid you with insults. You're a remarkable person to have taken a stand, particularly when it would have been far easier to just turn your back on me.

I'm sorry I let myself get into that state, and I'm particularly sorry that I made things so difficult for you. I won't let it happen again.

Thanks for caring enough to put up with me. You're a great friend.

Gratefully,

> - Acknowledge your behavior.
> - While an apology may be good enough, a promise never to repeat the behavior is even better.

Sorry I Can't Come to Your Party (14-08)

Dear Lorraine and Tom,

Did you ever wish you could be in two places at once? I'm feeling that way about the upcoming weekend. Your anniversary bash sounds like the event of the year. But the timing is bad for us. Our niece is making her First Communion in Atlanta and, as her godparents, Bill and I are committed to being there.

We're disappointed that we'll miss celebrating your twenty-five years of togetherness.

We'd like to toast you belatedly when we return. How about dinner at Smokey's? I'll call you to set a date. Meanwhile, congratulations!

Best always,

> - Let the reader know that you appreciate and understand the importance of the occasion.
> - If you value the friendship, be specific about why you can't attend, and suggest a future get-together.

Sorry I Forgot Your Birthday (14-09)

Dear Penny,

Some friend I am! Would it help if I said I forgot your birthday because I think of you as ageless?

If flattery won't earn your forgiveness, how about letting me take you to lunch at Chez Nous next Friday? Champagne and the works?

I'll call Monday to confirm.

Your chagrined pal,

> - A little self-deprecation doesn't hurt if you've overlooked an occasion.
> - Let the reader know your apology is sincere, and prove it by offering to make it up in some tangible way.

Sorry I Forgot Your Birthday, Poem (14-10)

Dear Lisa,

Somebody you know is a dope,
A husband who's quite without hope.
Your birthday's forgotten,
He's feeling so rotten
He doesn't know quite how to cope.

If he just could get back in your graces,
He would take you to fabulous places.
Let him make up to you,
(Which he's sure you would do,
If you just could see how red his face is!)

I love you. Will you forgive me?

Sheepishly,

- You can ease the sting of being forgetful with an admission of guilt, albeit a humorous one.

- A promise to make it up to the person may soften any hurt feelings.

Sorry I Forgot Our Anniversary (14-11)

Dear Nan,

Someone once asked Albert Einstein's wife if she understood the theory of relativity. She said, "No, but I understand Dr. Einstein."

Well, you might not understand how I could forget our anniversary, but you do understand me well enough to know that I'll try very hard to make my blunder up to you. In fact, when I get home from this interminable trip, I'm planning a special evening for us at Le Champignon and a surprise I'm sure will please you.

Please forgive me, sweetheart. I may have missed our anniversary date, but I treasure every day that we've been married. I love you very much.

Your devoted (but forgetful) husband,

- There's no sense making excuses for forgetting an occasion that's this important. If you blew it, just admit it and go on from there.

- A bit of suspense can be disarming and diverting. A little romance can salve hurt feelings.

Sorry I Blamed You for Something You Didn't Do (14-12)

Dear Molly,

I'm so embarrassed. I blamed you for spreading a rumor about me, and I just discovered you had nothing to do with it.

I feel foolish for jumping to a conclusion without knowing all the facts. My anger was totally misplaced.

There aren't enough words to tell you how much I value your friendship. I can't forgive myself, but can you forgive me?

With love,

- Accept the blame and ask for forgiveness.
- The details of the error aren't as important as the sincerity of your apology.

Sorry I Betrayed Your Confidence (14-13)

Dear Marsha,

Trust is an important part of friendship. I think of myself as a good friend and that's why I would never betray your trust without a valid reason.

I discussed your personal affairs with Mike in an effort to bring you two back together. I felt that our mutual concern for you justified my confiding in him. Now I realize that, however noble my intentions, I was wrong to intercede without your permission.

Will you forgive me? Please!

Your friend,

- Admit that you were wrong.
- Offer an explanation (not an excuse).

Sorry I Hurt Your Feelings (14-14)

Dear Sharon,

My intentions are usually good, but the execution is, on occasion, lacking. I don't always think about the consequences of my words, but you've made it clear that I will have to, if our relationship is to continue.

I love you very much, and I'm sorry I hurt you. I'm glad you care enough about us to let me know when I've stepped over the line.

Please forgive me,

- Make it clear that you take responsibility for the hurt.
- Ask for forgiveness. The request demonstrates you are not taking the relationship for granted.

Sorry I Lied to You (14-15)

Dear Betsy,

I've compounded an error and made a bigger fool of myself than even I thought possible.

First, in order to avoid you, I lied and told you I would be away for the weekend. My feelings were hurt when you won the ESTEEM account and I didn't. False pride kept me from telling you I was resentful, and I needed time to get over it.

Then, when we ran into each other at the movies, I was so embarrassed I couldn't speak; that's why I walked right past you. I've dug a hole for myself, and now I'm trying to climb out of it.

I value you as a friend and as a colleague. Please accept my apology for my childish behavior. It's time I grew up and dealt with my feelings more maturely.

Most sincerely,

- Tell the truth, accept the blame, then apologize.
- Explain why you want to set things right.

Sorry if I Misled You (14-16)

Dear Jack,

I feel I can discuss almost anything with you. In fact, I feel more comfortable with you than with many of my women friends. Lately, though, I've sensed some tension when we're together, and I think I'm to blame.

I'm afraid my warm feelings toward you have been misinterpreted, and you've begun to think I'm looking for something more than friendship. I'm not; and I'm sorry if I gave you the wrong impression.

I hope our relationship can weather this misunderstanding. I don't want to lose a good friend and confidant.

Always,

- Tell the reader what you value about the relationship.
- Define your view of the relationship.

Sorry I Misunderstood Your Intentions (14-17)

Dear Wayne,

I guess I've been reading too many romance novels. It didn't occur to me that a man could invite me to his hotel room without seduction in mind. I overreacted and I'm sorry.

I really <u>would</u> love to see the video of your lecture. Will you invite me again?

Cordially,

- Explain how the misunderstanding occurred.
- Tell the reader how you'd like to make amends.

Sorry I Was Inconsiderate (14-18)

Dear Lloyd,

My timing was off yesterday. I pressed you for a decision about our vacation plans without knowing that you'd just been notified of your Dad's illness. I understand why you were upset, and I'm sorry.

I'd like to be more sensitive to your feelings, but I need your help. If something is bothering you, please tell me. It's frustrating trying to read your mind.

At this moment, your father's health is our priority. Let's talk about how we can support him through this episode.

Love,

- If you're at fault admit it.
- Make a suggestion about how to avoid future arguments.

Sorry I Started a Fight (14-19)

Dear Bruce,

I'm sorry I jumped down your throat during our card game... particularly since I've discovered that I didn't know what I was talking about.

You had the facts right, and I had 'em wrong. You acted like a gentleman, and I acted like an idiot. Even if I had been right, I would still have been out of line.

I apologize. If you're willing to forgive my tantrum, I'll give you my word that I won't subject you to that kind of adolescent display again.

My apologies,

Sorry You Felt Slighted (14-20)

Dear Wendy,

When I saw you in the Commerce building lobby the other day, you were deep in conversation with a group of people. Even though I wanted to say hello, I decided not to intrude on what appeared to be an intense discussion.

Not only was there no slight intended, I'm disappointed that you'd think I would intentionally ignore you. I had no way of knowing your conversation was social and open to an "outsider."

Anyway, let's forget it, shall we? I think our friendship can withstand this misunderstanding.

Fondly,

240   *APOLOGIES*

Complaints 15

There's one in every crowd: the whiner. The person who complains about virtually everything. Unfortunately, complaining is rarely a prelude to action—it's an end in itself.

The person who takes the time to write a complaint letter, however, is action-oriented. That's the purpose of a complaint letter: to bring about a change in policy or behavior or to establish legitimate grounds for restitution.

Complaints to neighbors. A great deal of tact is required when writing a complaint letter to a neighbor. After all, you're going to have to face this person each day when you step outside to retrieve the morning paper or empty the trash.

If your neighbor is neglecting their property, begin your letter by invoking a sense of community pride. Impress upon them how hard you (and the other neighbors) work to keep your street looking its best. Mention the effect of an ill-kempt yard on real estate values. Then tell the reader what action you want taken.

If you want your neighbor to *cease* an action, describe how that activity affects you, your children, or your property. Offer a suggested remedy or two. Express your hope that the issue can be settled amicably—without taking legal steps. Try to end the letter on a cordial, "neighborly" note.

Complaints to companies about employees. Decide before you write this kind of letter exactly what action you're seeking. Do you want the person fired, or simply reprimanded? Unless the offense was egregious, (such as reckless driving by a trucker), you might not think it's worth having some poor fellow's pink slip on your conscience. Describe exactly what happened (who, what, when, where and how); then suggest to the reader what action you think is appropriate. A subtle reminder about personal grooming? A mandatory course in customer relations? Reparations for your damaged garage door? Think about what your demands are, then state them *firmly*.

Complaints to companies about products and services. These are straightforward, no-frills demands for restitution. You need to provide a detailed account of the facts and circumstances surrounding your complaint, and furnish documentation to back it up. Establish a reasonable deadline for response, and state your intention to work your way up the chain of command until your demands are met.

Clean Up Your Property (15-01)

Dear Lew,

If you were sitting in my living room, looking across the street at your home, here's what you'd see: a rusted water heater, a chipped, discolored bathtub, three out-of-commission lawnmowers, a bunch of broken screens and other unsightly items in your driveway.

I've waited over a year to ask you to move the material, because I just kept assuming you'd get around to it. By now, it may have reached the point where you're so used to it, you don't even see it. (I know that's happened to me: Until Julie told me that the paint on our house was cracked and peeling, I never noticed it.)

Please move the material out of sight or simply put it out with the trash. If you need help moving any of those items, my son and I would be glad to lend a hand.

Thanks for the consideration.

Sincerely,

- Try to make the reader see the situation as you see it, without attacking their integrity.
- An offer to help expresses willingness to cooperate with the reader.

Your Lawn Needs Mowing (15-02)

Dear Mr. Sloane,

I feel fortunate to live in a beautiful neighborhood like ours. That's probably why I take such pride in maintaining the appearance of my property. I wouldn't want real estate values to decline for <u>anyone</u> in Crestwood!

It concerns me that your lawn has gone unmown for weeks now, which diminishes the appearance of the entire street. If there is some reason why you have been unable to care for your property, I know the neighbors would be happy to pitch in to help.

Otherwise, everyone on Maple Grove Road would appreciate it if you would return to mowing your lawn regularly, as you always have in the past.

Thanks.

Sincerely,

- Explain that one overgrown lawn brings the entire street down a notch.
- Offer to help out if the homeowner is temporarily unable to care for their property.

Don't Use Our Pool without Permission (15-03)

Dear Joanna,

One of the joys of having a pool is being able to share it with friends. But along with pool ownership comes responsibility for the safety of everyone who uses it. In fact, the township requires us to have a fence around the pool area to discourage unauthorized swimming.

Twice this past week I came home from work and found Matt and Troy in the pool. There were no adults around.

Joanna, as I've offered in the past, anytime you or your boys want to swim, call me. If it's convenient, I'll tell you so. But for everyone's safety, be sure that the boys never use the pool without permission *and* supervision.

Thanks.

Cordially,

- Let the reader know that you're not inhospitable; there's a safety issue involved.
- Be specific about your rules and stick to them.

Your Workers Destroyed My Garden (15-04)

Dear Mr. Hoyt,

Your new fence looks great. I wish I could say the same for my garden. Your workers trampled the flowers I recently planted: six flats of impatiens, a dozen geraniums, and a dozen pansies.

I put a lot of effort and expense into my garden. I'm willing to do the replanting, but I'd like to be reimbursed for the cost of new plants, which was $63.

I'll call you at the end of the week to arrange for the payment.

Thanks.

Cordially,

- Make it clear that you expect to be repaid.
- Say when you intend to follow up.

You Forgot to Return My Tools (15-05)

Dear Howard,

I'm pleased to hear how well your deck turned out. I'm sorry I couldn't give you more of a hand, but at least my tools were there to represent me.

Now I need to get started on a few projects of my own by the end of this month...but I'm short on tools at the moment! Maybe we can kill two birds with one stone: Why don't you and Ellen plan to spend a day with us soon, and bring the tools along with you?

Call me or Mary Beth so we can make a date. We're looking forward to seeing you again. Maybe you can give me a few tips on remodeling my kitchen.

Cordially,

- Asking for something to be returned doesn't have to be confrontational or embarrassing.
- Even though the letter is friendly, make it clear that it's the reader's responsibility to return the tools.

You Broke My Lawnmower (15-06)

Dear Sam,

One of the things I like about our neighborhood is that people help each other. I was happy to lend you my lawnmower, because I felt confident it would be well cared for.

Unfortunately, since you used the lawnmower, I haven't been able to start it and one of the blades is bent. I had the mower serviced at the beginning of the season and had only used it once, so I know it was in good condition when you borrowed it.

I'm taking the mower to Howell's Lawn and Garden Center to be checked. I hope I can count on you to pay for the repair. When I have an estimate, I'll stop by.

Sam, let's not allow this mishap to interfere with the great relationship we've enjoyed these past years.

Cordially,

- Keep the tone cordial, but be clear about your expectations for the repair.
- Let the reader know you hope one incident won't spoil the friendship.

Your Dog's Barking Keeps Me Awake (15-07)

Dear Mr. McConaghy,

I'm a nurse who works long and hard hours. A good night's sleep is critical to my performance on the job.

For the past week, your dog has made it impossible for me to get any rest. He starts barking just as I'm trying to go to sleep, and he continues non-stop into the early morning.

The loss of sleep is starting to affect my work and I can't allow that to happen. Please find a way to keep your dog quiet.

Thank you.

Sincerely,

- Explain any special circumstances that might gain the reader's cooperation.
- Be cordial, but make your point.

Your Visitors Block My Driveway (15-08)

Dear Peg,

I've always enjoyed the sounds of happiness that come from your back yard. I really think you're the best hostess in the world. Where you get the energy to entertain nearly every weekend is beyond me; I seem to need my weekends just to recuperate so I can go back to work on Monday!

I'd appreciate a favor. Would you please keep an eye on where your guests park? I'm reluctant to interrupt your get-togethers to ask people to move their cars so they don't block my driveway. But it's becoming more than an occasional nuisance.

Thanks so much.

Cordially,

- Starting your letter with a compliment can ease the sting of a complaint.
- Even though you're clearly in the right, you can maintain a relationship by asking for help rather than demanding a correction.

Your Child is Bullying Mine (15-09)

Dear Mrs. Metzger,

For the past week my son, Billy, has been arriving home from school in tears. Yesterday he confessed to me that your son has been forcing him to turn over his lunch money every day this week. Peter threatened Billy with a beating if he told anyone what was going on.

Billy is seven years old. Peter is eleven. Naturally, Billy is intimidated by an older, bigger boy who is making threats.

I haven't reported these events to the school authorities because I wanted to give you the opportunity to deal with the problem privately with your son. However, if the behavior doesn't change immediately, I'll notify the school authorities and follow up with them until the matter is resolved.

Sincerely,

> - Describe the behavior that has prompted you to write the letter.
> - Notify the reader that if the offensive behavior doesn't stop, you'll take the problem to a higher authority.

Your Child Stole Something (15-10)

Dear Marla,

If my son or daughter had taken something without asking permission, I'd want to know about it. Knowing you as well as I do, I'm confident you feel the same way. Which brings me to the reason for this note.

When Richie stayed with us last weekend, he fell in love with Jesse's baseball card collection, particularly his Mike Schmidt rookie card. Richie kept putting the card in his shirt pocket, and Jesse kept reminding him to take it out.

Just before you picked Richie up Sunday evening, the card was missing again. Jesse insisted that Richie had it, but Richie denied it. I would have said something to you that evening, but I wanted to search through Jesse's room first.

Since the boys played with the cards only in Jesse's room, and since no one else was in the room that weekend, I'm asking if you would check with Richie. Jesse's so upset his card is missing (and so's his dad, who says the card is valuable).

Thanks for helping. I'll call you in a few days to see if Richie was able to shed some light on the disappearance.

Sincerely yours,

> - There's no easy way to suggest to a parent that their child took something. Asking for help in resolving the situation is better than making outright accusations.
> - Remember that you're dealing with both parents' and children's feelings.

Your Clerk Made an Ethnic Slur (15-11)

Dear Ms. Branch:

I'm annoyed at myself for not having the presence of mind to respond immediately to an ethnic slur made by one of your cashiers. The comment wasn't directed at me, but that didn't make it any less offensive.

As I walked past a checkout counter, I overheard one of your clerks telling a joke to another clerk. It didn't seem to matter to her that she told the joke loudly enough to attract attention, or that what she was saying was racist. In fact, she was so open about it, she may not have been aware of how insensitive her words were.

Rather than asking you to single out the young woman, I'd like your assurance that the store will review and enforce sensitivity training with your employees. And I'll give you my assurance that if I ever hear another racial comment in your store, (a) you'll lose a good customer, and (b) I'll register a complaint with the president of your company.

I look forward to hearing from you.

Sincerely,

- A "cool" letter can be very effective with a hot issue. This is far more effective than demanding termination or discipline.

- If you want a response, ask for it.

Your Waiter Made Sexist Comments to Me (15-12)

Dear Mr. Stavros:

I think the food in your restaurant is wonderful, but I may never have the chance to enjoy it again. At least not until one of your waiters (his name tag read "GIANNI") either leaves or is taught how to deal with women customers.

During lunch, your waiter felt free to comment on my figure and my clothes. And he topped it off by noting that I also needed to smile more, intimating that he might be of help in that regard.

I suspect you've lost more than a few customers due to this obnoxious employee. If you don't want to lose more, I strongly suggest you do something about his behavior.

Sincerely,

- The threat of losing business guarantees that your letter will be read by management.

- Detail what you considered offensive; otherwise the behavior can't be corrected.

Your Salesperson Has an Offensive Odor (15-13)

Dear Mr. Allen:

I visited your store near closing time on Tuesday, and approached a salesperson to ask some questions. But I was so repelled by the odor of cigar smoke, both from his breath and his clothing, that all I could think of was getting away from him. I mumbled that I was late for an appointment and left.

The next day, motivated by the good things I had heard about your pricing and service, I decided to make a return visit, this time in the morning. I didn't give it a second thought when the same salesperson smiled and started to walk towards me. Unfortunately, the odor was just as bad.

I didn't even make an excuse this time; I just spun around and left. I can't help but wonder how often this scene is repeated in your store. And I also wonder if the people who work there have a sense of smell. How can you stand it?

I don't know the salesperson's name, but you shouldn't have any trouble knowing who I'm talking about. You owe it to your customers—and this oblivious man—to do something about it.

Sincerely,

- People cannot correct problems if they're not aware of them.

- Any respectable business owner would want to be informed that sales are being lost due to a correctable problem.

Your Salesperson Was Rude (15-14)

Dear Sir or Madam:

One of your saleswomen offended me, and unless she's reprimanded and retrained, I won't be returning to your store. Her name is Clarice.

I was trying on bathing suits (as if that isn't traumatic enough!), and had narrowed my selections down to four. I asked Clarice which two she thought looked best. Her response was, "If you don't lose fifteen pounds, it doesn't matter which one you buy."

Obviously, she doesn't work on commission, but that's no excuse for her rudeness and insensitivity. I got dressed immediately and left the store without making a purchase.

If you expect to stay in business, you'd better pay more attention to your employees' attitudes. Please let me know how you plan to correct this problem.

Sincerely,

- Describe the offending salesperson's behavior.

- State your expectation of a response.

Your Cloak Room Attendant Lost My Coat (15-15)

Dear Mr. Luongo:

Last Friday evening, the coat I wore to your restaurant disappeared from your cloakroom while I was dining. It was bad enough that your cloak room attendant allowed my coat to "walk," but her complete indifference to the loss made it even more infuriating.

You can either (1) Produce the coat within a week (full-length leather, black, size medium, fleece-lined, with a Calla Newell label), or (2) send me a check for $425 to cover a replacement. And speaking of a replacement, you might consider hiring a new cloak room attendant who takes her responsibilities more seriously.

I'll expect to hear from you by October 2nd.

Sincerely,

> - Describe what was lost.
> - Specify what action you expect and when.

Your Deliverymen Damaged My Floor (15-16)

Dear Mr. Wilson:

Despite your assurances that it wouldn't happen, your deliverymen scratched my new hardwood floor when they delivered my refrigerator.

What makes this particularly galling is that we discussed the sequence of events before-hand. You strongly urged me to have the flooring put down before the delivery. You said it would be easier for the flooring people, and that there would be less wear and tear on the refrigerator if it didn't need to be lifted to install the new floor. As things turned out, it was easier on everyone but me.

The flooring company—at a cost of $375—will sand the floor and refinish it. Since your deliverymen caused the damage, and since you guaranteed that the delivery would be damage-free, I expect you to pay for it.

You can either mail the check to me this week, or I can pick it up on the way home from work. I'll call to confirm arrangements.

Sincerely,

> - There's plenty of time to negotiate later, if necessary. Take a strong stand and demand full payment to start with.
> - Be very clear as to whatever action you want taken (e.g., check sent, telephone response, etc.).

Your Mechanic Tried to Rip Me Off (15-17)

Dear Mr. Majors:

I may not be an expert in car repairs, but I know when I'm being ripped off.

I brought my 19XX LeBaron to your shop for repairs on October 23. Your mechanic, Steve, informed me that I needed a complete set of brakes. In fact, he stated that I risked an accident if I didn't have the work done immediately. After getting Steve's estimate (which was very high), I took the car to another repair shop for a second estimate.

I was informed that my brakes were in excellent condition and would require only a minor adjustment.

Because the two shops gave me such different diagnoses, I went to a third repair shop. They agreed totally with the second shop's opinion.

Your operation appears to be dishonest. I'm reporting Majors Auto Repair to The Better Business Bureau and the state consumer protection agency.

Sincerely,

- Give an account of your experience, stating why you believe you were ripped off.

- Inform the reader that you plan to report his business to the appropriate "watchdog" agencies.

Your Truck Driver Almost Drove Me off the Road (15-18)

Dear Mr. Slawek:

One of your truckers is driving recklessly and needs to be disciplined or dismissed.

This morning, at about 9:00, I was heading south on the Garden State Parkway near Rahway. I was traveling at the speed limit in the passing lane, when I saw a huge truck bearing down on me. As soon as it was safe, I signaled and moved to the right lane. The truck followed me there, again bearing down inches from my bumper. I moved back to the other lane and it followed. This dangerous cat and mouse game continued until I pulled off the parkway to escape. By this time I was shaking visibly.

The lettering on the truck said Northeast Distributors; the I.D. number was 84224NE. I was unable to get the entire license number, but the first three digits on the New Jersey plate were 893.

This driver is a menace. I'd like to know what you plan to do about him before I decide whether to take further action.

Very truly yours,

- Go right to the top with serious complaints. You're more likely to get quick action.
- Give all the details necessary to identify the vehicle.

Your Product Is Defective; Exchange It (15-19)

Dear Sir or Madam:

Last month I purchased the Misumi Audio Component System MSM-3220 from your Christmas catalog. The system is defective, and I want to exchange it for a new unit. All my CD's jump during play, regardless of how I position the unit.

Here's the information you need to process my exchange:

Date of Purchase: December 4,19XX

Method of Payment: Check #195, issued by Firstbank

Amount of check: $821.59

Please notify me when I can expect delivery of the new system and when the defective unit will be picked up.

Thank you.

Very truly yours,

- Identify the product and explain the defect.
- Give details of the purchase (e.g., date, method of payment, amount,etc.).

Your Product Is Defective; Refund My Money (15-20)

Dear Sir or Madam:

Re: Deckmate Picnic Partner
         Item No.: 1PP 23970
         Price: $189.50
         Date of Purchase: April 2,19XX
         Method of payment: Check #1209 Gibralter Savings

Trying to assemble your "Deckmate Picnic Partner" table and benches almost caused a divorce in my family. Finally, my husband and I realized that we weren't inadequate; your directions were.

I thought the problems had ended when we put all the pieces together, but that's when your product's poor design became apparent. The benches fit so close to the table that we could barely squeeze into the seats (we're of average weight).

Your product is impossible to use. I want to return the unit for a full refund, as guaranteed in your catalog.

I await a check in the amount of $189.50 and instructions as to the disposal of "Deckmate Picnic Partner."

Very truly yours,

- If you feel ripped off, say so.
- Let the reader know that your demand for a refund is non-negotiable.

Your Product Isn't What You Advertised (15-21)

Dear Sir or Madam:

Re: Money-Back Guarantee

I purchased your product based on a television advertisement that guaranteed satisfaction in the elimination of blood, pet and virtually any other kind of hard-to-remove stains from carpets. The ad claimed that Miracle Whiz Carpet Cleaner is used by hotels, theaters, offices and other high-traffic centers.

Those facilities must be satisfied to have unsightly stains on their carpets. I used your product—as directed—and found that it did nothing whatsoever. The stains just sat there. About the only positive thing I can say about Miracle Whiz is that it didn't damage my carpeting. I don't understand how you can make such outrageous claims about such an ineffective product.

I should probably complain to the FTC, but I'll settle for a prompt refund.

Sincerely,

- Address your letter to Customer Service. You may find they are willing to give you more than you ask for, just to generate good will for the company.

- A mention of the FTC (Federal Trade Commission) may also help expedite your refund.

Your Advertising Is Misleading (15-22)

Dear Mr. Elliot:

Early this summer, I purchased patio furniture from you. One week later, you ran an ad offering a 10% discount on all furniture. Since your advertised policy is to honor the reduced price on any merchandise purchased within 14 days of a sale, I brought my receipt to your service desk and was told the discount didn't apply to seasonal furniture.

Last week, I purchased bath towels, and then received a flyer that advertised 25% off on towels. When I tried to get the discount, I was told I had purchased towels that had already been marked down...that they were not eligible for the sale pricing. Your company always seems to have an excuse for not honoring its stated discounts.

Since I'd rather get the discount than file a complaint with the State Attorney General, I'll forego any action if you agree to honor your own policy. I've attached both sales receipts. I'll expect a positive response from you by Friday, September 12, or I'll take appropriate action.

Sincerely,

- State the policy in question and the violation.
- Be certain the reader understands the consequences of their failure to take action.

My Oven Still Doesn't Work (15-23)

Dear Sir or Madam:

First, the good news: Your serviceperson was prompt, pleasant and courteous. He actually removed his work shoes (his idea) because he had to walk across brand new carpeting to get to the kitchen.

Now, the bad news: My oven still doesn't work properly. Your serviceperson indicated he wasn't familiar with my particular model, which makes me wonder why he was sent out on my job.

I'd appreciate it if you would send a repair person who can perform the service required. I need my oven fixed before the holidays, and I need you to live up to your reputation for fast, efficient service.

Please call me at (718) 555-0388 to schedule a new appointment.

Very truly yours,

- You can express annoyance without tearing someone's head off.
- Tell the company what action you want taken; don't expect them to do what you want without their being told.

You Didn't Honor Your Warranty (15-24)

Dear Mr. Evans:

Have you ever noticed how television news loves to play up "Business Bilks Customer" stories? How the owners always come off as Scrooges and scoundrels? How businesses immediately sag when the stories air?

Well, brace yourself, Mr. Evans, because it's about to happen to you. Picture yourself as the feature story on the news this Thursday, as the local consumer reporter barges into your store demanding to know why you won't honor the warranty for a refrigerator purchased by a struggling single mother.

If you don't like the picture, I suggest you have a repairman here by Wednesday, June 12. I'm angry that your continual lies and broken promises have forced me to resort to this sort of action. I'll do whatever it takes to get you to fulfill your obligation to me.

Sincerely,

- Letters with time limits should be sent via a method that provides proof of delivery.
- Paint a picture to help the reader understand the consequences of your words.

My Phone Bill Has Calls I Didn't Make (15-25)

Dear Sir or Madam:

Re: (215) 555-2820 (residence)

My phone bill, dated June 7, has charges for calls I didn't make.

The following charges are erroneous:

April 18	9:42 a.m. to Los Angeles	(213) 555-7610	34 min.
April 18	10:30 a.m. to Santa Fe	(505) 555-6738	90 min.
April 18	1:10 p.m. to Denver	(303) 555-6833	68 min.

I was at my office from 8:30 a.m. until 5:30 p.m. on April 18. No one else was at my residence on that day.

I will not accept responsibility for these calls. Please delete them from my bill.

Thank you.

- List the erroneous calls as they appear on your statement.
- Explain why you're not responsible for the charges and direct that they be removed from your bill.

You Ruined My Dress, to Dry Cleaner (15-26)

Dear Felix:

Between tailoring and dry cleaning, I spend about $1,000 a year with you. That means you're willing to forego at least $10,000 to $15,000 in future business, because you won't compensate me for the dress you ruined.

In addition to the revenue you'll lose from me, I'll make it a point to mention to everyone in my club, office and church how you ruined my dress and refused to make good. That can easily extend to another $50,000 in lost business for you every year. That doesn't make you a very good businessperson, Felix.

We both know that accidents happen...and I'd like to think that I'm dealing with reputable businesspeople who take responsibility for them when they do.

Your refusal to pay me for my unwearable dress is going to cost you a lot more than it will cost me to replace it.

Sincerely,

- Although the seeming purpose of this letter is simply to tell an unresponsive businessperson that they will lose business, it may also stir him to make restitution when the potential loss is indicated in black and white.
- Don't threaten legal action when it's obvious to the injuring party there will be none (owner's loss is too insignificant).

Room Service Takes Too Long (15-27)

Dear Ms. Waters:

I've always enjoyed staying at the Alouette, but if room service remains as slow as it was during my stay last week, I won't return.

I had a 50-minute wait for breakfast one morning, and over an hour's wait another morning. In both cases, I had placed my order the night before to avoid delays. And my request for coffee during one afternoon meeting was never met.

I'm willing to pay top dollar for top service, but I resent paying for this kind of performance. May I have your assurance that the problem will be resolved? If not, I'll have no choice but to stay at another hotel when I'm in San Francisco.

Sincerely,

- Service establishments appreciate being told of problem areas. You're doing them a favor by being straightforward.
- Indicate what you plan to do if the hotel doesn't take action.

You Don't Have Enough Salespeople (15-28)

Dear Mr. Sweeney:

Trying to shop in your store is a frustrating experience.

Why? Because there are never any salespeople around. Yesterday I waited ten minutes for service in the housewares department before throwing my hands up and leaving the store. I lost my patience, and Conniff's lost a $98.00 purchase.

This wasn't an isolated experience. On several occasions I've had to scout up salespeople to ring up my purchases. There's hardly ever a salesperson in sight.

I've continued to shop at Conniff's because I like your merchandise and your prices. But now I'm questioning whether it's worth the effort.

If you'd like to keep a disgruntled customer from becoming a former customer, hire some more salespeople.

Very truly yours,

- Cite a specific example of your complaint.
- Warn the reader that they will lose a good customer if the service doesn't improve.

You Need Facilities for Handicapped People (15-29)

Dear Mr. Saltes:

My wife is confined to a wheelchair. To avoid uncomfortable situations, I always call ahead to be certain a facility can accommodate handicapped people.

Can you imagine our surprise—after being told that your restaurant had handicapped access—when we arrived and found that the access was through a delivery entrance? Can you understand why I was angry and why my wife felt humiliated? Offering to have her wheeled through the kitchen into the dining area does not constitute compliance with the Americans with Disabilities Act.

In addition to the embarrassment you caused us, I wonder if you have any idea of the fines you're risking with your non-compliance. I plan to help you find out, because I'm filing a formal complaint against your restaurant.

Sincerely,

- Letters are great for blowing off steam and for helping people understand their obligations.
- In many ways, a "threat" on paper has more power than a verbal confrontation. Use your pen to confirm your rights under the law.

My New TV Is Defective, Letter #1 (15-30)

Dear Mr. Jonczak:

I'm disappointed by your unwillingness to make good on the defective television you sold to me.

I'm tired of the delays and puzzled by your unresponsiveness. Your delivery man acknowledged that the console was damaged (see copy of my receipt), and I want a replacement unit or a refund in full.

If you ignore this letter as you have my calls, I'll take this issue directly to your store manager. Let's get it resolved, shall we? You need to live up to your "satisfaction guaranteed" motto.

I'll expect your call within the week.

Sincerely,

- Don't just call when you have problems. Create a "paper trail" that proves you attempted to communicate.
- Be clear as to subsequent action if your complaint is not acted upon. And be prepared to follow through.

My New TV Is Defective, Letter #2 (15-31)

Dear Mr. Lister:

I'm sorry to have to ask you to handle a transaction that your salesperson, Kevin Jonczak, should be taking care of, but I don't have any choice. He won't answer my calls or correspondence.

I want a replacement for the defective television I purchased from your store. It was delivered with a large gouge on the side of the console. As you'll see from the attached copy of my receipt, your deliveryman acknowledged the problem. All I'm asking you to do is give me what I paid for: a television in perfect condition.

If you can give me a delivery date for the new television, and an approximate delivery time, I'll be sure that someone is home to receive it. Call me during the day at (304) 555-3900 or in the evening at (304) 555-4896.

Sincerely,

- Let the manager know that you have been trying to "go through proper channels" without success.
- Ask for a delivery schedule to emphasize your expectations.

My New TV Is Defective, Letter #3 (15-32)

Dear Mr. Bunting:

The Best Value Appliances store in Irving, Texas has failed to live up to—or acknowledge—your satisfaction-guaranteed pledge.

I'm seeking a replacement for the damaged television that was delivered to me two months ago. As shown on the enclosed copy of my delivery receipt, the driver noted that the television was damaged in transit. In retrospect, I'm sorry I accepted delivery because the personnel at your Irving store have ignored my numerous calls and letters (copies enclosed), and I'm stuck with a defective set.

I'm ready to go to the local media to vent my displeasure with Best Value. My hope, however, is that you'll make that step unnecessary. I'd appreciate a call from you or a representative to let me know when I can expect a replacement unit. I can be reached during the day at (304) 555-3900, or in the evening at (304) 555-4896.

I expect a call by March 12. Thanks for your expected intercession.

Sincerely,

- Don't lose your rational tone or *you'll* be perceived to be the problem. Keep the focus on the store as the villain.
- Define your expectations and provide a deadline.

My New TV Is Defective, Letter #4 (15-33)

Dear Sir or Madam:

This is a formal complaint against the Best Value store in Irving, Texas.

I purchased a Nakamura console television in December. When it was delivered, the driver acknowledged on the receipt that there was damage on the side of the cabinet (a copy of the receipt is enclosed). I accepted the set, assuming that Best Value would make good, as promised. They've stonewalled me, disavowing any responsibility for the defect (see enclosed correspondence).

After four months of trying to settle this issue with unreasonable people, I'm turning to you for help. I want a replacement for my damaged television. And I'd like to see you take punitive action against Best Value to "send them a message" that this sort of irresponsible behavior will not be tolerated.

If you need more information before proceeding, you can reach me during the day at (304) 555-3900, or in the evening at (304) 555-4896.

Very truly yours,

- Most states have a consumer protection unit that will assist you. Put your tax dollars to work for yourself!
- Briefly explain the situation and tell what action you expect.

My Car's a Lemon—Replace It (15-34)

Dear Mr. Garfield:

It's obvious Pitcairn Motors, in Skokie, has no intention of making good on a bad car. Here's the sequence of events that's forced me to turn to you for help:

1. I drove my brand-new Spirit Rover out of Pitcairn's lot on March 3. Within one mile, the radiator exploded.

2. After waiting a week for the dealer to make the necessary repairs, I had the car for five more days when the electrical system caught fire.

3. After another week of Rent-a-Wreck, I anxiously took possession of my car again and, within two weeks, had a cracked engine block.

The dealer is now suggesting that I'm the problem, not the car. Before I go to the time and trouble of contacting attorneys and consumer agencies, I'm asking you for help. I want the new car that I paid for, not the lemon that's now sitting in the dealer's service bay.

Call me at my office at (312) 555-9339, or in the evening at (708) 555-1473. I'd like to reach an understanding by next week. I can't be without a car much longer.

With great anticipation,

- Regional offices are usually more responsive than local dealers. Turn to them whenever a serious issue arises.

- Explain what future actions will be taken if there is no satisfaction. It helps the negotiation.

My New Siding Is Falling Off (15-35)

Dear Mr. Denkenberg:

A red flag should have gone up when HomePride Construction gave me a price for siding that was 50% lower than its closest competitor. However, the combination of a tempting price and a persuasive salesperson sold me on the deal.

The workmanship was beyond shoddy. After the first rain, a number of panels fell off and many others shifted, exposing insulation underneath. Armed with my 25-year guarantee, I've called HomePride several times a week for two months, but no one will agree to make the repairs.

If you come out to my home, you'll see for yourself how HomePride has turned the exterior into a nightmare. I'll also show you their 25-year guarantee and their pie-in-the-sky literature.

I think you'll find this is a great visual story that will help many homeowners avoid a similar fate...and it should also have great ratings appeal, because every homeowner can relate to it. I'm usually home during the day, and you can reach me at (617) 555-5229. May I hear from you?

Sincerely,

- You need to offer visual images such as fallen siding, exposed weatherproofing and written guarantee when attempting to get television coverage.

- Remember: ratings determine coverage. Indicate why you think your problem will draw viewers.

I've Been Asking for a Refund for 6 Months (15-36)

Dear Mr. George:

Unless you'd like to have a conversation with the State Attorney General, I had better find a check for $1,015 in my mailbox by June 10. That will be exactly six months to the day that you picked up your defective sofa.

To be sure you have the whole story, here's a recap:

o   I purchased a sofa from Bilt-Rite on October 15, and gave a $300 deposit.

o   The sofa was delivered on November 28, and I paid the balance of $715.

o   On November 29, I called my salesperson when I realized that the fabric on the pillows and frame was from different dye lots.

o   The salesperson (Lois Waters) assured me that the sofa would be fixed within 30 days. Eleven days later it was picked up, and ever since I've received nothing but lies and evasions.

You've created an empty spot in my living room, a hole in my wallet, and a knot in my stomach. Now I'd like to return the favor. If I don't have my refund by June 10, I'll do what I should have done months ago, and report you to the State Attorney General.

Sincerely,

- Explain your position right up front.
- Summarize key dates and actions.

Encyclopedia Salesperson Was Unethical (15-37)

Dear Ms. Monte:

We were badgered and insulted by a regional representative of the Child Achievement Encyclopedia Company here in Tustin. We're contemplating legal action, but we also want your agency to warn other unsuspecting potential customers.

We inquired about the Child Achievement Encyclopedia and agreed (reluctantly) to have a salesperson visit our home. The sales call was a nightmare.

We couldn't get the representative, who called himself "Mr. Smith," to leave. We kept insisting we needed time to think about such an expensive purchase ($1,200). He actually had the gall to say that we seemed unconcerned about the future of our child.

After two hours of browbeating, my husband said we didn't want the encyclopedia. That's when Mr. Smith demanded that we give him $50 for his time. When I picked up the phone to call the police, he gathered his materials and left.

This company needs to be put out of business. Please tell us what steps you plan to take.

Sincerely,

- Don't be coy. Situations like these call for strong language when writing to organizations like the Better Business Bureau.
- Detail your specific objections and expectations.

Cancellation of Door-to-Door Purchase (15-38)

Dear Ms. Todd:

Re: Cancellation of contract

We've decided to take advantage of the "cooling-off period" provided by federal law, and we're canceling the purchase we made last evening of a Stay-Right adjustable bed.

In accordance with the rights guaranteed by the Federal Trade Commission, we expect to have our deposit refunded within 10 days, and the agreement for extended credit terms destroyed.

We'd appreciate your prompt attention to this request.

Sincerely,

- The Federal Trade Commission provides consumer protection through a 3-day cooling off period, during which a door-to-door sale may be cancelled.
- By specifically citing the sponsoring government agency and repayment terms, you demonstrate awareness of your rights and your willingness to fight for them.

Take My Name Off Your Mailing List (15-39)

To Whom It May Concern:

Please have my name and address deleted from all mailing lists. I do not wish to receive unsolicited mail.

Thank you for your attention.

Sincerely,

- Contact the Direct Marketing Association (attention: Mail Reference Service, PO Box 9008, Farmingdale, NY 11735) if you wish to have your name removed from all mailing lists.
- If you wish to remove your name from just one mailing list, write to the individual mailer.

Congratulations 16

A congratulatory note can add so much to an occasion worth celebrating. It gives the reader the "fifteen minutes of fame" that everyone is entitled to at least once in a lifetime.

Sending a congratulatory letter presents the writer as a magnanimous, aware individual. These qualities will serve you well in both your personal and professional life.

Remember that your letter should be about the *recipient*—not about you. Stifle the impulse to talk about yourself, and direct the spotlight where it belongs-on the reader.

Congratulations on event. Events such as birthdays, anniversaries, births, and the purchase of a new home warrant congratulations. Your congratulatory letter should be upbeat, warm, and as intimate as the relationship itself. Take this opportunity to say all the nice things that you've been storing up over the years.

Congratulations on achievement. After working hard to achieve a goal or to overcome an obstacle, everyone appreciates a pat on the back. Use a congratulatory letter to tell the reader that they deserve the good things that have come their way. Be specific in praising them for their accomplishments, and express your conviction that today's brimming cup of cheer will spill over into the future.

Saying it with a poem. If you have a whimsical mindset, putting your congratulations in the form of a poem can be as entertaining to write as it is to read. It doesn't require a talent for perfect rhyme and meter—the recipient will probably give you an 'A' just for effort, rather than judging your composition on artistic merit.

Congratulations on Birth, to Friend (16-01)

Dear Winnie and John,

We were all delighted to hear of the arrival of John, Jr., on May 1. We're looking forward to seeing pictures and perhaps the baby himself at the annual Fourth of July picnic.

Best,

- Like all personal notes, this should be handwritten. Use personal stationery with your company's letterhead if writing in an official capacity. Otherwise, use personal stationery or send a conservative card. Use your discretion about sending a gift.
- You don't need to be effusive. Simply acknowledge the birth and the parents' joy.

Congratulations on Birth, to Business Associate (16-02)

Dear Mandy and Howard,

What a relief! All of us at the office had been watching the calendar every day, awaiting word that your bundle of joy had finally arrived. He's already got a built-in fan club!

I understand that he has your bright blue eyes, Mandy, and your curly dark hair, Howard, and that he's beautiful. With your genetic combination, how could he be otherwise?

I am <u>thrilled</u> for all three of you, and especially glad that Howard survived labor and delivery without anesthesia!

Congratulations! I can't wait to get a firsthand look at the little one.

Love,

- This is a momentous, upbeat occasion. Let your words reflect that you share the joy.
- New parents feel that their baby is the most special person in the world. Your message should affirm that.

Congratulations on Adoption, to Friend (16-03)

Dear Wendy and Ira,

We're so happy for you! There's nothing quite like the joy of sharing your lives with a child. And we can't think of two people who will make better parents.

As delighted as we are for you, we're even more delighted for baby Michelle. She's lucky to have two wonderful, loving people like you to raise her.

Congratulations and good health. Send photos!

All our love,

- Treat the adoption of a baby as you would any new arrival. A baby is a baby.
- It's a confidence-builder to tell parents that you feel the baby is lucky to have them.

Congratulations on Adoption, to Business Associate (16-04)

Dear Sarah and Jake,

We were delighted to hear about the new addition to your family. It must thrill Lindy to have a new sister. We're looking forward to seeing all of you at the company Holiday party so we can greet Carol Cynthia Hudson in person.

All the best,

- Another obvious opportunity for a handwritten note, in which case you would not need the inside address.
- "The new addition to your family" is a much better phrase than "adoption," since the manner in which the child arrived is not important.

Congratulations on Your Engagement (16-05)

Dear Rebecca,

I think you and George belong on my roster of great couples:

> Antony and Cleopatra
> Lunt and Fontanne
> Wilma and Fred
> Rebecca and George

It may sound corny, but I've always thought you belonged together. That's why I'm delighted that you're engaged. Best wishes for a blissful marriage.

Fondly,

- Acknowledge that this is a special occasion and that the engaged pair is a special couple.
- Traditionally, "best wishes" are offered to the woman; "congratulations" are offered to the man.

Congratulations on Your Marriage, to Friend (16-06)

Dear Ava and Victor,

The news of your marriage has made me so happy and so smug. You've confirmed what I realized as soon as you met—that you belonged together.

I knew you'd make a great couple. You complement each other perfectly!

I wish you a lifetime of love and joy.

Your wise friend,

- Include something that makes your wishes unique, instead of the cliched "I hope you'll be very happy together."
- Let the tone of the message convey warmth.

Congratulations on Your Marriage, to Business Associate (16-07)

Dear George,

Mary and I wanted to send our very best wishes to you and Lonnie on the occasion of your wedding.

I understand you're honeymooning in Cancun and will return on the 20th. I hope we can all get together for dinner when you get settled.

Best,

- If you don't know both spouses, address the one you do know and mention the other one in the body of the handwritten letter. If you refer to your spouse, you should use a personal letterhead.
- It's pleasant, but optional, to suggest a dinner after the newlyweds get settled. If you send a gift, you can write a brief note on the card and skip the letter.

Congratulations on Your Anniversary (16-08)

Dear Madelyn and Dave,

When you two met and married as young kids, you probably gave no thought to becoming a statistic. Yet here you are, defying the odds by staying happily married for 35 years. You have the envy and the admiration of all your friends.

As wonderful as you are as individuals, you're even more remarkable as a couple. We wish you many more years of marital harmony and the blessing of good health so you can enjoy them.

All our love,

- Recognize that having a long-lasting and successful marriage is an accomplishment.
- Offer the couple your best wishes for the continuation of their happiness.

Congratulations on Your Bar Mitzvah (16-09)

Dear Michael,

After watching your bar mitzvah ceremony, it became clear why it's considered a rite of passage into manhood. You were so sure of yourself and so confident of your reading from the scriptures. You related so well to the congregation that no one could ever think of you as a child again. It's obvious how much preparation you put into your bar mitzvah, and that's the mark of a mature, determined person.

I've always known you had great talent and intelligence, and now I know you have the discipline to apply those gifts. I'm so pleased to see that you have what it takes to be successful in whatever you do.

I'm proud of you, Michael. Congratulations.

With love,

- A follow-up letter after the event has dramatic impact.
- Be specific in your praise, rather than just saying, "You did a wonderful job."

Congratulations on Your Retirement (16-10)

Dear Norm,

Face it. The time has come when you're going to have to confront some really difficult decisions:

> Whether to wake up early or sleep in.
> Whether to go sailing or hiking.
> Whether to paint a picture or a room.
> Whether to watch a movie or a sunset.

You've got some tough choices ahead, Norm. I hope you thoroughly enjoy every one of them.

Congratulations on your retirement.

Sincerely,

- Convey a sense of unlimited options to the reader.
- A little humor gets the message across.

Congratulations on Your New Home (16-11)

Dear Serena and Keith,

Buying a new home is a combination of joy and jitters. Don't let the former be over-shadowed by the latter.

May your housewarming be the first of many celebrations at 6 Carriage Way.

Congratulations and best wishes,

- Acknowledge the significance of the event.
- Express a positive outlook for the future.

Congratulations on Graduating High School (16-12)

Dear Julie,

We wish we had the organizational skills that you possess. Not only did you graduate with honors, you were also the school's sports and yearbook photographer. And you worked after school and on weekends! How did you do it?

We've been lucky to have someone like you as a neighbor. It's been a treat to watch you grow and mature into a wonderful young woman. It's so obvious to us that you have a bright future ahead of you.

Congratulations on your graduation. We're very, very proud of you.

Fondly,

- Comment on the positive characteristics of the graduate.
- Indicate that the future will be rewarding.

Congratulations on Your Child's Honor (16-13)

Dear Marie,

I was delighted to read that Josephine had been cited as a National Merit Semifinalist. It must make you very proud.

The paper also mentioned that Josephine would be going to my old college in the fall. If she would like some (relatively dated) information on what it's like, please have her call me. Since I'm active in the alumnae association, I may also be able to put her in touch with more recent graduates.

Again, my congratulations.

Best wishes,

Congratulations on College Acceptance (16-14)

Dear Kirby,

Your hard work paid off—congratulations! Waiting for college acceptance letters can be agonizing, but when they arrive—what a high!

You probably feel lucky that Wesleyan chose you. I see it from a different perspective: Wesleyan is lucky to have you.

Enjoy your college career.

Sincerely,

- Recognize the accomplishment.
- Acknowledge that the reader earned it.

Congratulations on Graduating College (16-15)

Dear Serena,

Like many of life's milestones, graduation is a paradox: It signifies a beginning and an end.

As you look back on your past and anticipate your future, I offer enthusiastic congratulations. You've achieved a history of academic excellence and you've established yourself as a person who's willing to take risks.

I'm confident that your diligence and determination will bring you great success and satisfaction.

Regards,

- Be specific, if you can, about special accomplishments, such as academic excellence.
- Express optimism for the graduate's future.

Congratulations on Medical Degree (16-16)

Dear Chuck,

I have always thought of doctors as being 50ish, dignified, and very wise. But now you come along and get a medical degree. I guess I'm going to have to rethink my image of physicians.

Seriously, Chuck, I'm really proud of you. And here's the ultimate compliment: I'll become one of your patients as soon as you open your practice. I can't think of anyone I'd trust more with my health.

I wish you much success, Dr. Cooper. Congratulations!

Affectionately,

- Generally, good natured humor is appropriate and appreciated among friends.
- Be sure to balance the humor with sincere praise.

Congratulations on Your New Job (16-17)

Dear Dan:

Whoever said, "Change is the only thing that offers new opportunity," must have been thinking of you. And so am I.

I'm excited and happy for you. And I think your new employer will be, too, when that fertile mind of yours starts to plow some new profits for them.

I know you have some reservations about changing careers at this stage, but I'm sure you'll come to feel at home in the insurance industry in no time at all. Congratulations and success.

Cordially,

- Starting with a quote adds a fresh element to any letter.
- Make it clear that you feel the new employer has made a wise decision.

Congratulations on Your Promotion (16-18)

Dear Sean:

I can't begin to tell you how happy I am for you. You worked for your new position, you waited for it, and when the opportunity presented itself you were ready for it.

When you have a moment or two to sit back and relax, I hope you'll have a sip of the enclosed and toast your continuing success. Congratulations and good luck.

Cordially,

- Let the individual know you realize how much this means to them.
- Enclosing something that signifies a celebration (for example, champagne or flowers) is a nice touch that will be remembered.

Congratulations on Your New Appearance (16-19)

Dear Mandy,

Even though there are 50 pounds less of you to love, you're still my favorite niece! You look sensational, but more importantly, you've added years to your life.

You've given me the incentive to lose some weight. Following your sensible diet, I'm going to try to muster some will power to start eating healthier foods myself.

I'm proud of you.

With love,

- People whose appearance has changed for the better are always pleased when the improvement is noticed.
- Let the person know that it's not just their appearance that's important to you.

Congratulations on Your Successful Surgery (16-20)

Dear Warren,

That loud sound you might have heard the other evening was a huge sigh of relief.

What great news! When Anita called to let me know that your surgery had been successful, it seemed as if a dark cloud that had been following me around had suddenly vanished.

Do us all a favor, will you? Do what the doctor says and take care of yourself. I'm looking forward to many more years of friendship with you.

I'll see you as soon as you're ready for visitors.

Fondly,

- When someone is recovering from major surgery, it's comforting to know that people really care. Take the time to write; it will be greatly appreciated.
- Don't get into medical war stories. Stay upbeat.

Congratulations on Starting Your Own Business (16-21)

Dear Juliet,

Congratulations on the grand opening of "Jewels by Juliet."

Your designs have been the rage of the neighborhood for years. It's about time your jewelry was available to a larger audience.

Your drive and creativity guarantee success. And your friends will help on the marketing side: We're already boasting that we've been wearing "Jewels by Juliet" for years!

Best of Luck!

Fondly,

> • Express an optimistic attitude regarding the reader's potential for success.
>
> • Back it up with specific positive references to the person's skills.

Congratulations on Winning Election (16-22)

Dear Zack,

Every time I was a little lazy—with schoolwork, sports, household chores—my mother would wag her finger at me and say, "If you want to eat the nut, you have to crack the shell."

That bit of wisdom sums up the sensational campaign you ran to become City Council President. Sometimes it seemed as if you were in three sections of the city at the same time. You outworked (and out-thought) your opponent, Zack.

You may be knee-deep in shells, but now you have the entire municipal streets department to clean up behind you! Congratulations on a much-deserved, hard-fought election. I'm proud to be your friend.

Sincerely,

> • No one wins an election without a lot of work. Let the reader know that the effort didn't go unnoticed.
>
> • Quoting someone can often make your point more emphatically. Acquire a book or two of great quotations, and have thousands at your disposal. And you can supplement those with sayings that have been part of your own history.

Congratulations on Your Award (16-23)

Dear Martha,

I love to hear your speeches and have often told you so. But you're so quick to pass off compliments as just flattery.

However, your recent award as Communicator of the Year is tangible proof of your ability as an orator. The Fairfield County Association of Public Speakers is a prestigious organization. And knowing how tough the competition was should add to your pride and satisfaction.

I congratulate you on this outstanding achievement.

With admiration,

- Acknowledge the person's talents.
- Point to the prestige of the award or quality of the competition that was faced.

Congratulations (General), Poem (16-24)

Dear Harley,

Hear! Hear! Congrats and Whoopdedo!
Salud! Hip Hip Hooray!
All hail! Best Wishes! Bully, too!
Yeah, man! Hot dog! Ole!
You really are a clever chap!
Three cheers! Thumbs up! Oh boy!
You hit the mark; you sank the putt.
You earned it, now enjoy!

Love,

- Be as enthusiastic as you care to be for a congratulatory poem. Whatever the occasion, it's a happy one.

Congratulations on Your Engagement, Poem (16-25)

Dear Gloria and Gary,

After years of resisting the urge,
I hear that you're right on the verge
Of a ring and a kiss
And marital bliss.
What great news—you've decided to merge!

Love,

- Your message should convey that you're 100% in favor of the step the reader is taking.

Congratulations on Your Marriage, Poem (16-26)

Dear Cheryl and Chuck,

In charting a course that's harmonious,
Avoid using words acrimonious.
Let giving and taking
And frequent lovemaking
Be guides for your ship "Matrimonious."
Congratulations on your marriage!

Love,

- You can use some "poetic license" in your wording (for example, "Matrimonius") to add warmth and humor to your message.

Congratulations on Your New Baby, Poem (16-27)

Dear Sarah and Marshall,

Who's sent to you from heaven?
Who's dressed in blue—not pink?
Who's held so tight?
Who cries all night?
Who oftentimes can stink?

Who's Sarah's little treasure?
Who's Marshalls's pride and joy?
Who's love and bliss
And a sloppy kiss?
Your bouncing baby boy!

Congratulations from
All your pals at work

- Parents are usually so delighted with their new arrival that it's hard to overdo a "new baby" congratulatory message.

Congratulations on Your Graduation, Poem (16-28)

Dear Jamie,

We knew that you could do it,
With awards you would come through it,
Making parents, friends and relatives so proud.
The diploma's in your hand,
Life's ahead, it should be grand,
For a girl who stands so far above the crowd!

Love,

- Recognize the achievement and be positive about the future.

Congratulations on Your New Home, Poem (16-29)

Dear Amy and John,

A mortgage
A mailbox
A lawn
And a mower;
A washer
A dryer
A dog
A leaf blower.

Then a basement
That's wet
And a crack
In a beam.
Get set
To enjoy
The American Dream!

All kidding aside, homeownership is wonderful. Welcome to the ranks!

Love,

- A little irony is okay, as long as it's presented with a sense of humor.

Congratulations on Your New Job, Poem (16-30)

Dear Christina,

You're newly relocated,
And much remunerated.
Upon the fastest track you have no peer.
I know you'll be successful,
Though the challenge will be stressful.
Kudos on your illustrious career!

Good Luck on Your New Job!

Sincerely,

- Everyone's nervous and excited about starting a new job. Build confidence when you congratulate the reader.

Congratulations on Your Promotion, Poem (16-31)

Dear Steven,

The boss says that you're number one;
A whiz who can get the job done.
All those hours of devotion
Have earned you a promotion.
Your climb to the top has begun!

Congratulations!

Warmly,

- Show that the boss is not the only one who recognizes the reader's accomplishments.

Correspondence to Family and Friends 17

When it comes to communicating by letter with family and friends, *you're* the best judge of what to say and how to say it. Each relationship is unique, so heed your internal barometer when deciding which topics are appropriate, how much information you want to share, and the degree of intimacy that's comfortable for you and for the reader.

Letters to your parents. Sometimes it's easier to communicate by letter than it is face to face. This is especially true with sensitive issues. Perhaps you've totalled the car. Writing a letter gives you the opportunity to compose your thoughts and deliver your news without fear of interruption (You what??!!), or verbal assault (How could you be so stupid??!!). A letter also gives the reader the extra time required to react to disappointing news and cool down before the next communication with you. Communicating bad news by letter isn't the coward's way out—it's simply a wise approach when emotions could be volatile.

If your letter contains negative news, a few sentences at the beginning of the letter should prepare the reader for what's to follow. Next, relate the information as clearly as possible, taking responsibility for your actions if you've caused the problem. Then state your intention to rectify the situation, and describe a plan and time frame in which you intend to carry it out.

If you're delivering news that you're happy about (Guess what? I eloped with a rodeo clown last weekend!), but believe will meet with the reader's disapproval, state your conviction that the decision has been well thought out and is the right one for *you*.

Good news. The good news letter is fun to write. It gives the author a chance to take a bow, take some credit, and accentuate the positive. Convey the information, share your feelings about it, and describe how you think it will affect your future. If possible, try to make the reader feel a sense of reflected glory.

Bad news. There's really no juxtaposition of words that can make bad news sound good. The first few sentences of your letter should gently alert the reader to unhappy tidings. Deliver the news candidly, but avoid unnecessary embellishments. If the reader can help in some way, describe how. Try to end the letter on a philosophical note.

Reminders. The reminder letter should be polite, but firm. State your position, your justification, and your expectation. In some cases, it's also necessary to describe the steps you'll take if the reminder doesn't produce results.

Holiday correspondence. Holidays provide the opportunity to put positive feelings about our lives and our relationship in writing so that those who care about us can share in them. Make the message positive, uplifting and optimistic. Holiday letters should spread warmth and cheer. Any bad news should be saved for a separate letter.

Dear Mom and Dad, My Grades Were Awful (17-01)

Dear Mom and Dad,

I wish I could rewind my life like a videotape. Then I could start the last semester over and study harder, receive better grades, and not have to write this letter.

Unfortunately, I have to face reality, and that means admitting that my grades were awful. I'm angry with myself for not doing better. I guess I put my social life and campus activities ahead of hitting the books.

I'm making a renewed commitment to apply myself next semester. I know I have the potential to earn good grades, and seeing how awful it feels to do poorly, I won't shortchange myself again.

Love,

- Don't make excuses. Take responsibility for your bad grades.
- State your commitment to improve.

Dear Mom and Dad, I Want to Move Back Home (17-02)

Dear Mom and Dad,

I was pretty cocky when I left home. I remember saying that I couldn't wait to be on my own.

Now I know that the reality of independence isn't as picture-perfect as the fantasy. The truth is, I'm not happy here, and I need a little time to think about my future. It would be great to be able to do that thinking in familiar surroundings.

That's why I want to come home. I need your support while I sort things out. I'm willing to get a job, and I'll certainly help around the house. I'll even cook. Just tell me its OK to move back home for a while.

Your loving daughter,

- Explain why you want to move back home.
- State your intention to contribute to the household in some way.

Dear Mom and Dad, I'm Living with Someone (17-03)

Dear Mom and Dad,

I've taken a major step in my personal life, and I want to share it with you.

For about three months, I've been dating a man I met at school. His name is Jonathan Merbrook, and he comes from Atlanta. He's a psychology major, too, so we have a lot in common.

Our relationship has become serious and, after much discussion, we've decided to live together. We both believe that it's the right thing to do, and we're looking forward to spending more time together.

l hope you'll support me in my decision.

Love,

- Give some pertinent information about the live-in.

- Indicate that the decision wasn't made impetuously.

Dear Mom and Dad, I Got Married (17-04)

Name

Dear Mom and Dad,

You taught me by example that a good marriage is life's greatest reward. That's why I promised myself that when I met the right person I would make the same commitment you two made.

Well, I met her and I kept my promise. Her name is Laura Patten, and we were married at City Hall on January 15.

Here's what you should know about her: she's 27, she's a graphic artist, she grew up in Chicago, she plays the clarinet and she's got a wonderful sense of humor.

We're so much in love, we just couldn't wait to get married, but I want you to meet Laura just as soon as we can get a few days off to travel home.

Laura and I are living at my place until we find a bigger apartment.

Mom and Dad, you were right—marriage is life's greatest reward!

Love,

- Let the readers feel that they contributed to your positive attitude toward marriage.

- Reassure them that you're confident you made the right decision.

Dear Mom and Dad, I'm Pregnant (17-05)

Dear Mom and Dad,

I've just gotten some very disturbing news, and I need your support.

I'm pregnant. I didn't plan it, and I don't know what to do about it. The baby's father isn't willing to make a commitment to me or his future child.

Whatever I decide to do will have enormous implications for my future, so I want to consider all my options. I'd really appreciate some advice.

No lectures, please. Just let me know what you think. I can't promise to do what you suggest, but I certainly promise to listen.

Love,

> - Acknowledge the significance of the circumstances.
> - Ask for support.

Dear Mom and Dad, Please Send Money (17-06)

Dear Mom and Dad,

I'm conscientious about money and, generally, I manage it well. But this past month I've encountered unforeseen expenses, and my bank account is depleted.

I need $200 to cover my outstanding debts. I would have preferred dealing with this problem myself, but I don't have the resources.

Could you please send me the money? I'll repay you as soon as I can.

Thanks.

Gratefully,

> - Reassure the reader that your financial situation is the result of unusual circumstances, not reckless spending.
> - Be straightforward about how much money you need.

Dear Mom and Dad, I'm Gay (17-07)

Dear Mom and Dad,

Every time you asked if I had a girlfriend yet; every time you questioned why this cousin or that friend was getting married and I wasn't; every time you asked aloud if I'd ever give you grandchildren...every single time, I wondered if you knew.

I think it's time I ended the speculation: Yes, I'm gay. I assume that this declaration simply confirms suspicions you've had for many years. And I also assume that our relationship won't change in any way.

I want your continued love and support.

All my love,

> - Suggest that your parents may have suspected the truth.
> - Make it clear that, as far as you're concerned, nothing about your relationship with your parents should change.

Dear Mom and Dad, I'm Engaged (17-08)

Dear Dawn,

I never believed in the phrase "happily ever after." It seemed so corny and naive. I certainly didn't think it would ever apply to me.

That was before I became engaged! Now I'm convinced of my everlasting happiness with the most wonderful man.

His name is Stuart Renshaw. He's an architect. He's smart, funny and sexy. We met about a year ago through mutual friends and have been together ever since.

We're planning a <u>huge</u> May wedding. Expect an invitation!

Love,

- Share some pertinent information about your fiance or fiancee.
- Give some indication of the kind of wedding you're planning, such as, "We're planning a <u>huge</u> wedding," "We're planning to elope to Tahiti," etc.

I Got Married (17-09)

Dear Brenda,

You know I've been dreaming about my wedding day for years, and I finally got to hear those wedding bells ring.

Seth and I made a decision to elope on Valentine's Day. We flew to Las Vegas and got married in one of those little chapels you always hear about. It was so tacky and romantic—the perfect setting for our offbeat relationship.

All our belongings are piled in boxes in our new townhouse on Lakeshore Drive. We're still in shock at the idea of actually co-habiting <u>legally</u>.

The truth is, I'm happy. Seth's happy. And I hope my lifelong friend will be happy for us.

Love,

- Share some details of when and how the wedding took place.
- Transmit the joy that you're feeling.

I Got a New Job (17-10)

Dear Ian,

My perseverance has paid off. On September 16 I became managing editor of children's books for Holiday Publishing!

I'm now a full-fledged New Yorker with a studio apartment in Manhattan. It's a short walk to work (or a cab ride in the rain). After months of financial uncertainty, I'm indulging myself. I've even enrolled in a health club.

I'm amazed at how my situation has reversed itself. The job search was a learning experience that proved the value of determination and staying power. It also proved the value of supportive friends like you. Thanks.

Fondly,

P.S. My new home phone number is (212) 555-2872

- Give some details, rather than just the bare bones, of your new situation.
- If the reader was helpful or supportive during your job search, express your appreciation.

I'm Retiring (17-11)

Dear Margaret,

I'm approaching the end of this month with a mixture of anticipation and disbelief. Can it be forty-two years since I taught my first sixth grade class? The calendar says yes, which is why I'm about to become a retired schoolteacher.

I plan to take full advantage of my year-round independence. I'm already researching a winetasting tour of France for September. Would you be interested in joining me?

And while I watch my garden grow this summer, I'm going to try my hand at writing a few short stories that have been simmering on my brain's back burner for years.

I'm looking forward to this new passage. As long as my health remains good, I feel ready to tackle anything.

The school is throwing a retirement party for me on June 23. The sixth graders are even composing an original song! I've been given "carte blanche" to invite friends and relatives, so I hope you'll come—I may need some "bucking up."

Give me a call and let me know if you can make it.

Kindest regards,

- Tell the reader how it feels to be approaching retirement.
- Share your plans and aspirations. If you're looking for companionship, say so.

Our Son Led His Team to Victory (17-12)

Dear Uncle Bart,

Wasn't it you who always proposed a round of touch football at holiday picnics? Those family free-for-alls were Todd's first introduction to competitive sports.

Since you taught your nephew how to throw a pass, you deserve some of the glory.

Last weekend, Todd made the winning touchdown for his team in the district play-offs. The Conestoga Pioneers won 14-13, and Todd's jubilant teammates carried him off the field on their shoulders. Now he's a school hero!

Todd's proud, we're proud, and you should be proud, too.

Love,

- State why you think the reader will be interested in the news.
- Relate some details about the event.

We're Expecting a Baby (17-13)

Dear Danielle,

A miracle has happened. At least that's how I feel.

I'm pregnant! While that announcement may be routine to some people, to Jim and me it's mind-boggling. We're still marveling over it. You know how long we've be trying, and what a difficult time I had conceiving.

The baby is due in October. So far, everything is proceeding according to the pregnancy textbooks, but I'm having amniocentesis next week to be absolutely certain that all is well.

This is all so new and thrilling. We'll keep you posted.

Love,

- People love to receive good news. Share your happiness with the reader.
- Tell when the baby is due, and promise to give updates on your progress.

We've Moved (17-14)

Dear Elsa,

We're celebrating our independence. We no longer have to:

1) Mow an acre of grass every week.
2) Mulch and plant several garden beds each Spring.
3) Weed those gardens when the mulch isn't thick enough.
4) Shovel snow.
5) Rake leaves.
6) Do all our own home repairs.

We've chucked homeownership for the carefree life of lakeside condo ownership. After one month, we've concluded that it was the best decision we've ever made. Relaxation has become a way of life.

We'd love to see you and show you our new quarters. Why not plan to take a drive to Marshall Lake for a visit. Please call us at (404) 555-1058. We'll roll out the red carpet (we have plenty of spare energy now).

Best regards,

- Tell the reader what factors affected your decision to move.
- Express how happy you'd be to see an old friend.

Dad Has to Have an Operation (17-15)

Dear Allan,

Dad has been so active since retiring that I often forget how old he actually is. Recently, however, he's been experiencing shortness of breath. His doctor put him in the hospital for a cardiac catheterization and the results were not good.

His arteries are blocked and he's at risk for a heart attack. Two consulting cardiologists agree that Dad needs a bypass without delay. The surgery will be performed on Friday, April 26 at University Hospital.

Dad's a brave guy, but he's shaken by the prospect of this surgery. There is risk involved, but the doctors seem optimistic. They say that Dad could be back on the golf course in eight weeks.

The operation starts at 8:00 a.m., and could last up to eight hours. Unless you decide to come, I'll phone you as soon as I have news.

Love,

- Give a reasonably detailed account of the situation so the person doesn't feel uninformed and left out.
- Stress the positive.

Grandpa Died Peacefully (17-16)

Name

Dear Tom,

I have some sad news to share with you. Grandpa died peacefully yesterday afternoon at about three o'clock. He was sitting in his chair, watching the ocean, when he closed his eyes and slipped away.

He was loved by so many people during his cantankerous eighty-seven years—not the least of whom were his grandchildren. We'll miss playing Trivial Pursuit and Scrabble with him. Even though he'd pound his fist when we beat him, he always loved the challenge.

He had asked to be cremated and to have his ashes scattered over the ocean. I hope you can be there in the spring when the family carries out his wishes.

I'll send more details when they're available.

All my love,

- When the reader is far away, they need to feel "connected" to the family during a time of loss. Let your words reflect this.
- Let the reader know about plans for a tribute or memorial.

A Relative Has Died (17-17)

Dear Stan,

We both know that Dad never seemed close to Aunt Betty. He only saw or spoke to her once or twice a year, and Mom always had to push him to do even that much.

Well, we just received word that Aunt Betty died last night, and amazingly, Dad seems devastated. (That's not an overstatement.) Mom and I think he feels guilty that he didn't stay in closer touch with her.

Anyway, I thought you should know. Dad would probably appreciate hearing from you. In fact, I'd like to hear from you, too. It's been too long.

Hope all is well.

Love,

- Explaining a situation in honest terms gives the reader the information they need to respond appropriately.
- If you're writing to someone who might not know what is expected of them, suggest a call or letter to comfort the bereaved.

Our Mutual Friend Is Very Sick (17-18)

Dear Tony,

I just had a call from Paul Irwin's dad. He wanted us to know that Paul had a serious heart attack. He's going to survive, but his heart is damaged. In fact, Mr. Irwin said that Paul will require extensive surgery.

It will be at least another week or two until Paul can see anyone, so don't even think about flying in for a while. I'll let you know how things are going. In the meantime, you can send cards or letters to:

Cardiac Unit
City Hospital West
1900 W. Poplar Street
Omaha, NE 68102

I've had no luck trying to reach you by phone, so unless I hear from you, I'll send you written updates as more information becomes available. Incidentally, it might be a nice touch to call Mr. Irwin (402-555-6936). He's lonely and scared.

Let me hear from you.

Best,

- Offer a mailing address for the sick person.

- If you're the person on the spot, you can be of great service by telling others what to send or do.

Our Mutual Friend Has AIDS (17-19)

Dear Darryl,

I've always tried to avoid television reports and articles about AIDS. The disease seemed so remote from my world, and I was naive enough to believe that it would never affect me, or anyone close to me.

Now I'm facing the reality that AIDS touches everyone. You probably know that Barry has, for months, been missing a lot of work because of a recurring "flu." Well, last night, he confided to me that he has AIDS. He asked me to share the information with you, but no one else.

I feel certain that he'd appreciate a call or a note from you. Come to think of it, so would I. We need to talk about what we can do to help Barry through the difficult times that lie ahead.

Best always,

- There's no way to sugar coat information like this. Don't even try. Just talk about how the situation might best be handled.

- If the information is confidential, be sure to state so clearly.

Our Mutual Friend Has Died (17-20)

Dear Flora,

Even with my absolute faith in the Almighty, this is a day that has severely tested my resolve. Our dear friend, Lorraine, suffered a cerebral hemorrhage early this morning, and died within hours. It was all totally unexpected.

I've spent the last few hours with Ed, helping him with some of the arrangements. He knows how close we all were with Lorraine but, at this point, he's insistent that the services and burial be strictly for the family. If he changes his mind (a possibility, given his current state), I'll call you.

Lorraine was so full of life. It's impossible to believe she's gone. I wish you lived closer; I'd feel so much better if you were here with me.

All my love,

- Although the news will be shocking wherever you insert it, give the reader a sentence or two to prepare for it.
- Give a brief summary of the circumstances. Details can be dealt with when you talk.

Our Relative Was in an Accident (17-21)

Dear Sidney,

As I write this letter, it occurs to me what a poor correspondent I've been. I'm embarrassed that I feel compelled to write only when there's bad news.

Aunt Kate was in an automobile accident last week and broke her hip. She'll be in the hospital for a few more days, then she'll be transferred to a rehabilitation center. The recuperation could take several months.

Her spirit needs a boost, and it would be helpful if you wrote or phoned her.

The address is:

> Memorial Rehabilitation Center
> Room 301
> Paoli, PA 19301
> Telephone: (215) 555-4989

Thanks, Sidney.

Love from your cousin,

- Tell the circumstances of the accident and the extent of the injuries.
- State what the reader can do to help.

My Dad Died (17-22)

Dear Alex,

I've always lived my life without much concern for the future, but at this moment I feel my own mortality.

My Dad passed away last week. Although, as you know, he'd been ill for months, losing him was a shock. I used to visit him every day, and I already miss our talks.

Our family has requested that any contributions in his name be made to the Boy Scouts of America. That's because, in so many ways, Dad was the quintessential scout. The years he spent as a boy scout were the happiest of his life. And he was the most beloved scout leader imaginable. Throughout his life, he embodied the bravery and loyalty that is the real meaning of scouting.

I hope that to some extent, at least, I'll find a way to follow in his footsteps.

With a heavy heart,

- There's no need to hide your feelings in a letter of this nature.
- Let the reader know your preference for commemorating the deceased.

I Had a Miscarriage (17-23)

Dear Ellen,

I'm a strong person, but right now I feel my strength is being tested. That's why I need support from you.

Ellen, I lost the baby. Even though my obstetrician says that miscarriages are common with first pregnancies, I have such a feeling of emptiness...and even failure. We wanted this baby so much!

Rather than getting a phone call, I'd appreciate one of your long, newsy letters. When I feel up to talking about this, I'll call you.

Thanks.

Love,

- This is a time when you need support. Don't be afraid to ask for it.
- Don't expect the recipient to be a mind reader. Tell them exactly how to help you (notify others, stay in touch with you by letter, etc.).

My Husband Was Laid Off (17-24)

Dear Mom and Dad,

Every article I read says that the recession touches everyone. Now I believe it. Last Friday Jack was laid off. We had heard rumbles about the plant cutting back, but hoped Jack's outstanding job performance record would protect him. It didn't.

On the bright side, he has a few leads on job possibilities, and we can manage on my income for a while. I know he won't be out of work for long, so I'd better not get used to his being home.

Please don't worry about us. We're going to be just fine.

My love to both of you,

- For the sake of everyone's pride, make it clear that the lay-off was the result of circumstances, not performance.
- Keep the letter upbeat and reassuring, especially if there's nothing the reader can do about the situation.

Our Business Failed (17-25)

Dear Mom and Dad,

As Maureen and I struggled to make a go of our recycling business, I listened to every motivational tape I could get my hands on. The more we fell behind in payments and payroll, the more I listened.

It took me a while, but I finally realized that it takes a lot more than motivation and enthusiasm to run a business. In retrospect, we weren't prepared emotionally, technically or financially to even start this business. I was too naive to know what I didn't know.

We're okay. Don't worry. Maureen already has a good job lined up, and as we're shutting down the business, I've been interviewing for an engineering job. But we both agree that as soon as everything settles down (in other words, when our finances are stabilized), we're going to take another shot at entrepreneurship.

I've borrowed my new motto from Henry Ford. I wrote it in big block letters on poster board, and hung it over our bed: "Failure," said Ford, "is the opportunity to begin again, more intelligently." We'll be back!

All my love,

- Taking responsibility for the loss demonstrates maturity and growth (which will be important if you decide to ask for future assistance from relatives!)
- Explain your plans. Don't let the reader wonder how you're faring, or what you'll do.

Our Mutual Friends Lost Their Home in a Fire (17-26)

Dear Nan and Bill,

You never expect to see people you know on the eleven o'clock news. But there they were—Jim and Judy Benson—being interviewed as their house burned in the background. Fortunately, no one was hurt, but the house was completely destroyed, along with everything else they owned.

I'm heading a drive to help Judy and Jim through this difficult time. Friends are being asked to contribute whatever they can: food, money, clothing (the Benson boys are five and nine), sheets, blankets—whatever! So far the response has been fantastic.

Can I count on your support? Donations can be left at my house any day this week, between 8 A.M. and noon.

My address is:　14 South Remington Rd.
　　　　　　　　　Manchester
　　　　　　　　　555-2403

If that's not convenient, someone will stop at your house for a pick-up—just call to set up a time.

Thanks,

- Some people cannot or will not contribute money. Offer alternatives.

- Make it as easy as possible for people to help out (in this case, by offering to pick up items at their home).

Return the Dress You Borrowed (17-27)

Dear Anna,

I was going through my closet yesterday, trying to plan what to wear to an upcoming Bar Association dinner. I thought of my black strapless dress with the matching shawl, and spent ten minutes searching for it. Then I remembered that you borrowed it last spring before you moved to Dayton.

Would you please mail it back to me by the end of next week? I have my heart set on wearing it to the dinner, and I need to be sure it still fits.

I'll call you to make sure it's on its way.

Thanks.

Best always,

- Telling the reader that you need the item by a specific date creates some urgency without sounding like you're reprimanding.

- Let the borrower know you'll be on their case and won't let the matter drop.

Repay the Money You Borrowed (17-28)

Dear Arnie,

I feel uncomfortable writing this letter. The subject of money is always an awkward one—especially between friends. But two months have passed since you borrowed a hundred dollars from me, and I'd like to be repaid.

I value our friendship and don't want it to be tarnished by an outstanding debt. Would you please send me the money by the end of the week?

Thanks. I'm confident that I can count on you.

Sincerely,

- Tell the reader that you dislike having to ask for your money.
- Set a deadline, and indicate that the friendship is in jeopardy if the deadline isn't met.

Pay Your Share of the Phone Bill (17-29)

Dear Mitch,

Here's a copy of last month's phone bill. I've circled the calls that I made during your stay here. The remainder are yours. By my calculations you owe $53.21.

The phone bill is due on the 21st so please send a check to arrive by the 15th.

Thanks.

Sincerely,

- Enclose a copy of the phone bill, indicating the outstanding charges.
- Be clear about your expectations.

It's Your Turn to Take Care of Grandma (17-30)

Dear Maggie,

I'm thankful that we've agreed to share the burden of Grandma's care. And I've actually enjoyed having her with us. But after fulfilling my six months' obligation, I'm ready for a break. It's not that she's been a problem, but having her here limits my freedom.

Could you pick her up after lunch on Saturday, April 6? We're planning to leave for Florida on Sunday.

I'll call you this weekend to confirm.

Love,

- Remind the reader that an agreement was made and you expect it to be honored.
- Set a firm date for the changeover and spell out how it is to take place.

Remove the Furniture You Have Stored in My Basement (17-31)

Dear Harry,

Last weekend I spent hours in the basement searching for a box of 45 rpm records. I was amazed at how much junk I've accumulated and how disorganized I am.

I vowed to bring some order into my life, and I'm starting with a major cleanup. That includes disposing of things I don't need or use. I've scheduled a yard sale for the end of the month.

I don't want the furniture you've stored here to be trashed or sold by mistake. Please make arrangements to remove it within the next few weeks. I'd be glad to help with the heavy lifting.

I'll call you in a few days to set a date for the move.

Best,

- Make it clear that you will no longer be responsible for the stored item.
- The tone of the letter can be friendly *and* assertive.

I Can't Be There for Christmas, from Parent (17-32)

Dear Donna and Mark,

I wish we could be together for Christmas. I'm thinking of you and missing you very much.

I hope you like the gifts I've sent. Maybe next month, when we get together, you'll model them for me. For now, I can only imagine how great they'll look on you.

I love you, and I can't wait to see you. Enjoy the holidays, and get ready for some extra hugs when I come out to see you in January.

Love,

- Separation from loved ones can be painful, especially during family holidays, such as Christmas. A warm letter can help to fill the void.
- Gift-giving is nice, but it's equally important to tell loved ones that they're missed and that you're thinking of them.

Holiday Update on Family News (17-33)

Dear Aunt Edith and Uncle Jack,

This has been an unusual year. Each of us has had to deal with significant change, but it's been 100% positive. For example, the company Scott works for was sold this year.

We heard rumors of massive layoffs, and we prepared for the worst. Not only did Scott survive, he received a promotion and a raise!

Both children have moved into apartments with friends. Lee is a copywriter with an advertising agency and Paula has a civilian job at Fort Benning. As for me, I "fell into" a home business. Lee's agency needed outside people to type envelopes, insert brochures, and hand-address special promotions. I volunteered, liked the work, and offered my services to other companies in the area. Would you believe I now have two employees? I may have to rent office space!

We're going to give ourselves another six months, and if things continue to go well, we're going to buy an RV. Scott's always wanted one, and he's promised that our first trip will be to visit you in New Mexico. If that news doesn't scare you off, let us know and we'll make definite plans.

Will you call or write to bring us up-to-date on how retirement is agreeing with you? If I know the two of you, you're up to your eyebrows in all sorts of activities.

Speaking for Scott and the children, have a wonderful Christmas and a happy and healthy New Year.

With love and affection,

- Stay positive in holiday updates.
- Make it clear that you want two-way communication. Ask the readers to reciprocate.

Reminder about Holiday Plans (17-34)

Dear Marlene,

I'm counting the days until Christmas! I've looked forward to your visit all year.

I'll try to balance the usual frantic holiday pace with long stretches of time for conversation and "hanging out." The most important thing is that we'll all be together this year.

Let me know the details of your arrival and length of stay (I hope you'll be with us through New Year's Day!).

Your presence is the best present you could give me.

Love from your baby sister,

- Remind the reader of their commitment.
- Emphasize how important the visit is to you.

Thank You for Everything, Dad (Father's Day) (17-35)

Dear Dad,

Now that I'm a father, I find I appreciate you more than ever.

Every time I'm about to tell my son I'm too tired to play with him, I do a quick about-face because of the example you set for me. It never occurred to me, until recently, that you might have been tired, or upset, or just wanted to be left alone when you came home from work. But you always had time for me, no matter what.

If I'm a good father—and I think I am—it's because you've been my role model. Thanks for everything, Dad. I'm thinking of you and I love you.

With great affection,

- Parents love to hear that you recognize what they've done for you.
- There's no greater compliment than to tell someone they provided a wonderful role model.

Thank You for Everything, Mom (Mother's Day) (17-36)

Dear Mom,

Being away for Mother's Day makes me feel sad on the one hand, but surprisingly upbeat on the other. I'm sad that I can't be there to give you a hug and a kiss and take you out to dinner. But I'm upbeat because the separation has given me some quiet time to reflect on our relationship.

All through my life, people have remarked on my positive outlook on life...how I look on the bright side, no matter the situation. Guess where that came from? I realize, Mom, that you've given me an attitude—a mind set—that's more valuable than any material reward.

For as long as I can remember, you've made me feel loved and secure, happy and successful, confident and assured. You've always taught me to take responsibility for myself, which has helped me grow and achieve.

I like the woman you shaped. And I love you for all the effort you put into doing it. I may not be with you physically, but I know you can feel my thoughts. I appreciate you and all you've given me. Happy Mother's Day.

Your loving daughter,

- A personal note is often worth more than the most expensive gift.
- Words that show caring such as "love" and "appreciation" make a parent happy.

Valentine Message to Dad (17-37)

Dear Dad,

Maybe it was the Valentine's Day ads that got to me, but as I started thinking about you a flood of wonderful childhood memories filled my head.

It makes me laugh to think how Mom would roll her eyes when she couldn't tear you away from a game of touch football with the neighborhood kids. You were as much a kid as any of them!

I thought about our family history: the stories you told us about your parents and grandparents, and your struggles to establish yourself and support us. I realized that your history is my history too. And I want Jody and Mark to feel it's their history, so I continue to tell your stories to them.

You're so unique and special, and you always made me feel that way, too. You've given me so much. I hope you know how much I love and appreciate you.

Your loving daughter,

- This kind of loving letter will be read again and again.
- Try to incorporate shared experiences. It helps set a nostalgic mood.

Valentine Message to Wife (17-38)

Dear Patty,

Whether you're carting diapers or dressing for dinner, whether you're pulling weeds or just out of the shower, the effect is always the same: You look absolutely wonderful to me.

You're as fresh and fascinating as the day we met. You're more than I ever dreamed possible, and I love you and need you so very much.

Please be my Valentine forever.

Your adoring husband,

- It's reassuring for the reader to know that you find them as attractive as ever.
- Saying "I love you" is important; saying "I need you" is equally important in some relationships, not so appropriate in others. Choose your words carefully.

Dealing with 18
Banks, Credit, Taxes

A well thought-out letter to an institution will accomplish four objectives. It will (1) save you time because you won't have to make a personal visit, (2) prevent an unpleasant confrontation if you are emotional about the issue, (3) help you set forth the facts, step-by-step, to get the results you want and (4) put you "on record" if a dispute ever occurs.

A letter to an institution should be different in style from one you write to a relative, friend or close associate. While Aunt Barbara may love reading a long, rambling, free-flowing letter, people at credit agencies, banks and government agencies do not. In fact, a letter that doesn't get to the point quickly may be misinterpreted or—still worse—ignored.

State your objective clearly and succinctly, and offer supporting data. If you sound overwrought, your message may be lost. Write for results, not for reactions.

Banks. Although there have been attempts in recent years to humanize the image that financial institutions present to the public, banks remain largely faceless and mechanical in their dealings with customers. Don't make the mistake of writing as if a caring friend will be reading your missive.

Avoid the temptation to include personal information in your correspondence; it's far more important that you provide the particulars the bank needs in order to respond. And as fine as your writing technique may be, it's no substitute for having complete, accurate records of all transactions at your fingertips, and presenting them plainly when called for.

When you write to a bank, always highlight your account number prominently. And if you expect a response to your correspondence, ask for it. Don't assume it will be sent automatically.

Credit. Problems with credit can haunt your chances to obtain loans, mortgages and credit cards. People often get so upset that they use inflammatory language to deal with credit disputes, when it's level-headed communication that is required to resolve them.

Keep in mind that you're not being singled out for persecution. Mistakes happen within every type of company, and if you're using credit, chances are you'll be the victim of a mistake or two by a credit organization at some point in your life.

As with a bank, clearly list your account number and state the problem or request. If you have supporting documents or evidence of an error, include them with your letter. Always ask for written confirmation of any adjustment or settlement.

Taxes. If you run into problems with taxes, you will have the dubious pleasure of dealing with bureaucratic agencies. If you have to respond to city, state or federal tax offices, your best bet is to work through an experienced CPA. But if you feel you can handle tax-related problems on your own, be certain to stick *only* to the area in dispute.

Identify yourself by your social security or tax ID number, and be certain to retain copies of all correspondence, including any required forms that may accompany your letter.

Insurance. Be specific about the name of the policy, your policy number, and any data that's to be changed, added or deleted when you write to an insurance agent or company. Since discrepancies about coverage may occur only after a tragedy occurs, it's imperative that you understand your coverage, and that your insurer understands your directives. Put your requests and inquiries in writing and ask for written responses so you have proof of each exchange.

I'm Closing My Account because of Poor Service (18-01)

Dear Mr. Krulisky:

You've lost a good customer. I've had my money in Bay Area Bank for twelve years, but I can no longer tolerate the rudeness and poor management.

What's wrong? Here are three examples:

1) At lunchtime on Fridays, the busiest time of the week, there are only two teller windows open and lines stretch to the street.

2) I have waited as long as ten minutes for one of your desk people to finish a personal call before letting me into my safe deposit box.

3) Last month my statement was inaccurate, and when I called to straighten it out, the person I spoke to was rude to the point of blaming me for the bank's mistake.

I have closed my personal checking account, my business account and my Money Market account. I'm switching to a bank where the customer matters.

Sincerely,

- Get right to the point.
- Be specific about your complaints. Your letter could be an instrument of change that will benefit customers and employees.

I Won't Be Responsible for Charges Made by My Ex-Wife (18-02)

Dear Sir or Madam:

Re: Card #2331 4534 2200

Due to our divorce, effective April 3, 19XX I will not be responsible for any charges made by Mary L. Darnell after that date.

Please issue a new card in my name only, and send it to the above address.

Thank you for your attention to this matter.

Very truly yours,

- Be sure to reference your credit card number.
- A simple, straightforward notification is all that's necessary.

I'm Closing My Credit Card Account (18-03)

Dear Sir or Madam:

Re: Acct.# 3009 4214 3200 0401

Please terminate my UNIVERSAL credit card account immediately.

Enclosed are (1) a check for the outstanding balance, and (2) my credit card, which I have cut in half.

The account is in the name of: Paula Berschler Levine
228B Needham Terrace
Claymont, DE 19703

Please send a confirmation that the account has been closed, and a statement reflecting a zero balance.

Thank you for your prompt attention.

Very truly yours,

- There's no need for explanation. State what you want done, and give the bank the specific information it needs.
- Ask for a confirmation that your instructions have been followed.

Increase My Credit Limit (18-04)

Dear Sir or Madam:

Re: Acct.# 4535 2111 3200 3101

I'm a good TRAVELON customer. I've had my card for two years, I use it frequently, and I always pay my bills on time.

Therefore, I'm asking for an increase on my line of credit from $1,500 to $3,000, effective immediately.

Please notify me of your action.

Thank you.

- Briefly mention your good payment history.
- State the amount of credit you're requesting.

Replace My Stolen Credit Card (18-05)

Dear Mr. Chalmers:

Re: Acct.# 2121 4767 4100 8432

As we discussed yesterday, my TRAVELON credit card was stolen on January 19, 19XX. This letter confirms my request to cancel it immediately, and to have a new one issued.

I understand that I will not be responsible for any charges over $50 made after January 18, 19XX.

Following is the information you will need to cancel the old card and process a new one:

> Julia F. Soloway
> 79 North Valley Road
> Wichita, KS 67233

Your quick response will be appreciated.

Very truly yours,

- State the urgency at the beginning of your letter. Make sure that you say you want a new card issued.
- Restate your understanding of your liability.

Remove My Name as Trustee on My Son's Account (18-06)

Dear Sir or Madam:

Re: Acct.# SA1111 346 9889 02

Please remove my name as trustee for my son's savings account as of January 25, 19XX. On that date he will turn twenty one, and will be legally responsible for administering his own affairs.

The account is now listed as follows:

> Jane Markham Petyk ITF Thomas Petyk

Please confirm the change in writing. The address remains the same. If you have any questions, please telephone me at my office (303) 555-2200.

Thank you.

Very truly yours,

- This is a no-frills letter. It simply requires stating your request, and giving the information necessary to make the change.
- Provide your phone number in case the reader has any questions.

Why Did You Bounce My Check, to Bank (18-07)

Dear Ms. Reilly:

Re: Account# LT3540001125

Confirming our phone conversation today, I was shocked to learn that one of my checks bounced, and I want to know why.

> Check number: 2003
> Written to: Blue Ridge Electric Company
> Amount: $147.35
> Dated: March 7, 19XX

My account balance has never dipped below five hundred dollars. Yet this check to my utility company has been returned marked "insufficient funds." They are threatening to turn off my service.

Please do the following to correct your error:

1) Put the check through again.
2) Remove the "insufficient funds" charge from my account.
3) Send me a written explanation of how this error occurred.
4) Send a written explanation and an apology to the Blue Ridge Electric Co.

Very truly yours,

- This should be a follow up to a phone call so that you have a record of requesting the corrections.
- Separate critical information from the body of your letter.

You Made a Billing Error (18-08)

Dear Sir or Madam:

Re: Account# 72-332069

My current bill, dated 4/22, is incorrect. It indicates that I purchased a pair of jeans for $49.95 at your Honolulu store. I've never purchased jeans from any of your stores. In fact, I've never been in the Honolulu store.

Please correct your records, and send a confirmation that my account has been properly credited. I'd appreciate your prompt attention.

Sincerely,

- Reference your account number to ensure that you are credited properly.
- There's no need to be antagonistic. The vast majority of credit disputes are resolved amicably and quickly.

There's a Charge on My Bill I Didn't Make (18-09)

Dear Sir or Madam:

Re: Account# 2207657-12

There's an error on my monthly statement, and I'd like it corrected immediately.

I've been charged $130.00 for a meal at Le Petit Jardin in Santa Fe, New Mexico on January 23. That charge is incorrect because:

1) I've never been to Santa Fe.
2) On January 23 I was in the hospital undergoing surgery (attached is a copy of my hospital bill.)
3) My credit card has never left my possession.

Please remove this charge from my bill.

Thank you.

Very truly yours,

- State your reasons for believing that the creditor is in error, and supply proof, if possible.
- Request that the charge be removed from your statement.

You Didn't Credit My Payment (18-10)

Dear Sir or Madam:

Re: Account# 28781A

I'm up-to-date on my payments, but I'm not being credited for them. Here is the chronology of events that will help you get my account current:

1. As part of a neighborhood protest for poor service, I paid half of my November and December bills (check #s 3965 and 3944 for $28.25 each).

2. Service problems were corrected in late December, so I sent the withheld balance (check #4009 for $56.50).

3. In January, I received a letter threatening to cut off my service. I ignored it, since I had made good on the deferred payments, and sent in my monthly payment (check #4020 for $56.50).

4. In February, I received another threatening letter, this time telling me I was two months in arrears. I decided it was time to write before things got out of hand.

Copies of cancelled checks, corresponding to the list above, are enclosed. If any questions remain, you can reach me by day at (913) 555-3387.

Sincerely,

- Don't be emotional. Just supply pertinent facts.
- Simplicity counts when trying to resolve payment problems. Using numbered lists presents information clearly.

Request to Set Up Payment Schedule (18-11)

Dear Sir or Madam:

Re: Account# 33807

I realize my account is in arrears, and I'm committed to bringing it up to date.

Your records will show that I've always paid my bills on time. But a recent illness has made it difficult for me to meet my financial obligations.

Now I'm working again, and I want to pay off my overdue electric bill as quickly as I can. I'd appreciate your cooperation.

Would this be agreeable? I'll pay each month's bill in full, and add $20 towards the overdue portion each month until the entire amount ($287) is paid off.

May I count on Northwest Electric Company to keep me out of the dark?

Very truly yours,

- Briefly explain that recent hardship has temporarily disrupted your good credit history.
- Offer a reasonable way to resolve your debt.

Response to Collection Letter (18-12)

Dear Mr. Albritton:

I won't respond to future collection letters; my attorney will.

I've called your credit department three times to discuss your billing error. Each time, a very pleasant—but apparently incompetent—person agreed that that the error was the store's, and would be corrected. Shortly after each call, I received a nasty collection letter.

I've enclosed copies of your letters, my telephone log with the dates of my calls and the name of the person with whom I spoke, a cancelled check showing that the bill was paid, and my cut-up Buckley's credit card.

I'll consider any subsequent collection letters as harassment, and I'll instruct my attorney to file a very public suit against you and your company.

Sincerely,

- When all else fails, take the offensive. Most companies will go to great lengths to avoid bad publicity.
- Carefully document your position.

Correct the Error on My Credit Report (18-13)

Dear Sir or Madam:

Re: Report #345870912

There is an error on my credit report which needs to be corrected.

The report shows an outstanding balance of $234.75 owed to Collier's Department Store. This balance was paid in full on May 16, 19XX. Attached is a copy of the canceled check.

Please do the following:

1) Remove the outstanding balance.

2) Send me a copy of the corrected report.

Thank you.

Very truly yours,

- Provide proof such as a canceled check, receipt, letter, etc. that the outstanding debt has been paid.
- Request a copy of the corrected report.

Send Me a Copy of My Credit Report (18-14)

Dear Sir or Madam:

Please send me a copy of my credit report. My address is noted above, and my Social Security number is 122-09-3551.

Thank you.

Very truly yours,

- Be sure to include your Social Security number when requesting a credit report.
- Keep your request simple. There's no need to give details of why you're making the request.

Why Have You Refused My Request for a Credit Card? (18-15)

Dear Sir or Madam:

Why have you refused my request for a POWERBASE credit card?

I'm a homeowner, I'm gainfully employed, and I have an excellent credit rating. If I'm not the ideal credit risk, who is?

Please send me an explanation. Better yet—why don't you review your decision and send me a credit card.

Very truly yours,

- Make your case as a good candidate for credit.
- Request an explanation for why your credit application was turned down.

Disputing Disallowance of Deduction (18-16)

To Whom It May Concern:

Re: Norman and Page Weller
SS# 160-55-3110 and 095-60-1683
Disallowance of Deduction on Form 1040 (19XX)

Your disallowance of our $4,000 deduction for IRA contributions is an error. On the notice you sent, you indicated the reason for the disallowance is that one of us is covered by a retirement plan.

As you can tell from the enclosed copies of our W-2 forms for 19XX, this is incorrect. Neither of the forms is checked in the pension plan block.

Since neither of us was covered by a retirement plan in 19XX, we request that you correct your records to (1) allow the IRA deduction, and (2) abate the tax and penalty we were assessed.

Very truly yours,

- The IRS makes errors, as does any organization. Contrary to public opinion, they also rectify their errors.
- State your case, supported by facts, and don't allow emotions to intrude. End by asking for a correction.

My Refund Check Was in Error, Too Little (18-17)

Dear Sir or Madam:

Re: Underpayment of refund
SS# 122-98-5462

I believe the refund check you sent me was incorrect.

According to my completed 19XX tax return, I am entitled to a refund of $1,287.65. Yet you sent me a check for $128.76, with no explanation regarding the discrepancy.

It appears that the amount due was incorrectly keypunched into your computer.

Please correct and acknowledge the error, and send me a check for the additional $1,158.89.

Very truly yours,

- Reference your social security number to identify yourself.
- Clearly state the discrepancy and request that it be rectified. Also request a written acknowledgement of error on the part of the IRS.

My Refund Check Was in Error, Too Much (18-18)

Dear Sir or Madam:

Re: Overpayment of Refund
SS# 141-48-0064

I was scheduled to receive a refund check of $1,142.67, but received a check for $3,478.00. I've enclosed a check for $2,335.33, which is the amount of overpayment you erroneously made. I trust this will close the matter.

Very truly yours,

- When the IRS makes an overpayment, problems may follow unless you immediately send a letter with a check in the amount of the overpayment. Send it return receipt requested.
- According to one CPA firm, the IRS has been known to penalize people who have received overpayments, even though they *verbally* reported the error.

My Social Security Number Was Incorrect on My Return (18-19)

Dear Sir or Madam:

Re: Resubmission of Form 1099

I filed my taxes with an incorrect Social Security number, so I've enclosed a new Form 1099, with the correct social security number.

Incorrect Number: 155-09-8735
Correct Number: 155-09-8753

I apologize for the error. If there are any questions, please contact me at (312) 555-4943.

Sincerely,

- If you file your return with an incorrect social security number, it's recommended that you refile a new return. Trying to correct the original error is often an exercise in futility.

- The new submission will be entered properly in the IRS computers, which will negate any problems that may arise due to the original filing.

Response to Notification of an Audit (18-20)

Dear Ms. Soldano:

Re: SS# 151-35-7007

Here are our answers to your three primary questions:

1. I haven't been able to locate my cancelled checks from 1996. I'm still looking, and I'll be back to you within a week.

2. The $32,000 in tax payments/prior year credit on line 31 of our 1996 tax return was paid/credited as follows:

Credit from 1995 return	$ 4,197
Paid on or about 12/31/96	17,803
Paid on or about 4/15/97	10,000
Total line 31	$32,000

3. I have no record of ever receiving the $4,756 refund or credit indicated on Form NJ-601, Notice of Adjustment, dated June 13, 1998. Therefore, it has not been applied as a credit.

I hope this resolves matters. However, if you need additional information, please call me during the day at (908) 555-3882.

Sincerely,

Change the Beneficiary on My Policy (18-21)

Dear Ms. Long:

Re: Change of Beneficiary
Life Insurance Policy# 0073A22A

My wife, Georgia, passed away nearly a month ago. I'd like to continue to carry my policy, but substitute co-beneficiaries, as follows:

Arlene Claire Gorham Ross (my daughter)
Harvey Edward Gorham (my son)

If any forms need to be signed, please send them to the address shown above. If any questions need to be answered, you can reach me at (404) 555-6693.

I'd appreciate your prompt acknowledgement and processing of this request.

Very truly yours,

Does My Policy Cover Damage from Storm? (18-22)

Dear Brad:

Re: Homeowner's Policy
#125-32-771B-363

I was one of the lucky ones when a twister visited my neighborhood last week. But I may not be so lucky next time.

I pulled out my homeowner's policy to check my coverage on storm damage, but I'm still not sure what's covered. Would you please give me a written summary, in everyday English, of what—if anything—I need to do to protect my investment in my home and grounds.

May I hear from you within the next couple of weeks?

Sincerely,

- Insist on a written answer; it may be of value in a dispute.
- Ask for a response within a reasonable time period.

Add the Following to My Valuable Items Policy (18-23)

Dear Ms. Smith:

Re: Policy# VI 277700546

I recently inherited a diamond ring from my grandmother's estate and I would like to insure it. I have enclosed a copy of the appraisal and a photograph of the ring.

Please confirm, in writing, that you have added the ring to my valuable items policy. Also advise me how the addition will affect my premium payments.

Thank you.

Sincerely,

- Attach a copy of the appraisal.
- Ask for written confirmation that your instructions have been followed.

Transfer Policy to My New Car (18-24)

Dear Marika:

Re: Policy# 520AZ-19930

As you requested, here are the details on our new car:

Make: Ford
Year: 1998
Model: SE Coupe
VIN: HAC58F6E5K812663
Anti-theft Device: Yes

I'm the primary driver and, as with our last car, it will be used to go to and from work each day (a round-trip commute of 20 miles). All coverage and deductibles will remain as before.

Thanks for your help, Marika. As always, it's a pleasure to work with you.

Sincerely,

- Although most insurers cover you from the moment you call, it's important to put the information in writing.
- This information is best faxed or sent via certified mail.

Make This Change in My Homeowner's Policy (18-25)

Dear Garson:

Re: Homeowner's Policy
#54-65-3112-7

When I heard how much my neighbor sold his home for, alarms went off in my head. It made me realize that my home is seriously under-insured.

Effective immediately, please upgrade my Homeowner's coverage as follows:

Dwelling:	$250,000
Personal Property:	$175,000
Personal Liability:	$500,000

Would you please acknowledge that the change has been made? I don't want to wait for your invoice to be certain I'm covered at the new levels. Thanks.

Sincerely,

- Indentations highlight key information.
- Ask for an acknowledgement. Don't assume anything.

Why Is My Premium So High? (18-26)

Dear Kent:

I suppose it was the latest rate increase that forced me to do some comparison shopping, and I don't like what I've learned. It appears that at least three other insurance companies charge less than the one your firm recommended for exactly the same automobile coverage.

If you want to retain my business, please call to explain why I'm paying so much.

Sincerely,

- By making it clear that they are about to lose your business, you can force your agent to respond promptly.
- State that you're willing to listen (otherwise you might not get a response). Chances are the agent will come up with some ideas that will lower your premium.

Employment 19

A successful job search is comprised of several facets. Though many job seekers focus solely on the interview as the most critical part of the process, getting the job you want is also dependent on presenting yourself well in correspondence and resumes. Because a prospective employer is likely to "meet" you on paper even before you get to your first interview, your written communications will often determine whether or not a face-to-face meeting ever takes place.

Gathering information. You may have interest in a given profession or company without knowing much about it. If this is the case, request an appointment to speak with someone who works in the field or knows specifics about the company. This is known as an information meeting or interview.

Although some information interviews, as well as job interviews, result from contacting people you find on your own, many are arranged at the suggestion of a mutual acquaintance. If this is the case, be sure to mention the source of your referral. Also you'll want to send thank you's to both the person with whom you met and the one who referred you.

Resumes and job interviews. Think of your resume, requests for interviews (cover letters) and thank you's after interviews as sales devices. They are meant to highlight your strongest assets, while downplaying any weaknesses. They should be constructed with the prospective employer's requirements, not yours, in mind. It's not what *you* find interesting, motivating or impressive that counts; it's what the *reader* might find of value that's important.

Your resume should spell out relevant experience, achievements, and skills, emphasizing those features that make you an outstanding candidate. If your educational background merits particular attention, for example, put that first. If, on the other hand, your experience is of greater importance, feature that in the most prominent position. While the resumes presented in this section vary in style and format, their function is always to communicate the best possible match between your skills and the employer's needs.

Responses to job offers. If you have no interest in the position offered, send a cordial and appreciative rejection letter, stating briefly the reason for your decision. If the offer is acceptable, send an acceptance letter confirming the details of the offer.

If you are interested in the position, but have further questions, thank the prospective employer and request an appointment to discuss your concerns. When you have decided you want the job, you can negotiate any remaining details in a clearly stated letter, and then accept or reject the final offer.

Resignations. No matter what the reason for leaving your current position, you'll do yourself—and possibly your future employment prospects— a great disservice if the departure isn't handled with dignity and thought.

Your resignation letter leaves your employer with a final impression, and it should summon good feelings, rather than stirring up memories of past slights or disagreements.

Throughout the job search process. Double and triple-check your correspondence and resume for errors in word usage, grammar, spelling and typing. Ideally, you should have another person proofread the material before you send it out. A slip-up in this area could doom your chances for a job.

Request for Advice (19-01)

Dear Bern,

I'm going through one of those periods in life when I wish someone would just grab me by the lapels, shake me, and tell me what to do. Since I respect your opinion very much, perhaps I can impose on you to help snap me out of my indecision.

Here's the situation: About six months ago, I took a sales job with a North Carolina-based company. I was assured that I could operate from Minneapolis where, as you know, I have family, friends and home. All of a sudden I started getting pressure to relocate to North Carolina. Management has decided that I have a lot to offer, and they want me to work more closely with them. This is a first step, I'm told, to moving into management.

While I'm flattered by the attention, I'm not sure I'm ready to alter my life so radically just now. It's taken me 38 years to reach a point where I'm doing what I want to do, and the thought of change has me frozen.

You know me as well as anyone. Will you give my situation some thought, and then call me at 612-555-4480? I'll fill you in on the specifics when we talk, but this will give you a headstart. You're so good at examining all sides of a question, I can't wait to hear from you.

Your friend,

- Don't beat around the bush; if you want advice, ask for it.
- Highlight the dilemma in broad terms; save details for a more in-depth discussion.

Request for Reference (19-02)

Dear Joel:

It was great to see you at the Financial Networking Conference last week. As I mentioned, I am thinking about moving on and have been putting out some feelers in the San Francisco area. One name that came up was Allied Bank, which is undergoing a major restructuring of its Bonds and Acquisitions Department.

I am writing to you because I want to follow up on it, and I was wondering if you knew anything about their plans for the future. I also know that you are a friend of Al Goodspell. I was hoping you could give me a good reference. It's always hard going into these things cold, and having my name mentioned to the Senior V.P. would be a big help. Since you had an opportunity to see me work in our five years together at WestBank, your reference would really mean something.

If you know of any other good leads, please let me know. I really appreciate any help you can give me. I hope that someday I can return the favor.

Thanks again.

Very truly yours,

- Don't beg, plead, or wheedle. Just ask. Everybody understands the importance of connections, and it's inherently complimentary to ask somebody to use theirs to help you.
- If you are asking for a reference from somebody who doesn't know your work history well, send them a resume.

Thank You for Referral (19-03)

Dear Phil:

Thank you for putting me in touch with Tom Stanley at Roth, Roche and Stern. We spoke on the phone at length on Tuesday, and I received a very favorable impression of both the company and Tom.

Tom has set up appointments for me with two managers who have openings in their departments, and he has been quite encouraging about my prospects at Roth, Roche and Stern. I look forward to pursuing my options there.

I'll keep you posted as things develop further. Thanks again for your help.

Best,

- Referrals are the life's blood of a job search. Thanks should be immediate and specific but not drawn out.
- Always offer to keep the person informed about the results of his or her efforts to refer you (and then do it).

Thank You for Help (19-04)

Dear Linda,

Thank you for dinner last night. It was a pleasure to reconnect after so long.

I was very glad to hear that your business continues to prosper, and I appreciate your offer to pass along my resume to Ron McMullin at Technology Park. I'm planning to call him when I'm in town.

I'll keep you posted on my job search. I look forward to seeing you at the Ancient China Exhibition next month.

Kind regards,

- This is a hybrid letter—a cross between a friendly note and a job-search letter. Because it's directed to a friend, it should be handwritten on personal letterhead.

Request for Information about Company (19-05)

Dear Ms. Cohen:

I am a recent college graduate interested in finding a position in a securities firm. I understand that Axiom Securities has an excellent marketing trainee program, and I am writing you to find out more about it.

Among the questions I have are: When does the program begin and how long does the training take? What qualifications make for a successful applicant? And, of course, I would like to know what the application procedures are.

I hope you can help me with this information. I look forward to meeting with you to discuss career opportunities at Axiom Securities.

Sincerely,

- Be clear and concise. Don't try to bowl them over; just get the information. There will be other chances to impress.
- Unless they have some prepared information—and most small and medium-sized companies will not—you will do better to ask specific questions. And always, if possible, ask for information about particular jobs. Don't go on a fishing expedition.

Thank You for Information about Company (19-06)

Dear Ms. Thompson:

Thank you for sending me the information I requested on Texmat's hazardous waste control services. Your brochure and the annual report give me a much clearer picture of the range of services Texmat offers and the nature of its clientele.

I enjoyed talking with you on the phone last week, and appreciate the effort you took in getting the materials to me quickly.

Sincerely,

- Follow up with written thanks whenever anyone helps you further your job search.
- Be sure to mention how you benefited from receiving the information.
- Close with thanks and some reference to your request.

Request for Information Meeting (19-07)

Dear Ms. Myren-Walker:

I'm writing you on the recommendation of Matt Newman. Matt has told me about your work and recent promotion within Crestwood Communities. I am very interested in a career in the administration of retirement communities, especially those that offer full-service health care. Would it be possible for you to meet with me to share some information about your profession?

My training is in social work with an emphasis on gerontology. After six years as a case worker with senior citizens, I returned to school to pursue a Master's degree in Business Administration. I graduated last month, and I'm excited about pursuing my goal of combining my experience and training in a management position on behalf of the elderly. I have enclosed my resume for your information and convenience.

I will call you next week to arrange an appointment, if possible. I will be in your area during the second week of March—perhaps we can meet then.

Sincerely,

Enclosure

- State your purpose for writing and your source of referral in the first paragraph.
- Help your interviewee learn about your interests and how you've prepared for this, or a related career, by offering brief biographical information and your resume.

Thank You for Information Meeting (19-08)

Dear Susan:

I want to express my thanks to you again for meeting with me last week. The information you gave me about your work at Crestwood Communities was very helpful. I appreciated your willingness to speak openly and to offer useful advice.

I have already contacted Jean Simsbury and Ed Hernandez for additional information interviews, on your recommendation. Both of them were able to fit me into their busy schedules, and both were pleased to hear about your promotion.

Again, Susan, thank you for your time. I will keep you updated as my job search continues.

Best wishes in your new position!

Sincerely,

- Though this is still business correspondence, this letter can be more personal than your original contact. Let your interviewee know that you appreciated the time and information.
- Acknowledge the names of additional referrals.

Update after Information Meeting (19-09)

Dear Susan:

I'm writing to share my good news with you. I have accepted a position as Director of Health Services with Casa del Sol, a retirement community in Phoenix, Arizona. I will be moving there within the month.

You were an important part of my getting this job, and I want to thank you for it. My interview at Casa del Sol resulted from my meeting with your colleague Jean Simsbury. Your referral was a key link in the chain.

I'm very excited about the work I will be doing. It calls for someone who has my experience in social service agencies, direct contact with the elderly, and training in business administration. It's a good match! Thank you again for your help, Susan.

Best regards,

- This kind of letter is appropriate for people who were especially helpful in your job search. Information interviewees often appreciate knowing how your search turned out. This letter not only updates them but maintains a professional network.

Request for Information from Outplacement Agency (19-10)

Dear Mr. Curry:

I enjoyed our interview Friday, and I wanted to get back to you as soon as possible. As you know, Co-Ark Chemical has given me a choice of two outplacement firms, and I do want to have a basis of comparison.

We agreed that:

- Curry & Associates will provide secretarial support for a 500-letter direct mail campaign, with each letter personalized and proofread.
- I will dictate an unlimited number of individual letters.
- I have full and unencumbered use of an office.

I need to know:

- Is there any limit on phone calls? Local? Long-distance? As you know, verifying names sometimes requires a great many brief calls.

I'll call you next week to discuss these items.

Sincerely,

- Outplacement firms offer a great many services, but it's good to pin them down to specifics.
- Just because you've been fired or layed off doesn't mean that you don't have a right to be assertive.

Resume: Chronological, Entry Level (19-11)

Tamara Paul
21 Schmidt Avenue
New Haven, CT 06514
(203) 555-5210

Education

1996-1998   Yale School of Management, New Haven, CT
Candidate for Master's degree in Public and Private Management,
May 1998. Emphasis in marketing and strategic planning.

1990-1994   Oberlin College, Oberlin, OH
BA in Economics
Comfort Starr Fellowship
Appointed student member of President's Advisory Committee on
Budgetary Affairs. Member of Student Organization Funding
Committee.

Experience

Summer 1997   American Consumer Products, Westport, CT
Corporate Market Analysis and Planning
Developed and evaluated forecasts by market sectors. Analyzed
sensitivity of demand to cannibalization, economic scenarios, and
technological change. Presented findings to top management.

1995-1996   Data Management Corporation, New York, NY
Project Director
Directed marketing research projects from study design through
analysis of data and report-writing.

Provided manufacturers/advertising agencies with primary research
data used to:
- develop marketing strategies
- forecast new product potential
- optimize product growth and penetration
- identify sales opportunities

1994   Thomas Marketing Research, New York, NY
                           Junior Project Director
                           Designed questionnaires, analyzed data, and wrote reports.
                           Account responsibility included Chesebrough-Ponds and Gillette.

Summer
1992-1993   Brewington Associates, Summit, NJ
                           Market Research Field Assistant
                           Acted as liaison between project directors and field force.
                           Aided in the direction and supervision of data-gathering staff of 60
                           supervisors and 200 interviewers.

**Professional
Affiliations**   American Marketing Association 1994-present
                           Junior Achievement Counselor 1995-present

- If your most recent educational credential is vastly more impressive than your work experience, you should highlight it by giving it star billing, providing it bears directly on the job you want.

- The job descriptions are functional and give the employer a "hook" so that he or she can think, "This woman can do what I need to have done—forecasts and market research reports—and her presentation skills must be first-rate."

Resume: Chronological, Early Career (19-12)

BRIAN B. POTTER
28 Trumbull Street
New Britain, Connecticut 06050
(203) 555-2943

1998-Present **LEGISLATIVE AIDE,** Connecticut General Assembly, Hartford, CT. Clerk for the Substance Abuse Prevention Committee. Review proposed legislation, organize public hearings and meetings. Prepare statements and letters for State Representative.

1997 **FLOOR DIRECTOR,** Tom McDonough Show. WTBV-TV, New Haven, CT. Directed all communications between talent and crew. Managed all aspects of studio while taping, ran camera. Show seen in 104 markets nationwide.

1994-97 **PUBLIC ACCESS COORDINATOR and PRODUCTION MANAGER.** Cable Times, Norwalk, CT. Responsible for creating community programming using community volunteers. Worked with the local governments and school systems in lower Fairfield County to produce programs.

1993-94 **NEWS and FEATURE ASSISTANT.** WCBC-TV, New York. Collected and organized facts on developing news for producers and reporters. Premium placed on interview skills, accuracy, and ability to work under a daily deadline.

1993 **VIDEO WRITER/DIRECTOR,** Training Center, Metro Railroad, New York. Produced training and promotional tapes for internal use.

EDUCATION

GRADUATE SCHOOL OF CORPORATE AND POLITICAL COMMUNICATIONS, FAIRLEE UNIVERSITY, Fairlee, CT. M.A. Thesis in progress. Media, Organizational Communications.

COLGATE UNIVERSITY, Hamilton, NY. B.A. 1992. Graduated with Honors in English. Emphasis on writing.

- Be thorough and clear. Put yourself in the best light but don't inflate or lie. If you get caught, you definitely ruin your chances for landing a job.

- Work experience is the most important category, so put it first. If you want to include an objective, that should go before work experience.

Resume: Chronological, Mid-Career (19-13)

Thomas Kitter
23 North High Street
East Haven, CT 06512
(203) 555-1813 (Home)

Business
Experience

1988-Present   CARLETON ASSOCIATES   Boston, MA
Consulting assignments for many clients, including development
of comprehensive business plan for publishing venture;
management control system and functional reorganization of
newly spun-off company; financial projections and cash flow
planning for entrepreneur.

1980-1988   TRIAD CORPORATION   New York, NY
Sales and Marketing Consultant for this OTC-traded company.
Responsibilities included identification of new markets for
company's "Dial Us" information retrieval and order-taking
services; cost analysis and development of pricing policy;
creation of new sales materials. Sold firm's services to major
prospects. Recommendations resulted in creation of new direct
marketing division, now making substantial contribution to
Triad's bottom line.

1979-1980   AMERICAN HOMES QUARTERLY   Springfield, MA
Assistant Director of Marketing. Responsible for devising and
implementing marketing strategies for this 150,000-circulation
magazine and executive relocation service. Created advertiser-
sponsored "welcome to Springfield" kit; developed relocation
business through direct mail campaign and personal contact
with personnel directors. Sold long-term advertising contracts to
major manufacturing firms.

1978-1979   WILSON TOYS   Providence, RI
Management training. Worked first as apprentice on assembly
line to acquire "feel" for how production really works. Then
completed training programs in Sales, Marketing, and Finance
divisions.

Thomas Kitter
Page 2

Education
1974-1978   BROWN UNIVERSITY
                   BA with concentration in urban and American studies. Feature
                   writer for *The Brown Daily Herald*.

References available upon request.

- Mid-career resumes may or may not have a "career objective" at the top. The writer clearly felt that including such an objective would be limiting, especially since there is no obvious "next step."

Resume: Achievement, Early Career (19-14)

BRIAN B. POTTER
28 Trumbull Street
New Britain, Connecticut 06050
(203) 555-2943

Proven Abilities to:

- Develop effective communications using a variety of media, including written and video communications.

- Work within the structures of public policy and government and anticipate the needs of public policy makers.

- Work with community leaders and public officials and enhance the image of the company within the community.

- Collect, organize, and analyze information clearly and effectively.

Achievements:

- Prepared testimony for State Representative. Handled sensitive constituent contact. Analyzed impact of proposed legislation.

- Participated in daily production of popular daytime talk show seen in 104 markets nationwide. Fluent in all aspects of video production: camera, directing, editing.

- Worked on the assignment desk in local news in New York City television. Set up interviews, investigated and created story ideas.

- Managed production crews for a variety of community television programs. Worked with community leaders to produce educational and informational programs.

Career Summary:

CONNECTICUT GENERAL ASSEMBLY, Legislative Aide, 1998-Present
TOM McDONOUGH SHOW, Floor Director, 1997
CABLE TIMES, Public Access Coordinator and Production Manager, 1994-97
WCBC-TV, New York, News and Feature Assistant, 1993-1994
METRO RAILROAD, Video Writer and Director, 1993

- This type of resume requires some tough editing. You must constantly ask yourself if information must be included and if it is being presented fairly and accurately. Don't over-inflate yourself, and don't be ambiguous. If you accomplished something, include it—don't dance around what was a group effort.

Resume: Achievement, Mid-Career (19-15)

George F. Shepherd
1209 Dixworth Avenue
Marietta, Georgia 30060
(404) 555-4096 (home)

OBJECTIVE: Entry into Commercial Development via position as Construction Representative.

EMPLOYMENT: HARTWELL CONSTRUCTION COMPANY, Atlanta, GA
Project Engineer/Manager, June 1994 - present

- Project experience includes:
600,000-square-foot, class A office building for major U.S. corporation ($45 million).
Structural steel retail building located downtown Atlanta on air rights ($2 million).
Ten-story state educational facility ($10 million).
New 60,000-square-foot country club facility with elaborate interior work. Also demolition of existing facility ($3 million).
Several urban office building renovations, including extensive base-building and tenant fit-up construction ($1-2 million each).
- Oversee all phases of project estimating, bid, proposal, start-up, contract negotiation, extensive drawing and specification review, change orders, coordination, scheduling, and close-out.
- Inherited one project running at a loss and brought to completion at substantial profit.
- Played a major role in successful negotiation for project with first-time client. Subsequent performance as Project Manager assured further business with client.
- Successfully and profitably managed complex project built over railroad air rights. Project had been declined by other contractors due to technical difficulty.
- Brought projects within budget by working closely with owners/architects on value engineering.

CHASE MANHATTAN BANK N.A., New York, NY
Trade Finance Department Officer, June 1989 - August 1993

- Acted as liaison between marketing and operations.
- Performed market studies to assess competition, pricing, areas for new product development, and other market characteristics.
- Assisted lending officers in problem-solving and developing marketing strategies and presentation for clients.

EDUCATION: GEORGIA INSTITUTE OF TECHNOLOGY, Atlanta, GA
Master of Science in Construction Management, School of Civil Engineering, 1994. GPA 3.6

- Intensive study of all aspects of construction management with a blend of academic and practical application. Heavy engineering and computer course format.
- Courses in Land Use Planning, Project Feasibility
- Analysis, Construction Accounting, Engineering Economics and Scheduling.
- Received research grant for work on computer programming of the CYCLONE scheduling model.

UNIVERSITY OF NEVADA-RENO, Reno, NV
Bachelor of Arts in Economics, 1989. GPA 3.7

- Graduated with distinction.

REFERENCES: Furnished upon request.

- This is an achievement-oriented resume with a chronological arrangement.
- The "objective" provides the needed focus.

Resume: Functional, Entry Level (19-16)

JESSICA MARIE COLLINS
29 Fairgrounds Road
Durham, California 95928
(916) 555-7483

CAREER OBJECTIVE
> A responsible position in the management and operations of a community service agency.

EDUCATION

Holmes School of Theology, Asuncion, New Mexico
Master of Divinity 1997

St. Dymphna College, North River, Minnesota
Bachelor of Arts in Religion and Social Services 1993

WORK EXPERIENCE
1993-Present

Archives Assistant
Holmes School of Theology, Asuncion, California
- Organized and processed archival papers of missionaries to China.
- Assisted patrons with research.
- Research Assistant for Asian Missionaries Indexing Project.

1995

Intern
California Food Bank, Chico, California
- Coordinated a four-month long, state-wide food drive in cooperation with the Governor's office.
- Recruited and trained food-drive volunteers throughout the state.
- Wrote instructional pamphlet for local food drive organizers.

1991-93   <u>Director of Children's Education</u>
                            Grace Community Church, North River, California
                            • Directed the Sunday School of 75 children and 9
                              teachers.
                            • Administrated all church activities involving children.
                            • Initiated and implemented numerous seasonal and
                              liturgical celebrations and events.
                            • Recruited, trained, and supervised over 25
                              volunteers.

RELATED EXPERIENCE
                            • Board member on Publicity and Budget Committees
                              of Asuncion Area United Way Board of Directors.
                            • Attended three-day conference on "The Challenge of
                              Hometown Hunger" 1993. Taught a workshop on
                              "Training Volunteers in Food Banks" at same event.
                              Have taken numerous workshops on community
                              service topics such as housing, daycare, and
                              fundraising.
                            • Researched and wrote a 40-page Senior Thesis
                              entitled "Conflict and Cooperation among Social
                              Service Agencies in the Greater North River Area."
                              Received Honors with Distinction.

References available on request.

- A combination chronological and functional resume is often a good choice for the entry-level applicant. It communicates recent career preparation and relevant experience.
- Note the careful choice of verbs to communicate skills in organizing, training, administrating, and working with the public. The more specific the verb, the better.

Resume: Career Change (19-17)

PETER A. HASKINS
1741 Lancaster Drive
Othello, Washington 98902
(403) 555-8784

Innovative <u>Human Resources Director</u> with in-depth fifteen years of experience in personnel development. Analytical, research-oriented, and persuasive with strong skills in teaching and writing. Highly motivated and enthusiastic about sharing both private and public sector expertise with graduate students in business or public administration.

<u>PERSONNEL ADMINISTRATION</u>

Director of Personnel and Employee Relations, 1990-Present
Freedland Mining Company, Reno, Nevada
> Reporting to the Division President, managed five assistants and coordinated functions in support of Division operations.
> - Initiated and managed a cost reduction campaign that resulted in 27% reduction in controlled operating expenses.
> - Identified division-wide training needs and priorities to improve existing program. Impact: reduced turnover in staff and notable improvement in services, productivity, and morale.

Manager of Personnel Services, 1982-90
West Coast Gas and Electric Company, Fresno, California
> Chief Officer for staffing, compensation, training, benefits, and labor relations. Was invited to implement a Management Development program. This resulted in:
> - Initiation of customized management training program that became a model for the West Coast region.
> - Expansion of college relations program with target MBA schools.

TEACHING AND TRAINING

Job-Related
- Designed and conducted numerous training events ranging from half-day seminars to five-day off-site events. Topics ranged from organizational behavior theory to recent legislative changes.

Private
- Taught night division course in Public Administration at University of Nevada at Reno, 1991-Present.
- Taught two courses in Personnel Development at Fresno Community College, 1985-87.

PUBLICATIONS

Training and Development Journal, May 1995. "The Role of the Personnel Director in a Downsizing Organization."

Personnel Journal, Winter 1991. "Does Your Company Know the Law?"

EDUCATION

Master of Public Administration. Rice University, Houston, Texas. 1982

Bachelor of Arts in Political Science, Cooper College, Ames, Iowa. 1979

- When you've got solid experience, focus your resume on your achievements and credentials. Stress the data that match the needs of the prospective employer and can lead to an interview.

- Be as specific as space allows when describing the impact of your work. Quantify the results when appropriate; for example, the percentage of costs that were reduced.

Resume: Curriculum Vitae (19-18)

CURRICULUM VITAE
RICHARD RUNDLETT
677 Vista Road
Virginia Beach, VA 29483
(407) 555-2938

Richard Rundlett is an attorney in private practice in Virginia Beach, Virginia. He specializes in litigation on behalf of organizations dedicated to ecological protection and social justice. Since earning his J.D. from the University of Virginia in 1980, his clients have ranged from small, local organizations to nationally recognized movements. Greenpeace, People against Acid Rain, Citizens for a Nuclear Free Future, The Crusade Against Hunger, and Mothers Against Drunk Drivers are among his clients.

Prior to his law career, Richard served parishes in New England and the Midwest as a clergyman in the United Church of Christ for 12 years. Following his graduation from Andover-Newton School of Theology, in Massachusetts, he pastored both urban and rural congregations. These included a "three-point parish" in northern Montana where he traveled to three churches in a 150-mile radius to conduct services every week.

Richard's deep commitment to social justice and ecological concerns grows out of his experiences in high school and college. During that time, he lived on Whidby Island in the Puget Sound near Seattle, Washington. He saw the consequences of marine and air pollution, oil spills, and inadequate planning for environmental impact. He also became active in protecting the fishing rights of Native Americans in the Pacific Northwest. While completing a Bachelor's degree in Political Science at Washington State University, he "tested the legal waters" by working as a paralegal in a community service agency.

Richard lives near Virginia Beach with his wife and has two grown children. He spends his free time gardening and doing amateur photography. He is a popular speaker on ecological and justice issues and the author of several articles on these topics.

- Curriculum vitae, or CV, is Latin for "course of one's life." It is a short account of your career and qualifications within your profession. It can serve as an elaboration of your resume and can give the reader a more three-dimensional picture of who you are.

- Write it factually and in reverse chronological order. Some CV's omit information about personal life in the last paragraph.

Request for Interview, with Referral (19-19)

Dear Mr. Barthman:

Since Riley and Santilli is merging with Mutual Corporation, I am discreetly exploring career alternatives. I understand from Jon Pritchard that Omega is seeking a potential partner, and I would welcome an opportunity to talk to you about that possibility. My resume is enclosed.

My experience with Riley and Santilli, first in operations and then in real estate development and finance, qualifies me to manage the growth of a major regional real estate company. Furthermore, I am eager to participate in the ownership of a growing firm while helping that firm build its net worth.

I will call you next week to see if we can find a mutually convenient time to talk.

Sincerely,

Enclosure

- Explain, early on, why you are seeking employment and the position you seek.
- State, as crisply as you can, what qualifies you for that position.
- Ask for an appointment.

Request for Interview, Cold Mailing—Broad Focus (19-20)

Dear Mr. Stewart:

I believe my experience and solid record of achievement make me an ideal candidate for an industrial sales and marketing position in your firm.

I have over 13 years of professional sales and marketing experience, with a four-year career base established with General Products. As my enclosed resume indicates, I have successfully managed sales programs in the pulp and paper industry. My experience includes distribution channel organization and training, product promotion and development in both the international and domestic markets, and advertising and collateral promotional materials origination.

Please call me at (804) 555-4168 after 6 p.m. if you need further information about my experience.

Sincerely,

Enclosure

- Generally, these letters are sent to so many people that individual follow-up is impossible. Providing a phone number and "best time to call" is the next best strategy.

Request for Interview, Cold Mailing-Narrow Focus (19-21)

Dear Mr. Kingman:

If you're like most successful sales managers, you're never satisfied with your company's sales. An extra push here, an additional call there, and your team could generate an additional ten percent.

Well, I'm the person who can supply that extra ten—or fifteen, or even twenty—percent. I've consistently set territory records at my current company...and I'd like the opportunity to do the same for you.

I'll explain why I want to work for your company when we meet. And I'll show you how you can put my successful experience to work for your future growth.

I'll call you next Wednesday at 10:00 a.m. to arrange an appointment. If you won't be available, please contact me at (302) 555-1886, or leave word when it would be convenient for us to talk.

Very truly yours,

- To get an interview, you must convince your "target" that you can achieve something that they need. Increased sales, more productivity, lower costs, etc.

- By being specific about the time of a call, you're more likely to make contact.

Request for Interview, Follow-Up to Ad (19-22)

Dear Sir or Madam:

Re: Executive Secretary Position
Advertised 6/23, Danbury Gazette

I've served as the "right arm" for senior executives for nearly twenty years. Although I don't have the associate degree you request, I think you'll find that my secretarial and office management skills (not to mention English and grammar skills) are superior.

I'm proficient in word processing (UltraWord), spreadsheets (ZoomPro) and databases (DBVII). Since I'm from the "old school," I'm also proficient in shorthand and dictaphone transcription.

When we have the opportunity to meet, I'll elaborate on my work experience—which seems to complement your needs—and supply you with strong references. I can be reached during the day at (203) 555-1818, or in the evening at (203) 555-5067.

I'm looking forward to discussing the position with you.

Very truly yours,

- Show how your skills or experience match the requirements listed in the ad.

- Be sure to identify the ad and the newspaper, otherwise your letter may not get to the right party.

Request for Interview, Follow-Up to Phone Call (19-23)

Dear Ms. Cullen:

After thinking about our phone conversation, I believe I have a lot to offer Worldwide Fashions. I've enclosed the resume you requested, with the reminder that it presents only a partial picture. By granting me an interview, you'll have the opportunity to see the full range of my work and my solutions to a number of design challenges.

Thanks for spending so much time on the phone with me. I'll call within a week to arrange a meeting date.

Sincerely,

- Don't just say that you want a meeting; explain why it will be beneficial to the prospective interviewer.
- Take the initiative by saying that you'll do the phone follow-up to arrange the interview.

Request for Interview, at Suggestion of Co-Worker (19-24)

Dear Mr. Whittaker:

Roger Neilson, in your manufacturing group, suggested that I contact you about the opening for a writer on the company newsletter.

One of the things Roger felt would be of great value to your company is my versatility; I can fill many roles. For example, I've been a reporter (Maplewood Community News), an advertising copywriter (The Tricewell Agency), and an editor (The Daily Report). That means that you have the flexibility to use my skills in multiple functions.

Roger said that he'd be happy to fill you in on why he feels I'd be an asset to your operation (you can reach him at Ext. 211). I hope you'll take him up on his offer. And I'd like to have the opportunity to meet you and present my credentials in person. I'll call you next week to set up an appointment.

Cordially,

- If an employee will give you an endorsement, it represents an excellent "leg up" on your competition.
- Remember: Your goal is to get an interview. Don't overload your letter with data.

Request for Interview, Career Change (19-25)

Dear Mr. Brooks:

I saw your advertisement for a news reporter, and I wish to apply for the job. Enclosed is my resume and some clips for your consideration.

Although I have made my living in banking, writing and news have always been my first love. I have been writing features for a couple of local newspapers while working at First Security Bank. I majored in journalism at Northeastern University and did an internship at *The Boston Globe* in my junior year. While I may not have all the hard news experience you are looking for, I certainly know how to write.

I look forward to an interview and hope to hear from you soon.

Sincerely,

Enclosures

- Do a little selling without overdoing it. Use the cover letter to refer to the resume by bringing out certain experiences or educational background. You do want them to read your resume the right way-as someone who is eminently qualified for the job.

- Make it clear that you are looking for an interview. Be positive!

Request for Interview, to Executive Search Firm— Specific Job (19-26)

Dear Mr. Coburn:

I understand that you are attempting to recruit a vice-president, marketing, for a small family-owned trucking firm in the Midwest.

I have enclosed my resume. We should talk because:

- I have 10 years of successively more responsible positions in marketing in the transportation industry. My achievements in each position were substantial.

- My family lives in Michigan, and I am eager to relocate to that area.

I will call you in a week to see if we can find a mutually convenient time to meet.

Sincerely,

Enclosure

- Executive search firms usually ignore unsolicited resumes. Don't waste your time unless you know that they're looking for someone with your credentials (it pays to network) and you can offer them something special or unique (your willingness to relocate to the Midwest, for example).

Request for Interview, to Executive Search Firm— No Specific Job (19-27)

Dear Mr. Kasten:

Every book I've read says you don't contact executive recruiters; they contact you. But my guess is you'll overlook protocol if the talent is highly marketable. And I am.

I'm skilled at putting ideas into action. In fact, I have 12 years of consistently high quality problem-solving and profit-producing achievements behind me...with the promise of many more successful years to come.

The enclosed resume will give you some idea of what I've done and for whom. A personal interview will help convince you that I can be a valuable addition to your executive bank.

I'll call within the week to arrange an interview.

Sincerely,

Enclosure

- George Bernard Shaw wrote that people who get on in the world are those "who get up and look for the circumstances they want, and if they can't find them, make them." This writer accomplishes that with this letter.

- Indicate that you will pursue the interview with a phone call, and be sure that you do.

Thank You for Interview, Interested in Job (19-28)

Dear Mr. Jackson:

Although you indicated you had more interviews to conduct before making a final decision, I want you to know how interested I am in the controller's position.

You made it clear that you're looking for someone who is every bit as good a manager as he is a creative financial planner. When you combine my accomplishments in management accounting with my industry-specific background, I think you'll find that I fit your profile perfectly.

Thank you for an excellent interview and the opportunity to gain some insight into an outstanding organization. I hope we have the chance to talk again.

Very truly yours,

- Enthusiasm sells. If you feel an interview went well, let the interviewer know it. It will mark you as someone who is in tune with others' feelings (a people person).

- Take the opportunity to reiterate how your abilities mesh with the job description.

Thank You for Interview, Not Interested in Job (19-29)

Dear Mr. Feyerherm:

I want to thank you again for interviewing me for the Sales Representative position with Golden Valley Computers. It was good to learn about the nature and operations of your business.

As you explained, the person chosen for the job must be prepared to travel one week out of three. After talking it over with my wife and children, I have decided to withdraw my application from further consideration. While our kids are still in school, my wife and I feel it is important for me to work near home.

Again, Mr. Feyerherm, I appreciated the opportunity to meet with you. I wish you and Golden Valley Computers all the best as your company continues to grow.

Sincerely,

- Make it short and sincere. Express your appreciation for the interview and explain briefly why you no longer want to be a candidate for the job.
- Finish the letter with personal good wishes.

Thank You for Interview, Second Interview (19-30)

Dear Mr. Smeakins:

Thank you for the opportunity to interview with you for the position of Senior Analyst in the Finance Department. I enjoyed talking with you, and with Charles Madden the day before. I've always had great respect for IDS's innovative product line and strong support network.

The position seems challenging and interesting. The responsibilities as you detailed them are a good match with my background.

I look forward to our next interview. One last personal note-you mentioned that you were a big Yankees fan, and I told you I supported the Red Sox. I went home last night and watched your Yankees crush my Sox 10-4. I just wanted you to know that I harbor no ill feelings!

I look forward to hearing from you soon.

Sincerely,

- This is an attempt to make a more personal contact with those doing the hiring and to get them to remember you. So, while you include a thank-you, look forward to the next time, and reiterate how qualified you are, the real meat of the letter is to make a personal comment to the interviewer.

Thank You for Interview, Keep Me in Mind (19-31)

Dear Mr. Morrissey:

It was a pleasure meeting you yesterday. I enjoyed learning more about the projects your company has underway and hearing about Holloway's ambitious plans for growth.

I came away from our meeting with a strong vision of how I might be a part of that growth. My skills and background dovetail closely with your company's growing need for experienced construction managers, and I believe I possess the talent, commitment, and energy you are looking for in prospective members of the "Holloway team."

Please keep me in mind as your plans to add staff take shape. I understand it will be a few weeks before you begin to schedule interviews for specific positions, and I look forward to hearing from you then.

Thank you again for meeting with me yesterday.

Sincerely,

- Following up each interview in writing is crucial in showing you are a serious job applicant. This is your opportunity to make a more lasting impression on your interviewer, and to remind him or her of your strengths.

- Refer specifically to what you discussed and comment on what you took away from the interview.

Thank You for Interview, Even though I Didn't Get Job (19-32)

Dear Mr. Yates:

I may not have gotten the job at Griffith, but I received a terrific education. I can't thank you enough for your time, effort and interest.

Armed with the feedback from my interviews, I'll work on the areas in which you feel I'm weak...and I'll polish the strong points, too. I was so impressed with you and Griffith Industries that I hope I'll have the opportunity to reapply in the future. I plan to be prepared when I do!

Thank you. I have a feeling we'll meet again.

Sincerely,

- Always acknowledge an interview, win or lose. It marks you as someone with class and savvy.

- Let the interviewer know that you understand and appreciate the effort that they put into the meeting(s).

Acceptance of Job Offer (19-33)

Dear Ms. Coulton:

Thank you for your offer to join Proteus Partners as a staff engineer. I'm delighted to accept at the salary of $36,000 with the standard benefits package that we discussed on Thursday. I am looking forward to working with all the talented and committed people I met while interviewing, and to being associated with such a fine company and a high quality line of products.

I will call you on Friday to give you whatever information you need prior to my starting work June 1. I look forward to seeing you again soon.

Sincerely,

> - First, express appreciation for the offer and state your acceptance. If salary has been an issue, reiterate the figure you finally agreed upon.
> - Mention *why* you look forward to joining the company.
> - State exactly *when* you will call again to clear up any details.

Thank You for Job Offer, Need Time to Think (19-34)

Dear Mr. Caldwell:

I appreciate the job offer. In fact, I'm flattered that you made me your first choice out of so many candidates. But I'm going to need a few days to think about it before making a commitment. Are you willing to wait for an answer until next Monday morning?

This slight delay has nothing to do with your offer or the position; both are outstanding. But there are family matters that must first be resolved, so that if I say "yes," it will be wholeheartedly.

I hope you can wait for my decision, particularly since your organization and the responsibilities you've outlined are so attractive. Unless I hear otherwise from you, I'll call you Monday morning at 9:00 a.m. sharp.

Thanks for the opportunity.

Sincerely,

> - This letter is appropriate only if you were the pursued, rather than the pursuer.
> - Don't leave the letter open-ended. Guarantee an answer by a specific time.

Interest in Job Offer, with Questions (19-35)

Dear Mr. Ambler:

Thank you for your offer to join the Flotronics Group as a sales associate. The salary and benefits package you propose is quite attractive, and I'm sure I would find the job challenging and enjoyable.

Before I make a final decision, I would like to discuss with you further your policy for reassigning sales associates to other locations after six months. Are you free to discuss this one day next week? I will call you on Friday to make an appointment, and look forward to talking with you again soon.

Sincerely,

Interest in Job Offer, with Conditions (19-36)

Dear Mr. Heitner:

Thank you for your offer to join Archer Industries as a graphic designer. I'm sure I will find working with such a talented design team both challenging and enjoyable. Archer Industries is a company I can feel proud to work for.

The salary and benefits package you offer is quite attractive and well within the range I've been seeking. I would, however, like to make my starting date June 9 to accommodate commitments I have already made for May. I will call you on Thursday to confirm this date and make final arrangements for joining Archer Industries.

I look forward to talking with you then.

Sincerely,

Negotiation of Job Offer (19-37)

Dear Ms. Drile:

I have received your revised job offer, and I agree that the details to be worked out are not insurmountable. They do, however, require further discussion.

Since I will have the same job title and responsibilities at Kidsworks as I presently have, my motivation for this move is primarily financial. But the base salary you have offered is only slightly better than what I currently earn. The 15% performance bonus is more along the lines of what I was hoping to receive. It is important that the criteria of the performance review, upon which the bonus will be based, be established at the outset, so there is no confusion later. It must be decided what sales targets I must meet, what managerial changes and improvements you desire, etc. I can't meet your performance expectations unless I know what they are, and the more explicitly, the better.

Secondly, at my present job I have a company car. Since replacing it at my own expense dilutes the financial motivation for making this move, I would like Kidsworks to provide me with a car for my own use.

I would like to meet with you and Mr. Weiss to discuss these matters. I will call you to set a date.

Sincerely,

> • Be tough and sure of what you want, but don't be obstinate. Remember that you are going to be working with these people soon. State your counter offer, explain your motivations (if that's appropriate), and keep communications open.

Rejection of Job Offer, Accepted Another Job (19-38)

Dear Mr. Bartel:

Thank you for your offer to join Weston, Inc. as a product manager. Although the prospect of joining the Weston team was quite tempting, I've accepted an offer from Fultrex, Inc. that would allow me to stay in the Chicago area.

I appreciate the time and effort everyone at Weston took to answer my questions and make me feel welcome. My favorable impression of Weston made my decision especially difficult.

Sincerely,

> • Despite your first impulse, never brag about your new job offer or demean a company when you turn down a job offer. Give a specific, preferably neutral reason for rejecting the offer (in this case, your reluctance to relocate).
>
> • Always express appreciation for the time and effort expended by the people involved.

Rejection of Job Offer, Staying at Current Job (19-39)

Dear Mr. Dorsey:

I'm flattered that you offered me the position as account supervisor on the Greenlea Pharmaceutical account. It's a prestigious position, and probably the answer to many an adperson's prayer. At this stage in my life, however, I'm not convinced that I'm ready to make the transition from publishing to advertising.

I appreciate the time you, your staff, and your executive recruiter gave me. I can't think of a group that I'd rather work with. But the attraction of my current position pulls hard. Leaving now would make me feel as if I were turning my back on unfinished business, from the company's as well as my own viewpoint.

Thanks again for the opportunity. I wish you much continued success. I hope we cross paths again in the future.

Very truly yours,

Resignation, Changing Jobs (19-40)

Dear Ralph:

Please accept my resignation from Tweed and Sons, effective April 1.

I have recently been offered an opportunity to move into sales management at Textrex, Inc. and have decided that this position best suits my professional goals.

Leaving Tweed and Sons was not an easy decision. My four years with the company have been both personally and professionally rewarding, and I appreciate the interest you have shown in my career since I joined the company. I wish the company only the best for the future. I will always be proud to say I started my career in sales with Tweed and Sons.

Thank you again.

Best regards,

Resignation, Because of Illness (19-41)

Dear Mr. Berg:

Your patience and understanding during the past several months have meant so much to me and my family. Thanks for adjusting my schedule to accommodate my trips to the doctor.

The news from the most recent round of tests is not good. I have a form of chronic leukemia which will require intensive treatment, and months of bed rest. The prognosis for recovery is uncertain.

It's very painful for me to have to say good-bye to my friends at Deluxe Packaging, but my illness leaves me no choice but to resign, effective immediately.

Thank you, Mr. Berg, for being a wonderful supervisor. I'll keep fond memories of my thirteen happy years at Deluxe.

Sincerely,

Resignation, Spouse is Being Transferred (19-42)

Dear Ian:

It is with great regret that I have to offer my resignation. My husband has received an offer to head the division of his company that's based in Northern Maryland. He and I agree that when something this good comes along for either of us, there's little choice but to take it, even if it disrupts the other's career.

I have so much to do to prepare for the move, I'd appreciate being relieved of my duties as soon as possible. But I'm willing to stay for up to three weeks if you need me.

It's been a pleasure working for you, Ian. You're a unique individual, and your insight, intelligence, and managerial style have helped me to grow personally and professionally. I hope we stay in touch.

Best wishes, and thanks for your friendship and support.

Sincerely,

Resignation, to Be a Full-Time Mom (19-43)

Dear Gale:

The years I've spent producing commercials at Abercrombie have been rewarding and challenging. But motherhood is proving to be rewarding and challenging, too.

I miss my baby when I'm at work. I find myself losing concentration. Giving less than 100%—at work or at home—is not in my nature. So, rather than turn out work that's below my standards, I feel I have to resign. This has not been an easy decision.

Advertising will always be a great love of mine. No doubt, when I no longer have little ones at home, I'll be contacting you again, storyboards and portfolio in hand. I hope you'll welcome me back.

It's been a joy working for you and with you.

Sincerely,

Resignation, Because I'm Moving (19-44)

Dear Ellen:

I wish I could pick this company up and put it back down someplace in the Phoenix, Arizona area. Since I can't, I have no choice but to offer my resignation.

As you know, my wife's family is concentrated in Arizona. That's one reason for the move. We both feel very strongly about the kids having family around them during their formative years, and we have no family here. Another reason for moving is the positive effect the doctor tells me the heat will have on my cranky, football-scarred knees. He says I'll finally feel <u>my</u> age...not my grandfather's!

Thank you for six wonderful years. I appreciate the guidance you've provided, your faith in my ability, and the many kindnesses you extended to me and my family. I can't tell you how much I've enjoyed working for you, and for Robertson Container. It will be very difficult to leave a work environment that can't be duplicated anywhere else.

We plan to leave in 30 days, Ellen, but I could give you an extra week or so if you need the time to ease the transition. I'll do whatever will help.

Sincerely,

Resignation, Because I'm Retiring (19-45)

Dear Will:

It's reached a point where what's going on outside my office window is more important to me than what's going on inside the office. So to be fair to both of us, I'm offering my resignation.

Because my retirement is a relaxed decision for me, I can work around your schedule. I'm willing to stay on to help you train a replacement (and do whatever else you feel is necessary to ease the transition), but by early Spring, Millie and I plan to start traveling in earnest.

If I can be of future help on any special projects or collaboration, I hope you'll call. I think you'll agree that my instincts and analytical skills are as sharp as ever—only my desire to work full-time has diminished!

Thanks for everything, Will. Let's get together to work out a non-disruptive departure schedule.

Sincerely,

- If you have a high-level position, it's a courtesy to give as much time as possible to create an orderly transition.

- If you're willing to consult in the future, be sure to make the company aware of it. Don't assume they'll call unless you invite them to.

Thank You, to Ex-Boss (19-46)

Dear Harry:

When you hired me, I thought I had a lot to offer...but I didn't know how much I had to learn. Now, as I take inventory of the skills, insight and understanding I'm bringing to my new job, I realize how far you've brought me.

It's ironic that I'm thanking you for giving me so much, since I've used it as a springboard to another position. I feel somewhat guilty for leaving, but I also feel pleased to have the chance to apply your management practices and principles elsewhere.

I don't know how to repay you, Harry, except to promise that I'll continue what you started. Now I can do for others what you did for me: turn the work place into a stimulating environment...a place of challenge, opportunity and growth.

Thank you so much for helping to turn me into the businessperson I've become. I hope we stay in touch.

With great admiration,

- If someone helped you achieve your potential, be certain to acknowledge their role.

- An ex-boss can become a boss again, or a very valuable resource. Use every opportunity to cement relationships.

I Don't Want to Lose Touch, to Ex-Colleague (19-47)

Dear Mark:

So far, my new job is everything I hoped it would be. I like the pace, the no-nonsense approach to forecasting, and even the demands it makes on me. This management group asks a lot, but they give you the tools you need.

I'd like to tell you more (I know you'll get a kick out of their unique perspective on customer service), so let's get together for lunch some day soon. We worked together for so long, I don't want to lose touch. Will you call me at 555-1300? I'd like to hear from you.

Kindest regards,

- If you would like a work-related friendship to continue after your departure, say so. The person "left behind" may need reassurance.

- Indicate that you still have some interests in common.

Expressing Opinions 20

When you believe strongly in an issue, it's natural to want others to share your view. Persuasion is the art of swaying others to your vision, and persuasion requires tact and the marshalling of facts.

You may wish to express your opinion to a public official, newspaper or a hero of yours. Prepare your letter with the same care you would give a letter to a prospective employer or the object of your affection, even though you're writing to someone you may never meet. The more coherent and convincing your letter, the better its chances of making your point.

Be clear that what you're saying is your opinion (I think, I feel), if that's what it is. Or, if you're stating something as fact, be able to back it up with supporting data.

Getting it off your chest. While it might satisfy your urge to "get even" by throwing an epithet or two at someone who is irritating you, it's far more constructive to state your disapproval or disagreement reasonably and admit that there may be other viewpoints. Then you can suggest the actions you feel should be taken.

Often it helps to spread a little honey at the start of the letter to get the reader on your side, then lead into the criticism or suggested change. Remind the reader that they stand to gain something from paying attention to you. Pressure is fine; abuse isn't.

When expressing an opinion, build credibility and trust by identifying your sources (newspaper article, reference book, tv documentary, etc.) and explaining your logic.

If the idea behind your letter is to simply make a statement and "speak your peace," that's fine. But if you want a response or an action, be sure to ask for one.

Fan letters. Mark Twain once said, "I can live for two months on a good compliment." He probably echoed the feelings of most people, whether they're in the public eye or not.

It's thoughtful to offer letters of praise for outstanding work, as well as for great performances. Rock stars and athletes aren't the only ones deserving of our admiration. A teacher or mentor can be a hero, too.

There are no hard and fast rules when it comes to writing a fan letter—which is really a letter of appreciation—but your best chance of having yours read is to keep it short and simple. Any accompanying requests (e.g., photo, autograph) should be reasonable.

Recipients of fan mail will be most likely to respond to your letter if it seems well thought out and heartfelt. Obsessive, overly doting letters are considered juvenile and may even be thought of as threatening.

Letter to the Editor Requesting Correction #1 (20-01)

Dear Sir or Madam:

Would you please print a correction in your paper. On December 3, you ran a story on page two, in the metro section of the Morning Call Gazette. The headline was, "Local Woman Wins Award." You listed me, Marion Elderson, as the recipient of the award. I presented the award. The correct name of the recipient is Alma Norris.

Despite the mix-up, we're pleased that you covered our event! Thank you.

Sincerely,

- Be specific about the date the story was published, and its location in the paper.
- Describe what the story said, then what it *should* have said.

Letter to the Editor Requesting Correction #2 (20-02)

Dear Mr. James:

I am sorry to have to bring this matter to your attention, but my calls to reporter Ann-Marie Newhardt have been to no avail. The article headlined "Small Potatoes — The City Coalition's Inner-City Garden Program" gave an inaccurate account of our group's efforts to establish a community self-help program. Specifically, it is not true that administrative costs consume 55% of our budget. As you can see from the attached annual report, our administrative costs are only 22% of our budget, well within the range of similar organizations. Ms. Newhardt may have been relying on verbal information from outside sources.

We would greatly appreciate it if you would print this letter and/or a correction in your next issue. We would not want a fine program damaged by an inaccurate impression.

Sincerely,

- Write *only* if you have already tried to talk to the reporter and if the error is major. Chances are, a greater number of people will notice the inaccurate charge when the paper retracts it than did the first time around. If you are refuting information, be sure to document your position.

Letter to the Editor Regarding New Shopping Mall (20-03)

Dear Ms. Sangree:

I'm concerned about plans to build a shopping mall in the vicinity of the Boynton Middle School for two reasons:

1) A mall will hasten the demise of the economy of our Main Street shopping area.
2) Malls are magnets to young people-for all the wrong reasons. From all I've read,

teenagers use the malls as hangouts and for buying and selling drugs, as well as committing other crimes.

I have two children who are students at Boynton. Although they're responsible kids, they are not impervious to peer pressure. I hope I won't have to keep them from becoming involved in the mall "scene."

We don't need another mall. Let's try to find a more positive use for the North Street property.

Sincerely,

- State your opinion or grievance clearly.

- Have a sound basis for your position.

Letter to City Councilperson Regarding Proposed Bill (20-04)

Dear Sir:

Re: New Stadium Bill

Published reports suggest that you are planning to support a bill to construct a new baseball stadium. I'm a sports fan, Mr. Charles, but I can't see sinking $75 million into a new stadium...particularly since it would require just $3-$5 million to bring our existing stadium up to code.

We live in a city overrun with homeless people, addiction-fueled criminals, dilapidated neighborhoods, racial hostility, and, to add to the overall discomfort, cracked sidewalks and potholed streets. There's no way you can justify spending $75 million to make millionaire athletes and fat-cat corporate types more comfortable!

If you vote "yes," I'll be in the forefront of a movement to see that you're not re-elected.

Very truly yours,

- The way to stave off an unfavorable vote is to get to a politician *before* the vote. Your opinion isn't worth much after the fact.

- Nonviolent threats are effective tools for swaying votes.

Letter to Mayor Regarding Preserving Historic Buildings (20-05)

Dear Mayor Blankenship:

Baldridge House and Morris Manor represent Vermont history and tradition, but they've been allowed to fall into disrepair. If city government can find funds to "beautify" hundreds of sterile municipal offices, it should also be able to afford a few gallons of paint to spruce up a piece of our rich heritage.

You ran on a ticket of preserving values. Here's an excellent opportunity for you to make good on your pledge to uphold them. These wonderful homes represent a link with our past. I expect you to lead a fight to maintain that link.

May I know how you stand on this issue?

Very truly yours,

- Politicians need to be held accountable for their promises. Writing letters is a primary means of pressuring government officials.
- If you don't ask for an answer, you probably won't get one.

Letter to School Board President Regarding Banned Books (20-06)

Dear Dr. Larken:

From everything I've read, your attempts at diplomacy have been interpreted by a small group of zealots as a "green light" to continue their attack on freedom of thought.

History books are full of examples of how poorly appeasement works as a mediation tool. Every retreat you make emboldens and strengthens the book-burners...and confuses the fence-sitters who mistake the silence of leaders for acquiescence.

You're a respected educator, Dr. Larken, and you've got to make your position clear. You must provide leadership before the extremists succeed in purging our libraries of anything that provokes thought or dissent. I'm sure you don't want to be remembered as the person who stood by while great literature was expelled from our schools.

We must stand firm against the continual assault and erosion of our basic liberties. Once we're told what we can read, our freedom is gone. Stand up for what you believe in or step aside.

Sincerely,

- Public opinion can give a politician backbone. Speak up.
- Plant the thought of history assessing the reader negatively. That's a strong incentive to do the right thing.

Letter to Councilwoman Regarding Condo Construction (20-07)

Dear Councilwoman Luganos:

I have no quarrel with the development of a condominium complex in our area. In fact, I believe a well-built, well-run condo attracts good neighbors and has a positive impact on tax ratables.

I do, however, have one major concern: traffic flow. I've lived in condos in different parts of the country, and I've seen surrounding neighborhoods become literally choked with traffic. There's never enough thought given to access roads. Thousands of cars move through narrow residential streets that were never intended for high volume traffic.

We can avoid endangering children if we simply take a hard look at traffic patterns <u>before</u> construction is started. Will you please work with us to make sure our neighborhoods aren't harmed? If you do, we'll work with you to make the complex a reality.

Sincerely,

- A reasoned approach will earn you an audience; ranting and raving will not.
- Concern for children's safety is always taken seriously.

Letter to State Representative Regarding Local Shelter (20-08)

Dear Representative Curran:

I wish to express my support for the Adams Street Men's Shelter in downtown Wilmington. I think the state should assume some of the burden for running this shelter for homeless men. The Lutheran Church should not be the only group to tackle what is surely a municipal problem.

I'm writing because I'm sure you are getting many letters attacking the establishment of a city-run men's shelter, and I wanted you to know that not everyone agrees with that view. I am a merchant in the downtown area, and I live within a half mile of the proposed site for the shelter. I reject the argument that this shelter will increase crime in our neighborhood, or lead to the concentration of bums in our city. These people already live here. Ignoring them is not going to make them invisible. I see them every day, and I don't think we are doing enough.

At least we can provide a bowl of soup and a safe place to sleep. At least we can know that some old, crippled man isn't going to starve on our streets while we sleep, or get beaten up by some kids who think it's amusing to prey on the helpless.

I believe we, the citizens, should do more. I think we should have the Adams Street Men's Shelter, and I hope you will join me in supporting it.

Sincerely,

- Never bully, never threaten; always make a reasoned argument. Make the most persuasive case you can. Think in terms of not only persuading the public official, but also giving them something *they* can use in making your argument as your representative. Remember that personal, self-interested arguments are not very persuasive to a public official—they must appeal to a broader constituency.

Letter to Animal Protection Organization (20-09)

Dear P.E.T.A.:

As someone who cares deeply about the humane treatment of animals, I urge you to investigate unethical practices at Jefferson University Research Center in Seattle, Washington.

A reliable source tells me that unanesthetized orangutans are being maimed in head trauma experiments.

The research supervisor is Dr. Emmet Widener. Over the past three years he has received $1.6 million dollars in Federal grants for these experiments.

I'm outraged that my tax dollars are being used to torture animals. Please use your resources to stop the experiments.

Sincerely,

- State your position on the research.
- Give as many details as possible about the research. (e.g., location, type of research, project director, etc.).

Letter to TV News Director Regarding Offensive News Footage (20-10)

Dear Ms. Case:

I was appalled at the graphic footage that appeared on your noon newscast on Thursday, November 3. A public official was shown throwing himself from a window.

Thursday was a snow day and my children were home from school watching television. What they saw on the news upset them so much that they couldn't fall asleep that night.

What was gained by showing that incident to your audience? Have you no sense of responsibility to the viewing public?

I watch the news for information—not to be shocked. You've turned your newscast into a tabloid show.

I won't watch your news broadcasts again. I'm also sending a copy of this letter to your station's General Manager, as well as to the FCC.

Very truly yours,

cc: Charles Eppley, General Manager, WHY-TV

- State the time, date and specific material that offended you.
- Send a copy of your complaint to whomever you think might influence future broadcasts.

Letter of Support to President (20-11)

Dear Mr. President:

I think the media has been unfair to you. Every report I see—in print or on television—seems to paint you with a broad brush, and a negative one, at that.

Of course, nobody likes to hear bad news. But it's far better for you to tell us the truth, negative though it may be, than to invent positive news, just to placate the American people.

I'm someone who <u>approves</u> of what you're doing, and I know there are millions of others who do, as well. Don't let media "gurus" dissuade you from your "Changing Horizons" agenda. It takes courage to initiate change, but the alternative is even more frightening for our country.

To quote Franklin Delano Roosevelt:

> "The country needs, and unless I mistake its temper, the country demands bold, persistent experimentation. It is common sense to take a method and try it. If it fails, admit it frankly and try another. But above all, try something."

Keep trying, Mr. President. And good luck.

Sincerely,

- Tell the President why you think he's doing a good job.
- A quote can often put your own thoughts into more eloquent language.

Letter of Praise to Congressperson (20-12)

Dear Representative Hauser:

Your recent appearance on "Inside the Beltway" was impressive. You overwhelmed your opponent, and you did it with insight and grace. I applaud you.

Most politicians consult a pollster before taking a stand. You appear to speak from conviction, not out of concern for your ratings in the polls. That's why I want to volunteer for your next campaign.

People like you <u>can</u> make a difference. And you've convinced me that I can make a difference, too.

Thanks for being my Representative.

Sincerely,

- Tell the Congressperson what inspired you to write the letter.
- If the reader spurred you to action, say so.

Fan letter to TV Newsperson (20-13)

Dear Ms. Morgan:

You have singlehandedly debunked the myth that female anchors are airheads! You're an intelligent, articulate and incisive journalist.

Over the past few years, I've admired many of your investigative pieces. The most recent one, "Cutting Edge," was a stunning expose, expertly researched and written.

You deserve an award—no—two awards: One for excellence in broadcasting and one for advancing the credibility of female anchors everywhere. Congratulations on a job well done!

Sincerely,

- Tell the broadcaster what you admire about their performance.
- Refer to a specific accomplishment, if possible.

Letter of Praise to Company President (20-14)

Dear Ms. Mikloscik:

Bravo! I applaud your decision to establish a free, on-site day care center for DeLeon employees. You're doing your part to provide working mothers (and fathers) quality care for their children, while freeing them to concentrate on their jobs.

I'm a working mother with a child in private day care. I spend my days with one eye on the clock—wondering how my son is. His day care center is thirty minutes from my workplace and transporting him back and forth is time-consuming. Needless to say, I can't "drop in" to check on him during work hours. And the added expense of private care takes a huge chunk out of my paycheck.

I hope you will serve as a role model for other local companies. All working moms and dads deserve company-sponsored day care. Just because we have to work outside of the home, it doesn't mean we don't care about our families.

By the way, I'm sending my resume to your Human Resources Department. I 'd like to work for DeLeon Cosmetics!

Sincerely,

- Relate why you feel the actions are commendable.
- Tell the company president what prompted you to write.

Fan Letter to Author (20-15)

Dear Ms. Estes:

Your murder mystery, "The Wellspring," kept me up all night. I'm an avid reader of crime stories and can usually predict the ending. But this plot was so intricately woven that I was stunned at the outcome. What a debut for a first-time novelist!

I particularly liked the character of the mother. It's to your credit as a writer that she was diabolical yet sympathetic!

I expect to see "The Wellspring" on the New York Times bestseller list. I'm doing my part by touting it to all my friends.

I await your next "whodunit."

Kindest regards,

- Tell the author what you admire about their work.
- Express an interest in the author's other books.

Fan Letter to Rock Star (20-16)

Dear Billy:

You're a poet as well as a musician. Your latest hit, "Pack it In," combines a great sound with an important message.

I own all your CD's and have enjoyed watching you mature as an artist. You made a quantum leap from "No Go" to "Speaking My Piece," and now you've scaled new musical heights.

I'm hoping your upcoming concert tour will include a stop in Detroit. You're an electrifying live performer and I look forward to hearing the new songs in person.

Could you send me an autographed picture?

Sincerely,

- Show your familiarity with the artist's music—past and present.
- There's no guarantee that a photo request will be honored, but it doesn't hurt to ask.

Letter of Praise to Athletic Coach (20-17)

Dear Coach Chisholm:

I'd like to congratulate you on another winning season as coach of the Bradford Bears. Your patience and determination have guided a young team toward maturity. But I admire you for more than your ability to coach basketball.

Under your guardianship, many disadvantaged young men have been transformed into disciplined, productive individuals. You build character on and off the court.

That's why I love to attend games at Bradford. I'm not just watching a team beat the odds to win a game. I'm watching them beat the odds to win at life.

Thanks.

Sincerely,

- Tell the reader what you admire about them.
- If your admiration extends to characteristics beyond the call of the job, be sure to mention that.

Gift Card One-Liners 21

How many times have you stood at the florist's stand, or at the department store counter, with your mind as blank as the gift card in front of you? Minutes tick by. The clerk impatiently taps a pencil. Finally you sigh in frustration and scratch out those boring old cliches: "Good luck" and "Best Wishes."

A clever gift card message is a condensed version of a well-written letter. It presents its own set of challenges. The first, and most obvious one, is time. Coming up with the perfect one-liner in the few minutes it takes to pay for a gift or send flowers is quite different from sitting at your desk and thoughtfully composing a letter. Secondly, the one-liner has to be succinct. The essence of your message must be conveyed in one sentence.

Here is an opportunity to flex your creative writing muscles. As long as your message is appropriate to the occasion, there's no limit to the ways you can recast the standard "Happy Anniversary," "Congratulations," or "Get Well."

If the circumstances warrant congratulations or celebration, humor and originality can be just as effective as sentimentality. Or the occasion may remind you of a line from a well-known song, or a familiar quote.

Congratulations (General) One-Liner (21-01)

Dear Eve,

I knew that you could. I knew that you would. And you did!!!

Congratulations!

Love,

- Try a different approach to a standard phrase.

Congratulations on Your Engagement, One-Liner (21-02)

Dear Marva and Will,

You're truly blessed. You've found what many only dream of.

Love,

- Convey your sense of sharing in the couple's joy.

Congratulations on Your Wedding, One Liner (21-03)

Dear Eleanor and Gene,

You've spoken the vows; you're Mr. and Mrs. Now you'll discover what marital bliss is.

Warmest wishes on your marriage!

Sincerely,

- Create a message that's upbeat and supportive.

Congratulations on Your Anniversary, One Liner (21-04)

Dear Liza and Malcolm,

If it ain't broke—don't fix it!

Happy Anniversary!

Love,

- Reflect the positive aspect of a lasting marriage.

Congratulations on Birth of Your Baby, One-Liner (21-05)

Dear Lorna and Stefan,

Good things really do come in small packages! Enjoy your beautiful little bundle.

Sincerely,

- Show that you share in the wonder of the new arrival.

Congratulations on Your Graduation, One-Liner (21-06)

Dear Gretchen,

Stand back, world! Here she comes! Congratulations, Graduate.

Warm regards,

- Make it sound as if the reader is the first person ever to graduate!

Congratulations on Your New Home, One-Liner (21-07)

> Dear Ina and Hal,
>
> May your hearts and hearth glow in the warmth of your new home.
>
> Congratulations and good luck.
>
> Fondly,

- A new home symbolizes a new beginning. Convey the wish that it be a joyful one.

Happy Birthday, 16-Year-Old, One-Liner (21-08)

> Dear Andy,
>
> Congratulations. Now you can take your "show" on the road!
>
> Happy 16th birthday—and drive safely!
>
> Love,

- Acknowledge the significance of the 16th birthday. (For many teenagers it means eligibility for a driver's license.)

Happy Birthday, 50-Year-Old, One-Liner (21-09)

> Dear Wally,
>
> Once you're over the hill, it's easy sledding. Happy 50th Birthday!
>
> Love,

- Show that there are benefits to getting older.

Get Well, Illness, One-Liner (21-10)

> Dear Howard,
>
> Get well quick—it's no fun when you're sick.
>
> Best wishes,

- Make the message upbeat and humorous.

Get Well, Operation, One-Liner (21-11)

> Dear Monique,
>
> Now that your surgery's over, you're perfect!
>
> Love,

- Convey a sense of warmth, humor and optimism.

Congratulations on New Job, One-Liner (21-12)

> Dear Kathy,
>
> You've achieved success the old-fashioned way: You've earned it.
>
> Congratulations and good luck.
>
> Best regards,

- It's okay to use a familiar saying if it expresses how you feel.

Congratulations on Your Retirement, One-Liner (21-13)

> Dear Eloise,
>
> May your days be filled with all the joys which had to wait until you had the time.
>
> Affectionately,

- Acknowledge that retirement presents the opportunity for personal pleasure.

I Love You, One-Liner (21-14)

> Dear Ronnie,
>
> No special occasion. Just to show my ever-lasting love for you.
>
> Always,

- Simplicity often expresses a sentiment best.

Merry Christmas, One-Liner (21-15)

> Dear Adele and Perry,
>
> Joy at this most beautiful time of the year.
>
> Merry Christmas!
>
> Fondly,

- Express the warmth you feel at holiday time.

Introductions and References 22

Think about the occasions when you've met people for the first time. Do you remember being a little unsure of yourself? Or wishing you had said something you only thought of saying later? One of the great advantages an introductory letter has over a face-to-face first meeting is that it provides the opportunity to craft your first impression. So take your time and be sure you get it just right.

Put yourself in the reader's shoes when you write an introductory letter. The person you're writing to has never met you, but is being asked to like you, understand who you are, agree with you, hire you, or endorse you. The reader can't see your body language or the expression on your face, or hear the sound of your voice. You have to create a picture with your written words. The overall tone of your letter will determine how you are perceived.

Introductions. Consider the circumstances, then decide what tone would be most appropriate. If, for example, you're introducing yourself to the friend of a friend, the tone might be informal or even humorous. If you're a teacher writing to a parent, you'll want to sound cordial and friendly, but somewhat more formal.

If you're writing about something that may be upsetting to the reader, or if your letter of introduction contains a surprise or a shock ("I'm your biological daughter"), try to balance the effect by sounding as calm and reassuring as possible.

References. The person who writes a letter of reference is putting their good name on the line. If you're requesting a letter of reference, realize that you're asking for a significant favor. Explain why you need the reference and how important it is to you.

Even though some might deem it presumptuous, it's reasonable for you to give the writer some "direction" as to the form the reference should take. It's nonproductive to ask for a favor that can't be used because the reader missed the point of the request.

If you're the one who's writing a reference for someone, stick to what you know about the individual. Don't comment on their scholarship, character or work ethic if you've never been in a position to judge them.

We Have a Mutual Friend (22-01)

Dear Carla,

Our mutual friend, Helene Peters, suggested that I contact you.

I've recently relocated here from Chicago, where Helene and I belonged to the same fitness club. Finding the right place to work out is almost as important to me as finding the right apartment, and I could use your expert guidance.

Helene tells me that you work out almost every day. I'd like to get together with you to hear your recommendations. Perhaps I could meet you to check out your club one evening. I hope you'll telephone me at work: (813) 555-9889 or at home: (813) 555-2136.

I look forward to meeting you, and perhaps to finding a new fitness friend.

Cordially,

- Mention your mutual friend by name, and reveal something about the nature of the relationship.
- Establish that you have a common interest with the reader (e.g. fitness, music, theater, etc.).

I'm the Child You Gave Up for Adoption (22-02)

Dear Mrs. Schaum,

I hope you will be at least a little bit pleased to read this letter, which is very difficult for me to write.

After conducting several months of research I have documented proof that you are my biological mother.

I was born on November 20, 19XX at General Hospital in Baltimore, Maryland. I was adopted by Mona and John Whitman. They have been wonderful parents, but I have always longed to know the woman who gave birth to me.

I am contacting you in the hope that we can arrange a meeting. I don't intend to disrupt your life—I only want to clarify mine.

Will you please respond by letter or telephone (404-555-4763)?

Hopefully,

- Don't set the reader up by saying you expect them to be very upset about the news.
- Give reassurance that you don't want to cause distress—you only seek information.

I'm Your Biological Mother (22-03)

Dear Regina,

Please forgive me if this letter comes as a shock to you. I don't know how much your parents have told you about your origins.

I am your biological mother. You were born on January 25, 1972 at Bay Bridge Hospital in San Francisco. I was a sixteen year old unwed mother, and at the time I believed I had no choice but to surrender you for adoption. The loss has haunted me all these years, and I felt compelled to find you.

I don't want to interfere in your life—I only seek reassurance that you are all right.

Will you contact me by phone at (714) 555-3218 or by letter?

I await your reply.

With great anticipation,

- Prepare the reader for the startling news.
- Supply details that confirm the relationship (e.g. date of birth, place of birth, etc.)

I'm Your Child's Teacher (22-04)

Dear Mrs. Gorman,

You have a bright ten year old! I say that with assurance because I'm Chad's teacher. I enjoy having Chad in my class. He is an imaginative child with exceptional reading ability.

I'm writing to tell you that I welcome comments and suggestions from the parents of my students. Please don't hesitate to contact me if there's something you'd like to discuss.

Sincerely,

- Make a specific reference to the special needs or abilities of the child.
- Establish a foundation for good parent-teacher communication.

Request to Teacher for College Reference Letter (22-05)

Dear Dr. Lankenau:

The All-Girls Choir was an important part of my teen years. It wasn't just the singing that I enjoyed—I also loved the rehearsals, the travel, the concerts, and the friendships that I developed.

I owe you a debt of gratitude for teaching me so much about music and discipline.

You've been a motivating force in my life. In fact, I plan to major in voice at college next year. That's why I'm asking for one more favor.

I'm applying to Westminster College, and I need a letter of reference from a music teacher. I feel confident that a recommendation from you would earn me serious consideration by the admissions committee. Just leave the audition to me!

I want to thank you for so many things, Dr. Lankenau. Mostly for showing me that music can be much more than a pastime.

Gratefully,

- Explain why you're requesting a letter of reference from this reader (e.g., "you've been a strong motivating force," etc.)
- Share your hopes and plans for the future.

Request to Employer for Letter of Reference (22-06)

Dear Mrs. Freund:

Before we moved, I enjoyed working at your pharmacy after school and on weekends. You taught me so much about how a business operates and how to deal with people. Now that graduation is approaching, I'll be looking for full-time work.

Would you provide a letter of reference? I believe it would impress future employers to know that you trusted me to open and close the store and to handle cash transactions. Anything else positive you could mention about my work habits and enthusiasm would also be appreciated.

I'll call you next week to be sure that you're willing to write the reference. If you are, perhaps you can tell me when you'll be able to complete it, because it would be a great help during interviews.

Thanks for everything.

Sincerely,

- If you're asking for a reference from a past employer, remind them of how pleased they were with your performance.
- By gently suggesting a time deadline, you might help speed up the process.

Reference for Former Employee (22-07)

Dear Ms. Golden:

Re: Lydia Wilson-McCune

I understand that Lydia Wilson-McCune has applied for a position as a copywriter with your ad agency. I hope you'll give particular attention to her application. She has much to offer you.

Lydia was my assistant for about a year at Elkman Advertising, where I'm a creative director. During that period, she proved to be an excellent writer, and I encouraged her to pursue a career in that field. She has a flair for the offbeat and the focus to carry a project from concept through storyboard.

I think Lydia has a terrific future as a copywriter. Her husband's relocation has forced her to leave our agency. I hope you'll be able to reap the benefits of her talent.

Sincerely,

- Give some background regarding your relationship with the person being referenced.
- State your evaluation of the person's qualifications for the new job.

Reference for Friend of the Family (22-08)

Dear Mrs. Harrigan:

I'm pleased to tell you about Lillian Heath, whom I have known since she was a child. Lillian is the daughter of a close friend, and I have had the opportunity to observe her in a variety of settings.

Lillian has substantial "people" skills. I have seen her converse with senior members of government and the gardener with equal ease and charm. As she once said to me, "You don't learn anything while you're talking." I feel that her empathy with other people and her desire to learn from them may be interpreted by some as shyness, but I can assure you that there is a core strength in Lillian that any employer would find valuable.

As you already know, Lillian has done an admirable job preparing herself for life, winning honors in high school and college. Her extensive summer work with college-bound inner city youths, which she has reported to me with great enthusiasm, has given her a good sense of what it would be like to work for the Admissions Department.

In short, I heartily recommend Lillian Heath to you—for her ability to deal with people, her record of achievement, and her energetic approach to dealing with life's vagaries.

Sincerely,

- Character references, like other reference letters, should be confined to the specifics of what you actually know. Whatever you do, don't resort to artificial phrasing and exaggeration—it will prejudice your reader against the applicant.

Request for a Letter of Introduction to Country Club (22-09)

Dear Neil,

I inquired about membership in the Cherry Valley Country Club, and the executive director, Monte Parker, was very encouraging. However, he said that before membership could be considered, I must first submit a letter of introduction from a club member.

May I ask you to write a letter on my behalf? It should comment on the length and type of our relationship (e.g., we're business <u>and</u> social friends), a statement of my character, and any comments you would like to make about my family and financial status. I'm not sure you should mention how poorly I play golf! That might get me blacklisted.

If there's any problem whatsoever about doing this, please let me know. Otherwise, I'll thank you in advance. This is a great favor, and I'm very appreciative of your help.

Cordially,

- When asking for a letter of introduction or a reference of any kind, it's a good idea to suggest what you'd like the writer to say.
- Make it hard for the reader to say no. Tell them, in advance, how grateful you'd be for the favor.

Invitations *23*

Although invitations may vary as much as the occasions for which they're used, there are some features that they all must contain. If the questions below are all addressed, your invitations—formal or informal—will always be understood and acted upon:

WHO? Name of celebrant and host (if someone other than the celebrant is giving the party).

WHAT and WHY? Type of event, for example retirement dinner, anniversary brunch, or child's birthday party.

WHEN? Date and time.

WHERE? Place.

RESPONSE REQUIRED? R.S.V.P. or phone call.

Invitations to formal occasions should have traditional wording and style, but most other invitations—adult's or children's—are limited only by imagination.

Adult invitations. When you send an invitation, you're really trying to persuade someone to come to the event, so make your appeal as strong as possible. Entice the reader visually to motivate them to attend. Using stationary or card stock in attractive colors and type faces evokes a positive reaction.

Most people love parties and special occasions, but sometimes it takes a real sales pitch to bring the attendees to an event. That's especially true if there's a charge involved, as with a fundraiser or community party, for example. With these, pull out all the stops when preparing your invitation to make the reader feel they'll be missing out on something very special if they don't attend. Give the reader some details about what will make this year's class or family reunion different—and better—than others, or how they'll be able to talk directly with the candidate at a political fundraiser. That's the way to get fence-sitters to make the decision to join you at your gathering.

Make it easy for the invitee to respond to your invitation. If you enclose a response card in a self-addressed, stamped envelope with a check-off or easy to fill in reply card, your response rate will increase dramatically. A deadline for responding will also help. For smaller events, you may choose to request a telephone response.

Children's invitations. Young children are delighted to receive mail. Always send party invitations directly to the child, even if it's a three-year-old. Most parents will make it a point to give the envelopes to their children so they can see their names and react to the invitation.

For a children's party, be sure to explain the event as completely as you can—including starting and ending times, special clothing or equipment to be brought, and what food or activities may be expected. Children's invitations should contain bright, creative, playful and unusual visual and verbal messages to make them appealing.

Invitation to Birthday Party, Formal (23-01)

Jack Morton and Melissa Morton-Crowley
invite you to join them
as they honor their father
Harold Morton
on the occasion of his
60th birthday.

Reception and dinner
Saturday, the seventh of May
at 7:00 O'clock
in the Sterling Hotel
East Ballroom
7 Oak Avenue
Santa Clara, CA

R.S.V.P. (408) 555-9508 by April 18

- Be sure to mention if there will be food service.
- There should be a deadline for responding.

Invitation to Rehearsal Dinner, Formal (23-02)

Rehearsal Dinner for
Carolyn Garner and Michael Went
Hosted by
Mr. and Mrs. Bernard Went
Friday, June 13, 6:30 p.m.
The Hideaway Restaurant
South Hannibal, NY 13074

R.S.V.P.   The Wents
W. Litton Street
Cleveland, OH 44179
(216) 555-8508

- A rehearsal dinner is usually given by the groom's parents the night before the wedding.
- Traditional invitees are the wedding party (and, often, spouses). In many cases, out-of-towners (particularly, close relatives) may be invited.

Invitation to Hotel Wedding, Formal (23-03)

Allison Winters Bernbach
and
Joseph Alexander Alesio
request the pleasure of your company
at the celebration of their marriage
Saturday, the eleventh of February
nineteen hundred and ninety-eight
at six o'clock
Regency Park Hotel
San Francisco, California

R.S.V.P.   *Black tie requested*

- The phrase, "honor of your presence" can be substituted for "pleasure of your company."
- A self-addressed stamped response card usually accompanies the formal invitation.

Invitation to Church Wedding, Formal (23-04)

Mr. and Mrs. Charles Alexander
request the honor of your presence
at the marriage of their daughter
Julia Marie
to
Mr. Ward Francis Landy
Saturday, the fourth of September
Nineteen hundred and ninety-eight
at half after eleven in the morning
Our Lady of Assumption Church
20 High Avenue
Charleston, South Carolina

R.S.V.P.

- This is the standard formal wedding invitation; however some of the language may be changed. For example, the bride and groom may want to issue the invitation themselves.
- An invitation to the reception is usually presented on a separate piece of stationery.

Invitation to Wedding at Home (23-05)

Dear Uncle Mort,

Harvey and I would be so pleased if you could join us as we celebrate our marriage in the presence of a small gathering of friends and relatives.

The ceremony will be in the garden of my parents' home on Sunday, May 22, at 2:00 P.M. Harvey's uncle, Judge Wyndham, will officiate. A small reception at the house will follow immediately afterward.

We look forward to sharing our wedding day with you. Please let us know by May 12 whether or not you can come. You may telephone me at (405) 555-1140. If no one is home, please leave a message on the machine.

Love,

- Stating that only a select group of close family and friends is invited makes the reader feel their presence really matters.
- Since the wedding itself is rather informal, the R.S.V.P. can be informal, too.

Invitation to Wedding, Fourth Marriage (23-06)

Dear Amy,

You're one of the very few people I'd like to have witness my marriage to Darryl. You've been to my first three weddings, and I'd like you to see me do it right for once!

We'll be married on Sunday, April 22, in the Emerald Suite of the Providence-Carstairs Hotel, at 1:45 p.m. (directions are enclosed). Refreshments will be served.

The only gift I want is your presence (bring a guest, if you'd like). Call me at (401) 555-2603 to let me know if you can make it. Please try; it would mean a lot to me.

Love,

- By the time you've reached a fourth wedding, standard rules need not apply. Invitations can be as informal as a letter, or as formal as an engraved invitation.
- Advise if no gifts are to be given.

Invitation to Surprise Party (23-07)

Dear Barbara,

Ssshh! It's a surprise!

Shana is celebrating her fortieth birthday on March 6, and I'm having a dinner party for her that night. I'm inviting some of her closest friends. Can you join us?

I'm asking everyone to meet at my house no later than 7:00 p.m. Please park in the mall lot across the street so Shana won't suspect anything. She'll be arriving with Diane at 7:30. (She thinks the three of us are going out to dinner.)

Please let me know if you can attend by calling me at home (201) 555-6589 or at work (201) 555-3500 no later than February 28.

We're pooling our resources to buy her that microwave she keeps talking about, so if you're agreeable, please send me a check for $25 for your share.

And remember—it's a surprise!

Best,

- Emphasize the need for secrecy.
- State what is requested of the invitee (for example, parking a car out of sight or chipping in for a gift).

Invitation to Anniversary Party (23-08)

Dear Aunt Jewel and Uncle Leo,

We're celebrating our twenty-fifth wedding anniversary with a renewal of our vows on Saturday, September 5. We hope you'll be with us at 11:00 a.m. at the Cathedral of Sts. Peter and Paul, 21st Street and Kinney Boulevard. Immediately following, we'd like you to join us for a luncheon at the Springhouse Inn, directly across the street.

Please let us know by August 16th if you will be able to attend. Call us at (718) 555-4002 or write to the above address. Your presence would add special meaning to the occasion.

With love,

- Informal invitations may be handwritten and individualized for each recipient (usually reserved for small functions).
- It encourages attendance when you tell people that their presence is important to you.

Cancellation of Invitation, Formal (23-09)

Mr. and Mrs. Cary Norton
are obliged to recall their invitations
to the marriage of their daughter
Lynne Grace
to
Mr. August Sparks
as the marriage will not take place

- Though printed or engraved announcements may be sent, if time does not allow, do whatever is necessary to get the notice out—including sending handwritten notes, telephoning, or sending overnight letters.

- If illness is the cause of the recall, you may wish to say so to avoid undue speculation (e.g., due to the illness of their daughter...).

Invitation to Baby Shower (23-10)

IT'S A BABY SHOWER

For: Linda Hauser
Date: March 15
Time: 2:00 p.m.
Place: The Riley Residence
142 Stenton Lane
Arvada, CO 80002
Given by: Linda's sisters,
Megan Riley and
Marcy Parrish

Let's shower Linda with baby gifts that befit a princess-
she's having a girl!

Call Megan at (303) 555-7355 to R.S.V.P. by April 30

- Include the baby's sex if it is known (and if the parents give permission); it helps in the gift selection process.

- There are many potential additions to a modern invitation. For example, to acknowledge the parent's wishes, you may request gifts of only cloth diapers or cotton clothing.

Invitation to Christening (23-11)

A white christening gown our baby will wear
On this wonderful day when he's placed in God's care.

Christening Celebration for
Charles Edward Foster, Jr.

Date: Sunday, November 14, 1995
Time: 4:00 p.m. (refreshments and buffet)
Place: The Foster Residence
14 Melbourne Street
Reston, VA 22091

R.S.V.P. (301) 555-5798

- This is an informal invitation, which is perfectly appropriate for home-based celebrations. However, if you're planning a larger, more formal function, a more formal invitation—similar to one used for a wedding-should be considered.

Invitation to Communion (23-12)

Mr. and Mrs. Amos Jordan
cordially invite you
to share their joy
as their daughter
Mary Catherine
makes her first communion.

St. Helen's Cathedral
Ivy Lane, Stockbridge, Michigan.
Mass will be held on Saturday,
May 3, at 10:00 a.m.

Luncheon immediately following
at the Jordan residence
6 Lancelot Court,
Stockbridge, Michigan

R.S.V.P. (517) 555-5622 by September 9

- To simplify matters for out-of-towners, be sure to include directions to each locale.
- If you're planning to send printed invitations, you need to allow at least 4-6 weeks lead time prior to the mail date.

Invitation to Family Reunion (23-13)

(Page 1...)

"If a boy is a lad and he has a stepfather, is the boy a step ladder?"

Best Groaner, 19XX Reunion
Winner: Uncle Frank Weston

Were you there when Aunt Dorothy fractured her foot when she kiddingly (?) kicked Uncle Sam?

Happened during the 19XX Reunion
(Does Dorothy still have a limp?)

Did you see cousin Wendy get hit in the eye with a watermelon seed during the family seed spitting contest?

A 19XX event. (Wendy married the
emergency room intern who treated her.)

(Page 2)

IT'S FAMILY REUNION TIME AGAIN!

Do you want to risk missing out on this year's fun? Who knows what might happen next? Here's the vital information:

McLeester Family Reunion
Sunday, July 13, from 11:00 a.m.-6:00 p.m.

Olympia Lakes Amusement Center
(BBQ grills available)
Route 280
Bridgewater, NJ 08807

(Conveniently located just 1/2 mile from the Kennedy Hospital Emergency Room)

R.S.V.P. Carl McLeester (609) 555-3312 by June 20

- A corny invitation like this will remind family members of the unique quality of your family—and should encourage them to attend your upcoming reunion.

- An informal invitation can be printed on two pages, or on one folded page—like a greeting card with writing on the first and third sides.

Invitation to Barbecue (23-14)

Come to
An Old Fashioned Neighborhood Barbeque
Hot dogs, Hamburgers, Horseshoes and Beer
Bring your Appetite and your Loudest Bermuda Shorts

Four o'clock Saturday, August 5
The Bradley's
826 Piedmont Way

Call if you can't come
555-3198

- This invitation gives a lot of specifics in a lighthearted, friendly way. The reader knows who will be at the party, what will be served, what the activities will be, and what to wear.

- Clearly state what kind of response, if any, is expected.

Invitation to Informal Dinner Party (23-15)

Dear Dale and Danny,

Stan and I have decided that the only way to escape the winter doldrums is to give in to them: build a fire, mull some cider and cook up a big pot of stew. Then invite some friends over to share it all.

Will you join us for a cozy surrender to January?

Please come on Saturday, January 12 at 7:30 p.m. I'll call you this week to confirm.

Hope you can make it!

Fondly,

- In the absence of an "official" special occasion you can create one by the tone of the invitation.

- For any invitation that doesn't have an R.S.V.P., be sure to arrange for some kind of confirmation if it matters to you whether or not a guest will be accepting.

Invitation to Country Weekend (23-16)

Dear Valerie and Sean,

Frank and I are planning to be at our country house the weekend of October 20th and 21st, and we'd love to have you join us. The fall foliage is gorgeous around that time, and the drive should be spectacular. We have no special plans, but if you enjoy the outdoors, there's a great hiking trail just down the road.

Come in time for lunch on Saturday, and stay through an early supper on Sunday. Lumberville is about a two-hour drive from the city, so if you leave around 10 a.m.you should arrive just in time for our famous fajitas!

We're <u>very</u> casual (even when we go into town for dinner), so bring comfortable clothes: jeans, slacks and sweaters are fine. A jacket is a good idea, too, because the autumn nights can get chilly!

We hope you can make it. Give us a ring by Friday of this week at (215) 555-3381 to let us know. We'll give you directions then.

Warmly,

- When inviting guests for a weekend, spell out the terms of the invitation, including arrival time, departure time and which meals are to be served.
- Give a general idea of what activities to expect, and what wardrobe is appropriate.

Invitation to Awards Banquet (23-17)

Dear Janice and Mel,

John is being given a special "Award of Merit and Excellence" at his company's annual meeting, and he's invited his close friends and relatives to share in his accomplishment.

The enclosed invitation from his company gives all the details, except one: how much it would mean to both of us if you could come. You've been great friends to us, and we'd love to have you with us on this special occasion.

I hope you can make it. In addition to the presentation, it promises to be a wonderful night of dining and dancing. Send in your response, as indicated, but also, please give me a call to let me know if you're coming.

Love,

- Invitations to most awards functions are sent by the organizations but you can personalize them by adding handwritten or typed notes to special friends and relatives.
- Be sure to tell the invitee to honor the formal response request. Otherwise their place may not be held at the function.

Invitation to Retirement Dinner, Poem (23-18)

Herb needs time to read a good book,
To smell the roses, take a lingering look.
He wants to travel the U.S. of A.
To hike a trail, swim Montego Bay.
Now that he's leaving his office environment,
Join us to celebrate Herb's impending retirement.

Retirement Dinner Party for Herb Wingate
Given by his children (Gail Lister and John Wingate)

Date: Friday, August 17
Time: 6:30 p.m.
Place: The Mansion, 422 W. Smalley Pike
        Littleton, CO 80120

R.S.V.P. by August 1 (303) 555-7981 (The Lister house)

- You can set a festive mood, even before the party starts, by sending an upbeat invitation.
- Include the names of the party-givers, so guests know who is hosting the party.

Invitation to Dinner Honoring Special Guest (23-19)

Dear Jamie,

Zeke Guyer will be in town the week of April 15 to promote his new novel. He's going to steal a few hours from his hectic schedule to join us for a small dinner in his honor. I'm inviting a group of friends from his pre-bestseller days, and you're at the top of the list.

We're meeting at Tiramisu, on Abraham Street, at 7:30 p.m. on April 18. Please let me know if you can attend (and if you'll be bringing a date) by calling me at (405) 555-7595 no later than April 11.

I look forward to reminiscing with you, and I know that Zeke does too.

Warm regards,

- State the reason for the get together, and tell why the reader's presence is important.
- Indicate whether or not it's appropriate to bring a date.

Invitation to Fund-Raising Dinner (23-20)

Dear Mr. Barillo,

I'm delighted to invite you to join a select group of community leaders to spend an evening with the woman who we believe will be the next Governor of Iowa, Barbara Clark Chasen.

Representative Chasen has asked me to organize a small pre-caucus dinner party at my home on Sunday, September 18 at 6:00 p.m.

This will be a unique opportunity for you to speak directly to the candidate. Representative Chasen will spend time at each table, sharing ideas with you and other supporters—all of whom represent the heart of the Davenport community.

Please circle the 18th on your calendar to reserve the evening for cocktails, dinner and conversation with Barbara Clark Chasen. Your contribution of $1,000.00 per person will go a long way towards ensuring Representative Chasen's election as the next Governor of Iowa.

Please respond by returning the enclosed card by September 1. See you there!

Warm regards,

- Stress the importance of the fundraising event.
- Assure the reader that there will be a benefit to them in attending.

Invitation to Class Reunion (23-21)

Dear Classmate,

What do a lawyer, exotic dancer, plumber, college professor, travel agent, circus performer, accountant and funeral director all have in common? They're your classmates from Northwestern High School's 19XX graduating class...and they'll all be part of a nostalgic evening of reminiscing, dining, dancing and guessing who's who.

Here's Part I of NW's Great Reunion Evening: Match the classmate with the occupation. Send your answers along with the enclosed acceptance card and you may be the winner of a $500 savings bond (announced at the reunion)!

19XX Yearbook Job Prediction	Current Occupation
A. Selma Blank (research pharmacist)	1. Lawyer
B. Thomas Parnell (dancer)	2. Plumber
C. Hazel Butler (tennis pro)	3. Accountant
D. Don Gottschalk (engineer)	4. Exotic Dancer
E. Lisa Grauten (photographer)	5. Funeral Director
F. Richard Kuttner (politician)	6. Circus Acrobat
G. Robert Maynard (pilot)	7. Professor
H. Steven Tanner (teacher)	8. Travel Agent

There will be lots of fun on Saturday, February 23, starting with a reception at 5:30 p.m., followed by dinner and dancing at 6:30, at the Oakland Street Catering Hall (details on the enclosed information sheet). Reserve your place now. Find out who's doing what...and more!

Enthusiastically,

- Think of a reunion invitation as a sales letter, because its asking people to spend money. Give reasons to attend.

- Curiosity is a great motivator for attending a reunion.

Invitation to Child's Birthday Party at Outside Facility (23-22)

Shelly loves crafts and bright, jazzy clothes
So a T-Shirt design bash is the party she chose!

Come to Shelly O'Connor's 10th Birthday Celebration!

Saturday, August 4, 2:00-5:00 p.m.
Where: Crafty Ann's Emporium
8 Country Crossing
Morgantown, PA 19543
(party room is in the rear)

You'll receive your own pastel T-Shirt, as well as paint,
glitter, decals and sample designs, to make your own
fashion statement. Birthday cake and other party refreshments
will be served!

Say YES to an afternoon of fun and fashion
at Shelly O'Connor's 10th Birthday Party.

R.S.V.P. (215) 555-0503 by July 27

- There are many unique facilities, offering interesting activities, that now cater to kids' parties. A quick look through the Yellow Pages will help you throw a memorable party. (Try Party Planning Services or, if your child has a particular interest, look under that category.)

- Be creative with the invitation. Perhaps the facility can give you pictures and suggest wording to include.

Invitation to Child's Theme Party (23-23)

WANTED: Josh Kolchins

FOR: A birthday Bar-B-Q for Phillip Lombardi

LAST SEEN: In Miz Horne's second grade posse

Kolchins is instructed to give himself up at 2:00 p.m. on Saturday, June 10. Sheriff's deputies will be waiting at the Lombardi Ranch, 24 Winding Way, Townshend.

REWARD: Ice cream, cake, games, and a chance to win a real cowboy hat!

Ring us up at the Lombardi Ranch by June 3 to say if you'll show: 555-8865

- Don't just state the theme of the party. Elaborate on it throughout the invitation.
- Some form of R.S.V.P. is required, even for children's parties.

Invitation to Child's Halloween Party (23-24)

All goblins and all ghoulies
All monsters, spooks and crones,
On brooms or feet, come trick or treat,
We'll dine on skeleton's bones!

The date's all Hallow's evening
The Haunted House is mine;
To get a shock, come at six o'clock
And plan to shriek 'til nine!

R. S. V. P. by October 25

Bobby Ruttenberg
(212) 555-6547

- With an amusing invitation like this, the fun starts even before the party begins.
- Give the date, time and address without breaking the theme mood.

Invitation to Child's Slumber Party (23-25)

Dear Samantha,

I'm having a slumber party on November 20 and I hope you can come.

Bring your sleeping bag, your warmest P.J.'s and your cutest stuffed animal. We're taking over the recreation room for the night.

I know it's called a slumber party, but don't plan on sleeping!

Come at 7:00 p.m. We're sending out for pizza at 8:00. See you then (I hope!). Let me know by November 13 if you can come (555-4024).

Love,

- Tell the reader what to bring to the party.
- If the party begins around mealtime, state whether the invitation includes food.

Invitation to Child's Pool Party (23-26)

Dear Jason,

I'm having a pool party, and you're invited!

Bring your bathing suit, a towel and a brown bag lunch. (We'll have drinks and dessert.)

> Date: July 8, 19XX
> Time: Noon
> Address: 1 Apple Orchard Terrace
>
> R.S.V.P: (503) 555-6620 by July 5

The party is on even if it rains. We'll be all wet anyway!

Please come!

Your friend,

- Be specific about what the reader should bring to the party (e.g. towel, picnic lunch, etc.)
- Indicate whether or not there is a rain date.

Invitation for Child to Spend Weekend (23-27)

Dear Jessica,

Can you spend the weekend of May 23 at my house?

We're planning to open our pool then and I want you to be here for the first swim of the season. There's a hitch, though.

Before we can swim, we have to help my mom and dad remove the pool cover. It's a big job but it's fun, too. And the reward is that we get to swim all weekend.

We can pick you up on Friday night after dinner and bring you home Sunday afternoon. Call me at 555-6831 to let me know if you can come.

Love,

- Describe the activities planned for the weekend.
- Make arrangements for transportation.

Letters to Builders and Landlords 24

Contractors are generally honest, hardworking people who sometimes make errors because they have so many details to manage. It's best if you can establish an amiable, rather than an adversarial relationship with them from the start. If you don't ask for the impossible, if you stick with the agreed upon deadlines, materials and fees, and make some allowances for the occasional error, you should be able to maintain a fine relationship with the folks who are doing construction work for you. The same is true for most landlords—a good relationship will work to your benefit.

Builders and contractors. A home represents the largest expenditure most people will ever make. So if things go awry when you're undertaking construction or remodeling of your house, the impact can be enormous, both financially and emotionally.

Begin to protect yourself from unforeseen occurrences by getting all information and agreements in writing. If you're promised something verbally, follow up with a letter stating what was said, and asking for confirmation. Then if something does go wrong, you have a good chance of correcting the situation by using the written agreement to guide, encourage, motivate, or threaten action, if necessary.

Deadlines, materials, numbers of workers and responsibility for repairing manufacturing defects should be part of any understanding. Often, while a job is in progress, you or the contractor might think of an enhancement or two. Don't just give a verbal "go-ahead," no matter how good you feel about the work. You need to agree in writing about the specifics of the changes, including costs. Builders and contractors who are unwilling to give you what you want in writing—including references—are not worth the risk.

Landlords. Occasions arise where you need to ask for something you'd like or something that's owed to you by your landlord. Don't always make the assumption that the landlord will be unwilling to do what you want. In some cases, you can gain compliance or favors by being creative. Try to think of ammunition that will convince a landlord to work with you. Can you offer a promise to extend or renew your lease, in return for a favor? It can be of value to mention a positive as a counterpoint to a negative. And remember, the problem that's plaguing you may not be your landlord's fault.

Blame a power or phone outage on your local utility and save your displeasure with your landlord for things over which they have control.

If you know you're dealing with an irresponsible or obstinate landlord, using an assertive tone may help stir action. List the history of your past attempts at solving a problem (phone calls, meetings), including time frames and unmet deadlines. The more you have on paper, the better the chances you'll succeed if you need to seek legal redress later on.

I Need Your Guarantee in Writing (24-01)

Dear Mr. Grant:

You're receiving this letter instead of a signed agreement because the 25-year guarantee we discussed was not included in your contract. As soon as you produce the completed document, written specifically to fit this job, I'll sign and return it to you with the initial check.

I'm looking forward to getting started.

Sincerely,

- Don't get into a narrative of who said what when. Just state your concern.
- By promising a check, you're likely to get action. If that doesn't work, find another contractor.

I Need Your Price Quote Broken Out (24-02)

Dear Mr. Cwalina:

I appreciate the time and thought that went into the plans for our grounds, but I'm not sure we can afford to do everything at once. So I'd like you to resubmit your quote, breaking the pricing down as follows:

    o Regrading/installation of French drain

    o Addition of a sprinkler system (front and back)

    o Landscaping and Spring clean-up around new porch

    o Landscaping and trimming at rear property fence

We'd like to make a quick decision. To save a day or two, please fax your revised quotation to my office (207) 555-3887. Be sure to mark it to my attention.

Thanks for your patience. I'll be in touch.

Sincerely,

- Be specific as to what you want broken out, or you may frustrate yourself and the contractor.
- Often, a contractor will drop the overall price, rather than lose an element of a job.

I'd Like to Change Your Suggested Payment Schedule (24-03)

Dear Clayton:

I like everything about your proposed contract except the payment schedule. I'm reluctant to give you what amounts to 90% of the total by the time the job would be only 50% completed.

Here's what I suggest:

Upon agreement	20%	($6,000)
In two weeks	20%	($6,000)
In four weeks	20%	($6,000)
Upon completion	40%	($12,000)

If you agree, send a revised contract and I'll return it with two signatures: one on the agreement, the other on a check for $6,000.

Thanks for working with me.

Sincerely,

- Virtually any aspect of an agreement is negotiable. Don't be afraid to ask for better terms.
- The prospect of immediate cash is a strong incentive to make changes quickly.

I've Decided to Use Another Builder (24-04)

Dear Mr. Yarnall:

Thank you for giving my husband and me the opportunity to consider your proposal for the addition to our house.

Your ideas are impressive, but we've decided to hire a builder who has more experience refurbishing older homes.

However, we've recommended you for another job. An acquaintance of ours is soliciting bids for a master bedroom suite. We've given him your business card.

Good luck and thanks for your time.

Very truly yours,

- There's no need to detail the specifics of your decision.
- The offer of a referral is a friendly gesture.

You Didn't Complete the Work As Promised (24-05)

Dear Mr. Koch:

You might not think that a couple of missing shingles are of cosmic importance. But my porch roof looks lousy without them and I expect a leak any day.

I've now been waiting six weeks for you to send someone to finish what appears to be a 15-minute job. (I didn't have to wait five minutes for you to appear whenever a payment was due.) I'm frustrated, not just because you haven't completed what you contracted for, but because you haven't had the courtesy to respond to any of my calls.

I don't understand why you would jeopardize your reputation over something so small. If my roof isn't finished by the May 12th, I'll contact the Better Business Bureau and town construction officials.

Sincerely,

- Recount the reason for your disappointment or frustration.
- Make it clear that your patience has a time limit.

Your Workmanship Is Unacceptable (24-06)

Dear Mr. Arnolfini:

Every spring I see news reports about fly-by-night contractors who do lousy work—then take the money and run. It's made me a cautious consumer.

I hired you to pave my driveway because your price seemed fair and you had good references. Now I'm questioning my judgement. Only two weeks have elapsed since you completed the work, yet my driveway is cracking.

I want you to come back and do the job right.

I've left five messages on your answering machine, but you haven't returned my calls. If I don't hear from you by the end of the week I intend to report you to the Better Business Bureau, the Consumer Advisory Board and the Department of Consumer Affairs.

You can contact me at work: 555-8000, or at home: 555-0907.

Very truly yours,

- Tell the contractor why you're dissatisfied with the job and how you want it to be corrected.
- State what you intend to do if your demand isn't met.

May I Keep a Pet in My Apartment? (24-07)

Dear Ms. DeMoss:

Would you agree that Tim and I have been model tenants? The rent is always paid on time, we don't throw wild parties, we help with the upkeep of your lawn, and we're active in neighborhood affairs.

I've recited that partial list to justify asking for a favor. My sister is moving to Canada and can't take her cat with her. I'd like your permission to bring the cat here.

Melissa is a house cat. She's never been out of my sister's home, and would never leave my apartment. She's de-clawed, so she couldn't do any harm to the apartment. As you know, Tim travels quite a bit and I'd like to have a pet to keep me company when he's gone.

I'd be happy to sign a waiver against any damage. This is very important to me, and I really need you to say "yes."

Very truly yours,

- There's nothing wrong with asking for a favor in return for "good behavior."
- Explain the circumstances and the import you attach to the request.

May I Sublet My Apartment? (24-08)

Dear Mr. Maloney:

My company has offered me a one-year assignment in Saudi Arabia. This is an important opportunity for me, and I want to say "yes." But I can't afford to pay for housing there and here. So, before I say yes, I need your permission to sublet my apartment.

As you can tell from a check of my record, I'm a responsible tenant. And I'll bring you someone who will maintain an equally prompt payment schedule and good neighbor policy. Since I'll be resuming my lease when I return, I obviously want to do everything possible to be sure you're pleased with whomever replaces me.

I must let my company know by next week if I can take the Middle East job. That means I need to hear from you no later than Monday or Tuesday. I'll call for your response. Please be positive; you'll have no regrets.

Cordially,

- The best technique is to be pleasant, and hope the landlord will comply.
- Give a firm deadline for an answer.

Would You Let Me Out of My Lease Early (24-09)

Dear Mr. Herrmann:

When Nina and I leased our apartment, we hadn't planned on having children. Two-and-a-half years later, we have two!

I know we have six months remaining on our lease but, as you can imagine, we've run out of living space. And that's an understatement. We don't have a legal leg to stand on, but we're appealing to you to let us out of our lease.

While our preference would be to find a home, we'd be willing to move to a larger apartment within Pheasant Run if that would satisfy our obligation. But it's imperative that we find more spacious quarters quickly...while we still have a shred of sanity.

We're in your hands, Mr. Herrmann.

Hopefully,

- Don't make threats when you have no negotiating position.
- Most people are willing to help others in need. It's up to you to ask in a way that evokes compassion and, hopefully, cooperation.

The Snow Hasn't Been Removed (24-10)

Dear Mr. Braman:

As I look out my bedroom window at a snow-covered parking lot, it seems as if the world is at a standstill. Nothing is moving.

The problem is, that as I and hundreds of other tenants sit trapped in our apartments, we're able to watch television and see that the rest of the city is back in action. Major arteries are open, side streets are navigable, and walking doesn't seem any more perilous than usual.

Even after repeated phone calls to your office, you have not lived up to your end of the lease agreement by plowing the lot and access roads to the highway. Many of us have missed work along with much-needed income.

This isn't the first time you've been slow to respond to our needs, Mr. Braman. But I promise you that you'll be suffering along with us if this pattern of neglect continues. Perhaps a rent strike will better convey our frustration than words.

Sincerely,

- It's always helpful to point out that dissatisfaction is based on a contractual—rather than an emotional or ethical—violation.
- Threats can be effective if the recipient believes you have the power to deliver on them.

My Apartment is Overdue for a Paint Job (24-11)

Dear Sir or Madam:

According to my lease, my apartment is to be repainted every three years. But I've been here for 41 months, and I haven't been advised that your painters are planning to do the work.

Perhaps I should have contacted you earlier, instead of waiting to be notified. In any case, please accept this letter as confirmation that I want my apartment painted, as promised in our agreement. I'd appreciate it if the job could be scheduled and completed within the next 30 days.

May I hear from you next week? Please call me at my office during the day (219) 555-2000, ext. 223, or in the evening at my apartment (219) 555-0448.

Sincerely,

- Explain the issue in the first paragraph.
- There's no need to be accusatory. Just tell what you want and when you want it.

I'm Escrowing Rent Until You Do the Repair Work (24-12)

Dear Mr. Armstrong:

Because you've been so uncooperative, my attorney has directed me to place all future rent payments in an escrow account. When the water pressure problems and leaks are finally resolved, he'll be happy to discuss disbursement.

If you have any questions, please contact my attorney directly:

> John O'Hara, Esq.
> Butterfield and O'Hara
> 4200 Skyway Drive
> Rapid City, SD 55702
> (605) 555-1900

Let's get this resolved right away, shall we?

Sincerely,

- Once you've engaged an attorney's help, let them handle negotiations and interactions. Simply refer the landlord to the attorney.
- Rent escrow accounts are an acceptable method for making unreasonable people act reasonably.

I'm Frustrated By Your Unresponsiveness (24-13)

Dear Mr. Althorp:

I'm not sure which is more frustrating: my broken refrigerator or your unwillingness to deal with it.

Since I started calling you three days ago, I've had to throw out all my food, and I've done without ice. And I still have no idea when you plan to fix it and reimburse me for my losses.

Since you have an aversion to answering my calls, I'll have to take matters into my own hands. If I don't hear from you by the end of this week, I'll bring in my own repairman and subtract the cost from future rent payments. And there had better not be a complaint about the cost.

Very truly yours,

- Let the reader know what action will be taken, and when it will happen.

- Send the letter via an express service so the reader receives it in time to take action. This also gives you proof of delivery.

My Rent Will Be Late; Please Work with Me (24-14)

Dear Mr. Kimball:

I need your understanding and patience for about 30 days.

One of my freelance accounts just sent me a note (attached) advising that they're changing accounting procedures. This change-over will cause them to be approximately 30 days late with their payment.

I was expecting a substantial check from that company this month. Without it, I can't pay my rent. So will you work with me? Will you accept 50% payment this month, and let me make it up next month? This is a short-term cash crunch which will resolve itself by the end of next month.

I'll be grateful if you'd make allowances during this temporary setback.

Very truly yours,

- It's better to inform your landlord of an impending problem and to ask for help in resolving it, than to wait until it escalates into a crisis.

- Assure the landlord that the difficulty is temporary,

You Have No Right to Withhold My Security Deposit (24-15)

Dear Mr. Dreyer:

Your refusal to return my security deposit is pushing me to take legal action. I'm sure neither of us wants to incur attorneys' fees, but I don't know what else I can do to force you to return the $450 you owe me.

After four years of an excellent tenant/landlord relationship, I can't understand what has prompted this poor-faith action on your part. I followed the lease to the letter: No pets, no permanent alterations, no wallpaper. I even spackled the few nail holes I made. There was no damage of any kind; you had nothing to do to prepare the apartment for the next renter.

You won't receive any more calls or letters from me. I'll wait until November 1, and if I haven't received a check for the full $450, I'll let my attorney work it out for me. If you want to call, you can reach me during the day at (504) 555-0959.

Sincerely,

- Although appeals to reason rarely work with unreasonable people, it's worth reminding the landlord of your impeccable tenant record.

- Let the landlord know that you are willing to pursue the matter, even if it means incurring legal costs.

Letters to Professionals 25

Dealing with professionals can be intimidating for a number of reasons. Doctors, lawyers, accountants and other service professionals often speak in technical terms that may be indecipherable to laymen. In addition, some professionals have an air of self-importance or even arrogance. And finally, the circumstances under which most people have to deal with professionals are often stressful—an ailment, a law suit, a tax audit.

Professionals depend on your patronage, just as other business people do. Yet, many people are uncomfortable questioning a professional. Individuals who have no problem returning damaged goods or withholding payment for shoddy work, often lose their nerve when confronting professionals. A well written letter will hold a service professional as accountable as any other "supplier" with whom you do business.

Doctors. You might expect that physicians would be constantly vigilant, to ensure that their practices run smoothly and that their patients are pleased with the service they receive. Yet, many people say that their doctors are unaware of problems with their staff, their billing procedures or their own demeanor.

Surprisingly few people make these complaints directly to their physicians, and things are unlikely to change unless the physician is given a reason to change them. Letters that suggest potential loss of patients, reputation and billings are strong motivators.

Lawyers. Some lawyers use the skills they learned in law school to put you at a disadvantage. They can turn phrases cleverly and couch their answers to your questions in obscure or evasive terms. Don't be put off by these techniques.

Ask as many questions as you need to, until you satisfy any doubts you might have about your representation (e.g., How many of these types of cases have you undertaken? How many went to trial? What were the results? What do you consider to be your specialty?) And demand that the answers be in plain language that you can understand. If you're dissatisfied with the service you've received, let the lawyer know that you have "reasonable doubts" about them and that you plan to take your business elsewhere.

Accountants. Accounting can sometimes be as much an art as a science, and if you feel your accountant has missed the boat in guiding you, or has led you astray, you need to question them. You needn't start out by being antagonistic; just raise the issues you wish to have addressed. It's important that you have confidence in your financial advisor.

If you've ever had a dispute over fees, you understand the importance of having costs quoted in writing. Even hourly fees can be misleading if there's no estimate of the number of hours required to perform the work. If you can't get a written quote from an accountant or other professional, you might want to start looking elsewhere.

Explain Nature of My Condition (25-01)

Dear Dr. Moore:

Our conversation has left me confused and anxious. You told me that my condition was "serious." You also told me that I have "nothing to worry about." Which is it?

I need written clarification from you on the following:

       1) What is the exact nature of my condition?

       2) What is the best treatment for my condition?

       3) What is my prognosis?

Please answer my questions candidly and in language that I can understand.

Thank you.

Sincerely,

- List the questions that you would like answered.
- Request that the answers be forthright and in layman's terms.

Explain Charges on My Bill (25-02)

Dear Dr. Walker:

Could you please explain the charges on my bill dated August 19.

I visited your office on that date for a throat culture, but I've been charged $165.00. I know we're in the midst a of health-care crisis, but this is ridiculous!

I'm going to withhold payment until I receive clarification. Please review your records and have someone from your office call me with an explanation. I can be reached at the following numbers:

      Work: 555-5000
      Home: 555-7997

Thank you.

Very truly yours,

- State the reason for your inquiry.
- Say that you're withholding payment pending an explanation.

Send My Records to Another Doctor (25-03)

Dear Dr. Adamczyk:

I appreciate the time and thoroughness you've put into my examination, testing and recommendation for surgery. However, before I agree to any invasive procedure, I'd feel a lot more comfortable if I obtained a second opinion.

To help me reach that comfort level, please have a copy of my complete records sent to:

> Dr. Richard Grossman
> Hardaway Medical Center
> 48 N. Brighton Avenue/Suite 2A
> Kansas City, KS 66111

After I meet with Dr. Grossman, and he confers with you, I'll call you to discuss the next step. Thanks for your help.

Sincerely,

- Many people feel it is a slap in the primary physician's face to request a second opinion, and they avoid taking that important step. In fact, most physicians will gladly provide the name of another doctor for a second opinion, if it's requested.
- Keep your request cordial and non-confrontational.

You Kept Me Waiting Too Long in Examining Room (25-04)

Dear Dr. Telgheider:

I've been taken advantage of. I arrived at your office in pain last Thursday, with my back in spasm. I was ushered into an examining room, instructed to undress, and assured that you would be with me "in a few minutes."

I couldn't sit on the stool provided because it had no back support. I couldn't lie on the examining table because lying down was too painful. I couldn't return to the waiting room (at least it had comfortable seating) because I was undressed. I waited for you for fifty minutes. When you finally arrived you were brusque and unapologetic.

The Hippocratic oath includes "never abusing the bodies of man or woman." I feel abused, physically and mentally.

You'll need to convince me that what I experienced last week did not accurately represent the way you run your practice, or I'll never seek your services again. I hope to hear from your office.

Sincerely,

- Be descriptive about your frustration. It strengthens your position.
- Explain the consequences of the behavior that disturbed you.

Your Nurse Wasn't Supportive (25-05)

Dear Dr. Hecksher:

Your nurse, Mrs. Barnett, handled my recent phone call to your office in a callous fashion.

I called on Tuesday to learn the results of my Pap smear. Mrs. Barnett informed me the test was positive, and scheduled me for an appointment to see you. When I expressed concern about my condition, she cut me off, saying that you would discuss my situation when I came to the office.

I spent an hour fighting off panic and contemplating my great misfortune.

I called back for clarification, and a different nurse pulled my records and assured me that the this test often produces false-positive results, and that the need for a retest is not at all uncommon.

I'm still unnerved by Mrs. Barnett's insensitivity. She needs to be instructed that patients are naturally worried when they hear about medical problems, and that everything possible should be done to allay their fears.

Very truly yours,

- Describe how you were mistreated.
- Relate the emotional impact the treatment had on you (and might have on others).

Your Phone Manner Is Brusque (25-06)

Dear Dr. Lindquist:

What ever happened to the <u>care</u> in health care?

When I telephoned you last Friday for reassurance about my upcoming surgery, you were brusque to the point of rudeness. As a result, I felt foolish for expressing apprehension about my operation.

This isn't the first time your phone manner has offended me. I need to feel that my physical <u>and</u> emotional well-being are important to you. If that's asking too much, perhaps I should start looking for another doctor.

Very truly yours,

- Be candid about how the offensive behavior affected you.
- Let the reader know that they risk losing you as a patient.

Your Insensitivity Offended Me (25-07)

Dear Dr. Borler:

When my father passed away in January, I telephoned your office to inform you and your staff of his death. Your receptionist assured me that she would give you the message.

My dad was your patient for many years, and I was surprised that you never contacted me to express your condolences.

I was particularly offended, however, when your receptionist telephoned a few weeks ago to schedule a physical exam for my father. As you can imagine, the conversation left me unnerved.

I don't know whether to blame the oversight on poor interoffice communication or insensitivity, but I believe you owe me an apology.

Sincerely,

- Tell the reader why their behavior offended you.
- Request an apology.

I'm Changing Doctors (25-08)

Dear Dr. Waggoner:

While I feel you have excellent medical skills, you and your staff are so short on people skills that I've decided to change physicians.

My move is based on three factors:

1. There's no respect for my time. Every visit involves at least a one-hour wait. There has to be a way to better anticipate your time with each patient.
2. Your receptionist acts perturbed whenever anyone approaches her with a question.
3. Your medical technician is rude, and has a heavy hand. She's drawn blood from me three times and has bruised my arm severely each time. An expression of pain is met with a roll of her eyes.

I suspect you wouldn't put up with this sort of treatment from <u>your</u> personal physician (or any other professional). Unless you take some positive steps—soon—mine won't be the only such letter you receive.

Sincerely,

- A physician is selling a service. If you're not happy with the service, express dissatisfaction, just as you would with any other service provider.
- By listing your complaints, you increase the chances that your letter will be read completely.

Your Special Concern Meant a Lot to Me (25-09)

Dear Dr. O'Hara:

You've restored my faith in the medical profession. I wish that your style of doctoring was universal.

Your sensitivity and concern during my recent illness made a lasting impression on me. I'm sure it helped to speed my recovery.

"Bedside manner" seems to be a lost art among many doctors today. But you have it. And I'm very grateful.

Thankfully,

- Express your appreciation for the special care.
- Tell how you were affected by the concern that was shown.

I Didn't Like Your Attitude (25-10)

Dear Mr. Glenby:

Your attitude at our preliminary meeting yesterday only advanced the stereotype of the greedy, arrogant attorney.

Before asking even one question about the nature of my case, you stated your retainer requirements. Then you launched into a ten-minute tribute to your litigation skills. When you finally turned your attention to me, and I began (somewhat painfully) to relate my story, you interrupted me twice to take phone calls.

When I hire a service professional, I need to feel that he or she will be on my team. Since you made no attempt to reassure me that you had any interest in my case other than financial, I'll be seeking counsel elsewhere.

Very truly yours,

- Make your point at the beginning of the letter.
- Let the reader see their actions from the standpoint of the client and tell what action you plan to take.

You Weren't Available When I Needed You (25-11)

Dear Mr. Herschel:

You've lost a client.

I understood that the purpose of a retainer fee was to retain your services—that is, to purchase your attention <u>and</u> your availability.

Last week I needed to speak to you on an urgent matter concerning my company's lease. I placed several calls to your office throughout the day. Although I emphasized the critical nature of the calls, each time your secretary said you were "unreachable."

You did not return my call until <u>three</u> days later. By then, it was too late. The deadline for resolving the issue in my favor had passed.

Please return the $15,000 dollar retainer fee I recently paid you, along with all files, records and paperwork pertaining to my case by next Friday, April 23.

If I don't receive the check and documents I have requested, you and I will still have our "day in court"—but we'll be opposing one another.

Very truly yours,

- Tell the reader why they have lost you as a client.
- If you seek restitution, tell what kind, and state your intention to follow up.

You Misrepresented Yourself (25-12)

Dear Mr. Delaney:

I'm disappointed in both of us. <u>I</u> should have asked you how much experience you had in criminal law, and <u>you</u> should have told me without being asked.

It was quite a shock to find that I'm being defended on a case of criminal trespass by someone who specializes in divorce cases. You should have told me in advance that you had no experience in that area of law, and referred me to someone with a record of achievement in criminal practice.

Please accept this letter as notice of your dismissal. And don't waste your time sending an invoice. If you do, I'll make a formal complaint to the Pennsylvania Bar Association Ethics Committee.

Sincerely,

- Detail your complaint, particularly if there may be further action taken by you or the attorney.
- A "cause and effect" statement is very powerful (e.g., "If you send an invoice, I'll go to the ethics board.")

I Hired You, Not Your Paralegal (25-13)

Dear Ms. Whitman:

In the seven months you've been handling my case, I've seen you once. At that initial meeting you impressed me with your credentials and your competence. You never mentioned that all work on my behalf would be performed by a paralegal.

Since then, I have made five calls to your firm and had three follow-up meetings. In each case, I asked for you and was intercepted by your paralegal. The last time I looked, my monthly legal bills had your name as the payee, but I can't imagine why. Your paralegal fields all my questions, has apparently done all the research, and has filed motions and paperwork on my behalf.

It's obvious that my case isn't important to you. Unless you can convince me by the end of this week that I should continue to use you—not your paralegal—I will seek new counsel. I'm very disappointed in your lack of interest and follow-up.

Sincerely,

- Unless you speak up, nothing will change. If you're not being treated as you wish, it's up to you to take steps to correct the situation.
- The threat of loss of income is a powerful motivator.

You Missed a Deduction (25-14)

Dear Dennis:

As you know, I'm very involved with Kingsford Hospital, and serve as its fundraising chairperson. This unpaid position requires a tremendous amount of driving time, as I go to meetings with potential donors throughout the county.

On one of my driving trips, a fellow volunteer mentioned that he took a $1,200 mileage deduction on his tax return. As we spoke about it more, he was surprised that I had never taken advantage of this allowable. I told him my accountant had never mentioned it.

Is he right, Dennis? Have I been missing a significant deduction every year? Please check my returns and call me immediately. If there was an oversight, can we recover for previous years?

Waiting to hear from you,

- Don't jump to conclusions based on information offered by a nonprofessional. Your circumstances may be different from theirs.
- A calm, reasoned request will bring about a reasoned response. Your primary objective is to get an accurate answer.

Your Bill Seems High (25-15)

Dear Alan:

I don't understand your current invoice. It's nearly 30% higher than previous invoices, and there's no explanation attached.

I can only assume this was sent in error because we've never discussed an increase in rates or services. Will you please have your billing department issue a corrected invoice at the usual rate? As always, it will be paid promptly.

Cordially,

- Never accept an invoice for higher than the negotiated rate without asking for an explanation.
- Treat the incorrect invoice as an error. You have nothing to lose, and you might stem an increase by doing so.

Praise and Thank You's 26

In a society where time is measured in nanoseconds, and communication has been reduced to your machine talking to my machine, the value of a personally written note of thanks or praise can't be overestimated. A well-composed thank you letter is more than just an expression of gratitude. It's more than a spur-of-the-moment, easy-to-make phone call. It's written proof that civilized society is not entirely obsolete.

Praise. Whether you're praising a life saving rescue effort or a well-coordinated church bake sale, the purpose of the praise letter is to tell the reader how their actions effected a change for the better. While the objective of this type of letter is to make the reader feel appreciated, don't make the error of being excessively effusive, or you'll be perceived as insincere.

Describe what you admire about the reader's actions—be specific—and relate how those actions affected you on a personal level.

Thank you's from adults. Keeping in mind that the objective of the thank you letter is to make the reader feel appreciated, acknowledge the need or desire that the reader fulfilled. Describe the positive results of the gesture and how it affected you. Finally, if appropriate and possible, offer to reciprocate in some way.

Thank you's from children. A child's thank you letter should look and sound age-appropriate. A perceptive reader will quickly detect the "voice" of a letter from a child that has been dictated by an adult. Talk your child through the thoughts that they want to express in their thank you. Then act as a gentle guide to help the youngster write the letter in their own words.

Thank you's in business. When writing a business thank you, the degree of familiarity or formality with which you address the reader should be dictated by the closeness of your professional relationship. Refer specifically to the event or circumstance for which you're appreciative.

Thank you's to organizations. A cordial approach should be used when writing a thank you letter to an organization. Bearing in mind that the letter may wind up on the company bulletin board, make your thank you all-inclusive, so that each employee will feel appreciated. Convey your belief that the organization's good deed will have far-reaching effects.

You Make Me Proud (26-01)

Dear Mark,

As graduation nears, I want to tell you why I always knew that you would be successful. Not just in academics and sports, but in your personal relationships.

One day, when you were 8 or 9, there must have been 20 boys in our back yard playing baseball with you. As I watched from inside the house, I saw little Joe Benjamin (who was thought of as the neighborhood nerd) timidly approach you and ask if he could play.

Most of the other boys started hooting at Joe, calling him names and telling him to go home and play with dolls. As Joe choked back tears and turned to leave, you stood up to the whole crowd. I remember it as if it were yesterday. You announced that Joe was your friend, and that anyone who didn't want to play could leave.

I knew then that you would always have the courage to do the right thing...and I've never been disappointed. You've accomplished virtually every goal you've set for yourself throughout school, and I'm confident that you'll achieve equal success in the work world.

You deserve everything good that's come to you. I'm very proud of you. You've made fatherhood a joy for me.

Love,

- A description of a significant act or event is an excellent way to illustrate why someone is praiseworthy. (It gives meaning to the words, "I'm proud of you.")
- People never tire of hearing compliments, even if you think they must already know how you feel about them.

You Showed Patriotism (26-02)

Dear Joey,

When I saw you salute the flag after you received your medal, I cried.

I'm proud of you for "serving with distinction," especially since public opinion wasn't always on your side during the recent conflict. Your loyalty is heartening—even inspiring. I wish more young people felt the same passion you do.

Congratulations, Sergeant Calvo. And thank you for awakening a patriotism in me that's been dormant for too long.

I salute you.

Admiringly,

- Acknowledge the achievement or endeavor that prompted the letter.
- Give the reader a sense that their actions command respect.

You Showed Courage (26-03)

Dear Jerry,

When your mother told me how you and your friend pulled someone from a burning car, I felt weak in the knees. What a remarkable, selfless act.

While there's a part of me that wants to tell you never to put yourself in that kind of danger again, it's overruled by the part that admires your courage.

Uncle Marv and I are very proud of you. You deserve all the praise that's been coming your way.

Love,

- Recognition from family members is cherished.
- Demonstrate that you know just what the accomplishment was.

You Improved Your School Grades (26-04)

Dear Heather,

Your "new and improved" school transcript is testimony to the power of commitment. Congratulations!

You took responsibility for your academic situation and set out to improve it. You succeeded. What a giant step toward maturity.

I'm so proud of you. I look forward to celebrating your future triumphs. There are sure to be many of them.

Love,

- Acknowledge the commitment that was required to bring up the grades.
- Convey your feeling of confidence in the reader.

You Led the Team to Victory (26-05)

Dear Thad,

I'm still hoarse from cheering! Your winning touchdown was the most exciting moment I've seen in high school football. You must have jumped five feet to make the interception.

It was a thrill to see you in action. Your ability to perform under pressure is impressive and demonstrates not only your serious athletic ability, but also your nerves of steel. You're a hero to your classmates and your friends.

Congratulations on a great game!

Sincerely,

> - Compliment the reader on their specific skills.
> - Acknowledge the effort required to win the game.

You Responded Well in a Crisis (26-06)

Dear Matthew,

Your quick response when Uncle Frank began having chest pains probably saved his life.

I'm so grateful that you insisted on calling the ambulance despite Uncle Frank's protests that he was only experiencing "indigestion." Your composure and resolve (while the rest of us were barely functioning) were remarkable. You could teach a course in crisis management.

Thank you for taking charge. I don't want to think about what might have happened if you hadn't been there.

Love,

> - Let the reader know that their response affected the outcome of the crisis.
> - Make a specific reference to the action that made a difference.

You Did a Great Job Tutoring My Child (26-07)

Dear Mrs. Barry,

Robbie struts to the school bus these days, and his new confidence is thanks to you.

Prior to your tutoring sessions, Robbie was restless and unmotivated. Computer games had triumphed over good study habits, and Rob's grades reflected that. Now he's transformed, and the credit is yours.

Your work with Robbie has been a successful blend of teaching, psychology and cheerleading. Thank you for helping him to understand the subject matter, and even more importantly, thank you for helping him to feel good about himself.

Sincerely,

> - Give some background that puts the reader's contribution into perspective.
> - Describe the positive changes that have resulted from the reader's efforts.

Thank You for Taking Care of Dad (26-08)

Dear Gavin,

Thanks to the care you provided for Dad, his morale has received a boost and so has mine. We both needed some "R and R!"

Taking care of him is a full-time job. I often feel that I'm the parent and he's the child. The responsibility eventually wears me down, and that's why I appreciate your giving me a "breather."

It's great to know that I can count on you.

Sincerely,

- Express the positive results of the care.
- Praise the reader for being someone you can depend upon. This leaves the door open for future requests for assistance.

Thank You for Helping Our Family during Crisis (26-09)

Dear Trish,

It's taken me almost a week to even begin to realize how much you've done for me and my family since Tom was injured.

You've handled everything, from seeing to it that the kids were taken care of, the right people notified, our home looked after, mail and deliveries sorted, parents called and calmed, and heaven knows what else.

You've made it possible for me to concentrate on Tom's recovery and deal with doctors, nurses, rehab centers, police, lawyers, insurance agents, and dozens of other people and details. I don't know how I'll ever be able to thank you.

You're a dear friend, and I'm very, very grateful for everything you've done.

With great affection and appreciation,

- People who come through for you in a crisis should be told how much their contribution is recognized and appreciated.
- Acknowledge just what was done for you.

Thank You for Contributing in Our Name (26-10)

Dear Evelyn and Jack,

You two are special people. Although we've received so many wonderful Christmas cards and greetings, your donation to the American Cancer Society in our name really stands out as capturing the essence of the season.

Thank you for the thought. We hope you both have a particularly healthy and prosperous New Year.

Fondly,

> • Always recognize a gift/contribution/donation in writing.
>
> • Refer specifically to the cause.

Thank You for Inviting Me to Your Party (26-11)

Dear Jim,

I felt at home at your party even though you were the only person I knew. I was so comfortable, so relaxed, and had so much fun that it seemed as if I were with old friends. I thoroughly enjoyed getting to know everyone.

The food, by the way, was wonderful, too. You're a remarkable host, and I hope you'll allow me the opportunity to reciprocate soon.

Thanks again for a terrific evening.

Cordially,

> • Select something about the party to comment on (e.g., guests, food) in addition to saying "thank you."
>
> • A suggestion of reciprocity is an indication that you enjoyed yourself.

Thank You for Lending Me Your Book (26-12)

Dear Gene,

I'm usually skeptical when someone insists I see a favorite movie or read a much-acclaimed book. The reality never seems to match the expectation. But the book you lent me was an exception. It left a mark.

I had heard of Bernard Malamud, but had never read any of his books. If the rest of his works approach the standard set by The Fixer, I have a lot of catching up to do.

Thanks for insisting!

Cordially,

> • People love to have their recommendations (books, movies, restaurants, etc.) endorsed.
>
> • Don't write a book report. Just tell the lender you enjoyed it.

Thank You for Standing Up for Me (26-13)

Dear Mr. Thomson,

I never thought that supporting the rights of high school children to read books such as Tom Sawyer, The Last of the Mohicans, and Catcher in the Rye would generate such scorn and loathing.

Just when I was wondering if the self-righteous zealots who packed the school board meeting were going to tar and feather me, you joined my team. And that was all it took. Emboldened by your support, others gathered their courage. Eventually, we were able to force a withdrawal of the censorship motion.

Thank you for your willingness to stand up for a principle. I know this fight isn't over, but now we have the nucleus of a group that should be able to withstand the onslaught of the book-burners.

I'll be in touch.

Very truly yours,

- Explain why the support meant so much to you.
- Describe how the reader affected the outcome of the event.

Thank You for My Wedding (26-14)

Dear Mom and Dad,

I've attended many weddings that reflected what the parents wanted, but you let Will and me make our wedding our own. You were so supportive and helpful through the whole planning and preparation period that you made the actual event a joy for everyone.

I don't know what the wedding cost—you never let me worry about it—but I know it was a stretch. I'll never forget what you did for Bill and me, and how you helped me begin married life exactly as I'd always hoped.

With all my love and thanks,

- By writing a letter of thanks, you're giving a memento that may be saved and re-read again and again.
- Weddings are often stressful. Comments about supportiveness during this period are much appreciated.

Thank You for Offering Financial Help (26-15)

Dear Len,

Thank you for being so sensitive to our needs. It was really thoughtful of you to offer financial help, but we're confident that we can weather the storm.

Sarah's job is solid, and as long as we continue to keep a tight rein on our expenditures, we'll be fine. I plan to take part-time work until something opens up for me again. Being an eternal optimist, I know that a good job is just around the corner.

You're a great friend, Len. We appreciate your caring about us.

Fondly,

- An offer to help monetarily should not be taken lightly. Be sure the reader understands that you feel good about the intent. Don't let pride stand in your way.
- Although you do not have to give a reason for refusing a cash gift or loan, an explanation can be very reassuring to the individual making the offer.

Thank You for Repaying the Loan (26-16)

Dear Joanne,

Thanks for the final payment. From what I've heard, it sounds as if your business is back on its feet. And that makes us so happy.

Just remember: If you ever run into a cash crunch again, we expect you to come back to us for help. We may not be wealthy, but we have enough to help our favorite niece.

Let us know how things are going. Will we see you at the family reunion in San Angelo?

All our love,

- When the final payment of a loan is made, thanks are in order (from both parties).
- If the dealings were satisfactory, you might suggest that the family "safety net" will remain in place.

Thank You for Get Well Flowers (26-17)

Dear Judith,

When I awoke after surgery, I thought I was in a garden! There was a beautiful blur of pink and white next to my bed.

Now that I'm fully alert, I can appreciate the arrangement you sent even more. The sight of all those lovely tulips and roses has lifted my spirits.

I'm feeling stronger each day. Thank you so much for the thoughtful gift and encouraging words.

Fondly,

- Express how much the thoughtfulness meant to you.

- Make a specific reference to the flowers (for example, "tulips and roses" or "basket of daisies").

Thank You for Gift, to Friend (26-18)

Dear Jeff,

You're the best listener! You remembered that I said I never had enough steak knives when company came over. And you also have great taste: The Honnenger set you gave me is perfect. I can't wait to use it during my next dinner party.

Thank you for a very thoughtful gift.

Fondly,

- An enthusiastic response by the recipient of a gift pleases the giver and rewards the effort they put into the choice.

- Noting you're aware that the person paid attention to something you said adds a personal touch that's often lacking in thank you notes.

Thank You for Gift, to Relative (26-19)

Dear Aunt Anne,

It's hard to believe the magnificent crystal candlesticks you gave us have survived bombs over London, a trans-Atlantic journey to the United States, the Depression, and four generations of Babcocks!

Mark and I will keep these cherished treasures in the family, in accordance with your wishes. And we'll display them prominently in our home. They're so beautiful, we want to share them and their history with everyone.

You could not have given us a more wonderful or appreciated gift. Thank you so much.

With love and affection,

- A meaningful "thank you" is often based on relating your understanding of the gift's significance. For example, if a family heirloom is given, show your appreciation of its history by retelling the story.

- Assure the giver that their gift is important to you, and that any directives attached to the gift will be honored.

Thank You for Baby Gift (26-20)

Dear Mia,

The photo album you sent was beautiful! Where did you find it? The lovely antique lace cover just invites people to look at it.

I can't wait to start filling the album with pictures of Chelsea. Thank you for a gift that will contain wonderful memories for us.

With appreciation,

- Comment on at least one aspect of the gift.
- If possible, tell how it will be used.

Thank You for Serving on the Board (26-21)

Dear Craig:

You've been just what the doctor—or a higher authority—ordered. You've brought a business sense to the church board, and you've helped put us on a firm financial footing for the first time that Reverend Dayman and I can remember.

Because of your vision and skillful management ability, we've been able to expand many programs, the most important of which has been our day care facility. It's had the effect of attracting lots of young families first to the center, and then into the church.

I knew you'd make a contribution as a board member, but I had no idea how substantial it would be. Speaking as a friend, I hope that our growth has been as rewarding to you as it's been to me and the entire church community, and that you'll continue your leadership role for many years to come.

Thanks for everything. You're an inspiration.

Sincerely,

- One reason people do volunteer work is for the thanks they get. If you give it to those who deserve it, they'll continue to work on your behalf.
- Offer a specific example of a praiseworthy accomplishment.

Thank You for Sponsoring My Membership (26-22)

Dear Charlie,

I just completed my first round of golf as a member. I played as poorly as ever, but somehow it felt better!

Thank you for sponsoring us; being a part of Richland Hills means a lot to me and my family. Ellen and I would like to say thanks by having you and Carolyn over for dinner. I'll call you shortly to see when we can mesh schedules.

I'm pleased that our business friendship has turned into a personal one.

With heartfelt thanks,

- When someone does a good turn for you, make it a point to tell them how much it means to you.

- A major favor may warrant a tangible acknowledgement, such as a dinner invitation or a gift.

Thank You for Your Guidance (26-23)

Dear Tom,

Henry Wadsworth Longfellow said, "A single conversation across the table with a wise man is better than ten years' study of books." By that measure, I must have the equivalent of five or six Ph.D.'s.

Without your guidance, I'd still be struggling with my life, chasing after all the wrong things. With your help, I've become secure in myself and my faith. And now that I have my personal life in order, material rewards are starting to follow.

You've been more than my minister, Tom. You've been my life support system. Thanks for helping me find my way.

With deep respect,

- Mentors of any stripe usually find their reward in the helping; however, a letter of thanks may be the best affirmation of all (other than seeing your personal growth).

- The thanks becomes more meaningful when you explain how the relationship/ mentoring has changed things for you.

Thank You for Your Advice (26-24)

Dear Louis,

Sometimes a problem can be overwhelming. That's when the advice of a trusted friend is invaluable.

I was so baffled by my predicament that I didn't think there was a solution. Your wise counsel proved me wrong—what a relief!

I feel lucky to be the beneficiary of your wisdom and experience.

Thank you.

Gratefully,

> • Express your gratitude.
>
> • Indicate to the reader that the advice paid off.

Thank You for Being My Friend during Divorce (26-25)

Dear Phil,

It's been a heck of a year for me, hasn't it? I've lost my mother, been divorced from my wife, wrecked my car, switched jobs, and moved. And there are still two months to go!

The only thing I could always count on was that you'd be there for me. Whenever I needed a go-between with Doreen, you were there. When I foolishly tried to drown my sorrows in a glass of beer, you drove me home. If I needed to talk about my job, family, or the meaning of it all, you were willing to listen.

I sometimes felt that I would have needed a padded cell if it hadn't been for you. You're a great friend, and I appreciate everything you've done for me. I owe you a lot, and I won't forget it.

Gratefully,

> • Even though people help people because they want to, it's rewarding to receive a heart-felt "thank you."
>
> • Mentioning what was special to you is appreciated.

Thank You for Being My Friend during Difficult Time (26-26)

Dear Gail,

It's easy to be a friend through the good times. The real test of friendship comes during adversity.

Thank you for your unwavering support during the awful period I've just gone through. You listened without judging. You made me laugh. You dragged me to the movies!

You have my respect, my admiration, and my gratitude. When I "grow up" I want to be just like you!

Love,

> • Tell the reader why you appreciate the friendship.
>
> • Give examples of what the friend has done for you.

Thank You for Helping Me Move (26-27)

Dear Kevin,

When my other "friends" called in sick on moving day, I wanted to climb into one of the empty crates and stay there.

Then you and your buddies appeared at my door, ready to work. I was so grateful and relieved. Your hard work and enthusiasm rescued me from disaster.

I'd like to repay all of you. How about dinner at my new apartment? I'll call you this week to set a date.

Thank you, Kevin.

Gratefully,

- Express your appreciation openly.
- Suggest a way you'd like to repay the favor.

Thank You for Your College Letter of Recommendation (26-28)

Dear Ms. Shearer,

You can't imagine how thrilled I was to receive my acceptance to Northwestern University. And your letter of recommendation was a very important addition to my application.

Attending Northwestern has been my goal since sixth grade. Their drama program is outstanding, and now I'll have the opportunity to participate in it!

I don't know how to thank you enough for writing such a glowing description of me. But I'll remember you each time I take a bow in a Northwestern production.

Gratefully,

- Acknowledge the importance of the favor.
- Convey a sense of your gratitude.

Thank You for Use of Your Vacation Home (26-29)

Dear Hal,

Thanks for the most relaxing vacation I've had in years. Your house provided the perfect setting for unwinding. I spent two weeks contemplating sunlight and moonlight on the changing tides. It was blissful.

The house is ideally situated between the ocean and the bay—especially from the vantage point of the hot tub.   (But I guess you know that!)

I appreciated every amenity—from the sauna to the automatic ice-maker.

You own a piece of paradise. I'm so thankful you invited me to share it. When you see me, you'll hardly recognize the revitalized version of your "burned-out" friend.

Fondly,

- Refer to specific aspects that appealed to you.
- Express gratitude for the invitation.

Thank You for "Babysitting" Our Dogs (26-30)

Dear Arlene and Len,

I know you think we're a little (a lot?) crazy for refusing to kennel our dogs. That makes us even more appreciative that you were willing to babysit for Freckles and Choco last weekend. Without your help we couldn't have attended our nephew's graduation party.

Thanks a million. We owe you one...or two!

Your devoted friends,

- Comment on why the help was appreciated (e.g., special event).
- Make it clear that you're ready and willing to reciprocate.

Thank You for Being a Good Teacher (26-31)

Dear Miss Obermyer,

I like having you as my teacher for three reasons:

1) You always answer my questions and never make me feel stupid for asking them.
2) You read stories with a lot of expression.
3) You sent me a card when my dog died.

Thank you for being my favorite teacher. I hope you like having me in your class as much as I like being there.

Love,

- Tell the teacher exactly what you like about them. Your thoughts can inspire them to become even better at their job.

Thank You for Taking Me on Vacation (26-32)

Dear Mr. and Mrs. Shanahan,

I had such a good time at the seashore that I didn't even miss my parents! I loved swimming in the ocean every day and walking on the boardwalk at night. Rehoboth Beach is a neat place.

Thank you for taking me on vacation with you. You made me feel like a part of your family.

Gratefully,

> • Describe what you liked best about the vacation.

Thank You for Taking Me on Overnight Hike (26-33)

Dear Mr. Forgione,

The overnight hike was so much fun that now I'd like to sleep outside all summer.

I felt proud that I learned how to pitch a tent and build a campfire. But the thing I enjoyed most was telling ghost stories in the firelight!

Thank you for teaching me how to be a good camper.

Your friend,

> • Tell what you learned as well as what you enjoyed.

Thank You for Having Me while Parents Were Away (26-34)

Dear Mrs. Blackburn,

I thought I would be sad while my parents were away. Instead I was happy. You took such good care of me that the week passed quickly. I had fun too.

You make the best spaghetti I've ever tasted. And I like your parakeet, Sky.

Thank you for letting me stay with you. I hope I'll be invited again.

Love,

> • When you tell the reader exactly what you liked about staying with them, they know you put some extra thought into writing the letter.

Thank You for Gift, from Child (26-35)

Dear Aunt Georgia,

Do you have ESP? You always give me the present I'm hoping for.

I've already watched the "Snow White" video three times. I'm going to memorize all the songs and sing them to you.

Thank you for being such a good mind reader. You're a good aunt too.

Love,

- Make the reader feel that the gift is special to you by describing what you like about it.

Thank You for Doing a Great Job on the Project (26-36)

Dear Louise,

I just left Jordan Makefield's office where I received a very enthusiastic pat on the back for an exceptionally well-run manager's meeting. Mr. Makefield said it was the finest such event in the company's 17 years.

I told him that you made the difference, and that I've never before had an assistant who paid such loving attention to detail. You did us both proud, Louise. I'm very appreciative of the work you put into this project. Thank you!

Sincerely,

- Recognition is a major reward, particularly for young people who have aspirations to grow within an organization. Praise is a powerful motivator.
- Send the thank you letter as soon as possible after the good job was completed. That's when it will have the greatest impact.

Thank You for Being a Great Employee, with Bonus (26-37)

Dear Lucy,

There are times when I wonder how this department ever functioned without you. You've upgraded virtually every office function, and you've also brought a sense of professionalism and grace to what had been a tense atmosphere.

In the rush of the day, I may not always sound as appreciative as I should. So I hope the enclosed bonus check will help say it for me. Thank you for being such a positive influence in the workplace, and thank you for making it possible for all of us to do a better job.

Yours truly,

> • Taking time out to tell someone they are noticed and appreciated is both thoughtful and rewarding.
> • Tying a letter of praise to a bonus check or pay increase doubles the effect.

Thank You for Supporting My Position (26-38)

Dear Charlie,

I'd been warned that manufacturing management was conservative, but I had no idea they burned innovators at the stake. I never thought that advocating a change in procedure was heresy, but it's obvious that <u>they</u> do.

If you hadn't been at the Monday meeting, I wouldn't have stood a chance. And a procedural change that you apparently agree will save tens of thousands of dollars would never have seen the light of day.

Thanks for the support. I hope I can return the favor some day.

Sincerely,

> • You earn points in business (and elsewhere) by taking the time to thank people who are supportive. A handshake is fine, but a handwritten (or typed) note means special recognition.
> • Acknowledge that the proposal/presentation/project may not have succeeded without support.

Thank You for Helping Out When I was Sick (26-39)

Dear Cheryl,

I don't know whether to be pleased or disappointed that some people didn't even know I was out of work for a week. You did such a wonderful job filling in during my illness, everything just sailed along.

I'm not sure how you managed double duty so well, but I appreciate every minute you put into it. I'd like to express my heartfelt thanks over lunch one day next week. I'll call to see when it will be convenient for you.

Thanks for helping out in my absence.

Gratefully,

> - Tell the reader you're aware how well things went in your absence.
>
> - A tangible reward, such as lunch or dinner, is a nice way to make your "thanks" particularly meaningful.

Thank You for Recommending Me (26-40)

Dear Bert:

I got the account!

I can't imagine what you told Don Bryson about me, but he acted as if I were doing <u>him</u> a favor by showing up for the appointment. I've never made an easier sale.

I hope you know how grateful I am for the recommendation. Please be my guest for dinner next Thursday when I'm in town for a meeting. It's just a small way of saying thanks. I'll call on Monday to confirm.

This couldn't have come at a better time for me. It's tough for freelancers right now.

With much appreciation,

> - An enthusiastic response is a great reward for someone who has taken the time to make a recommendation.
>
> - If the recommendation paid off, be sure to say so.

Thank You for Allowing Me to Use You as a Reference (26-41)

Dear Mr. Tyrell:

I had an interview this morning that I felt was going very well. When the interviewer—Harry Olin, of Great American Enterprises—asked for references and I gave your name, the interview immediately progressed to the next level. Mr. Olin was very impressed that you would "stand up" for me.

I won't know until next week if I have the job, but I do know how much I appreciate your allowing me to use your name as a reference. Thank you for your help.

Sincerely,

> - Even if you can't offer an anecdote about how the use of the person's name was helpful, a simple "thank you" is mandatory.
>
> - If someone is nice enough to allow you to use their name, make it a point to offer an occasional update on your job search.

Thank You for Hospitality, to Business Associate (26-42)

Dear Charles,

I want to thank you and Charlotte for making my first business trip to the New York area a pleasant one. To be shown around by two "native New Yorkers" gave me a view of the city I would never have gotten by seeing New York on my own.

I expect to reciprocate when the sales convention is in my home town of San Francisco next fall.

Please give my best to Charlotte, and thanks again to both of you for a most pleasant two days.

Kindest regards,

- Be sure to thank both host and hostess, if it applies.

Thank You for Gift, to Business Associate (26-43)

Dear Len,

Thanks so much for the crystal book-shaped paperweight. I have admired these beautiful paperweights in the magazine ads, and I very much appreciate your thoughtfulness.

Let's have lunch soon.

Best wishes,

- Any gift should be acknowledged, in writing, as promptly as possible.
- Use your company stationery or write the note by hand on personal letterhead.

Thank You for Flowers, to Business Associate (26-44)

Dear Kit,

Thanks so much for the beautiful flower arrangement. It brightened our new office for over a week and fit in perfectly with our color scheme. We're sorry you missed the open house but hope you will stop by the next time you're in the area. You ought to see where your people are working. The coffee pot is always on.

Best,

- It's always a good idea to end a thank-you with some kind of invitation.

Thank You for the Favor, to Business Associate (26-45)

Dear Jerry:

I tried to catch you before you went on vacation, but I was too late. Thank you so much for keeping an eye out for Super Delivery while I was away last week. One of the disadvantages of a one-person outfit is the inability to be all places at once, and the checks you collected from Super Delivery were very important to me. I wouldn't have had time to chase them down.

I'll do the same for you—anytime.

Best,

- Thank people for any out-of-the-ordinary favor in person, if possible. In this particular case, writing a note is preferable to waiting until you see the person, thereby risking forgetting entirely.

Thank You for the Contribution (20-46)

Dear Ms. Lapham:

The contribution your company made to the Bobby Gallagher Memorial Fund was a godsend. First, you should be aware that it was the single largest gift we've ever received.

Second, I want you to know that the dollars have been earmarked to provide motorized wheelchairs to spinal cord injury victims.

As the administrator of the fund—and, more personally, as Bobby Gallagher's mother— I want to thank you so much for your touching and generous contribution.

With gratitude and appreciation,

- Always acknowledge a contribution of any size.
- If possible, indicate how the dollars will be spent.

Thank You for the Grant (26-47)

Dear Mr. Penney:

I don't know who first said it, but your company embodies the sentiment: "We make a living by what we receive. We make a life by what we give."

Your creation of five annual $1,000 grants to college-bound seniors will help "make a life" for many deserving students who might otherwise have had to forego a higher education. NTA's strong sense of social responsibility marks it as a company that cares about the future of our country.

On behalf of the students who will benefit from your generosity, and for the faculty and staff of St. Mary's, thank you. Please express our gratitude to everyone involved in this wonderful decision.

Sincerely,

- When you use a quote, make sure its connection to the point you're making is obvious.
- Explain the value of the grant or scholarship.

Thank You for Creating an Apprenticeship Program (26-48)

Dear Mr. Engelson:

I'm excited that you've agreed to create an apprenticeship program. I think you'll find that this arrangement will pay immediate dividends: (1) It will give many young people an opportunity to learn a trade, and (2) You'll get first crack at what will be a potential new employee pool...with each student trained the way you like.

Speaking for myself and, I think, for nearly every other student at Madison County Vo-tech, thank you. This is a real boost to our program and our future.

Very truly yours,

- Remind the company that the benefits of participation flow two ways.
- Indicate that the results of cooperation will have a widespread effect.

Thank You for Sponsoring Our Team (26-49)

Dear Mr. Marley:

Thank you for sponsoring our team in the Kahului 10-12 year-old summer baseball league.

No matter what happens on the field this summer, Pacific Hardware is in first place with 25 very happy girls and boys (and their parents and coaches!). As soon as the uniforms arrive, I'll bring my son to model one for you.

The first game is Tuesday, July 6, at 7:00 p.m. We'd consider it an honor if you'd throw out the first ball.

Thanks again for your interest and support. We appreciate your contribution to Kahului's children.

Very truly yours,

- Be sure a sponsor is made to feel involved and appreciated.
- Keep the sponsor notified of every event.

Thank You for Providing a Speaker (26-50)

Dear Mr. Guiness:

Thanks to the fascinating presentation of your telecommunications specialist, Linda Giordano, everyone who attended our dinner feels like a communications expert. We were all enthralled by her discussion of how upcoming innovations will enable us to communicate more effectively in the future.

On behalf of the Tampa Area Small Business Association, I thank you for providing us with such a stimulating speaker. Many of our members have already expressed an interest in putting Atlantis systems to work for them.

Best regards,

- Tell the reader how the audience responded to the speaker.
- Let the reader feel that their organization benefited by providing the speaker.

Requests for Information and Assistance 27

A simple request for information requires that you be brief and direct; a request for assistance requires more of an explanation. In either case, it must not seem as if you're making a demand. When your request is asking for effort or commitment on the reader's part, it should be tailored to their needs (Why should they contribute? What will be gained by participating?)

Education. When requesting information that could have a bearing on your future (student aid, scholarships, admissions, transfers), you need to do some homework. Are you sending your request to the right department? (If not, you run the risk of a delayed answer or no answer, either of which could have a negative impact.) Is there a deadline for submission? (Missing a cut-off date can have disastrous consequences.)

If you're trying to persuade an educator to do something for you, express your request in terms of the institution's goals. For example, if you want a dorm transfer, it should be because you feel it will positively affect your academic performance, not because your roommate likes country music and you prefer rock.

Organizations. When you're writing as a representative of a civic or charitable organization, don't assume the reader knows your organization and the work it performs. Whether you're asking for assistance or a contribution, answer the reader's basic question: "How will I benefit?" or "How will my contribution help someone?"

Institutions and agencies. Large companies, bureaucrats and politicians are besieged by letters, requests, suggestions and complaints every day. Although most do a good job of responding, the speed and quality of the response is largely based on the clarity of the initiating letter.

For example, if you want information about a congressperson's voting record or position on an important issue, don't offer a lengthy preamble about your feelings; just ask for the specific information. If there is data that identifies the subject of your letter, such as the name or number of a form, the name or number of a piece of legislation, or the location of the property in question, display that data prominently.

Senior citizens. Letters are links to the outside world, particularly if you have limited mobility or access. They can be effective in (1) obtaining necessary information, and (2) pressuring businesses and officials to pay attention to your specific needs.

There are record numbers of senior citizens today who can use their collective power to gain the attention and services they want and need. Focus your letter of request on a reason why a merchant, institution, or official should cater to you (e.g., gaining business, backing or votes).

Travel. Travel plans can be dramatically simplified if you state your requirements in writing, and request written recommendations and confirmations, as well. With a written record of what was said and quoted, there's little room for error. Ask for confirmation numbers, dates when information was given, and the names of people who supplied it. Then, if certain accommodations were promised in writing but weren't delivered, you'll have recourse.

Request for College Catalog and Application (27-01)

Dear Sir or Madam:

I plan to enter college as a freshman in the Fall of 19XX.

Would you please send me a catalog and an application for admission?

Thank you.

Very truly yours,

- There's no need to embroider a letter such as this. Simply ask for what you need.
- Specify when you plan to start college.

Request for College Interview (27-02)

Dear Dean Andrews:

Now that I've applied to Mount Holyoke for the Class of 19XX, I'm anxious to share my goals with you in a personal interview.

I'm planning to visit the campus in February and I'd like to schedule a meeting for any Friday in that month.

Please let me know which date is most convenient for you.

I look forward to getting acquainted with you and with Mount Holyoke.

Sincerely,

- Convey an assertive attitude.
- Allow plenty of lead-time to schedule a mutually convenient date for the interview.

Inquiry About Scholarships and Loans (27-03)

Dear Admissions Officer:

I would like to receive information on your scholarship and student loan programs.

I'm a National Honor Society junior with a special interest in drama. I'm impressed with the scope of Penn State's Theater Arts program, and hope that I will be able to participate in it.

I'm exploring ways of financing my education, and I look forward to learning what Penn State has to offer in this regard.

Yours truly,

> • Give the school some idea of your interests and achievements. There may be special scholarships available.
>
> • State when you're planning to attend college.

Request for Reinstatement after Suspension (27-04)

Dear Dean Hoechst:

I appreciate the university's decision not to press charges for breaking and entering. When we decided to take your door off its hinges and run it up the flagpole on the ROTC grounds, we thought of it as a prank, not as a criminal act.

In the light of day, I understand the implications and consequences of my actions. I deeply regret my behavior, not just because I made a fool of myself and earned a suspension, but because I displayed such poor judgment.

I apologize for the concern and consternation I caused you and the university. I hope you'll consider a reinstatement for next semester. There will be no recurrence.

Thanks for your kindness and fairness. I look forward to the opportunity of redeeming myself.

Very truly yours,

> • Don't defend indefensible actions.
>
> • By taking responsibility, you demonstrate the maturity that is required for forgiveness.

Request for Professor's Assistance (27-05)

Dear Professor Worthy:

I'm in trouble, and I need your help.

I signed up for Astronomy 101 because (a) I need three science credits to complete my degree requirements, and (b) you have a reputation for bringing science to life. It never occurred to me, however, that a background in chemistry and physics would be helpful in understanding the material. As an Art & Architectural History major, I have neither.

I'm not afraid of hard work, and I'll do whatever's necessary to catch up. But I don't even know what I don't know. Perhaps you could direct me to some resources that would be helpful, or give me the name of a graduate assistant who can tutor me. I'll do whatever it takes.

Since I already enjoy the class, imagine how much more I'd like it if I really understood what you were talking about! I'll check with you after Friday's class.

Sincerely,

- Asking for help always grabs the reader's attention.
- Be specific about the type of help you require.

Request for Dorm Transfer (27-06)

Dear Dean Williams:

Re: Request for Room Transfer

My dorm adviser has told me that no mid-semester room transfers are permitted. So I'm appealing to you to make an exception.

Doing well in college means a lot to me. It's a struggle financially. I work for my meals at the Student Union Building and tutor local high school students in math.

I hope that conveys the idea that I'm serious about my responsibilities. My roommate may be serious, too, but not in a compatible way. For example, he studies with loud music in the background; I need quiet. He doesn't mind constant interruptions from his friends; I can't handle breaks in my concentration. He doesn't seem to need sleep; I can't function without it.

Will you please authorize my transfer to another dorm, or at least to another room in this dorm? I would appreciate your help. I'll move <u>anywhere</u> to find a more compatible roommate. My dorm phone is 555-3382.

Sincerely,

- Headline the request to get the attention of the reader.
- Back up your request with factual information.

Letter to Board of Education Regarding Bad Teacher (27-07)

Dear Ms. Finegold:

How would you respond if you were in the fourth grade and your teacher just told you that the question you asked was the stupidest question she'd ever heard?

If you're anything like my son, you'd respond by withdrawing emotionally, and falling behind in your schoolwork because you'd be afraid to ask another question.

It took two months of counseling to discover why my son's attitude toward school had changed so dramatically. But the teacher (Mrs. Camilla Swilling) and the administration of the Elverson Elementary School are unwilling to discuss the issue. So that puts it squarely in your lap.

What action will you take against a teacher who demonstrates an astonishing lack of understanding and sensitivity to young children? How will you protect the 22 children in her classroom? What steps will you take to try to undo the damage she's wreaked on my son?

I'll expect an answer within the week.

Very truly yours,

- An emotional appeal is warranted in situations like this.

- Asking direct questions tells the reader you expect a response.

Would You Canvas Neighborhood for Fundraising? (27-08)

Dear Mrs. Nathanson:

One hour of your time could bring months of relief to hundreds of starving children. That's why I'm appealing to you for help.

Eight years ago I was privileged to accompany GLOBALERT officials on a world-wide fact-finding mission. The devastation and despair that I witnessed remain with me to this day.

Upon my return to the U.S., I vowed to dedicate myself to freeing the children of the world from starvation. Today I'm the regional representative for GLOBALERT.

We are making a difference, but there are so many hungry children! Will you join the fight and take a few moments to canvass your neighborhood for tax-deductible contributions?

Together we can weave a tapestry of hope that will nourish starving children into the next millenium.

Thank you.

Gratefully,

- Appeal to the reader's compassion by stating the urgency of the cause.

- Let the reader know how their help can make a difference.

Would You Offer Items for Charity Auction? (27-09)

Dear Mr. Peterson:

As a highly acclaimed author and illustrator who resides in Minneapolis, you have a high profile. You draw crowds.

As chairperson of the Hahnemann Heart Hospital charity auction, I'm hoping to draw crowds to our celebrity event on February 18 at the Four Seasons Hotel. Will you help?

Would you be willing to donate a personal item or service for sale to the highest bidder? An autographed first edition of one of your books, a tour of your studio—whatever you decide. I'm confident that any item with the name "Arvin Peterson" attached to it will set off a frenzy of bidding and generate needed revenue for the hospital.

Hahnemann Heart Hospital is the leading cardiac facility in the Great Lakes region. With help from celebrities like yourself, we can grow even stronger.

I'll call you next week to find out what you'd like to put on the auction block.

Sincerely,

- Give the reader some flexibility regarding the type of donation they might make.
- Stress the importance of the reader's participation.

Would You Serve as Honorary Chairperson for this Event? (27-10)

Dear Mr. Evergast:

Congratulations on your recent ratings triumph. I'm not surprised that "Plant World" dominates the radio airwaves. Southern California would turn brown and wilt without your daily doses of gardening advice.

The Santa Barbara Arboretum would be honored if you would act as honorary chairperson for our annual "Flora Extravaganza" to be held at the Arboretum on May 6-8. As you know, this event is Santa Barbara's pride, and it draws more than 10,000 visitors each year. The enclosed brochure should answer any questions you might have.

Although we'd love for you to be actively involved, we'd be more than grateful if you would just give us permission to use your name and photo on our program and advertising materials. We'd also like to honor you at a preview reception for media and invited guests on March 5 at 6:00 p.m. at the Arboretum.

Your name and our event seem to be a perfect match. I hope you'll honor us with your participation.

Sincerely,

- Express your regard for the reader and your reasons for making the request.
- High-profile people have busy schedules. Be candid about the amount of time the honorary role will require.

Offer to Volunteer My Services (27-11)

Dear Sir or Madam:

I'd like to offer my services as a volunteer. I'm available Tuesday or Thursday afternoons from noon to 4:00 P.M., and one Sunday afternoon per month.

I'd love to share my gift for storytelling and reading with the children on the pediatric floor. Ideally, I'd like to establish a regular weekly story hour in the children's lounge.

If you can't use my help in pediatrics, I'd be happy to deliver books and magazines to patients via the hospital mobile library.

I realize that it may not be possible to accommodate my specific requests. I ask only that I not be assigned to the Critical Care area.

I look forward to joining the Abington Memorial Hospital volunteer staff. I'll call your office in a few days to arrange an introductory meeting.

Very truly yours,

- Be specific about your availability and areas of interest.
- If you feel you would be uncomfortable working in a certain area or doing a certain task, say so.

Come to Our Neighborhood Action Meeting (27-12)

Dear Neighbor,

Would you like to see the vacant lot on Downing Street turned into a playground? And a traffic light installed at the intersection of Lawton and Park before someone is killed? Perhaps you'd sleep better if a Neighborhood Watch Team were patrolling the streets. And maybe you'd enjoy seeing trees line the sidewalks, adding beauty and shade to the area.

Too good to be true? Not if we all join forces. Not if you meet with your neighbors-on Tuesday, May 22, at 7:00 p.m.-to form an action committee. Jane Redpath, of nearby Mt. Airy Street, is going to tell us how she and her neighbors accomplished similar "miracles" in their section of town...and how we can do the same.

There really is strength in numbers. Together, we can add to the quality of life in our neighborhood. Join us for coffee and cake at my home next Tuesday (address above), and help us launch the Oak Lane Action Committee! We're going to make this neighborhood better for our families.

If you have any questions about the meeting, please feel free to call me at 555-6329. And before you put this letter away, mark your calendar! I'll see you on the 22nd.

Your neighbor,

Would You Like to Join Our Civic Organization? (27-13)

Dear Sandy and Jules,

Wouldn't it be wonderful to have musical concerts in our community, instead of having to drive 30 miles into St. Louis? And wouldn't it be terrific to have regular "issues" discussions, with speakers such as State Senator Trevor Hauseman and noted psychologist Dr. Zora Winkowski? I know how much that appeals to you. And you can help us make it happen.

As you know, I've been very active in the Allentown Civic Association, and I'm proud of many of the things we've done to improve the quality of life in the community. But to create some of the activities and events we have in mind, we need the help of committed people like yourselves.

I'm extending a personal invitation to you. Will you join us for a "get to know you" meeting on Wednesday, March 12, at 7:00 p.m., at my home? You'll have the chance to meet many of your neighbors, to hear the plans we've made to upgrade the cultural life of our community...and to learn the role you can play in helping us do it.

It would be great if you could join us. And I think you'd enjoy being a part of the group. I'll call to confirm your attendance.

Sincerely,

Would You Speak at Our Meeting? (27-14)

Dear Ms. Markey:

I was impressed with the recent article in the <u>Lincoln Times</u> describing your work with victims of sexual abuse. The article illustrated how compassion and experience combine to ease the trauma of rape victims as they pass through your emergency room.

I've just been named Director of the newly established Crime Victims Center. We're a support group, counseling service, and follow-up facility for victims of sexual abuse.

Our volunteer counselors and staff would benefit enormously from your experience and expertise. Would you be available to speak at our monthly meeting on Thursday, May 13 at 7:00 p.m. at the Center? We'd like to allow about an hour and a half for your remarks and follow-up questions.

Our goal at the Crime Victims Center is to restore dignity and self-respect to victims of sexual abuse. We would greatly appreciate your participation.

I'll call you next week to see if you'll be available on May 13.

Sincerely,

- Give the reader an idea of who the audience will be.
- Be specific about time, date, location, topic and length of speech.

Resignation from Organization (27-15)

Dear Winifred:

Five years ago, you conceived a plan for an arts education program to enrich the lives of school children all over the Cleveland area. Today the Institute for Arts Enrichment has reached tens of thousands of youngsters—and is still growing. You have my respect and admiration. As one of the original board members, I'm proud to have played a role in launching such a worthwhile project.

Now that the Institute has "grown up," I feel it's time for me to step aside as Secretary. You need fresh energy and new ideas, and I've become distracted by other commitments.

Please accept my resignation as Secretary and board member effective the date of our next board meeting. Also, please accept my gratitude. It was a privilege to work with you.

Very truly yours,

- Praising the work of the organization should help offset any antagonism that your resignation might cause.
- Be sure to state the date when your resignation becomes effective.

Request for Copy of Annual Report (27-16)

Dear Sir or Madam:

Please send a copy of your current annual report and any other information that may help me evaluate your company for future stock purchases.

Sincerely,

- Most public corporations will gladly honor a request for financial data.

- If you ask only for the annual report, that's what you'll get. An expanded request may deliver additional information that will help you determine the character and investment potential of a company.

Request to Charity for Position on Issue (27-17)

Dear Mr. Driscoll:

I received a solicitation, under your name, for a contribution to help fund an expansion of your facility.

Before I consider writing a check, I need to know your position on animal rights in research. In other words, (1) do you use animals and, if so, (2) how are their rights protected, and (3) what sorts of experiments are routinely conducted?

My support is based on your answer.

Very truly yours,

- Ask for whatever information you desire. There is no reason to hide your motive.

- If an action of yours depends upon the response, say so.

Request to Senator for Position on Bill (27-18)

Dear Senator Richter:

I read in the March 15 issue of <u>Time Magazine</u> that you are sponsoring a bill to freeze immigration into the United States. If enacted, such a law would affect members of my family who are hoping to come to this country and ultimately to become citizens.

Would you please send me a copy of the bill and tell me your justification for proposing it?

Very truly yours,

- If you know which congressperson is sponsoring the bill, write directly to them.

- Identify the bill as specifically as you can. (If you know the number of the bill, include it.)

Request to Consumer Product Safety Commission (27-19)

Dear Sir or Madam:

Has there been a recall on the "Babykins" doll manufactured by Tidy Tot? I saw part of a news story about it on TV last night and I am concerned.

To avoid risk, I've taken the doll away from my two-year-old. However, her refusal to eat or sleep without it is upsetting the household. If the doll is safe, I want to return it to my daughter as soon as possible.

Please rush whatever information you have about the "Babykins" doll. I'd appreciate being added to your mailing list so I can receive information on hazardous toys.

Thank you,

- To avoid unnecessary confusion and delay, make sure you send your inquiry to the appropriate government agency.

- Save yourself from having to write another letter like this by asking to be on the mailing list.

Request to Pharmaceutical Company about Drug (27-20)

Dear Sir or Madam:

Re: Benzodiazepine

I read an article that listed you as one of the manufacturers of an anti-insomnia drug known as benzodiazepine. I'm planning to visit a physician for treatment of insomnia, and I'd like to discuss this very promising drug with him.

Please send whatever literature is available, including data on potential side effects, non-compatible medicines, food or beverages to avoid, etc. Thanks for your prompt attention.

Sincerely,

- You may be bringing your physician information that is new to them.

- Highlight the name of the product you're inquiring about to help the reader to assist you more quickly.

Letter to Tax Assessor about Real Estate Tax (27-21)

Dear Sir or Madam:

Re: Lot 515, Baldwin Hill

After checking on the assessment of neighbors' homes which are comparable to mine, it's apparent that the township has erred in its assessment of my property.

For example, the neighbor to my left (a corner lot) was assessed at $3,211—nearly $900 less than my assessment. The neighbor to the right was assessed at $3,062—more than $1,000 less than mine.

We should be able to work this out without going through the formal appeals process.

My guess is that a clerk made a calculation error, or the assessor made a series of mistakes in identifying improvements.

Would you please review my records, then call me at 555-8374. I'd like to resolve this promptly.

Sincerely,

- Demonstrate that you've done your homework, in this case "comparison shopping."

- Offer some reasons as to how the error could have been made, and ask for a review.

Letter to Police Chief Requesting Neighborhood Patrol (27-22)

Dear Chief Lebeau:

During the past few weeks, our neighborhood has been repeatedly awakened in the early morning hours by the sounds of blaring rock music, crashing beer bottles, and screamed obscenities. A far more serious problem has accompanied these incidents: There's been a dramatic increase in vandalism. Garages have been spray-painted with graffiti, shrubs and flowers have been uprooted, and windows have been broken.

We need a more visible police presence. None of the incidents occurred during neighborhood watch patrols, so it seems reasonable to assume we can eliminate the problem if it's known that police are patrolling the neighborhood.

If you need more specific information, call me at 555-3920. I'll be more than happy to cooperate in any way. Thanks for your help.

Sincerely,

- Don't assume that other people are reporting a problem so you don't have to. Besides, the more pressure there is to perform, the better the results.

- Explain the incidents that led to your request.

Letter to School Board about Late School Bus (27-23)

Dear Mr. Whalen:

You've constantly reminded the community to have our children ready to board when the school bus arrives each morning. I'd like to make a similarly reasonable request: Please have the bus arrive on schedule.

It's wrong to make the kids wait 20-30 minutes beyond their scheduled pick-up times. They get rambunctious, they run over people's lawns, they dart into the street, and they're taught that there's no need to be prompt.

Speaking for the parents whose children take bus #39 each day, I'd like your assurance that the bus will show up on time...or that the schedule will reflect a more realistic arrival time. You can write to the address above, or call me at 555-4391.

Don't you agree that for the children's well-being this should be resolved as quickly as possible? I'll expect an answer by Friday, February 2.

Sincerely,

- Let the reader know that a "contract" is a two-way street.
- Don't make your complaint personal; the children are the issue.

Letter to Town Sanitarian about Septic System (27-24)

Dear Ms. Tartaglione:

Six weeks have passed since I reported that sewage smells were leaking from the town's septic tanks, 300 feet behind my home. While there's been a flurry of activity since then, the odor has become more oppressive.

Although you've assured me that the gas is non-toxic, you haven't supplied any test results or scientific data. I'm not willing to wait any longer.

Since I'm being treated as a bother, rather than as a taxpayer, I'm turning this problem over to my attorney. She'll be in touch.

With concern,

cc: Mayor Eldon Briggs

- When dealing with an unresponsive or incapable municipal department, create a written record. Always follow up phone conversations with letters. They have more legal weight.
- Send copies of the correspondence to higher local, county and state officials.

Letter to Zoning Commission Requesting Variance (27-25)

Dear Sir or Madam:

Re: Variance Request
Lot 515A, Block 23

The enclosed plans for a building addition fall well within the township's structural requirements. Although the positioning of the "mother-in-law suite" brings it one foot closer to my neighbor's property line than township regulations currently allow, my neighbor has no objection to the construction (copy of letter enclosed).

I think you'll agree that the structure is consistent with the architecture that's prevalent in the neighborhood. And the builder, DeMartini Brothers, has a well-deserved reputation for excellence. I'm assured that the suite will appear to have always been a part of our house.

Since the only person even remotely affected by this request has approved the variance, I trust you will, too. If there is no need for a hearing, please send the necessary work permits to me in the enclosed self-addressed, postage-paid reply envelope.

Sincerely,

- If you don't ask for something, you'll never get it. There are always exceptions to rules.
- Document your requests to save time and energy.

Letter to Jury Selection Board Requesting Postponement (27-26)

Dear Sir or Madam:

While I believe that jury duty is a solemn responsibility, I respectfully request that my selection be deferred to a later date.

During the dates in question, I will be in the middle of intense labor negotiations that will affect the well-being of hundreds of employees. I've put months of preparation into these upcoming meetings, and it would be impossible for my union to replace me at this point.

I would be more than happy to fulfill my obligations to the community at a later date. But it would cause an extreme hardship to many people if I had to serve at this time.

Thank you for your consideration.

Respectfully,

- Use a respectful tone, and indicate your belief in the system.
- Explain the specific circumstance that you feel should cause the board to reschedule you.

Provide Seats in the Waiting Area of Your Restaurant (27-27)

Dear Mr. White:

Because you combine fine food with moderate pricing, you enjoy the patronage of many of the area's senior citizens. In fact, I can't remember ever coming for dinner when there wasn't a wait for a table. However, you're losing customers because there's no seating in the waiting area.

It's tough enough to get up the stairs to your entrance. Standing during a 20- to 30-minute wait once we get there is more than many of us can handle. If you would simply place a few benches in the entryway, you'd be (1) telling your regular customers that you appreciate and respect them, and (2) increasing your business because most of your lost diners would return. Favorable word of mouth would generate new customers, as well.

A little bit of TLC with seniors, Mr. White, will pay off in a big way. May I have a response?

Sincerely,

- A good suggestion letter benefits the sender and the receiver.
- By asking for a response, the reader knows you are expecting action.

Provide Home Delivery for Your Customers (27-28)

Dear Mr. Sherman:

Do you know why my daughter buys my various pharmaceuticals in her neighborhood and brings them to me on weekends? Because I have no way of getting them myself. You're only a half-mile from my apartment, but I can't drive (bad eyesight), can't walk that far (arthritis), and you don't deliver.

If you multiply my circumstances by that of only 100 senior citizens in the area (and there are a lot more than that!), my guess is that you're losing at least $5,000-$10,000 in business each month. Seniors buy lots of pills! Since it would probably cost you no more than $600-$800 a month for a part-time deliveryperson, it seems to me that you're cheating yourself out of a lot of business.

The minute you offer a delivery service—even if there's a small charge—I'll start to use your drug store. You'll dramatically increase your revenues, and I'll give my daughter a break. That would help everybody!

Sincerely,

- Telling your personal problems can help to make a strong case.
- Money talks! Use increased income as an incentive.

Request to Bus Company for Senior Discount Information (27-29)

To Whom It May Concern:

I'd like to take advantage of your senior citizens fare discount. Would you please send me information describing:

Hours the fare is in effect
Routes covered
Discounted fare

How fare is paid (e.g., cash when I ride, or do I need to
obtain tokens in advance?)
Identification required.

I appreciate your help.

Sincerely,

- Don't miss out on an age "perk" simply because you're not sure of cost, procedure, availability, etc. Most organizations have literature readily available to answer all your questions.

- State exactly what information you need.

Disputing Payment, to Medicare (27-30)

Dear Sir or Madam:

Re: Claim# 10239A53

I recently had cataract surgery, and was given dark glasses to wear for a period of time after the surgery. According to my physician, Medicare is supposed to pay for the glasses, as well as the surgery. However, payment for the glasses has been denied, apparently in error.

Would you please recheck your paperwork? I'm certain the glasses are covered, and I'd like your confirmation that the bill has been paid.

Sincerely,

- When questioning a claim, put the claim number in a prominent place.

- Ask that a confirmation of payment be sent to you.

Notification to Social Security Administration of Death of Spouse (27-31)

To Whom It May Concern:

Re: SS# 157-62-7002

My husband, Ronald Morley, passed away on March 22, 19XX, at the age of 68. A copy of the death certificate has been forwarded to you by the Smith-Hardy Funeral Home.

Would you please send a copy of your publication, <u>Survivors</u> (05-10084), to help me understand death benefits and procedures? Thank you for your help.

Sincerely,

- Normally, funeral directors forward copies of death certificates to their local SSA office. However, you should check with the funeral parlor to be sure.

- Include the deceased's social security number, as well as your own, to make it easier for SSA personnel to help you.

Request to Social Security Administration for Benefits Report (27-32)

To Whom It May Concern:

Please send me a copy of <u>Request for Earnings and Benefit Estimate Statement</u> at the address listed above.

Sincerely,

- In response to this letter, the SSA will send a form for you to complete that will help them project your retirement benefits. The entire process will take about six weeks.

- Don't clutter the letter with information about your retirement. It's a waste of your time and can distract from your request.

Request to Travel Agency for Estimate of Travel Costs (27-33)

Dear Mr. Davis:

After spending many enjoyable hours reading through the literature you provided about Las Vegas, we've decided on the trip we'd like to take. Here are the pertinent details:

1. Two adults.
2. 10 days, including travel time, from Saturday, June 12, through Monday, June 21.
3. Add a side trip to the Grand Canyon. Does it make sense to spend four days in Las Vegas, three in the Grand Canyon area (we'll need a mid-size rental car), and then three more in Vegas? I assume it's less expensive to fly home from Las Vegas?
4. Fly coach.
5. Stay in first-class hotels (we prefer a king or queen-size bed).

If you need any other information, call me during the day at (803) 555-7799, or in the evening at (803) 555-0247. Once you've determined available dates and costs, please give me a call and we'll meet to finalize our vacation schedule. Thanks so much for your help.

Cordially,

Request for Confirmation of Travel Costs (27-34)

Dear Jules:

We're inches away from giving you a deposit on the Italy-Switzerland-France tour you've recommended. But we can afford this trip only if we aren't hit with a lot of extras. So help us be certain there are NO surprises.

We need answers to the following questions. Does the price you gave us ($2,221 each) include:

	Yes	No	Add Extra $$$
All air and ground fares	___	___	$_____
All hotel rooms	___	___	$_____
All meals	___	___	$_____
All taxes/tips	___	___	$_____
All tour guides/attractions	___	___	$_____
Anything else	___	___	$_____

We need to work from a set budget, and we need your help to stay within it. The sooner we have your answer, the sooner you'll be able to book our space.

Thanks for your help and your patience.

Sincerely,

Request to Travel Agency for Travel Information (27-35)

Dear Sir or Madam:

My husband and I are planning to take a two-week vacation in mid-July. We want to do an in-depth tour (as much as possible within two weeks) of Italy. We're open to suggestions as to type of travel (e.g., air or boat), tour or independent, itinerary, etc. Here are our requirements:

1. We want to stay in deluxe hotels.
2. We prefer to visit locations that are rich in art and architecture.
3. Even though we plan to travel in July, we want to avoid the crowds as much as possible.
4. We're willing to spend up to $6,000 total for a first class trip.

Please send brochures, recommendations and any other descriptive material that will help us make a decision. If you need more information, please call me at (215) 555-5832.

Very truly yours,

- The more specific your request, the better information you'll receive.
- Don't be afraid to indicate how much you're willing to pay. It will help the travel agent zero in on the best choices for you.

Confirmation of Reservation (27-36)

Dear Sir or Madam:

I'd like to confirm a reservation made by phone earlier today for your eight-day "Island Paradise" package plan. According to your brochure, this plan includes the following:

- 7 nights at the Lanai Majestic, oceanfront room, king size bed, double occupancy.
- Full breakfast daily
- Island helicopter tour
- Honolulu and Pearl Harbor tour

Total cost of the package for two is $1,650.00 plus tax and gratuities.

Please send written confirmation of our reservations.

We look forward to our stay at the Lanai Majestic.

Very truly yours,

- Don't leave out any important details in your confirmation (e.g., oceanfront room, dietary restrictions, type of bed, etc.)
- Request written confirmation.

Cancellation of Reservation (27-37)

Dear Gail:

Once, when I was younger, my boss listened to me complain endlessly about something that had gone wrong at work. And then he said, "Adversity can't do you in, it can only reveal your spirit."

I hope that has as much meaning for you as it did for me, because I'm about to test your spirit. There's been a shake-up in my company, and all vacation plans have been put on hold. That means we have to cancel our European trip. I apologize for all the time and effort you put into finding us super rates and top accommodations.

Mary Ann and I are hoping that things will settle down quickly and we'll be able to resume our vacation plans. Even though we can't make the trip now, perhaps all the research you did on our behalf will still be applicable in the future.

I'd appreciate it if you would fax cancellation confirmations to my office as soon as possible at (313) 555-1828. Thanks for everything.

Sincerely,

- If someone has worked hard on your behalf, and especially if they are only paid via commission on a completed sale, it's thoughtful to tell them how much their effort is appreciated.

- Always ask for cancellation confirmations or you may end up paying for a trip you never got to take.

Request for Passport Application (27-38)

Dear Sir or Madam:

Please send me an application for a passport, along with any guidelines and specifications for material I'll need to obtain a passport.

Since I have to go out of the country in less than two months, I'd appreciate your prompt response.

Thank you.

Sincerely,

- Since you need items such as an official birth certificate (not a copy) and a passport photo, and because it requires 2-4 weeks to process an application (and possibly longer during peak travel times), be certain to start in plenty of time or you may, literally, miss the boat.

- Visit your local county passport office to pick up an application and start the ball rolling if time is a factor.

Request to Travel Agency about Health Issues (27-39)

Dear Toni:

Please send us guidelines on whatever health precautions are necessary during our upcoming trip to Central America. We've received so much advice (much of it contradictory), we'd appreciate whatever "official" information you can provide.

This is a much-anticipated trip for us, and we're anxious that nothing we sip, swallow, touch, or breathe interferes with our ambitious travel schedule. We appreciate the help (and patience) you've provided on every detail.

Sincerely,

- Make your request in the first sentence.
- Express some of your concerns to be certain that you get the correct information.

Sensitive Issues 28

Sensitive issues can be explosive if they're not handled with tact, diplomacy and a regard for the reader's feelings, as well as your own. A thoughtfully composed letter will help you avoid miscommunication while putting your desires, convictions and expectations "on the record." Just be certain that you write what you mean and you mean what you write. Once on paper, there's no guarantee your feelings will remain private. Be careful what you say and to whom you say it.

Love letters. A "love" or relationship letter is the most personal letter you can write. It takes courage to tell someone how much they mean to you. But if you don't do it, you may never know if your feelings are reciprocated. On the other hand, if your intention is to *extricate* yourself from a relationship, be considerate of the reader's feelings. Explain your decision and be firm. Vacillating only confuses the other person and prolongs an inevitable breakup.

Telling it like it is. If you've arrived at a point where you're ready to "tell it like it is," you might be so fed up with a situation or an individual that you don't care if your letter ends the relationship. As long as you recognize that possibility and are comfortable with it, go ahead and say whatever's on your mind. Describe how the reader's action (or inaction) is affecting you. State what you want from the reader, and tell what will happen if they fail to respond.

You hurt my feelings. This kind of letter shouldn't be about blame or laying a guilt trip on the reader. It should be about *you and your feelings*. Phrases like, "I felt sad (angry, scared, etc.) when you..." help to explain, in a non-judgmental way, how the reader's actions affected you. When you talk about the person's unacceptable behavior, rather than the person as a whole, the relationship can be salvaged.

Saying no. The "saying no" letter might have the same repercussions as the "telling it like it is" letter—it could end the relationship. To avoid second thoughts or regrets, be absolutely certain that you're comfortable with your position before saying "no." List reasons for your negative response. Once you put your refusal on record, make it clear that your decision is final.

Dear Jane Letter (28-01)

Dear Anne-Marie,

As you know, it isn't easy for me to express my feelings. My discomfort with emotion has been frustrating for both of us. Since I'm not a great verbal communicator, I've decided to write to you.

Lately I've felt a distance growing between us, and I realize that I'm responsible for it. I admit that my mind has been elsewhere. I know it's painful to be with someone who's not really "there," and I don't want to hurt you. That's why I think we should stop seeing each other. You are a fantastic person, and you deserve 100% of your partner's attention.

I don't know where my restlessness will lead me. I do know that wherever it is, I'll think of you often.

Affectionately,

- Take responsibility for breaking up the relationship.
- Leave the reader with positive feelings about herself and about you.

Dear John Letter (28-02)

Dear Zach,

You've probably sensed a problem between us lately, and I owe you an explanation.

I've begun to realize that our relationship has been based mainly on our physical attraction for each other. Our priorities and interests are just not as compatible as I first thought.

I think you're a terrific person who will make a great partner for the right person. I suspect she'll come along very soon.

I'll always cherish the time we've spent together. Hopefully, we can remain friends.

Fondly,

- Assume responsibility for your feelings and actions.
- Acknowledge the value of the relationship but be firm about your decision to end it.

I Miss You (28-03)

Dear Wendell,

I said I wanted to be alone. I said I needed time to think. Well, I've been alone and I've had time to think.

My conclusion?

I think I don't want to be alone.

Missing you,

- Be forthright about your feelings.
- Humor can help to make your point.

May I See You Again? (28-04)

Dear Brandon,

When something makes me feel good, I like to repeat the experience.

Being with you made me feel great. Here's why:

1) You're a good listener.
2) You have a wacky sense of humor.
3) You can whistle a Mozart concerto.

Let's get together again? Soon?

Fondly,

- Tell the reader what you like about them. Be specific.
- Be candid about your desire to pursue the relationship.

I'd Like to See You after All These Years (28-05)

Dear Franco,

For years you've floated in and out of my thoughts. For the past few days you've been my only thought. Now I have an irresistible urge to write to you.

I've changed a lot since we last met. I'm sure you have, too. I'd love to bring you up to date.

Might I interest you in a little deja-vu?

Hopefully,

> - Arouse the reader's curiosity (e.g., "I've changed a lot," "I'm involved in a fascinating project," etc.).
> - Suggest that you'd like to meet.

Will You Marry Me (28-06)

Dear Janine,

Lately I've been thinking about a quote I read in college:

> "Absence is to love as wind is to fire. If the flame is weak, the wind will extinguish it. If the flame is strong, the wind will help it grow."

Our separation has made my feelings for you even stronger than before. I miss you, I love you, and I can't imagine a future without you.

There's only one thing we can do. Will you marry me?

With all my love,

> - Tell the reader what led to your proposal.
> - Convince the reader that the only response possible is an affirmative one.

Letter to Dying Friend (28-07)

Dear Alan,

Just when I was wondering how and when I'd have a chance to see you, I was told that I'd be going to a trade show in Milwaukee next month (June 17-20)! I'm giving you as much notice as possible so you can reserve an evening or two for me. Your mom said you'd be finished with your round of treatments by then.

Instead of my usual written update on the comings and goings of our mutual friends (wait 'til you hear the lowdown on Beth and Marty!), I'll keep you in suspense so you'll have to see me when I'm in town.

While you're counting the days until I get there, here's something that will entertain you: Rent a video called Success Song. It's two hours of sheer joy. What a pleasant surprise; a low-budget movie that has more going for it than most $50 million productions.

And if you're looking for something with a little more weight to it, you can read all about the decline of morality in <u>America: Satan's Brew</u>. It's written by a theologian, but it reads better than most novels. It will give us plenty to talk about (not that we ever need help in that area!).

As soon as I'm given my hours and responsibilities for the show, I'll call you to work out the details. It will be wonderful to have the chance to see you.

With love,

- Don't focus on the person's illness in your correspondence. Write about the day-to-day occurrences that anyone would want to hear about.

- Avoid platitudes such as, "I just know you'll have a complete recovery."

Letter to Dying Relative (28-08)

Dear Artie,

Do you remember when we were younger, and we used to sit around and philosophize? One time, when we were debating religion, I asked if you believed in an afterlife. You said, "No, when you're dead, you're dead." So I asked if that meant you were an atheist, and you joked, "No, I don't believe in that, either."

I don't know how long either of us will be around, but I do know how many great times we've shared and how much I have enjoyed having you for a brother. Even when we disagreed, we always respected each other. I've always felt sorry for brothers who haven't had a relationship like ours.

I don't think I ever said these words to you, but it seems appropriate now, especially since we're both getting on in years: I love you. You've been a great friend as well as a great brother, and I cherish the time we've had together. Thanks for bringing so much to my life.

Your devoted brother,

- Often people regret having unexpressed thoughts after a loved one is gone. A letter like this "sets the record straight," particularly for people who have difficulty verbalizing their thoughts.

- A shared vignette or two will bring a smile of recognition.

Stop Stalking Me (28-09)

Carl,

On several occasions I've told you that your attentions aren't welcome. Yet you persist in telephoning me, lurking around my office, and following me.

I'm giving you notice that if this stalking doesn't cease <u>immediately,</u> I will notify the police. There are stalking laws in this state, and I will file charges.

> - Make the reader understand that you consider their behavior to be stalking. They may be surprised to hear this.
> - State what you plan to do about it.

Stop Harassing Our Daughter (28-10)

Dear Mr. Luff:

Our daughter has repeatedly told you that her relationship with you is over, yet you continue to harass her. Your refusal to accept Michelle's decision is causing her mental anguish and disrupting her studies.

If you don't stop this threatening behavior immediately, we will notify the police. Our daughter's well-being is in jeopardy and we intend to safeguard it.

With great concern,

> - Take a firm stand.
> - State the consequences that will result if your demands aren't met.

Stop Interfering in My Life (28-11)

Dear Penny,

You say that you want what's best for me. That's what I want, too. Unfortunately we don't agree on what "best" is.

I know you mean well when you tell me how to handle things, but I prefer to make my own decisions. While I welcome your friendship and support, I won't tolerate your interference.

Sincerely,

> - It's important to sound sure of yourself when you're dealing with a meddler.
> - State your terms for continuing the relationship.

I'm Having an Affair with Your Wife (28-12)

Dear Kevin,

My intention in writing this letter isn't to hurt you. It's to end the duplicity and the tension.

My relationship with Charlotte has developed beyond friendship. It wasn't planned; it just happened.

We're in love with each other. That may seem incomprehensible to you, but our feelings for each other have grown over time.

We realize the pain that this revelation will cause you. But it's time for complete honesty. Charlotte and I can't keep our feelings secret any more.

We don't expect your forgiveness, but we do hope for some level of understanding.

Charlotte thought that if this news came to you in a letter, it would give you a little time to digest the information before you and she talked about it.

Sincerely,

- Be forthright about your own feelings and your intentions.
- Explain why you're delivering this news in a letter.

Stop Seeing My Husband (28-13)

Ms. Sudmeyer:

Actions have consequences. The consequences of your association with my husband have been pain and embarrassment for my family.

If you don't end this adulterous relationship, you will be the one who suffers consequences.

1) I will tell your husband.
2) I will go to your office and tell your boss and co-workers.
3) I will post a notice on your church bulletin board describing your behavior.
4) I will take additional action without prior warning.

My husband has acknowledged his responsibility in this affair and has expressed his intention to end it. Do not write to him, telephone him or try to see him.

Adamantly,

- State your demands.
- Explain what you'll do if they aren't met.

You Are No Longer Welcome in Our Home (28-14)

Dear Lillian,

People often comment on the peaceful atmosphere of my home. I think the harmony exists because of my family's commitment to tolerance, flexibility and humor.

I expect the same from my guests. That's why I was stunned by the racist remarks you made here last weekend. Your comments upset the other guests and ruined my dinner party.

Your attitude is inconsistent with everything we believe in. Given the circumstances, you won't be invited again.

Regretfully,

- Tell the reader why the behavior was offensive to you.
- Leave no doubt in the reader's mind about future social interaction with you.

You Have a Problem with Alcohol (28-15)

Dear Stuart,

Writing this letter could cost me your friendship, but I care enough about you to take the risk.

I'm concerned about your drinking. Take an honest look at your repeated absences from work, your constant money problems, and your history of DWI's and accidents. They are all alcohol related.

Out of concern for you, I've done some research on the subject. I've even started attending Al-Anon meetings. I hope you'll let me share what I've learned.

You are a valuable human being. I'd like to help you. Please let me—for both our sakes.

Fondly,

- Tell the reader why you think they have a problem with alcohol. Don't be judgmental.
- Stress your desire to help.

Pay the Child Support You Owe (28-16)

Dear Gene,

Up until a few months ago, I thought we had been succeeding at keeping any animosity from our divorce under wraps. We've both been better off for it, and the kids have certainly benefited from the lack of sniping and confrontation. So it doesn't make sense that your child support payments have suddenly stopped coming.

School starts in less than two weeks and that means the kids need some new clothes, school supplies and lunch money. Without your payments, I can't even buy the bare essentials.

If I don't have at least two payments by next Friday, Gene, I'll have to ask my lawyer to notify the court. Please help me avoid a step neither of us wants to take.

Sincerely,

> - Avoid statements that blame the other party. They only cause anger and resentment.
>
> - By asking someone to help you avoid taking unpleasant action, you demonstrate that both of you will benefit.

You're a Bigot (28-17)

Dear Lance,

You're a puzzle to me. You always seem to function well in multi-racial, multi-ethnic settings. You never seem to have a problem mixing with people of all colors, shapes, and backgrounds. And yet, when you're in a more homogeneous group, your whole demeanor changes.

I've heard you tell jokes that are mean, not funny. I've seen you characterize entire groups as being murderous, miserly, or thieving. I've listened to you talk, in the most derogatory terms, about people who are "guilty" only of being of different faiths.

Perhaps you're not aware of the impact your words have. Perhaps you're trying to appeal to the base nature of one or two people whose approval is important to you. Perhaps you're trying to downplay your education and intelligence, for whatever reason.

But on the off-chance that you're not aware of it, I, and others in our crowd, have come to think of you as a bigot. That's an ugly term, Lance, and I doubt you'd like it applied to you. I think you need to look in the mirror and decide who you are.

With concern,

> - Giving the reader the "out" that they may not be aware of their behavior makes the letter less threatening.
>
> - Take responsibility for your words. Say "I think," "I've heard," etc. Don't hide behind what others say.

Your Coaching Style Is Destructive (28-18)

Dear Coach Arroyo:

I encouraged my son Greg's participation in after-school team sports because I believed it would give him a sense of belonging and self-esteem. The plan has backfired.

Because of your coaching style, Greg is more withdrawn and unsure of himself than he was before he joined your team.

I've attended every game and watched my son sit on the bench. During the entire season, he has never been given an opportunity to play, and he tells me that you constantly humiliate him by calling him "super spazz."

This is enrichment? This is team spirit? You need to re-think your obligations as an educator and a coach. Kids need to learn less about competition and more about playing the game.

I'm sending a copy of this letter to the director of athletics and the superintendent of schools. Perhaps you can be persuaded by them, if not by me, to give each member of your team a shot at success.

Sincerely,

- Express your grievance, and back it up with specific examples.
- Tell the reader how you would like their attitude or behavior to change.

I'm Gay, to Friend (28-19)

Dear Bonnie and Richard,

Someone once said to me that friends are people who know all about you and like you anyway. I hope I can count on you to live up to that definition.

Over the years, I convinced myself that I wasn't hiding anything by not telling you I was gay. After all, I reasoned, our friendship had nothing to do with my sexual orientation.

Times have changed, though. I now believe that I was deliberately hiding my homosexuality from you. I'm not sure why, since it's part of who I am, and I'm comfortable with myself and my life.

I've finally decided that keeping the truth from you has been causing me a great deal of discomfort. So now you know.

I hope this news won't change our relationship in any way. Your friendship and support mean so much to me. Please keep in touch.

Faithfully,

- Using an adage, like this one about friends, can set the tone for the entire letter.
- Giving people the impression that you expect them to take news well makes it more likely that they will.

You Didn't Understand My Needs (28-20)

Dear Elizabeth,

I dealt with my mother's death by withdrawing from people. I felt a need for complete privacy, and asked all my friends—including you—to respect my desire to be alone.

You're the only one who viewed my grieving process as a personal rejection. Even though you were the first person I called after my isolation, you were abrupt and almost confrontational.

I had the right to work my way through a devastating loss on my own terms. I'm disappointed that a month has passed since that conversation and you still haven't made any attempt to contact me.

We've known each other for a long time, Elizabeth, but you let me down when I really needed your understanding and support. I guess we didn't have much of a relationship, after all.

With many regrets,

- If you've been severely disappointed by someone close to you, you may wish to tell them so, even if it means ending the relationship.
- Be sure to explain yourself so there can be no mistaking your message.

My Guests Felt Snubbed by You (28-21)

Dear Lizette,

You achieved a unique record. Virtually everyone at my dinner party had a comment to make about you.

The men seemed to enjoy your company. At different times, each one conveyed to me that he felt you were bright, witty and charming. The women were also of a unanimous opinion; they felt ignored by you. They claimed that every word you uttered was directed to the men, with no attempt made to include the women or even acknowledge them.

I'm not repeating any of this to make you feel uncomfortable. I just thought you should be aware of how you're being perceived. I feel badly that my women friends dismissed you; I was hoping you would become a part of our social group.

If you'd like to talk about doing some repair work, give me a call.

Your friend,

> - People often "play to an audience," without being aware of the consequences of their actions.
> - If you're willing to discuss the behavior, tell the person so. You may be preventing their being excluded from future events.

Your Behavior Embarrassed Me (28-22)

Dear Kent,

There's a school of thought that says an individual is only responsible for his own behavior...that he can only embarrass himself. I don't subscribe to that belief; I was totally embarrassed by your behavior.

I brought you to the meeting because you asked for an invitation; I didn't drag you there against your will. It was bad enough that you felt a need to smoke in a non-smoking room. But to get into a shouting match about the rights of smokers was unconscionable. You were my guest, and I expected you to act like one.

If you still have hopes of joining the organization, you'll have to start with a letter of apology to the entire group. And then you'll need to find a different sponsor. I won't put myself in that position again.

Sincerely,

> - There's no need to tip-toe around the issue.
> - Briefly describe the behavior that embarrassed you.

You Had Your Facts Wrong (28-23)

Dear Claudia,

I'm sorry that you're angry with me, but your anger is based on misinformation. I told Erin that if you needed a ride to the dance you should call me, and I'd arrange one for you. I didn't say I'd pick you up.

I don't know if Erin misstated what I said, or if you misunderstood her. I would never have said I would pick you up because you live nearly an hour out of my way. There are at least three people—all within a few miles of your apartment—who would gladly have picked you up if they had known you needed a ride.

I feel badly that you waited for a ride that never came. The only thing I might have done differently was to deliver the message personally, instead of through a third party. Since this was a misunderstanding, can we put this incident behind us?

Please let me hear from you.

Your friend,

- It's often easier to analyze what went wrong in writing, rather than verbally.
- If the reader's reaction was based on bad information, and you want to maintain the friendship, tell the reader there are no hard feelings.

You Set a Bad Example for My Children (28-24)

Dear Dad Brown,

Ray and I work very hard to teach the kids respect for all beliefs, so it's disheartening to hear them parrot some of your comments about other people's religion.

They've told one neighborhood child that they didn't want his kind around any more, and threatened to beat him up. When I asked them where they got such ideas, the response was, "Grandpa Brown said..."

There are many different beliefs, and it's important that we treat others with kindness, and set a good example for the children.

From now on, will you please keep your thoughts about this subject to yourself.

I appreciate your understanding.

Fondly,

- Anger usually causes more anger. A firm, but moderate, tone is less antagonistic and equally effective.
- State what you feel is unacceptable to eliminate confusion and misunderstanding.

You Didn't Show Up for the Party I Gave for You (28-25)

Dear Patti,

After knocking myself out to help you become established in this area, I asked myself a lot of questions this weekend:

Why wouldn't you show up at a party I arranged, at your request, to help you meet new people?

Why were you at a club less than a mile from my apartment, when you were supposed to be here? (A mutual acquaintance saw you there.)

Why would you put me in the awkward, embarrassing position of trying to explain to my friends why the guest of honor didn't show?

How could you let the weekend go without so much as a call or attempt at an explanation?

Suddenly, the answer to every question hit me: You're a jerk.

Completely disgusted,

- Using a series of related questions builds to a climax.

- If it's more important to get something off your chest than to create a dialogue, saying something shocking works wonders. Just think about the potential consequences before sending the letter.

You Didn't Invite Me (28-26)

Dear Kim,

I was hurt that I wasn't invited to your daughter's wedding. For months preceding the event, you spoke about it so much, I couldn't imagine not being there to celebrate with you. In fact, I told my husband to get ready for what I was sure would be a spectacular affair.

With only a few weeks remaining before the wedding, it finally occurred to me that an invitation would not be forthcoming. I was disappointed because we've worked together for so long, I thought we had a relationship beyond that of colleagues.

I'm happy for you and your family, and I'm truly glad to hear that the wedding was such a success. However, I'd appreciate it if you'd stop talking about the wedding in my presence, since it hurts me every time you mention it.

Sincerely,

- It's healthier to express your feelings, rather than have them build up.

- If you see the person who offended you on a regular basis (as with a coworker), it's a good idea to send a letter that expresses your feelings without alienating them.

You Didn't Act like a Friend (28-27)

Dear Ross,

Maybe I have unrealistic expectations. But I believe in the Golden Rule. I treat people the way I'd like them to treat me.

I've been a loyal friend to you. That's why I don't think it's unreasonable to expect loyalty in return.

Your failure to defend me against unfair accusations is a great disappointment to me. If this is the way you behave towards friends, I'll have to reevaluate our friendship.

I feel betrayed. Perhaps you can offer an explanation.

Sincerely,

- Tell the reader how they disappointed you.
- Ask for an explanation.

You Ignored Me (28-28)

Dear Dale,

I was flattered that you asked me to attend your company picnic. It meant you thought enough of me to want to introduce me to your friends and colleagues. At least that's what I originally thought.

But as soon as we arrived, you jumped into a softball game that lasted nearly two hours. I was alone on the sideline, not knowing a soul, feeling very awkward about having to introduce myself to strangers. And this pattern continued throughout the day. You'd bring me something to eat or drink, then run off to talk with your buddies.

How could you be so insensitive? Didn't you realize how I'd feel among two hundred strangers? You invited me to spend the day with you, but the only thing we shared that day was being in the same zip code.

I'm disappointed in you, Dale. Your lack of sensitivity is a real threat to our relationship.

Sincerely,

- Someone who is insensitive won't "get it" on their own. You need to spell out the offending behavior.
- By ending with a statement of disapproval (as opposed to termination), you're leaving enough room for the other person to respond.

I Won't Babysit for You Anymore (28-29)

Dear Theresa,

I know from personal experience how quickly "cabin fever" can overwhelm a young mother. That's why I agreed to babysit occasionally for Jennifer. I guess I should have defined "occasionally."

Last week Jennifer spent three afternoons at my house. And on two of those occasions you dropped her off without even calling first. Jennifer is a darling child and I enjoy spending time with her, but I feel I'm being taken advantage of. That's why I'm withdrawing my offer to babysit.

Sincerely,

- Explain how a change in the situation has affected your decision.
- Accept responsibility if part of the problem is your fault.

I Won't Come to Your Event (28-30)

Dear Mark,

The invitation to your financial planning seminar came within days of my father's death, and it offended me. I would have preferred to receive a note of condolence before receiving an offer of advice on my inheritance.

Don't expect me at your seminar. At this time, financial planning is the farthest thing from my mind.

Sincerely,

- Be clear about your reason for declining the invitation.
- If you are annoyed about someone's behavior, a succinct letter can sometimes say it better than you could in person.

I Won't Give to Your Charity (28-31)

Dear Bill,

In the past, when you asked me to contribute to charitable causes, I never hesitated. But this time I'm saying no.

A few months ago I saw an unfavorable news report about Helping Hands, and it stayed in my mind. The report showed convincing evidence that the administrators of Helping Hands are pocketing a high percentage of the contributions.

Unless I can be certain that my donations are going to be well spent, I don't write a check.

I'd be glad to consider any future requests for worthwhile causes.

Sincerely,

- Explain your reason for not contributing.
- Put the onus on the reader to change your mind by providing additional information.

I Won't Give You a Letter of Reference (28-32)

Dear Brett,

Your request for a letter of reference puts me in an awkward position. I require evidence of three qualities before I'll recommend someone for a job:

    1) A willingness to work hard
    2) A desire to learn
    3) A positive attitude toward coworkers

You've shown that you can be a hard worker and you're receptive to new ideas, but I think you need to examine your attitude toward your colleagues—specifically, editors.

You may be great at researching articles, but without the contributions of the editors, even your best work wouldn't be polished enough to print. Yet on several occasions I've seen you treat the editors with disdain.

I regret not being able to write you a letter of reference. But I hope you'll benefit from my comments about your attitude.

Sincerely,

- State your criteria for giving a reference.
- State how the reader doesn't meet the criteria.

I Won't Lend You Money (28-33)

Dear Marilyn,

Your recent request for a loan made me think of a quote by Shakespeare—not the cliched section about borrowing and lending, but the rest of the passage, which has personal meaning for me. It continues, "For loan oft loses both itself and friend."

My experience has been that hard feelings ensue when money is at stake. I don't want to lose your friendship, so I'm going to pass on the loan. It's a matter of principle, and I'm not comfortable making an exception.

I hope you understand.

Kindest regards,

- Explain your reason for not lending money.
- State firmly that you won't make an exception.

I Won't Let You Borrow My Dress (28-34)

Dear Ellie,

It isn't easy saying no to a friend. Especially when the request seems so simple. But a recent experience has soured me on the idea of lending my clothes.

I lent an outfit to someone, and it was returned to me with permanent stains. I made a vow that I'd never lend my clothes again—to <u>anyone</u>!

I know how responsible you are, but I just can't risk damage to the dress—or worse—damage to our friendship.

Please understand.

Love,

- Explain why you won't lend the item.
- Tell the reader that your decision is based on past experience, not on a character judgement.

I Won't Lie for You (28-35)

Dear Peter,

I'm willing to assume responsibility for my own actions, but not for yours. I won't lie for you, and I resent your asking.

This is your problem. Please leave me out of it.

Sincerely,

- State your position firmly.
- It's O.K. to sound irate when someone has asked you to compromise your values.

I Won't Support Your Addiction (28-36)

Dear Alex,

I've run out of patience and I won't rescue you again. You need help for your addiction, and until you make an effort to get it, I'm withdrawing my support.

Reading about addiction has taught me three things:

1) I didn't cause your addiction.
2) I can't control your addiction.
3) I can't cure your addiction.

I'll help you find a recovery program. I'll drive you to meetings. But I won't support your habit.

I care very much about what happens to you. Now you have to care, too.

Fondly,

- Tell the reader what you *won't* do. Then tell them what you *will* do.
- Explain your motivation.

Sympathy and Condolences 29

When writing a letter of sympathy or condolence, don't claim the reader's grief or disappointment as your own. By carrying on endlessly about your *own* emotions, you defeat the purpose of the letter—which is to respectfully acknowledge the reader's misfortune. If you've experienced a similar loss, it can be helpful to share how you overcame your own ordeal, but keep the focus of your sympathy on the reader.

Sympathy. The sympathy letter is the antidote to the song, "Nobody Knows You When You're Down and Out." It's an expression of support, designed to help the reader through a tough time. Let your letter convey a sense of caring and concern. State your desire to help in a specific way (i.e., providing transportation, lodging, helping with meals, babysitting, etc.). Finally, express a positive outlook.

Condolences. Many people quake at the thought of writing a condolence letter, out of fear of saying the wrong thing. It's true that words of condolence should be carefully chosen, but the extra effort will be appreciated by the reader. Convey your shock or sadness upon hearing the news. Convey a sense of sympathy about the reader's loss. Share a meaningful recollection about the person who has passed away. Offer to help in any way you can.

The approach you take with your condolence letter will vary according to the circumstances. The death of an elderly person after a lengthy illness would be acknowledged differently from the sudden death of a healthy person. The death of a child would be acknowledged differently from the death of an adult. Similarly, the reader's relationship to the deceased will influence the overall tone of your letter.

A condolence letter can't reverse tragic or unfortunate events. It *can* offer comfort and support.

Sorry You Didn't Get into Your First Choice College (29-01)

Dear Mike,

I thought of you this morning as I was thumbing through an old Sports Illustrated article. Wayne Gretzky (your idol, as I recall) was quoted as saying, "I skate to where the puck is going to be, not to where it has been." Does that make sense to you? Gretzky was saying that if you don't look ahead, you fall behind.

You're my favorite nephew, Mike, and I don't like seeing you concentrate on what didn't happen, rather than on what did. You're putting all your energy into not having been accepted at an Ivy League school, instead of preparing for the wonderful experience that you'll have at Strathmore.

I'll see you during Christmas break...and I can't wait to hear about your first taste of college life. Congratulations on your acceptance to Strathmore; it's a great school!

Love,

- A quote from a celebrity is often helpful in making a point.
- Congratulate the reader on positive achievements.

Sorry You Didn't Pass the Bar (29-02)

Dear Shelly,

It's understandable that you'd feel disappointed you didn't pass the bar exam on your first try. That's only natural after all the effort you put into preparing for it.

But when we spoke, you sounded as if you were ready to throw in the towel. From what I hear, many successful attorneys need two or more attempts to make it.

When I was younger and thought I had hit bottom (more than once), your grandfather would sit me down and say, "The fight's not over 'til you're down for the count."

In other words, you've only begun to fight. You've got everything it takes to make a great lawyer. But you'll never make it unless you believe that. I do.

Love,

- Don't minimize the disappointment, but remind the reader that it's only a temporary setback.
- Reaffirm your faith in the individual's abilities.

Sorry You Lost Your Job, Fired (29-03)

Dear Vic,

Alfred Fuller, the man who started the Fuller Brush Company, was fired from his first three jobs. The fellow I currently work for admits to being fired twice prior to building his own business. (His wife once told me he was "modest" about his past; that he had actually been fired an amazing five times!)

The point, of course, is that you're too good to let this one bad experience get you down. You sounded awful on the phone, and right now you don't have the luxury of feeling sorry for yourself. You have to get your resume out, hit the road for some interviews, and get your confidence level back up.

Why don't you send me a copy of your resume and I'll see what I can do to help update it. I'll also tell the guys at work to keep their eyes and ears open.

I'll talk to you soon. Keep your chin up.

Your friend,

P.S. If it makes you feel any better, Lee Iacocca was fired by Ford, Ronald Reagan by Warner Brothers, etc., etc.

- It's helpful to put a firing in perspective. The message is that others have been fired and rebounded from it.
- If you're going to offer help, be sure that you'll deliver on it.

Sorry You Lost Your Job, Laid Off (29-04)

Dear Rick,

On the one hand, I'm sorry to hear that you were caught in a surprise layoff. The consensus is that your company overreacted to a down business cycle. Chances seem good, based on what I've been reading in the paper, that there may be a callback very soon.

On the other hand, you might choose to think of this "break" as giving you an opportunity to look at other employment possibilities. For example, I've wanted you to apply for a job at my company for a long time, and now you have the incentive to do so.

In fact, there are a number of companies you ought to check out while you have the time to interview. I'd be happy to give you some suggestions.

You're too talented to be out for long, Rick. Just make the most of your time off. Keep thinking of Thomas Edison's credo, "Everything comes to him who hustles while he waits."

Best,

> • Encourage the reader to seek other employment unless rehiring is guaranteed.
>
> • Bolster the reader's sense of self-worth.

Sorry about Your Accident (29-05)

Dear Jeb,

It's frustrating to be put on "hold" when you're making a phone call. It must be <u>awful</u> to have to put your whole life on hold because of an accident.

I'm sorry that you've been sidelined by the car crash. I hope your discomfort is minimal and that your broken leg heals quickly.

I'd feel that I was contributing to your recuperation if you'd let me feed your fish, water your plants or pick up some groceries for you. Just say the word. (P.S.—I don't do windows.)

In the meantime, get well. And call if you need HELP!

Fondly,

> • Try to lift the reader's spirits with a mixture of humor and compassion.
>
> • Offer to help out in any way you can (e.g., run errands, make phone calls, take care of pets, etc.).

Sorry about Your Divorce (29-06)

Dear Carrie,

I know you're experiencing a difficult transition, and I'd like to offer you a sympathetic ear.

Facing life as a single person, after years of togetherness, is a scary prospect. The motto that's been most helpful to me is "one day at a time." If that doesn't work, try "one <u>hour</u> at a time!"

We're rarely prepared for change, but frequently it can be a blessing. At the very least it's an opportunity for growth.

I'm confident that you'll emerge from this passage with a new sense of yourself. I did.

Fondly,

> - Offer the reader your support and compassion.
> - Share your own experience (or one you're familiar with) as proof that a positive transition is possible.

Sorry You Lost Your Home in a Fire (29-07)

Dear Marcy and Donald,

We've said a prayer of thanks that your family escaped the fire unharmed, but my heart goes out to you at the destruction of your home.

We can't fathom the emotional toll of such a loss, but we hope you'll let us help in any way we can.

Please accept our offer of food, clothing, transportation, or a place to stay. You've just got to get the family out of that motel.

We'll call in a couple of days, after you've had time to decide how we can be of greatest assistance.

Affectionately,

> - Express your sympathy.
> - Offer the kind of assistance that you can follow up on.

Sorry about Your Miscarriage (29-08)

Dear Maddie,

What a terrible disappointment you've had. You and Bob were so excited about becoming parents. It must be extremely painful to deal with the loss.

I hope the support of your family and friends will ease your sadness. Please let me know what I can do to help.

Love,

> - Acknowledge what a difficult time this is for the reader.
> - Remind the reader that family and friends can be helpful in overcoming the grief.

Sorry Your Wife Is Sick, to Business Associate (29-09)

Dear Cal,

One of the things I admire about you is your ability to juggle ten projects at once and make it look effortless. Knowing the stress that you're experiencing in your personal life makes your unflappable demeanor even more impressive.

I'm sorry that Ruth is not well. It must be a real challenge for you to shoulder the responsibilities of home and work simultaneously.

Your wife's health is your top priority, and it's important that you spend time with her. If there's anything I can do to lessen your load at work, please tell me.

As your friend and colleague, I offer my support and my sincere wishes for Ruth's full recovery.

Cordially,

- Acknowledge the reader's stressful situation.
- Offer to help out in any way that's feasible.

Get Well, after Operation, to Friend (29-10)

Dear Art,

My instinct is to say, "I hope you're feeling better after your operation!"

My experience tells me, however, that most people feel <u>worse</u> after an operation—at least temporarily. May you be the exception!

But you can't keep a good man down. That's why I know you'll recover in record time.

Get well soon.

Fondly,

- You don't need to get specific about the nature of the surgery. The point is to let the reader know you're thinking of them.
- Keep the tone of the letter optimistic and light.

Get Well, to Business Associate (29-11)

Dear Hildy,

The office is positively dismal without you. We miss your energy and creative stimulation. That's why I'm insisting that you get well ASAP!

If I can tie up any loose business for you, just give a yell. But don't expect me to inspire the troops—that's what we've got you for!

Kindest regards,

> - Reassure the reader of their value to the company.
> - Try to make them feel an ongoing connection to the workplace.

Get Well, to Relative (29-12)

Dear Aunt Edith,

I was sorry to hear that you've had to endure another bout of phlebitis. But I was happy to learn that you're recovering well. Uncle Jim tells me that you're following the doctor's orders and staying relatively immobile.

You know how much my kids love you, don't you? Well, I promised them a trip to see you next month, assuming you're feeling better. Kathy said she's not sure if that's such a great incentive for you to get well fast! The children can be a bit rambunctious.

We'll keep tabs on you. And assuming you're up to a visit, we'll set a date with you in a few weeks. Be sure you listen to the doctor and Uncle Jim.

I love you. Hope to see you soon.

Your nephew,

> - When someone is ill and vulnerable, it's important for family to acknowledge the illness and offer support.
> - Many people do not like drop-in visits when they're ill. It's best to say you'd like to see the individual, and to make sure they want to see you, too.

Get Well, to Friend—Humorous (29-13)

Dear Bud,

We decided to hold our regular Friday night poker game, even though you couldn't be there. The other guys might not admit it to you, but I will: It wasn't the same without you.

You know how much Ron gripes about your cigars? Would you believe he said he missed the "aroma"? Arnie complained that you're the only one who ever tells decent jokes, and that he was bored with the rest of us. And Dave said that he missed having a patsy to take advantage of.

The point is, we all miss you and hope your knee's on the mend. (I haven't been very conscientious about my morning jog without you to push me.) As to the card game, as soon as you can get around on crutches, we expect you back. I hope the doctors left a few dollars for us!

Get well soon!

Best wishes,

- People love to know they're missed. Make it a point to say so to a friend who's layed up.
- Personal quotes from acquaintances help the sick party feel less isolated.

Get Well, to Friend—Serious (29-14)

Dear Joe,

I was very sorry to hear that you weren't well. I'm sure that someone with your energy is very frustrated by the forced inactivity, but it's only for a short time.

Suzie tells me that you can have visitors in a couple of weeks. I'll be sure to come see you then.

Best,

- This kind of letter must be handwritten, unless your handwriting is indecipherable. A get-well card is also acceptable.
- Don't go on and on. Be positive but not maudlin. If you say you'll do something— visit, call, whatever—note it on your calendar and then do it.

Condolences on Death of Child, after Illness (29-15)

Dear Marilyn and Jon,

I'm so sad that Eddie's brave battle with cancer was unsuccessful. Your loss is more than any family should have to bear.

You gave your son the best: medically, emotionally and spiritually. He had splendid parents during his short time on earth; of that I'm certain.

Eddie taught me more about courage than any ten grown-ups. It's a lesson I'll never forget. Just as I'll never forget Jonathan Edward Bascomb, Jr.

My thoughts and prayers are with you.

With love,

- Express your conviction that the reader gave their best to the child.
- Communicate a personal memory of the child or your view of the legacy they left behind.

Condolences on Death of Mutual Friend (29-16)

Dear Phil,

Whenever I think of Tony, I think of you. You were such close pals that you used to finish each other's sentences. That's why I understand how empty you must feel without him.

I hope you realize how much he admired and respected you. He often told me that your encouragement provided the incentive he needed to turn his life around. He was very grateful, and he let everybody know it.

If you need someone to talk to, I hope you'll call me. I'm no substitute for Tony, but I'd be happy to fill in the gaps any way I can.

Sincerely,

- Acknowledge the reader's close relationship with the deceased.
- Share a positive memory or anecdote.

Condolences on Death of Spouse, after Illness, to Friend (29-17)

Dear Rosemarie,

I'm so sorry that Walt has lost his struggle. You both fought so hard. Your fortitude in the face of Walt's illness has been remarkable.

I believe you found your strength in the relationship that you and Walt shared. You'll always have memories of the wonderful years you spent together.

Please let me know how I can help you through this lonely time.

Fondly,

- Express your admiration for the reader's courage.
- Inject a positive note about the future, and offer any help you can.

Condolences on Sudden Death of Spouse, to Friend (29-18)

Dear Bob,

The news of Hannah's sudden death has shaken me. I feel angry that Fate has delivered such a cruel blow to you and your family.

Hannah was a vibrant person: at home, at work, and in the community. She brought out the best in people by setting high standards for herself. It's inconceivable that she's gone.

I'm placing myself at your disposal. If you need a babysitter, a cook, an errand-runner or a sympathetic ear—please call me. I hope you'll allow me to help you get through this.

With deepest sympathy,

- Acknowledge the shock that is caused by a sudden death.
- Convey the sense of loss that you share with the reader.

Condolences on Death of Parent, after Illness, to Friend (29-19)

Dear Florence,

This past year has been a really trying time for you.

I've admired your dedication to your mother during her illness. She couldn't have asked for a more devoted daughter.

Just as you brought comfort to your mother, I hope that her memory will bring comfort to you. She was a courageous, energetic woman with a wonderful sense of humor.

I see the same traits in you. What a legacy she has left!

With love,

- Acknowledge the stress of a long illness.
- Offer an uplifting thought about the lasting connection between parent and child.

Condolences on Sudden Death of Parent, to Friend (29-20)

Dear Lauren,

It's much too soon to have to write this letter. You and your Mom should have had many more years together. She was supposed to see her grandchildren grow up.

Even those of us who were not related to her felt her love and caring. I already feel her absence.

If you feel like talking, please pick up the phone. I know you and your Mom enjoyed late night gabfests. I'm an especially good listener in those hours between midnight and dawn.

My thoughts and prayers are with you.

With love,

- It's all right to express a sense of anger and disbelief.
- Offer to make yourself available to the reader as they go through the grieving process.

Condolences on Death of Parent, to Business Associate (29-21)

Dear Tara,

There isn't any way to prepare for the loss of a parent. I remember feeling so vulnerable when my Dad died—suddenly, the loving parent I had always turned to was gone. I felt as though I had to act grown up, but I felt very child-like.

You have my sympathy as you make your way through this passage. It won't be easy, but you can rely on the support of all your friends.

I didn't know your father, but he must have been quite a guy. Just look at his daughter.

Fond regards,

- If you can, share the wisdom you've gleaned from losing a loved one.
- Convey the thought that the parent lives on in the child.

Condolences on Death of Parent, to Employee (29-22)

Dear Tim,

I was very sorry to hear of your mother's death. It must be very hard to lose a parent.

I'm sorry I was out of town and unable to attend the funeral. You were in my thoughts.

My deepest sympathy,

- If you didn't get to the funeral, apologize. Sending flowers or a plant to the house or making a contribution in the person's name might be called for, depending on the relationship.
- If you didn't know the deceased, keep your handwritten note short. You can usually safely say it's hard to lose a parent.

Condolences on Death of Child, to Business Associate's Family (29-23)

Dear Mr. Markham,

I was very sorry to hear of Joy's death. We will miss her very much. Joy was a kind person you could always depend on—for a smile, for a humorous "lighten up, guys" when we needed it most, for doing more than her share, and more.

My deepest sympathy,

- Sympathy notes must be handwritten. They should never include comments like "I know how you feel" or anything else that presumes on a nonexistent intimacy.
- If the person was a business associate, refer to something that made him or her a good person to work with.

Condolences on Death of Spouse, to Business Associate (29-24)

Dear Pat,

This note may be late in coming (I just found out about Ralph's death), but the message is heartfelt.

Reading about Ralph made me appreciate how much he contributed during his life and why you always spoke so admiringly of him. I feel especially saddened that I never had the opportunity to meet him. What a unique person he must have been.

With deepest sympathy,

- It's better to be late than not to respond.

- If you haven't met the deceased, don't talk about them as if you did; it will make you seem insincere.

Condolences on Death of Co-Worker, to Spouse (29-25)

Dear Pete,

I was devastated to hear of Joy's death. We shared so many good times together—on our Sierra Club hikes, for example—and we were always part of the team "that made it happen" here at work.

There's never anything that can be said that will make it better, but Joe and I hope you will count on us for help—with the kids, for example, or for anything else you need. We'll call you.

With my deepest sympathy,

- Handwrite any sympathy note. Refer briefly to your association and friendship with the person who died.

- Offer to help, but don't expect an immediate response from the grieving person. It may be better to wait awhile and then call him or her and make a very specific offer—for example, "Can we take you and the kids to dinner Wednesday?"

Condolences on Death of Co-Worker, to Employee's Family (29-26)

Dear Mrs. Brightwell,

Everyone here was very sad to hear about Mason's death. We counted on him—he was always here to open up and greet our first customers. People said it was a pleasure to do business in a place where "customer service" wasn't just a phrase. Mason always put the customer first—and the customers knew it.

We'll miss him very much.

Our sympathy,

- If you're the boss, you handwrite the letter and refer to the rest of your staff's sadness.

- If you have business details, like benefits or distributions to discuss, write another letter at a later date. Don't include such issues in a sympathy letter.

Condolences on Death of Pet (29-27)

Dear Mary Ellen and Wayne,

We were sorry to learn that Thor passed away. He was such a great and loyal companion. It's hard to believe that he won't come racing out to greet us the next time we visit.

We understand your sense of loss. We still miss Corky, even though he's been gone for six years.

With sympathy,

- Treat the loss of a pet as you would any other loss. (This is hard for non-pet owners to understand, but valid nonetheless.)

- An example of how the pet will be missed personalizes your message.

Response to Condolence Letter (29-28)

Dear Monica and Al,

We so much appreciated your note; it was filled with such kindness and love. We need all the support we can get right now. Our hearts ache.

Patrick was a son who shared all his joy with us. He was so happily married—for two short years—and was such a doting father to eight-month-old Erica. We're hoping Patrick's wife and the baby will spend some time with us this summer.

Thank you for your thoughtfulness.

With affection,

- When someone cares enough about you to express sympathy, it's equally thoughtful to respond with a thank you.

- Since people are interested, you may wish to share some information on how the family is coping.

Index by Title

Index by Subject

(**Boldface** numbers indicate chapter introductions. Numbers in parentheses are document numbers found at the top of each letter. They are followed by page numbers.)

of new personnel (1-28, 2-12, 2-21), 15, 42, 48
of new policy (9-23, 9-24), 169, 170
of new product or product line (1-25, 2-13, 2-19), 14, 43, 47
of new salesperson, to client (3-06), 268
of new subsidiary (2-10), 40
of price change, to sales force (1-26), 14
of sales programs (1-21, 1-22), 12
Apologies, business
for billing error (4-02), 73
for computer error (4-03), 74
for damaged goods, with refund (3-39), 70
for damaged shipment (4-06), 75
for delayed shipment (1-39, 1-43, 4-04), 22, 23, 74
for employee rudeness (4-07), 75
for incorrect payment (6-28), 107
for late payment (6-29, 6-30), 107, 108
for missed meeting (3-23, 3-24), 63
for missing documentation or instructions (4-08), 76
for shipment error (4-05, 11-08), 75, 196
Apologies, personal, **229**
about event
for being out of town for your award (14-04), 232
for being unable to come to party (14-08), 234
for breaking CD player (14-05), 232
for burning hole in sofa (14-06), 233
for drinking too much (14-07), 233
for forgetting our anniversary (14-11), 235
for forgetting your birthday (14-09), 234
for forgetting your birthday, poem (14-10), 235
for my child misbehaving (14-01), 231
for my pet causing trouble (14-02), 231
for spoiling your party (14-03), 231
about feelings
for being inconsiderate (14-18), 238
for betraying confidence (14-13), 236
for blaming you (14-12), 236
for hurting your feelings (14-14), 236
for lying to you (14-15), 237
for misleading you (14-16), 237

for misunderstanding (14-17), 238
for slighting you (14-20), 239
for starting a fight (14-19), 238
Applications
credit, inquiry to bank regarding (8-02), 133
job (13-06), 214
job, response to (7-05), 117
Appointments (*See also* Meetings)
confirming (3-20), 62
setting up (3-19), 61
Appraisals, job performance (7-24, 7-25), 126, 127
Appreciation letters (*See also* Congratulations; Thank you's)
for answering questionnaire (1-33), 17
to customers
for complimentary letter (3-15), 60
for meeting (3-21), 62
for opportunity to quote (1-48), 25
for order (1-37, 1-38), 21
for payment, with information regarding other products or services (3-29), 65
for suggestion (3-14), 59
for helpful advice (8-34), 149
for help in job search, **313**
to hotel/facility for service (8-41), 152
for job application (7-05), 117
for permission to use name as reference (1-11), 7
for printing article (2-28), 52
for setting up sales call (3-22), 63
to supplier, for cooperation during difficult project (6-22), 105
Approach letter (10-01), 177
Approval
of credit (5-05), 86
of drawings (1-63), 32
request for immediate (11-16), 200
Article
enjoyed your (3-13), 59
offer to write (10-20), 185
thank you for printing (2-28), 52
Assignments
follow-up to meeting (9-04), 158
Authorization letter
to return product (4-16), 79
to transfer funds (6-27), 107

B

Background information
  use of, in longer press release (2-27), 51
Backorders
  letter notifying of shipment (1-43), 23
Bad news, **277-278** (*See also* Telling it like it is)
  about business
    announcement (9-27), 171
  about illness and death
    Dad is having operation (17-15), 285
    friend has AIDS (17-19), 287
    friend has died (17-20), 288
    friend is very ill (17-18), 286
    Grandpa died (17-16), 285
    my dad died (17-22), 289
    relative has died (17-17), 286
    relative was in accident (17-21), 288
  about misfortune
    business failed (17-25), 290
    friends lost home in fire (17-26), 291
    had miscarriage (17-23), 289
    husband was laid off (17-24), 290
Balance sheet formats (13-07, 13-08), 216, 217
Banking services
  inquiring about (8-16), 140
Banks, **297** (*See also* Credit)
  closing account because of poor service (18-01), 135
  credit card
    close account (18-03), 299
    increase credit limit (18-04), 300
    replace stolen card (18-05), 301
  inquiry to, about outstanding credit application (8-02), 133
  remove my name as trustee (18-06), 301
  why did check bounce? (18-07), 302
  won't be responsible for charges made by ex-wife (18-02), 299
Benefits
  employee
    clarifying (9-18), 167
    description of (7-21), 124
    request to Social Security Administration for report of (27-32), 450
Bids (*See* Quotations)
Billing (*See also* Invoices)

arranging terms of (6-02), 96
clarifying (4-01, 25-02), 73, 403
error in (4-02, 15-25, 18-08, 18-09, 18-10), 73, 254, 302, 303
questioning size of (25-15), 409
sending duplicate, per customer's request (3-36), 68
under consignment terms (1-61), 31
Birth of child (*See* Congratulations; Gift cards; Invitations)
Birthday (*See* Congratulations; Gift cards; Invitations)
Bonus
  to employee (26-37), 426
  explaining program, to sales force (1-30), 16
Borrowing (*See* Complaints; Saying no)
Broadcast advertising (*See also* Media)
  requesting rates for (2-07), 38
Brochures, use of (*See also* Catalogs)
  in announcing new product (3-01), 54
  in promoting workshop (1-20), 11
  in requesting appointment with potential customer (3-19), 61
  in requesting opportunity to quote (1-47), 25
  in welcome letter (1-01, 1-03), 3
Builders and contractors, letters to, **391**
  change payment schedule (24-03), 394
  decided to use another (24-04), 394
  disappointed in unresponsiveness (24-05), 395
  driveway is cracking (24-06), 395
  need guarantee in writing (24-01), 393
  need quote broken out (24-02), 393
Bullets
  in announcements (9-23), 169
  in recommendations (9-15), 165
  in reports (9-12), 163
  in resume (19-14, 19-15), 325, 326-327
Business association
  acceptance to serve in (10-17), 184
  declining to join (10-18), 184
  inquiry to (8-18), 141
Business forms (*See* Formats, letters and forms)
Business plans
  cover letter for (8-32), 148
  executive summary (8-31), 147

C

Cancellation
  of door-to-door purchase (15-38), 260
  of order (6-18, 13-12), 103, 221
  of reservation (27-37), 452
  of wedding (23-09), 379
Career summary (*See also* Curriculum vitae)
  including, in resume (19-14), 325
Car leasing (*See* Leasing)
Cash flow problems (3-31), 66
Catalogs, enclosing (*See also* Brochures)
  when acknowledging return (3-37, 3-38, 3-39), 69, 70
  when issuing duplicate invoice (3-36), 68
  when merchandise ordered is unavailable (1-41), 22
  when responding to request for information (1-09), 6
  when welcoming new customer (1-04), 4
Change of address
  format for (13-19), 228
  notification of (2-09, 13-19), 39, 228
Checks
  missing, new check issued (6-31), 108
  returned, request for payment (3-25, 3-26, 3-27), 64, 65
  sent (6-32), 108
Children, letters from (*See* Letters home, to parents; Thank you's)
Children, letters to (*See* Holiday correspondence; Invitations; Praise)
Christening (*See* Invitations)
Client
  conveying information about, to colleague (11-17), 201
  questionnaire to inactive (1-35), 19
  use of list, in requesting opportunity to quote (1-47), 25
Collection agency (*See also* Collection letters)
  response to letter from (18-12), 304
  as ultimate threat, **83**
  warning customer of using, to collect on returned checks (3-27), 65
Collection letters (*See also* Collection agency)

moderate tone (5-08, 5-09, 5-10, 5-11), 88, 89
  sequence of, **83**
  stern tone (5-12, 5-13, 5-14, 5-15, 5-16), 90, 91, 92
College (*See* Congratulations; Gift cards; Education; References)
Commission program
  explaining (1-30), 16
Community service, **175-176** (*See also* Fundraising)
Companies and organizations, requests to
  for consumer product safety information (27-19), 443
  for copy of annual report (27-16), 442
  for information about drug (27-20), 444
  for position on issue (27-17), 443
  to provide speaker (10-21), 185
Company not responsible letters (4-09, 4-10, 4-11), 76, 77
Complaints, **241** (*See also* Complaints about employees; Complaints to hotels; Complaints to neighbors; Complaints about products and services; Government, letters to; Telling it like it is)
Complaints from customers (*See* Apologies; Company not responsible; Customer dissatisfaction; Customer misunderstanding)
Complaints about employees,
  clerk made ethnic slur (15-11), 246
  cloak room attendant lost coat (15-15), 248
  deliverymen damaged floor (15-16), 249
  mechanic tried to rip me off (15-17), 249
  salesperson has offensive odor (15-13), 247
  salesperson was rude (15-14), 248
  truck driver almost drove me off road (15-18), 250
  waiter made sexist comments (15-12), 247
Complaints to hotels
  about maid service (8-42), 152
  need facilities for handicapped people (15-29), 256
  room service takes too long (15-27), 255

request to provide home (27-28), 448

Discount offers
    for cash orders (5-06), 87
    inquiring about (6-04, 8-14), 97, 139
    in prepayment option (1-16), 9
    request to bus company for senior (27-29),
        448
    in sales program (1-22), 12
    in store opening (1-19), 11
    in thank-you for permission to use name
        as reference (1-11), 7
    for timely payment, **83,** (3-28, 3-30), 65,
        66

Doctors, letters to, **401**
    complaints
        kept me waiting (25-04), 404
        lack of concern (25-07), 406
        nurse gave inaccurate information (25-
            05), 405
        phone manner is brusque (25-06), 405
    I'm changing doctors (25-08), 406
    inquiries
        charges on bill (25-02), 403
        nature of condition (25-01), 403
    send my records to another doctor (25-
        03), 404
    your concern meant a lot (25-09), 407

Documentation
    apology for missing (4-08), 76
    request for missing (6-17), 103

Donation letters (*See* Fundraising letters)

E

Education, **229**
    inquiries and requests
        for college catalogue and application
            (27-01), 435
        for college interview (27-02), 435
        for dorm transfer (27-06), 437
        for professor's assistance (27-05), 436
        for reinstatement after suspension (27-
            04), 436
        about scholarships and loans (27-03),
            435
    letter to Board of Education regarding bad
        teacher (27-07), 437

EEOC compliance
    request for verification of (1-64), 33

Employees (*See also* Personnel relations)
    acknowledgment of compliment to (3-15),
        60
    announcement of new (2-12), 42
    apology for rudeness of (4-07), 75
    complimenting supplier's (6-25), 106
    motivating (7-28, 9-25), 129, 170
    press release announcing achievement of
        (2-22, 2-23), 49
    request for help in recruiting (7-02), 115

Employment (*See* Job search; Resignations)

Employment agency
    performance unsatisfactory (6-19), 103
    requesting information from (8-24, 8-25),
        144, 144
    requesting information from temporary
        (8-26), 145
    requesting interview, to (19-26, 19-27),
        336

Employment application (13-06), 214

Employment verifications
    providing (7-20), 123
    requesting (7-19), 123

Enclosures
    catalog (1-04), 1-09, 4, 6
    contract, for signature (1-62), 32
    invoice (1-57), 29
    payment (6-26), 106
    proposal (1-48), 25
    refund check (3-35), 68
    with questionnaire (1-32), 17

Engagement (*See* Congratulations; Invita-
        tions; Love letters)

Equipment
    confirming rental of (8-40), 151
    inquiring about office (8-06), 135
    recommending purchase of (9-14), 164

Estimates (*See also* Quotations)
    offering free, in soliciting new business
        (1-12), 7
    request to travel agency for (27-33), 450

Evaluations, job (*See* Job performance)

Event planning services
    inquiring about (8-13), 139

Executive search firm
    approaching (19-26, 19-27), 336
    requesting information from (8-25), 144

Executive summaries
    of business plan (8-31), 147

of business report, **155**
of final report (9-12), 163
of progress report (9-11), 162
Expressing feelings (*See* Apologies; Complaints; Expressing opinions; Hurt feelings; Love letters; Saying no; Telling it like it is)
Expressing opinions, **349** (*See also* Fan letters; Getting it off your chest; Praise)

F

Family correspondence, **277-278** (*See also* Bad news; Good news; Holiday correspondence; Letters home, to parents; Reminders)
Fan letters, **349** (*See also* Praise)
  to author (20-15), 358
  to rock star (20-16), 358
  to tv newsperson (20-13), 357
Faxes
  apologizing for shipment error (11-08), 196
  to associate about client (11-17), 201
  canceling order (11-12), 198
  confirming order (11-06), 195
  confirming phone conversation (11-18), 201
  correcting prices (11-05), 195
  cover sheet
      master (11-01), 193
      for resume (11-02), 194
  notifying of shipment (11-07), 196
  to order (11-10), 197
  for quotation (11-04), 194
  requesting approval (11-16), 200
  requesting decision (11-15), 200
  requesting permission to return shipment (11-11), 198
  requesting quotation (11-09), 197
  responding to request for information (11-03), 194
  setting time for phone call (11-19), 202
  to supplier who does not return phone calls (11-13), 199
  with urgent data (11-14), 199
  uses of (1-54), 28, **191**
Feedback
  in advertising campaigns (1-23), 13

and customer dissatisfaction, **71**
and questionnaires (1-34), 18
soliciting, in proposal cover letter (1-52), 27
in updates of products (1-27), 15
Feelings (*See* Apologies; Hurt feelings; Love letters; Saying no; Telling it like it is)
Flyer (1-14), 8 (*See also* Catalogs)
Follow-up letters
  for booked speaker (10-23), 186
  to employment ad (19-22), 334
  in fundraising, **176,** (10-08), 180
  to interview (19-28, 19-29, 19-30, 19-31, 19-32), 337, 338, 339
  to job offer (19-33, 19-34, 19-35, 19-36, 19-37, 19-38, 19-39), 339, 340, 341, 342
  to meeting (9-04), 158
  to phone call, to prospective employer (19-23), 335
  to proposal (1-51), 27
  to questions regarding request to bid (1-53), 28
  recommending other products or services to current customer (3-29), 65
  regarding an order (1-37), 21
  in sales, **1-2**
Formats, letters and forms
  agenda for meeting (13-03), 210
  balance sheet, manufacturing company (13-08), 217
  balance sheet, service company (13-07), 216
  business letter, full block (13-11), 220
  business letter, full block, 2nd page (13-12), 221
  business letter, modified block (13-13), 222
  business letter, modified block, 2nd page (13-14), 223
  change of address (13-19), 228
  employment application (13-06), 214
  income statement, manufacturing company (13-10), 219
  income statement, service company (13-09), 218
  invitation, formal (13-18), 227
  invoice for goods (13-17), 226

to state department of taxes for information (8-21), 142

to tax assessor about real estate tax (8-27, 27-21), 145, 444

to town sanatarian about septic system (8-23, 27-24), 143, 446

to zoning commission requesting variance (27-25), 446

"Grabber," uses of, **1**

H

Help (*See also* Job search; Networking)

requesting

from elected representative (8-22), 143

for name of sales rep (8-33), 148

in recruiting new employees (7-02), 115

thank you for

during crisis (26-09), 415

with employee search (12-05), 206

financial (26-15), 418

in getting legal advice (8-34), 149

in job search (19-04), 316

in move (26-27), 423

during sickness (26-39), 427

Hiring process (*See* Employment; Job approaches)

Holiday correspondence, **278**

can't be there for Christmas, from parent (17-32), 293

reminder about holiday plans (17-34), 294

thank you for everything, Dad (Father's Day) (17-35), 294

thank you for everything, Mom (Mother's Day) (17-36), 295

update on family news (17-33), 293

Valentine message

to Dad (17-37), 295

to wife (17-38), 296

Hotels

appreciation to, for help/good service (8-41), 152

complaining, about service (8-42), 152

requesting rates (8-38), 150

reserving meeting facilities (8-39), 151

Hurt feelings, **455**

my guests felt snubbed by you (28-21), 465

you didn't act like a friend (28-27), 468

you didn't invite me (28-26), 468

you didn't show up for your own party (28-25), 467

you didn't understand my needs (28-20), 465

you embarrassed me (28-22), 466

you had the facts wrong (28-23), 466

you ignored me (28-28), 469

you set a bad example for my children (28-24), 467

I

Illness (*See* Bad news; Sympathy)

Incentives

in announcing opening of new branch store or office (2-15), 45

in questionnaire cover letter (1-32), 17

in welcome letter, (1-01), 3

Income statement formats (13-09, 13-10), 218, 219

Industrial products

generating leads for sales of (1-13), 8

Inquiries, **131** (*See also* Government, inquiries to)

accounting services (8-05), 135

car leasing (8-07), 136

consulting services (8-08), 136

credit card (8-03), 134

credit terms (6-03), 96

discounts (6-04, 8-14), 97, 139

event planning services (8-13), 139

to franchisor (8-09), 137

insurance (8-04), 134

medical plans (8-15), 139

office equipment (8-06), 135

office lease (8-01), 133

to Planning and Zoning (8-12), 138

product (6-01), 96

scholarships and loans (27-03), 435

telephone (8-10), 137

Insurance, **298**

changes to policy

add my new car (18-24), 310

add valuable items (18-23), 310

change beneficiary (18-21), 309

change homeowner's (18-25), 311

J

Letter formats (*See also* Formats, letters and forms)
    business letter, full block (13-11), 220
    business letter, full block, 2nd page (13-12), 221
    business letter, modified block (13-13), 222
    business letter, modified block, 2nd page (13-14), 223
    personal letter (13-15), 224
Letterheads (*See also* Letter formats)
    for community service letter (10-04), 178
    for personal letters (16-01, 26-42, 26-43), 264, 429
Letters home, to parents, **277**
    I got married (17-04), 280
    I'm gay (17-07), 281
    I'm living with someone (17-03), 279
    I'm pregnant (17-05), 280
    I want to move back home (17-02), 279
    my grades were poor (17-01), 279
    send money (17-06), 280
Letter to the editor (20-01, 20-02, 20-03), 351
Limited time offers
    use of, in store opening announcement (1-19), 11
Love letters, **455**
    Dear Jane (28-01), 456
    Dear John (28-02), 456
    to dying friend (28-07), 458
    to dying relative (28-08), 459
    I miss you (28-03), 457
    I would like to see you after all these years (28-05), 457
    I would like to see you again (28-04), 457
    marriage proposal (28-06), 458

M

Magazine advertising
    requesting rates for (2-06), 38
Managing your business, **131** (*See* Inquiries; Requests)
Maps
    use of, in trade show announcement (1-18), 10
Marketing, **1-2** (*See also* Advertising, goals of; Advertising campaign)

role of sales letter in, **1**
use of questionnaires in (1-33), 17
Media (*See also* Broadcast advertising; Letter to the editor)
    procedures for dealing with (9-17, 9-29), 166, 167
Medical plans
    inquiring about (8-15), 139
Meetings, **53** (*See also* Appointments)
    confirming (3-17), 61
    to discuss employee problem (7-13), 120
    to discuss program development and cost (3-16), 60
    to discuss services and fees (2-02, 2-17), 36, 46
    follow-up to (3-21), 62
    notifying of (8-36, 8-37, 9-01), 149, 150, 157
    recap of (9-06), 159
    requesting associate attend (3-18), 61
    rescheduling (3-23), 63
    to review sales performance (1-31), 16
    to submit quote (1-47), 25
Memos, **114, 155-156** (*See also* Reports)
    announcing assignments (9-04), 158
    announcing job opening (7-01), 115
    announcing motivational award (9-25), 170
    bad news (9-27), 171
    planning (9-05), 159
    policy (9-18, 9-19, 9-23, 9-24), 167, 169, 170
    procedure (9-17, 9-20), 166, 168
    recommendation (9-14, 9-15, 9-16), 164, 165, 166
    regarding benefits (7-21), 124
    regarding job performance (7-12, 7-13), 120
    requesting change in project (9-09), 161
    requesting employee participation in charity drive (9-10), 162
    resignation (9-26), 171
    thanking employee for suggestion (9-07, 9-08), 160, 161
Merchandise
    being shipped (1-42), 23
    ready for pick-up (1-44), 24
    unavailable (1-40), 22
Messenger

use of (1-54), 28
Motivation letter (7-28), 129

N

Negotiation
of job offer, **314**, (19-37), 341
Networking (*See also* Job search)
announcement of new business (12-01),
204
offer to exchange referrals (12-04), 205
request
for feedback on new product (12-02),
204
for help with employee search (12-
05), 206
for names of professionals (12-06),
206
thank you for input (12-03), 205
News (*See* Bad news; Good news; Letters
home, to parents)
Newspaper advertising
requesting rates for (2-05), 37

O

Objective, career
placement of, in resume (19-15, 19-16),
326, 328
Opening sentence
and "grabber," **1**
Opinions, expressing (*See* Expressing
opinions; Fan letters; Getting it off
your chest)
Orders, **2**
acknowledging (1-37, 1-38, 1-39, 1-40, 1-
41), 21, 22
canceling (6-18), 103
received, unable to process (1-41), 22
rejecting proposed substitution of (6-21),
104
sent by fax (11-10), 197
special, customer misunderstood terms of
(4-14), 79
Organizations, **433**
charity
offer to volunteer services (27-11),
440
request to canvas neighborhood (27-

08), 438
request to offer items for auction (27-
09), 438
request to serve as honorary chairperson (27-10), 439
civic
come to neighborhood meeting (27-
12), 440
join organization (27-13), 441
resignation from organization (27-15),
442
would you speak at meeting (27-14),
441
Outline format (13-04), 211
Outplacement firm
requesting information from (19-10), 319
Overnight service
uses of (1-54), 28
Overpayment
rectifying with refund check (3-35), 68

P

Parents, letters to (*See* Holiday correspondence; Letters home, to parents;
Thank you's)
Party (*See* Invitations; Thank you's)
Payment due, **53** (*See also* Collection letters)
for goods received (1-46), 24
for money you borrowed (17-28), 292
for phone bill (17-29), 292
for services rendered (1-45), 24
Payments
cover letter for (6-26), 106
crediting for (3-32), 67
and customer dissatisfaction (4-13), 78
debiting account, in lieu of (3-33), 67
explaining delay in (6-30), 108
inquiring about terms of (6-05), 97
notifying of change in policy regarding
(6-15), 102
offering discounts for timely, **83**
requesting additional, due to overlooked
charges (3-34), 68
withholding, until work or order is
complete (6-14, 6-15), 101, 102
Performance (*See also* Warning memos to
employees)
complaining of unsatisfactory, to service

company (6-20), 104

complaining of unsatisfactory, to temporary employment agency (6-19), 103

regarding sales (1-31), 16

Personnel relations, **113-114** (*See also* Benefits, employee; Employees; Job descriptions; Job offers; Job openings; Job performance)

and business reverses (9-27, 9-28), 171-172

policies affecting (9-24), 170

Planning and Zoning Commission

inquiry to (8-12, 27-25), 138, 446

Poems, **263** (*See* Apologies; Congratulations)

Policies

announcing changes in (3-05, 6-15, 9-20, 9-21, 9-23, 9-24), 55, 102, 168, 169, 170

clarifying, in memo (9-18), 167

recommending changes in (9-19), 167

Postscript

use of, to generate response (1-32), 17

Praise, **411** (*See also* Thank you's)

to athletic coach (20-17), 358

to child

you improved your school grades (26-04), 413

you led the team to victory (26-05), 413

you made me proud (26-01), 412

you responded well in crisis (26-06), 414

you showed courage (26-03), 413

you showed patriotism (26-02), 412

to company president (20-14), 357

to congressperson (20-12), 356

to President (20-11), 356

to tutor (26-07), 414

Premium

use of, as incentive to new customer (1-17), 10

Prepayments

as discount option (1-16), 9

requiring, after repeated delays in payment (3-31), 66

Press releases, **35**

for anniversary celebration (2-26, 2-27), 51

announcing employee achievement (2-23), 49

announcing merger (2-24), 50

announcing new employee (2-22), 49

announcing new partner (2-25), 50

announcing new product or product line (2-19, 2-20), 47

long version (2-27), 51

short version (2-26), 51

Pricing

correcting of (11-05), 195

explaining change in, to sales force (1-26), 14

notifying customer of changes in (3-02, 3-03) 54, 55

notifying dealer of changes in (3-02, 3-03), 54, 55

Probationary period, confirming, **114**

Procedures (*See also* Policy)

announcement of new (9-20, 9-21), 168, 169

Products

announcing new (1-25, 2-13, 2-19), 14, 43, 47

dealing with customer misunderstanding of (4-15), 79

explaining, in sales letter (1-13, 1-25), 8, 14

inquiring about, to supplier (6-01), 96

requesting change in (9-09), 161

updating specifications of (1-27), 15

Professionals (*See* Accountants, letters to; Doctors, letters to; Lawyers, letters to)

Promotions

and relationship with ad agency (2-03), 36

of sales program (1-21, 1-22), 12

use of, in announcing opening of new branch or office (2-15), 45

use of contest for (1-15), 9

use of testimonials in (1-17), 10

Promotions, job

announcing, **156**, (2-22, 9-22), 49, 169

notifying of (7-26), 128

Proposals, **2** (*See also* Quotations)

enclosed in thank you for opportunity to quote (1-48), 25

follow-up to (1-51), 27

U

V

Venture capital firms
    inquiry to (8-19), 141
    writing executive summary for (8-31),
        147
Verification of employment
    providing (7-20), 123
    requesting (7-19), 123
Volunteer service
    offering (27-11), 440
    refusing (10-15), 183
    requesting (10-11), 181
    welcoming to (10-14), 182

W

Warning memos to employees (7-12, 7-13),
    120 (*See also* Appraisals; Job
    performance)
Welcome letters
    to new board member (10-14), 182
    to new business, from supplier (1-02), 3
    to new client (1-03), 3
    to new customer (1-04), 4
    to new resident (1-01), 3
Workshop promotion letter (1-20), 11